Wake Up With the Word

A 365 Day Daily Devotional

Wake Up With the Word

A 365 Day Daily Devotional

Dr. William Luffman

Dedication

I would like to dedicate this book to my beautiful wife, Ginger, who has always been my biggest supporter, and to my three awesome children, J.T., Rebecca and Rachel. They have sacrificed time with me throughout the years and allowed me to fulfill my call to help others. Without their understanding and support, I would not have been able to carry out God's will for my life!

I would also like to dedicate this endeavor to my five terrific grandchildren, Kayla, Tracy, Madyson, Ayden and our newest Janel (with more to come I hope).

In addition, this book is dedicated to the memory of my late mother, Mildred Perry, and late step-father, Steve Wolfe, and B.J.

Foreword

by Dr. Mark T. Barclay

I believe Dr. William Luffman has hit an absolute homerun. He has worked so hard on this project to provide you the material needed for your personal development. May it advance you into a closer daily walk with Jesus Christ and His Word. The insights in this book are so refreshing, I found myself fighting to wait until the next day to see what was written. (I must admit, I cheated!) With our extremely busy lifestyles and the decay we face all around us in these last days, *Wake Up With the Word* will provide solutions and answers for life and bring the inspiration and perhaps even the "spiritual medicine" to strengthen your walk. I believe it will improve your personal discipline as you pick up the book each day and read the verses, thoughts and revelations Pastor William has written on each page. I'm sure you're going to want to share this with your friends and family members.

I have known this author, pastor and Bible teacher for many years. I have watched him humbly work in this Kingdom, and God has promoted him tremendously. He and his wife, Ginger, pastor one of the fastest growing and most successful churches in his entire region. It is something to witness—accomplished by no compromise to the great Holy Spirit and sticking right with the Word of God. You will feel his love and the shepherd's heart as you spend some time every day of the year with Pastor William. May this book touch your heart, build you up and make you the best Christian you can possibly become.

Foreword

by Dr. Larry Huggins, D.D.
President/The Commonwealth of Christ, Washington, D.C.

I f you wait until you need faith, to get faith, you're too late. Faith has to be fed every day. *Wake Up With the Word* is a faith devotional, written by a man devoted to faith. William Luffman knows what it means to wake up with the Word – he's done it all his Christian life. It's a discipline that's made him a successful leader, and has made Faith Outreach Church one of the most successful churches in the country.

Wake Up With the Word flows from the heart of a man who knows how to build faith. He wrote this book with you in mind: to inspire you, to bless you and to feed your faith. It's written in a clear and concise format, with lessons, prayers and affirmations that you can easily apply to your life.

Wouldn't it be wonderful if everyone could wake up with the Word? Get copies for all the special people in your life, so they can wake up with the Word. And always keep your copy beside your bed, so you can wake up with the Word.

A Note by the Author

*T*his project is a culmination of over 30 years of research and everyday living. I trust it will inspire, inform and challenge you in the toils of daily life. I recommend you make your own notes each day and reflect on them each night. This devotional is written in such a way as to be used again each year. May God richly reveal himself to you as you Wake Up With the Word.

JANUARY 1
A NEW DAY IS COMING

Zephaniah 3:5
"...Morning by morning he dispenses his justice, and every new day he does not fail, yet the unrighteous know no shame." (NIV)

Have you ever noticed how different one day to the next can be? One day the children of Israel were toiling under the heavy hand of Pharaoh, as they had been for over 400 years, then God delivered them through His servant Moses. They left with healed bodies and the riches of Egypt, never to see the Egyptians again. (Exodus 12:35-36; 14:13-14; Psalms 105:37-38) God not only delivered them, but He promoted them! It was almost as if their deliverance came overnight. Of course, it really did not, but it must have been amazing to be working as a slave one day, and marching out with the wealth the next!

Sometimes we may find ourselves in a place of disappointment or distress with no apparent deliverance in front of us, but we must remember God is preparing a new day for us. He is arranging new things, new relationships and new challenges.

Just think of some of the most difficult seasons of your life in days gone by. It probably felt like those days would never pass. Yet, you were able to overcome the hardships and continue to press ahead!

Joel 3:10 says, *"Beat your plowshares into swords, and your pruninghooks into spears: let the weak say, I am strong."* (KJV) You must begin to say the things you desire to see! Whatever you may have experienced in the past year must be put behind you. You must begin to believe God for something new. Our faith moves things. It opens the door to new things.

As you prepare to go forth into this upcoming year, consider the previous year finished. Just like the Egyptians, you will never see it again. This is a new day. Let your faith arise!

APPLICATION:
1. What do you need this year you have not seen before?
2. Look through the eyes of faith and prepare for your deliverance!

PRAYER:
Lord, I will move into some new things this year. Guide me in the things you have prepared for me. Amen.

JANUARY 2
FILL IN THE GAP

Ezekiel 22:30
"And I sought for a man among them, that should make up the hedge, and stand in the gap before me for the land, that I should not destroy it: but I found none." (KJV)

Have you ever driven through a countryside that has many farms side by side? It is not uncommon to see aged and rusty fences with pieces of sheet metal placed at the intervals where the fence has broken through. This is not meant for a permanent repair, but serves the purpose until the proper fencing can be put in place. Often, neighbors repair each other's "gaps," if they become aware of it before the owners do. The truth is because their farms are adjacent to one another it is advantageous to help their neighbors out, so that their livestock does not get mixed up. This type of caring makes for a special kind of community, which is sadly fading from American culture.

In this verse, the prophet explains how the Father has spotted "gaps" in the fences of His Kingdom, but there is no one aware or concerned enough to fill the gaps in, at least until they can be permanently stabilized. This is often the case of His people as well. There are people who have lost their way, or let down their guard, and they are exposed. Some are not even aware of it. They need someone in their lives who cares enough to step in and prevent any outside enemy from coming in!

We are living in a time, now more than ever, when we need to "cover" each other. We need not be so busy with our own lives that we take no notice of the plight of those around us. We must be willing to make a sacrifice of our own time and help preserve the well-being of those around us. We need to become inter-cessors through our prayer life until permanent help from Heaven comes. Let us pause, take a good look around and make it our cause to fill in the "gap" of the lives of those surrounding us beginning today!

APPLICATION:
1. Open your eyes to those who are struggling around you.
2. Put their names in your mouth and in your prayer time.
3. Reach out to those you are able to reach out to.

PRAYER:
Lord, open my eyes to those around me whose lives are exposed. Help me to not be critical, but concerned. Amen.

JANUARY 3
HE REMEMBERS

Luke 23:42
*"And he said unto Jesus, Lord, remember me when thou comest
into thy kingdom."* (KJV)

A churchgoer once wrote a letter to the editor of a newspaper complaining it made no sense to go to church every Sunday. "I've gone for 30 years now," he wrote, "and in that time I have heard something like 4,000 sermons. But, for the life of me, I can't remember a single one of them. So, I think I'm wasting my time and the pastors are wasting theirs by giving sermons at all."

This started a real controversy in the *Letters to the Editor* column, much to the delight of the editor. It went on for weeks until someone wrote this clincher: "I've been married for 30 years now. In that time my wife has cooked some 32,000 meals. But, for the life of me, I cannot recall the entire menu for a single one of those meals. But, I do know this: They all nourished me and gave me the strength I needed to do my work. If my wife had not given me these meals, I would be physically dead today!"

Although we may fail to remember all of the things we hear about Christ, and most of what we promise Him, He remembers what He has said about us and to us! God does not forget those who cry out to Him.

Joseph was sold as a slave and his dreams were seemingly out of reach. It appeared that not only his family had forgotten him, but his God as well. Still, God remembered Joseph, even when others did not. (Genesis 40:9-23) As a result, he lived his dream!

As I look back over my journey in life, I see more clearly His plan was working for me all of the time. Everything He said about me has, or is, coming to pass before my very eyes. He has remembered me when others have forsaken me. He has brought me into His promises. Regardless of what may be going on right now, consider that God has not forgotten you! You are on your way to your destiny!

APPLICATION:
1. Restate the things God has said to you, out loud.
2. Refocus your faith in Him.
3. Restart your dream!

PRAYER:
*Lord, thank you for remembering me and for listening to my cries and my dreams.
Amen.*

17

JANUARY 4
THERE IS AN APPOINTED TIME

Habakkuk 2:3
*"For the vision is yet for an appointed time, but at the end it shall speak,
and not lie: though it tarry, wait for it; because it will surely come,
it will not tarry."* (KJV)

We live in a world that is time driven. Schedules are posted on our walls, in our wallets, on our televisions and on our phones. They are everywhere. We seemingly never have ample time to complete the tasks set before us. Sometimes, we just cannot balance it all and something is inevitably overlooked or omitted.

God has appointments He is setting up for us that we can not afford to miss. Sometimes, it seems as if He has forgotten us, but just ahead is the first stage of the next part of our lives, a part that will bring fulfillment and contentment!

The words of this verse remind us our future is not in question. God is arranging some things just for our lives. Delays do not mean defeat. Pauses do not mean prevention. As a matter of fact, often we look back and realize we were not really prepared when we thought we were. When things finally came to pass, it was really the right time after all! Just like in our daily schedules, there may be appointments or tasks we can not attend or complete; however, they must certainly be rescheduled!

David was anointed king by Saul, but went back to the sheep and sheepfold for a season. It appeared he missed his appointment; however, God was merely waiting for a more opportune time for David to become king. Although it must have seemed to David that God had revoked his appointment, God was forming the stability and confidence in David's character he would need to possess to be king!

Even if it seems you have been "left out," just remember God has some things just ahead for you in your life. They will surely come to pass, if you continue to trust and follow Him! Your appointment has been made and if you continue to trust Him, He will lead you to it!

APPLICATION:
1. Continue to follow and serve Him in your present condition.
2. Be faithful where you are now, and continue to do what you are doing!

PRAYER:
Lord, I will wait upon you. Help me to not become weary or discouraged. I know you have something just ahead for my life. Thank you for today! Amen.

JANUARY 5
HE CALLS YOU BY NAME

John 10:3
"...and he calleth his own sheep by name, and leadeth them out." (KJV)

Last year, I was in New York City with my wife and another couple on our way to the old Yankee Stadium for an afternoon of baseball. The only way to get there on time was to take the subway. It was crowded as usual. My wife, Ginger, and I got separated in the crowded station. The train was getting ready to leave when I heard someone call out, "William, where are you?" I am sure there was probably someone else within earshot that was called by the same name. *William* is a fairly common name; however, when my wife called it out, I was the only one who even considered responding.

God also knows our name. Even though there are plenty of people who probably have the same name, when He calls our name out, it clearly becomes distinguished. When He calls our name out, it is always to lead us into a better place or to help us find our way.

It is not that He did not call our name before we knew Him. He called young Samuel three times before Samuel finally consulted Eli to discover it was indeed, God. He keeps calling our name out until we recognize it is Him.

Yet, it takes time to distinguish His voice from that of the enemy. Like every relationship, it takes effort to develop trust and confidence in someone else's call to us. God is consistently good, but the thief comes to steal, kill and destroy. If God is calling out to you, you can be assured there is something you are not seeing that He wants to point out to you!

He knows how to lead us out of trouble as well. Sometimes it seems as though we may have exhausted every possibility for our deliverance; however, there is an escape route He has prepared for us. If we will listen, He will call our name out and lead us into victory!

APPLICATION:
1. Make it a point to listen for your name.
2. Trust Him to make a way for you in a time of trouble.
3. Believe that He knows where you are and what you are going through.

PRAYER:
Lord, I will listen for you to call my name. When you call me, I will listen and trust you to lead me out. Amen.

JANUARY 6
YOU HAVE A STANDING INVITATION

Hebrews 4:16
"Let us therefore come boldly into the throne of grace, that we may obtain mercy, and find grace to help in time of need." (KJV)

I heard a story about a son who found himself in legal trouble in a city hundreds of miles from his home. Preparing to go before the judge, he was certain he would be found guilty and sentenced because the "witnesses" were co-conspirators, and actually the perpetrators of the crime. He could only imagine the court would be "fixed" against him as well. When he went into the courtroom, he trembled as he heard the judge's door open. To his utter surprise, his father walked through and took the judge's seat! He had not seen his father in years and had lost contact. He did not realize his father had moved there and become a prominent leader and judge. He was still worried his father might hold his past, irresponsible actions against him.

Yet, when his father saw him, he could only see the little boy he had gone fishing with, played pitch with and carried up to his bedroom at night when he fell asleep. The judge quickly discredited the "witnesses" and found them guilty of perjury. Later, he and his son met privately and reconciled!

This is the picture of our relationship with the Father. He has already forgiven our past and has accepted us for who we are now! He has already pardoned us and adopted us into His family. We have Kingdom rights!

Our accuser has been discovered and discredited! The writing on the wall against us has been wiped clean by the blood of the spotless Lamb of God! We, who were guilty, have been totally acquitted! There are NO charges against us!

We have a standing invitation to approach the Creator of the universe whenever we are in need or in prayer. Do not let the accuser fool you! You have access to His throne anytime!

APPLICATION:
1. Never be afraid of going before His throne.
2. Do not worry that your past will be used against you!
3. Remember, you are a child of God and you belong!

PRAYER:
Lord, thank you for giving me a standing invitation to come before you! I will not be afraid to approach you for any reason! Amen.

JANUARY 7
WILL YOU BELIEVE HIM?

Job 39:12
*"Wilt thou believe him, that he will bring home thy seed, and gather
it into thy barn?"* (KJV)

Every farmer knows the most important season of the year is harvest time. All of the early hours of the day spent plowing and planting, all of the times in the hot sun weeding and even watering when possible are in preparation for harvest time.

Days turn into weeks, and weeks to months. Sometimes it seems all has been in vain, but it is too late to turn back! Everything has been invested in the harvest!

Your whole life is pointing towards the day of harvest. Regardless of how tired you get, no matter how weary you feel, you must continue on! Everyday when you rise, you are one day closer to the harvest! Every night when you go to bed, you are one minute closer to reaping from all of your long, hard days of sacrifice and labor!

Then, just when you think the hardest work is over, you have to find a way to dig even deeper because now the day of harvest has arrived! You have to do whatever is necessary to get the harvest in on time before it spoils in the field. Jesus said the whole Kingdom operates on the principle as if a man cast seed into the ground. If you have been serving God for a long time, now is not the time to quit, let up or give up. Now, more than ever, you must be even more determined.

The payoff is coming! When the harvest is brought in, all of the hard work, long hours and waiting are worth it. Then, you will be able to enjoy the fruits of your labor.

Sometimes we forget the harvest is closer than we think. We fail to believe God will help us gather the seeds we have planted. Remember, it is not determined just by what you have planted, but by what you believe God will do with what you have planted!

APPLICATION:
1. Be sure you believe God for what you have planted.
2. Do not get discouraged by the "heat."
3. Be sure to keep yourself in position to receive the harvest.

PRAYER:
Lord, I call the seed that I have planted, home. I fully believe what I have planted is on the way to becoming the greatest harvest of my life! Amen.

JANUARY 8
DEALING WITH LIGHT AFFLICTIONS

II Corinthians 4:17
"For our light affliction, which is but for a moment, worketh for us a far more exceeding and eternal weight of glory;" (KJV)

Only someone with Paul's résumé could have written a verse like this. A close examination of his experiences is outlined in II Corinthians 11:24-28: *"Of the Jews five times received I forty stripes save one. Thrice night and a day I have been in the deep; In journeyings often, in perils by waters, in perils of robbers, in perils by mine own countrymen, in perils by the heathen, in perils in the city, in perils in the wilderness, in perils in the sea, in perils among false brethren; In weariness and painfulness, in watchings often, in hunger and thirst, in fastings often, in cold and nakedness. Beside those things that are without, that which cometh upon me daily, the care of all the churches."* (KJV)

Despite the intensity and frequency of Paul's trials, we know Paul never faltered, and finished strong. He never used his harsh experiences as an excuse for quitting or giving up.

Somehow, Paul maintained his focus on the prize ahead. Despite being so severely tested and tried, Paul endured and overcame all! He wrote what is referred to as the "joyful" epistle of Philippians—while imprisoned! Sometimes our life experiences are hurtful and extreme. We lose our focus on what God has already brought us through and let go of our faith in Him.

Before we let our circumstances, no matter how extreme, get the best of us, perhaps we should look around closely. There are probably some "Pauls" in our own lives we can draw strength and courage from! Although it does not seem so in the present, these afflictions may be lighter than we first believed!

APPLICATION:
1. Be sure you stay even closer to the things of God if you are presently in an intense trial.
2. Consider others around you who are going through even greater tests.
3. Draw on the comfort He has delivered you before, and He will deliver you again!

PRAYER:
Lord, forgive me for griping about my circumstances. I am confident that you will deliver me and vindicate me! Amen.

JANUARY 9
YOUR DECISIONS AFFECT OTHERS

Luke 6:39
"Can the blind lead the blind? Shall they not both fall into the ditch?" (KJV)

Every elected official makes countless decisions not only affecting him/her, but hundreds, perhaps thousands, of others. I heard a story of an elected official who was very frustrated about the lax of traffic violations in his city. As a result, he decided to work very hard to change the laws. He promoted a new zero-tolerance law, which not only required a fine to be paid, but also a minimum of 24 hours served in the local jail.

The law was to be strictly enforced with no exceptions. There were numerous people fined and jailed in just the first few days of the law going into effect. This was very satisfying to him. Then, one day, when the official arrived home from the office, he found an empty house. He asked neighbors if they knew where his wife and children were, but no one knew. Shortly thereafter, a police officer drove up and knocked on his door. The officer explained that earlier in the day, his wife had run a stop sign and was incarcerated. If the official wanted to see her, he would have to visit her at the jail! By the end of the year, the official worked to have the laws changed to a fine only, for first time violators!

Sometimes we do not realize how our decisions affect those around us. For instance, people who drink alcohol say they are only hurting themselves and not others. However, anyone raised in a house where alcohol was the norm knows better! As a little boy, I remember many times when we had little or no food in the house, but somehow my family seemed to find money for beer on the weekends. I remember we had a big family Bible on the coffee table with an ashtray full of cigarette butts on top of it, and beer cans beside it! Had I not been led to church when I was a teenager, I am sure I would have followed their example. They decided their appetites for sin were more important than their children's hunger. We must realize our actions always affect others around us.

APPLICATION:
1. Examine the decisions you are making now. Are they positively or negatively affecting others?
2. Do you need to reconsider how you are judging others?

PRAYER:
Lord, help me to be more thoughtful about the decisions I am making and less selfish in my intentions. Amen.

JANUARY 10
YOU ARE DESTINED TO WIN

II Corinthians 2:14
"Now thanks be unto God, which always causeth us to triumph in Christ, and maketh manifest the savour of his knowledge by us in every place." (KJV)

Have you ever considered how successful people achieved success? The truth is they failed miserably first! Michael Jordan did not even make his high school basketball team at first. The player, who would become what almost every basketball purist believes to be the greatest player ever, suffered a great disappointment and setback in the beginning. Despite this seeming defeat, he was recruited by the University of North Carolina, where he won a national championship, became player of the year and was drafted by the Chicago Bulls, where he won six World Championships!

God works through our losses and failures. He finds a way to bring us through them and causes us to gain valuable experience, which becomes a source of great strength for us and others later in life.

He uses them as a billboard later to broadcast to the world that what was once a mistake or failure, was not able to destroy us after all! Instead, those same failures become points of reference of God's intervention in our lives.

The Word of God reminds us no matter how dark the past failures of our lives may have been, we have a much brighter path just ahead of us. It is hard to imagine how God is going to bring us back into a life full of meaning and joy when we are hurting, but He has appointments for us down the road that will cause us to rise again and live!

Sometimes, our negative experiences teach us more about ourselves than success does. Thomas Edison said, "I have not failed. I have found 10,000 ways that do not work!" You have not failed; you have found ways that do not work!

APPLICATION:
1. Reconsider your failures.
2. Did you use those experiences to learn?
3. Do you use those experiences to help others with similar problems?

PRAYER:
Lord, forgive me for not recognizing the ways you help me even in times of failure. I believe you will cause me to live in victory again! Amen.

JANUARY 11
TURNING TO THE UNSAVED

Jeremiah 8:20
"The harvest is past, the summer is ended, and we are not saved." (KJV)

One year I composed a list of goals, which included witnessing a certain number of conversions to salvation by the end of the year. Despite having a record number of people make commitments to the Lord that year, it dawned on me my focus should not have been so much on how many had been converted, but instead on how many others had not.

No matter how successful our efforts are in reaching the lost for Christ, the truth is there are untold millions of people who are perishing every day. People you work with on a daily basis, people you come in contact with on a regular basis and even your own family members need your prayers and interest in their souls.

When my wife and I traveled the country before the GPS was invented, my wife insisted on having a roadmap. Of course, being a man, I did not want to look at directions and certainly did not ever ask for them! As a result, we, all too often, ended up lost and off the path to our destination.

The world is also full of lost people! Without our intervention, there is no way they will be able to find their way. They are destined for eternal destruction!

They are much more desperate than they will admit. Many are just waiting for someone to come along who knows the way. We have to care enough to pray for them and to share the Good News of the Gospel of Jesus Christ with them, which changed our lives!

Our work, as believers, is far from over. We have a vast field waiting for us to harvest. If we are willing to share His love with those who are lost, He will honor our efforts!

May we all make it our personal charge to be soul winners everyday of our lives, starting now! The prodigals are waiting on you!

APPLICATION:
1. Consider the people you come in contact with everyday and be willing to share your faith when possible.
2. Ask God to lead you to those who are searching for Him.

PRAYER:
Lord, please use me to reach those who are lost. Amen.

JANUARY 12
LOVE AT FIRST SIGHT

Genesis 29:9-11
"And while he yet spake with them, Rachel came with her father's sheep; for she kept them. And it came to pass, when Jacob saw Rachel the daughter of Laban his mother's brother, and the sheep of Laban his mother's brother, that Jacob went near, and rolled the stone from the well's mouth, and watered the flock of Laban his mother's brother. And Jacob kissed Rachel, and lifted up his voice, and wept." (KJV)

What a love story! It has all of the necessary ingredients: a young man, a young woman and a perfect setting. The scenery included a plush field where the flocks grazed and a well with cool water for thirsty travelers.

Jacob was the son of Isaac and the grandson of mighty, wealthy Abraham. He could have had any young lady, but he chose Rachel. The Bible describes Rachel as beautiful and well-favored. There was something about Rachel that distinguished her from the other girls. She had a radiance about her that caught Jacob's eye. He did not see any other girls after seeing Rachel. It was love at first sight.

This story reminds me of our youngest daughter, Rachel. We knew she would be the last child we would have, and we did everything to prepare. I was so sure we were going to have a boy, that my wife and I never discussed a girl's name. All clothing and toys we purchased were blue. In those days, you were unable to determine the sex of the child and had to wait until the birth. This did not affect me because I knew I was going to have a baby son.

On the day of the baby's birth, I watched as this miracle took place. Then, the moment came, and the doctor handed me my beautiful, healthy daughter. In a moment's time, all of my previous thoughts seemed to disappear, and it was love at first sight.

God has given us the blessing of love from the people He has placed in our lives. Do not miss this love!

APPLICATION:
1. Love the people God has placed in your life and put them first after Him.
2. Tell someone you love them.

PRAYER:
Lord, thank you for placing people in my life to love. Amen.

JANUARY 13
MIND YOUR OWN BUSINESS

John 21:22
*"Jesus saith unto him, If I will that he tarry till I come,
what is that to thee? Follow thou me."* (KJV)

There is a story of a man who recently sued the company he worked for claiming he was unfairly compensated for a job he signed a contract for. He stated he suffered mental anguish when he heard a more recently hired employee was making more money than him. He cited he should have been notified, if the other employee was going to be paid more. He won the case!

What happened to the days when an employer had the right to pay whatever wages they deemed right to whomever they wanted without the fear of a lawsuit, especially if there was a signed agreement?

We are living in a time when people in the Church are exhibiting the same attitude. Much like Peter, we are way too interested in what God is doing in others' lives and we compare ourselves to them. Thus, we are often frustrated by what we see.

We get infuriated when God places His favor on someone other than us; instead, we should be rejoicing for, and with them! We accuse God of not being fair and just. However, if there is one attribute of God that can be counted on, it is He is fair and equitable with all who serve Him!

Jesus hit the target when he reminded Peter his focus should not be on God's movement in the lives of others. In reality, it was none of Peter's business! Instead, Peter should have focused on what was required of him in his own faith and just continued to follow Him!

Too often, we get caught up in the affairs of others. We assume we know God's business better than He does. It is an age old accusation that God has forgotten what we have done for Him. Yet, nothing is unnoticed in His sight!

APPLICATION:
1. Examine yourself and be sure you are not comparing yourself to others.
2. Be honest. Ask yourself, "Am I doing what He told me to do?"
3. Do not be jealous of God's plan for others.

PRAYER:
Lord, search my heart and expose any jealousy in me. I repent for not following you to the fullest. May this be the year I become the closest to you. Amen.

JANUARY 14
LAZINESS LEADS TO LACK

Proverbs 12:27
"If you are lazy, you will never get what you are after, but if you work hard, you will get a fortune..." (TEV)

I was raised in a very, very poor environment. My father was rarely in the house. He would disappear for years at a time. My mother was older when I was born, and I was the last of nine birth children. Jobs were scarce. She received a government check from her second husband, who had died years before, but it was not nearly enough to make ends meet. There were winters when we had no heat in the house. There were days when food was scant, but my mother never conceded we would not make it. People would bring her baskets of laundry that needed to be starched and ironed. She would charge five to fifteen cents per piece. She made just enough to sustain us until the first of the month when the check arrived. I remember her saying to me when I was very small, "Son, you do what you have to do in life. Never forget it!"

Although I made some poor choices in my teen years, including dropping out of high school, I was never lazy. I went to work immediately at the age of 15 and have never been unemployed. Over the years God has blessed the work of my hands. I am not rich, but I am certainly not poor.

God has a plan to bless your life beyond your dreams and expectations according to Ephesians 3:20, but He will not do it if you are a lazy person.

Even God worked! Genesis says He worked for six days and rested on the seventh. We should never expect the blessings of God to manifest in our lives, if we are unwilling to do our part. God prospers all we put forth our hands to do!

It is time to quit making excuses for the lack in our lives. If we will be willing to work, God will make sure we never go without!

APPLICATION:
1. Are you a hard worker or a complainer about what you do not have?
2. Are you willing to do what you have to do in life?
3. Ask God to bless the work of your hands. You will discover that He already is!

PRAYER:
Lord, bless the work of my hands. Thank you for the ability and good health to work! Amen.

JANUARY 15
LEAVE SIN BEHIND YOU

Job 11:13-17
"Before you turn to God and stretch out your hands to him, get rid of your sins and leave all iniquity behind you. Only then, without the spots of sin to defile you, can you walk steadily forward to God without fear. Only then can you forget your misery. It will all be in the past. And your life will be cloudless; any darkness will be as bright as morning!" (TLB)

Have you ever visited a larger city and observed the homeless people? Many are there because of tragedies they could not overcome. Surprisingly, some of those people are there because they have developed a lifestyle they actually enjoy! I have watched people who tried to help someone get off the street, perhaps for a night, who rejected the offer. The reason was they did not want to leave the spot they were begging from because they were afraid they would lose it, and be unable to get it back!

Many Christians are the same way. They do not want to leave their past behind them completely. They still want to enjoy the "pleasures of sin" for a season. They have convinced themselves living for God is unfulfilling and drab. Although they see the destruction that accompanies their lifestyle, they will not let go of it! Doing so, would not leave anything for them to cling to, drag along or be excused by. Somehow, they have been deceived into thinking they cannot really trust God with all of their lives. They have found a false security in their sin!

We should never be deceived. The only way to truly enjoy today is to let go of yesterday!

APPLICATION:
1. Check yourself. Are you holding on to your past?
2. Are you holding on to sins you need to let go of?
3. Decide, today, to let go of your past and your sins!

PRAYER:
Lord, forgive me for dragging my past into my future. I repent of my sin and iniquities. I am ready to go on to what you have for me! Amen.

JANUARY 16
FOREVER WITH GOD

I Samuel 1:11
*"And she vowed a vow, and said, O LORD of hosts, if thou wilt indeed look
on the affliction of thine handmaid, and remember me, and not forget thine
handmaid, but wilt give unto thine handmaid a man child, then I will give him
unto the LORD all the days of his life…"* (KJV)

Hannah prayed a prayer for a son and God answered her. When Samuel was born, she recognized he did not belong to her, but to God. Her son was, in reality, His son!

Our children are a gift from God. They are on "loan" from Heaven. Before they were even formed in their mother's womb, they were with Him. God knew them before we did. There was a relationship we did not know about. No matter how long, or short, of a time we have with our children, we must remember they belonged to Him, first!

What if a child's days end prematurely or they are stillborn? What if a child is killed, dies from a sickness or in some tragic way? Will they go to Heaven? I believe the Bible clearly answers these questions.

Even in the Old Testament, we see how God considered any person less than 20 years of age exempt from the curse on the children of Israel. Anyone older could not enter into the Promised Land. They were considered fully responsible for their actions. Yet, anyone under 20 was allowed to enter in. Numbers 14:29-31 says: *"Your carcasses shall fall in the wilderness; and all that were numbered of you, according to your whole number, from twenty years old and upward, which have murmured against me, Doubtless ye shall not come into the land…But your little ones, which ye said should be a prey, them will I bring in, and they shall know the land which ye have despised."* (KJV)

Jesus came that we might have life. He overcame death, Hell and the grave. The problem of sin has been dealt with. If we have a child who has been taken from us, we will see them again! They began in His presence, and they are still in His presence. Their life here may have been interrupted, but their life in Heaven is secure!

APPLICATION:
1. If you, or someone you love, have been affected by this, consider the place the child has in Heaven now.
2. Rejoice in the promise ahead!

PRAYER:
Thank you, Lord, for Heaven! Amen.

JANUARY 17
HOW MUCH WILL YOU SPEND?

Luke 15:14

"And when he had spent all, there arose a mighty famine in that land; and he began to be in want." (KJV)

Over many years as a pastor, I have watched untold numbers of people come to God, after wasting away most of their best years. Of course, God is always merciful and forgives them, but sadly, many of them come so late in life they have missed what should have been their best years. They have spent so much of their lives chasing their own lusts and desires, leaving little left to give when they realize they need a Savior. God still uses them and forgives them, but their best years are gone forever.

I knew a man who ran from God for many, many years, and even mocked Christians. One day he laughed when someone told him they had become a Christian. He bragged about his sinful life and how ridiculous it was for anyone to give up his/her party life for Christianity. Late in his life, he finally gave his heart to the Lord, but he died in the same year. He spent all of his good years partying and had nothing left to give to God at the end. Did he make it to Heaven? More than likely, but the Bible says our works will be tried by fire!

With each passing day, we have one less opportunity to get it right. We have one less opportunity to fulfill our destiny. We have one less opportunity to help those around us in need.

Where are you today in your life? Have you truly surrendered all or will it cost you more of your life before you do? Do not wait until you are all spent. Get busy and become what you are meant to be!

APPLICATION:
1. At the present time, evaluate your commitment to God.
2. Be sure you are not holding on to your best, but giving all now.

PRAYER:
Lord, I make a conscience decision to give my all to you, today. Amen.

JANUARY 18
DO NOT BE A FOOL

Proverbs 26:11
"As a dog returneth to his vomit, so a fool returneth to his folly." (KJV)

Did you hear about the crook who robbed the same store three nights in a row? The first night, he fled the scene, but forgot his own wallet after pulling it out as if to buy something before pulling a gun and getting the cash from the register. The second night, he showed up just before closing, and this time, forgot and left his gun after grabbing the cash from the register. By the time he came in the third night to rob it, a police officer was posing as the clerk. He reached in his pocket to get his gun. When he realized he did not have it, he tried to run, and ran into the door! The officer came over and handcuffed him. When he awakened, he was in jail.

It seems when people get into the cycle of sin in their lives, they keep going over the same ground, even if it always ends up in failure! Even Christians get trapped into this deception. They often return to the "scene" of sin, imagining they will find something new. Yet, every time, they only make their lives worse!

There is an old saying: "Fool me once, shame on you. Fool me twice, shame on me!" There is much truth in this proverb. As someone wise once said, "If you don't like the results that you are getting in your life, then you are going to have to stop doing what you are doing!"

We must make every effort to leave behind the habits and patterns that once had us bound and torn. There is nothing there, but disappointment and heartache. May we slam every door of our past sinful lives and shut and lock it!

APPLICATION:
1. Be sure you are not leaving any doors of your past open!
2. Think of what you have been brought out of and stay clear of past stumbling blocks!

PRAYER:
Lord, I purposely examine myself, today, where my desires are concerned. If there is anything pulling me back towards my past, I ask you to help me shut the door forever! Amen.

JANUARY 19
YOU GUIDE ME WITH YOUR COUNSEL

Psalms 73:24
"You guide me with your counsel, and afterward you take me into glory." (NIV)

No matter where we eventually find our lives at, it is always a result of the counsel we have received in our lives, good or bad! The counsel we receive can make a difference in our life and transform us into what we need to be, or not be!

A Jewish man had a son who did not take his faith seriously. The father warned him if his attitude did not change, he would send the boy to the Holy Land to become a good Jew. The son continued to refuse, and true to his word, the father sent the son off to the Holy Land. Six months later, the son returned, and to his father's dismay, the boy had become a Christian. The father was dumbfounded, so he went to share his confusion with his best friend. His friend replied, "Funny you should mention. I, too, had trouble with my son. I sent him to the Holy Land to become a good Jew, and he, too, came back a Christian. What do we do?" After discussing it awhile, they decided to go seek counsel from the Rabbi. They said, "Rabbi, what do we do? We both have the same problem. We both had trouble with our sons. We both sent them to the Holy Land to become good Jews, and they both came back Christians." With an incredulous look, the Rabbi replied, "Funny you should mention. I, too, had trouble with my son. I, also, sent him to the Holy Land to become a good Jew, and he, too, came back a Christian. What do we do?" After discussing it for awhile, they decided to pray. They said, "God of Abraham, Isaac and Jacob, what do we do? We all three sent our sons to the Holy Land to become good Jews, and all three sons came back Christians." Then lightning flashed, thunder clapped, and a booming voice said, "Funny you should mention..."

APPLICATION:
1. Whose counsel are you following? Where are they leading you?
2. If you continue to follow them, what will you become?

PRAYER:
Lord, I make a quality decision to be guided by you, and you alone. If I am following anyone who will lead me astray, please reveal it to me and give me the strength to stop. Amen.

JANUARY 20
BE THE GIFT

Hebrews 11:4
"By faith Abel offered unto God a more excellent sacrifice than Cain, by which he obtained witness that he was righteous, God testifying of his gifts: and by it he being dead yet speaketh." (KJV)

What will be said about you when you are gone? God testified about Abel's gifts. Abel was undoubtedly taught by his father, Adam, the need to bring a blood offering to God. He understood he was a fallen man and brought a firstling to offer for sins. This offering of gratitude showed his unselfishness towards God. It took faith to offer the sacrifice with the belief God would accept him because of his offering (gifts).

Although he physically died, God testified for him before the courts of Heaven because of the faith he had. The "gifts" God was speaking of was not so much the offering of the firstling, but the gift of him (self). Do you realize your life is a gift? Your life was prepared before you were born. You were pre-engineered to make a difference. Exodus 4:18-19 tells us when Moses returned from the wilderness, he returned with his life! Then, he immediately gave his life as a gift to God to be used to deliver His people. He understood his life now was to rescue others.

It reminds me of this story: "Give me a sentence about a public servant," said a teacher to her students. A small boy wrote, "The fireman came down the ladder pregnant." The teacher took the lad aside to correct him. "Don't you know what pregnant means?" she asked. "Sure," said the young student confidently, "it means carrying a child."

Although God has great plans for our lives that will more than fulfill us, part of that plan is to be someone else's answer. When I visit the nursing home weekly, I always take the residents things they like to eat or drink. However, I must take more than food. I am to take the God in me! Be sure you are offering yourself to others. You have a gift inside you. Do not just bring a gift—be the gift!

APPLICATION:
　　1. Be sure you are "carrying" someone who needs you.
　　2. Offer yourself, today, to Him.

PRAYER:
Lord, I offer myself and my abilities to you, today. Use me! Amen.

JANUARY 21
WE NEED EACH OTHER

Romans 12:4-5
"For as we have many members in one body, and all members have not the same office: So we, being many, are one body in Christ, and every one members one of another." (KJV)

I have always had a firm belief every human being is intentionally created with certain flaws, requiring us to seek out the help of others. I have absolutely no skills or abilities when it comes to working on cars. I have had some really bad cars over the years, and every time one has broken down, I have had to pay for someone to repair it. I am thankful someone is able to do what I cannot do!

When you become a Christian, this is magnified even more. You are placed in a church body with mostly strangers and asked to somehow reach the world. It does not take long to realize this is an impossible task—without the assistance of others. It will take every member of the body doing what he/she does best, together, to get the job done!

This thought is probably best illustrated in the following way: You would not want to get on a plane and hear the pilot say, as you were taxing, "We do not have any flight attendants aboard today because they believe we do not think they are important. You probably also noticed there was no security check at the gate because the security guards did not think we would miss them. You probably did not notice, but the mechanics did not check the plane because no one ever gives them recognition. Also, we will not have any air traffic controllers to guide us to our destination because they feel too disconnected from the whole process. Have a nice flight!"

No one in his/her right mind believes the pilot can do it all! Be sure to give yourself to the cause of the Gospel. Your part is not just a duty, it is a necessity.

APPLICATION:
1. Be sure to offer your service to your church.
2. Be respectful to the others who serve as well.

PRAYER:
Lord, I am willing to take my place in your body. I am ready to work with those you have sent me to work along side of. Amen.

JANUARY 22
GOD WANTS US TO STRETCH
OUR BOUNDARIES

Isaiah 54:2-3

"Enlarge the place of thy tent, and let them stretch forth the curtains of thine habitations: spare not, lengthen thy cords, and strengthen thy stakes; For thou shalt break forth on the right hand and on the left..." (KJV)

When an elephant is a baby, if it is to be kept in captivity, it must first be chained to a steel rod that is deeply placed into the ground. This helps to establish its perimeters or boundaries. By the time it is grown, it can be kept at bay by merely tying a rope to its foot attached to a wooden stake. It will not break free, although it has increased in physical strength. The believer is much like this. We have certain boundaries we are tied to for much of our life and even after we are freed, we are fearful to go outside of our previous boundaries.

The longer we serve God, the more freedom we should be walking in. Too often, we let our senses pull us backwards instead of "growing up" into Him in all things.

As we grow in His Word, and develop a walk in the Spirit, He desires to lead us into places larger than we can dare to dream. Yet, too often, we forget we now possess the power to break out of the old patterns and boundaries, which formerly held us down.

Despite having some insight into some of the things God desires to accomplish through my life, I, too, find I am hesitant to attempt to "go for it." Somehow I "tie" myself down with doubt and unbelief, thus failing to walk in the authority He has given me. Every time I exercise my new "strength," I always seem to be able to do something I never before attempted or dreamed I could do.

Do not get bored or content with the same things of life. Go to God and He will help you break some new ground.

APPLICATION:
  1. Are you reaching for something new in your walk with God right now?
  2. Be willing to believe God for something bigger than your present state of being.

PRAYER:
Lord, I am willing to stretch my faith for the bigger things you want for my life. Give me a vision that can only be accomplished with your help. I trust you for it! Amen.

JANUARY 23
QUIT REPEATING YOUR LIFE

Deuteronomy 2:3
"Ye have compassed this mountain long enough; turn you northward." (KJV)

The children of Israel spent 40 long years in the wilderness. A whole generation died without seizing the moment and entering the Promised Land. All because they continuously complained and murmured about their plight and rebelled against God. They circled the same mountain, repeatedly, without getting out of the rut and never arrived at the destination God had pre-ordained for them. It is estimated the Israelites were as close as 11 miles from their Promised Land, but it still took over 40 years to cover the ground!

I watch many Christians do the same thing. God has ordained for them to enter the promises for their lives, but many years pass and they are still circling the same mountains of their lives! They are so very close to getting it right, but they never seem to reach their appointed destination.

It reminds me of the 90's film Bill Murray starred in, *Groundhog Day*. Bill Murray plays a selfish, self-centered weatherman named Phil Connors. He goes to Punxsutawney, Pennsylvania, to cover the story of their annual Groundhog Day festivities. He does not want to be there in the first place, but he ends up getting stuck living Groundhog Day over and over again. He is not allowed to move on to the next day until he finally uses the day to correct the wrongs around him in others, and thereby the things in his own life.

It is time for God's people to break out of the patterns, which have held them back for so long! It is time to get on the path leading us into the land that flows with milk and honey for our lives!

APPLICATION:
1. Assess the path you are on. Are you making progress or just circling the same ground?
2. Make a decision to shake off the hindrances holding you back.

PRAYER:
Lord, forgive me for my stubbornness and rebellion. It is my desire to enter into the things you have in mind for my life. Amen.

JANUARY 24
HE ALWAYS STANDS BY HIS COVENANT

Psalms 105:8
"...the commitment he made to a thousand generations." (NLT)

The well-known and respected Pastor, Dr. Charles Stanley, makes the following observation in his book, *Confronting Casual Christianity*: "Why do you suppose there are close to 100 million church members in America, yet they are not making more of a moral and spiritual impact? Why is it Sunday morning thousands of churches have more empty pews than full? Why is it that the average Sunday school in America has less than 66 people in attendance and that the average worship service has 84? Why is it only 50 percent of the number of any church membership can be expected to attend? If Christians really believe in real Heaven and real Hell, how can we be so silent? The answer to all of these questions is tragically simple. God's people have made a decision about Jesus, but have never made a commitment to Him."

Sometimes I wonder why so many believers are puzzled by the lack of impact the Church has on this crazy, confused world. I wonder why they are disappointed by the seemingly ineffectiveness of their prayer lives.

The answer lies within the lack of commitment in their lives. They always have an excuse for their lack of participation in church outreaches and functions. They just do not want to be committed to His work, but they always expect God to be committed to them.

Let us make a firm and lasting commitment to Him.

APPLICATION:
1. Decide today to re-establish your previous commitments to Him.
2. Look closely at the things you are passionate about and decide to at least match that intensity with your commitment to Him.

PRAYER:
Lord, search my heart and reveal the places I lack commitment to you in. Let me not be content with half-commitments, but only with a whole heart attitude! Amen.

JANUARY 25
IT IS WHAT YOU SAY AFTER YOU PRAY

Proverbs 18:21
"Death and life are in the power of the tongue: and they that love it shall eat the fruit thereof." (KJV)

How many times have you been around someone after they have prayed for something, then, heard them say something completely contrary to what they asked God to do? How many times has the person been you? As a pastor for well over a quarter of a century, I have observed this phenomenon many times. This kind of person almost always eventually becomes frustrated, and even angry, because things do not come to pass.

There is a spiritual law in motion. Not only is it important what we pray, but even more critical is what we say after we pray.

Our words will either support the prayers we have offered or they will undermine them. It is so important we continue to speak out what we desire. We should not be talking about our problems, but rather, talking to them!

I heard the world renowned minister, Jerry Savelle, preach a powerful message entitled: *What You Must Do Between the Amen and the There It Is!* He pointed out the most critical time of our lives comes after we pray. It is so important our words line up with our prayers. We nullify so many answers by confessing something contrary to what we have said is our will in our requests.

When we say something opposite of what we have prayed for, we are actually admitting we really did not believe our prayers would come to pass. This is something that has plagued Christians for centuries. It has been a source of great frustration for so long it has caused the body of Christ to abandon a vibrant prayer life. Remember, it is what you say after you pray that makes the difference!

APPLICATION:
1. Make an honest assessment of what you are saying regarding what you are praying about.
2. Change your confession now! Ask God to correct any words you speak undermining your prayers.

PRAYER:
Lord, if I speak anything not supportive to my prayers, correct me on the spot! Remind me of what I have prayed about in my spirit that I will not negate my own prayer. Amen.

JANUARY 26
WATCH FOR THE SNARES

Proverbs 6:2
"... you have been trapped by what you said, ensnared by the words of your mouth." (NIV)

How important are your words? They affect every part of your life. Your words have painted the landscape of the life you have lived. Your words are painting the map of the road you are traveling on right now. Most importantly, your words will paint the landscape of your future.

Your words aim you towards your destiny. Your words determine your harvest. Yet, at the same time, they also can ensnare you and trap you, thereby keeping you from God's best for your life.

I knew a young man who seemingly had everything going for him. He had a great paying job. He had a beautiful young lady whom he was engaged to. Everything pointed towards him living a long and totally happy life. However, every time I was around him, somewhere in his conversation, he would say, "I probably won't live much past 30."

Just after his 30th birthday, he was out on a lake one day, enjoying a beautiful summer day. He decided to jump in the water to cool off, and he never resurfaced. He drowned.

When I heard the tragic news, the first thing that entered my mind was his words, "I probably won't live past 30." He was snared with the words of his own mouth.

Snares seem to catch their prey suddenly, but in reality, they usually have been strategically positioned in a place, and left there for a time, before they accomplish their mission.

It is the same way with our words. It may not seem like they matter, but with each passing day, they are setting you up to be "caught," and snared by them.

Be sure to pay attention to what you say before the trap is sprung on you!

APPLICATION:
1. Be sure to never say anything that is not your will.
2. Repent of anything you have said contrary to God's plan for your life.

PRAYER:
Lord, please cause any words I have spoken against your will to fall to the ground! Amen.

JANUARY 27
DO NOT LET YOUR CONFLICTS
BECOME OFFENCES

Luke 17:1
"...it is impossible but offences will come..." (KJV)

On one of several occasions, in which I was led to preach on being offended, I ran across the following definition: Offence – 1. stumbling block, the movable stick or trigger of a trap, a trap stick, snare, 2. any impediment placed in the way and causing one to stumble or fall; i.e. a rock which is a cause of stumbling; a person or thing whereby a person is drawn into error or sin.

Too often, we let our conflicts with people turn into offences and thereby cloud our judgment. The following illustration points this out: Rodolphe Kreutzer was a famous violinist and composer. Beethoven dedicated his great sonata for a violin and piano, Opus 47, the sonata universally known as the Kreutzer Sonata, to him. It was only an accident and a whim of the composer's, which gave Kreutzer this celebrity. Beethoven originally planned to name Opus 47 after his good friend, George Bridgetower. However, Beethoven and Bridgetower quarreled over a very common subject, a young lady. As a result, the friendship was broken off and Bridgetower's name was erased from the title page and replaced with Kreutzer's name. However, the peculiar part is Beethoven is said to have only known Kreutzer slightly, and more than that, Beethoven had never physically met him! (Encyclopedia of 15,000 Illustrations, Hughes, pp. 179-192. Naming of the Kreutzer Sonata.)

Too often, we allow petty disagreements to become larger than they should ever be. We do not know how to disagree, but still maintain harmony. Conflicts should ultimately strengthen our relationships, not destroy them!

We should never practice spite, but we should practice forgiveness! May we keep ourselves from offences, no matter what the conflicts are.

APPLICATION:
1. Ask yourself: "Have I truthfully asked God how to deal with the conflict I am having with someone?"
2. We cannot be offended in Him! (John 16:1)
3. Offence leads to betrayal. (Matthew 24:9-10)

PRAYER:
Lord, forgive me for being so easily offended. Amen.

JANUARY 28
DETERMINATION LEADS YOU TO YOUR DESTINATION

Joshua 1:9
"Remember that I have commanded you to be determined and confident! Do not be afraid or discouraged, for I, the LORD your God, am with you wherever you go." (TEV)

The famous boxer, Smokin' Joe Frazier, became heavyweight champion of the world with a left hook to the jaw of Muhammad Ali. When Frazier was a beginning boxer, he was an overweight kid and not a very good prospect at all. Most respected trainers did not give him much hope to be a good fighter, but one man saw something in Joe that caught his eye. He noticed how determined Joe was to become a good fighter and how powerful his left arm was. When he asked Joe why he was so strong in his left arm, Joe answered, "When I was very young, my father lost his left arm in a farming accident. I had to quit school to help him. I stood at his left side and became his left arm. Whatever he needed to do with is left hand, I did it. Over time, my left arm became super strong because of that!"

The very word determination suggests that the outcome of something is relative to the will and efforts preceding. If a person truly decides to do something, and do it well, then puts forth the necessary effort, it will determine his/her success.

It is often said how much determination a person has determines how far and high they will go. We should be the most determined people on the earth as God's people!

Stop making excuses and letting the hindrances of your life determine your destiny. Instead, become more determined than ever to follow the plan God has just for you.

APPLICATION:
1. Are you truly determined to be the best at what you do?
2. Are you truly putting forth the effort necessary to be the best?
3. Make adjustments now to develop into the best you can be!

PRAYER:
Lord, search my heart and reveal to me the things I must change to become the best I can be. Amen.

JANUARY 29
GET OUT OF THE BUILDING

Proverbs 11:30
"The fruit of the righteous is a tree of life; and he that winneth souls is wise."
(KJV)

On September 11, 2001, every person in America, and around the world, watched in horror as the Twin Towers fell to the ground. It was not the buildings falling that brought tears and shock to us; it was the contents—as many as 50,000 people had entered the buildings that fateful morning. However, 2,799 did not make it out.

One lady who made it out alive, Elia Zedeno, was on the 73rd floor of Tower One. She said, "I heard a booming explosion and felt the building actually lurch to the south, as if it might topple." You would expect her first instinct was to flee, but she actually did the opposite. "What I really wanted was for someone to scream back, 'Everything is ok! Don't worry. It's in your head.'" Fortunately for Elia, one of her colleagues responded differently. "The answer I got was another co-worker screaming, 'Get out of the building!'" she remembers now. Years later, she still thinks about that command. "My question is, 'What would I have done if the person had said nothing?'"

This world is going to come to an end. It will be when it is least expected. "The building is on fire!" and God's Word gives us an evacuation plan! It is not time to be quiet! We must be bold, and show others the way. People's lives are on the line.

Just like the fire drills we had in school, we likely never really had to face an actual emergency. Yet, the day is fast approaching when the trumpet will sound and the Lord will appear from Heaven with the trumpet of God sounding the alarm!

It is time for us to shout, "The building's on fire! This is not a drill! Get out of the building of sin! It's collapsing!" Let us point them to the only way out—Jesus.

APPLICATION:
1. Are you witnessing to those you come in contact with?
2. Make it your assignment to tell at least one person every day about the "fire escape provided through salvation."

PRAYER:
Lord, open doors of opportunity for me to witness. Give me the boldness I need to speak your Word with love and conviction. Amen.

JANUARY 30
THE BELIEVER'S SIXTH SENSE

Hebrews 11:1
"Now faith is the substance of things hoped for, the evidence of things not seen."
(KJV)

Dr. Martin Luther King, Jr. said, "Take the first step in faith. You don't have to see the whole staircase, just take the first step."

I can remember many times in my life when everything pointed towards making a particular decision, but something on the inside of me put me in check and I decided to follow my faith instead. Never on any of those occasions was I disappointed with the outcome.

One instance that stands out took place when our congregation was looking for a building to move into. We had outgrown our first building, but were not ready to build yet. We looked at dozens of possible locations, but none really resonated until we looked at the last location. It was an abandoned jail headquarters. It had been vacant for over two years. It was dilapidated, dingy and badly decayed.

After we took the tour, I left totally unimpressed. I told my wife later that night, "That is one place I will not have to pray about!" Needless to say, God dealt with me about it that night. The next day, I notified the realtor that we wanted the building. That was the complete opposite of what I saw or perceived to be the right decision.

The lease payment was going to be five times that of our present building at the time. How would we be able to pay it when we had struggled so much making it where we were?

I knew it would be a leap of faith, but I knew God wanted us to have that building. Something inside of me overrode my natural senses. It was the best decision, up until that time, that I ever made as a pastor. We grew from 70 to 1,200 people! Thank God for the sixth sense!

APPLICATION:
　　1. Are you making decisions according to your senses?
　　2. Use your sixth sense to help guide you.

PRAYER:
Lord, help me to sharpen my sixth sense. I desire to walk by faith and not by sight! Amen.

JANUARY 31
FAITHFULNESS BRINGS PROMOTION

Proverbs 28:20
"A faithful man shall abound with blessings..." (KJV)

Of all of the qualities that produce God's favor, faithfulness stands alone. God measures His people not by perfect actions, but by persistent behavior! When Joshua was appointed by God to succeed Moses, it was not his courage that stood out. God had to immediately address his lack of courage. It was not his birthright. He was not a priest. It was not his direct relationship with Jehovah God. It was Joshua's faithfulness. He was faithful to Moses. He was called his minister or servant. When the children of Israel broke ranks and began to party while Moses was on Mt. Sinai with God, Joshua held his post. He was close enough to the bottom of the mountain to hear the sounds of revelry. He was also close enough to the top to see the glory cloud. Despite the pull of the sounds of the people, he remained faithful! You cannot have real Bible faith if you, yourself, are not faithful.

You cannot separate faith and faithfulness. Faithfulness will help you overcome all of your shortcomings and your deficiencies. Joshua had already proven he possessed faith when he and Caleb went to Canaan and spied out the land. He refused to be intimidated by the giants there. He used his faith to overcome, thus leading to his eventual promotion. Most would have thought Aaron or Hur would have taken Moses' place, but their unfaithfulness disqualified them!

When we come to the end of our earthly journey, may we hear him say, "Well done good and faithful servant!" No matter what you do, be faithful. If you are, then promotion will certainly come your way.

APPLICATION:
1. Are you being faithful over the things God has given you to be faithful over?
2. Be sure to use your faith, even when your senses suggest failure!

PRAYER:
Lord, strengthen me so that I might be found faithful! Amen.

FEBRUARY 1
GET GOOD COUNSEL

Psalms 16:7
"I will bless the LORD, who hath given me counsel: my reins also instruct me in the night seasons." (KJV)

A pastor by the name of James May recited the following: "I read a short story once where a couple had left their home to go on a trip from New York City's Grand Central Station to the Main Terminal in Philadelphia, Pennsylvania, and back. Their journey was by train in the early days of America. When they reached Grand Central Station, the crowds were tremendous with people going in every direction and loudspeakers constantly announcing the departure and arrival of trains to and from many destinations. It was all so confusing to this couple who had not traveled much before. Soon the wife began to give advice to her husband, 'Why don't you ask that man which way we should go? He seems to be pretty knowledgeable.' As any husband knows, we hate to ask anyone for directions. We would rather find it for ourselves than to appear ignorant. The man decided right then and there to cure his wife of this once and for all, so that is just what he did.

Each time they would appear to be lost, he would take his wife's advice and ask for directions, and each time he would follow those directions to the letter. Soon, they were on the wrong trains, going to cities that were far from Philadelphia. This went on for quite some time until they found themselves in the city of Calcutta, India. It was then the wife decided to quit giving instructions and told her husband to use his own judgment. 'Use your own judgment,' she said, 'I just want to go home.' Soon they were on a steamer and entering New York Harbor."

So, what is the point? Be careful when you chart the course of your life based on people's advice. Regardless of their good intentions, you owe it to yourself to seek other counsel when their counsel has constantly failed you.

APPLICATION:
    1. Carefully consider who you are receiving counsel from.
    2. Be sure to always ask God first for guidance!

PRAYER:
Lord, please guide me and lead me into your perfect will. Amen.

FEBRUARY 2
LIVE FOR TODAY

II Corinthians 6:2
"For he saith, I have heard thee in a time accepted, and in the day of salvation have I succoured thee: behold, now is the accepted time; behold, now is the day of salvation." (KJV)

Both the hummingbird and the vulture fly over our nation's deserts. The only thing the vultures see is rotting meat because that is what they look for. They thrive on that diet. The hummingbirds ignore the smelly flesh of dead animals. Instead, they look for the colorful blossoms of desert plants. The vultures live on what was. They live on the past. They fill themselves with what is dead and gone. Contrastingly, hummingbirds live on what is. They seek new life. They fill themselves with freshness and ongoing life. Each bird finds what it is looking for.

The truth is we generally get what we look for in life. If we spend our time looking back to where we have been or trying to resurrect things that have died, we will fail to see what is prepared for us today. What we have left behind is gone. Even if we could go back and change some things, it still might not make a difference anyway.

Life is about new seasons and new challenges. It is about new horizons and adventures. If we get too caught up in yesterday, we will fail to do the things today, which are meant to take us into our destiny.

I have found every time I let go of something of the past, God always brings something new and better. Twice a year, I go through my closet and give away suits, shirts and ties to congregation members in need. Every time I do it, I have had a new suit, shirt and tie bought for me!

When we awakened this morning, God already had some things preordered for us. We must be determined not to waste the opportunities before us. It is important for us to seize the moment and walk in this present day!

APPLICATION:
1. What are you presently feeding on? Does it promote God's plan for you or hinder it?
2. What are you looking for in your life today? Be sure it is what you really desire.

PRAYER:
Lord, search my heart and show me the life you have in mind for me today, so I might walk in it! Amen.

FEBRUARY 3
STAYING IN COVENANT

Mark 14:3, 10

"...as he sat at meat, there came a woman having an alabaster box of ointment of spikenard very precious; and she brake the box, and poured it on his head... And Judas Iscariot, one of the twelve, went unto the chief priests, to betray him unto them." (KJV)

Covenant and loyalty are foreign words to our culture. A covenant is a solemn pledge entered into that constitutes full support of the parties involved at all times.

The Bible is a book of covenants God has entered into with man. Yet, many times, man was disloyal to the covenant because of his greed and selfishness.

Judas became jealous of the display of affection shown to Jesus. He had a heart problem, with money at the root of it.

The Devil craftily, fully divided Judas from Jesus. He used his own personal desires of power and greed to point out what seemed to be inconsistencies in Jesus' life, and Satan entered his heart. He was "appalled" when Jesus allowed the alabaster box to be poured over him and the money not "given" to the poor. His offense cost him his future and his life!

Loyalty to a cause or a person means to be completely committed to the point no division is possible by anyone for any reason. It is personal between the parties. Even if there is a question, it is worked out between the parties only. It cuts much deeper than a contract. A contract has a time limit on it. Covenants are meant to be perpetual. Before we cut people out of our lives, we must consider the entire body of someone's life before we let ourselves be cut off from them.

APPLICATION:
1. Evaluate the motives inside of you concerning the relationships you are presently in.
2. Ponder what it would take for you to be willing to cancel that relationship.

PRAYER:
Lord, please help me put the right value on my relationships and not let outside circumstances and influences determine my commitment to them. Amen.

FEBRUARY 4
THE WORLD IS WAITING FOR YOU

Mark 16:15
"He said to them, 'Go into all the world and preach the good news to all creation.'" (NIV)

Ministry is unlimited in nature. There are countless opportunities all around us. People everywhere are hurting. People everywhere are searching. The fields are ready to harvest. Our predecessors have laid the groundwork for us. The world has never needed the Gospel more than now. You and I, as disciples, have an enormous task, but also an enormous opportunity. Arthur Preston said, "The church has many tasks, but only one mission!" The Son of God is still the same. He is the Savior! He is coming again, like He promised.

I heard a story of a mother who was waiting at a train station for her son, who had been to war for several years. She did not have any contact with him during that time. No letters, no phone calls, nothing to even verify if he was still alive. However, someone told her he would be on a particular train. The train rolled into the station. Person after person got off and walked by the little gray haired woman. Finally, the conductor got off. The woman's countenance dropped. "He must have been killed and I was not notified," she thought. Then, the conductor stopped in front of her and whispered, "Mom, it is me!" The Army postmaster responsible for mailing his letters misplaced them and never mailed them to her. She was so overwhelmed with joy when she realized this was her son. He had been released from war and joined the railway to help transport other soldiers home!

The Son of God is still coming back. We must be sure we deliver the letters He gave us to deliver for Him to a lost and dying world.

APPLICATION:
1. Ask yourself, do you deliver His letter of love to those around you?
2. Have you placed the spreading of the Gospel on your task list?

PRAYER:
Lord, stir up the desire in my heart to be a carrier of your Gospel. May every person I come into contact with be notified through me! Amen.

FEBRUARY 5
DO NOT BE PARALYZED

Psalms 118:6
"The Lord is on my side, I will not fear: what can man do unto me?" (KJV)

John Madden, former great football coach of the Oakland Raiders and retired expert football commentator, always crisscrossed the country many times each fall in a customized bus because he was afraid of flying. He logged over a million miles and countless hours on the road, which could have been greatly minimized if not for the paralyzing effect of fear.

A few years ago, one first-round draft choice in the NBA quickly ended his career with an unconditional release by his team due to his paralyzing fear of flying. What could have been a potentially brilliant career was cut short because of the trepidation of fear. All he had dreamed and worked so hard for was stopped cold because he could not seem to get over his fear of flying!

The truth is fear has a paralyzing effect on you. It will stop you from moving with God's plan. It steals away the dream God has placed in your heart. It convinces you something adverse is inevitable. It prevents you from walking in faith.

In the Garden of Eden, it was fear that caused Adam and Eve to hide from the presence of God. It was fear that caused Peter to sink when he was walking to Jesus on the water. It was fear that caused Job to suffer the loss of his children. Job 2:24 says, *"The thing I greatly feared is come upon me."* (KJV)

God's Word is the answer to anything bringing fear into your heart. Make sure you always refer to the Word of God and apply it to the things causing you fear. For instance, if you are afraid of a doctor's report, immediately speak I Peter 2:24 and Matthew 8:16-17. You will soon feel the power of God being released over your life.

Faith is the answer for fear! It neutralizes its effect and brings peace! Remember: God is on your side!

APPLICATION:
1. Be sure fear does not prevent you from doing what you need to do.
2. Apply God's Word to your fears.

PRAYER:
Lord, I will not fear. Your Word is alive and more powerful than anything troubling me. Amen.

FEBRUARY 6
STAY ON TRACK

Galatians 5:7
"You were running a good race. Who cut in on you and kept you from obeying the truth?" (NIV)

In a past NCAA cross-country championship held in Riverside, California, 123 of the 128 runners missed a turn, and got off track. One competitor, Mike Delcavo, stayed on the 10,000 meter course and began waving for fellow runners to follow him. Delcavo was able to convince only four other runners to go with him. Asked what his competitors thought of his mid-race decision not to follow the crowd, Delcavo responded, "They thought it was funny that I went the right way." Delcavo was the one who ran correctly.

I have observed during the years as a pastor, many good people running the race who became distracted or sidetracked. They let others who were weak or offended influence them. Before they knew it, they were out of the race. These were leaders in the race, people everyone expected to finish. People who were seemingly way out in front of the others, somehow, somewhere along the way became side tracked or tripped up and were disqualified.

I have also seen those who stayed on track and did not let any kind of adversity stop them. Although they were weak and bruised at times from the battle, they did not let anything or anyone keep them from continuing towards the finish line. They even helped others along the way, who were also wavering make it to the finish line.

As we go along in our Christian lives, there will be numerous opportunities to quit. People will disappoint us. Circumstances will become, at times, unbearable. There will be moments when turning back or dropping out will seem like the only option. We must continue to run the course of our lives with patience and persistence. Yet, we have the responsibility of staying on course because it not only affects our lives, but those who are behind us!

APPLICATION:
1. Evaluate the people you are following. Are they leading you in the right or wrong direction?
2. Are you leading your followers in the right or wrong direction?

PRAYER:
Lord, show me, today, the right path to take. If I am on the wrong track, forgive me and restore me to the place I should be. Amen.

FEBRUARY 7
FORGIVE AND LIVE

Proverbs 17:9
*"If you want people to like you, forgive them when they wrong you.
Remembering wrongs can break up a friendship."* (TEV)

Recently, a survey was conducted of 200 married adults regarding forgiveness. The researchers were wondering how one's ability to forgive others would affect their marital satisfaction and personal well-being. The results were astounding! This research suggests a large correlation between marriage satisfaction and forgiveness. In fact, it appears as much as one-third of marriage satisfaction is related to forgiveness.

Not only does the inability to forgive negatively impact the marriage relationship, but also significantly contributes to personal, emotional distress. As forgiveness ability increased, individuals reported fewer symptoms of depression, anxiety and fatigue.

This survey reveals something about forgiveness often overlooked. When we forgive someone, we are actually doing ourselves a favor.

Mahatma Gandhi said, "Forgiveness doesn't make the other person right, it makes you free." Stormie Omartian, author and wife of famous music producer, Michael Omartian, said this about forgiveness: "The weak can never forgive. Forgiveness is the attribute of the strong."

The one obstacle standing in the way of your freedom is most often the unwillingness to forgive. We somehow convince ourselves we have a right to hold a grudge or to be bitter towards someone, even someone as close as a spouse.

Reach down within your spirit, today, and find the strength to forgive. Something very powerful will begin to happen. When you forgive the other person and release them, you will begin to really live!

APPLICATION:
1. Make a decision, now, to release those who have hurt you.
2. Offer forgiveness to them, if possible.

PRAYER:
Lord, I make a decision to forgive all of those who have hurt me. By faith, I forgive them and receive my own forgiveness and healing. I am ready to truly live! Amen.

FEBRUARY 8
LOOK AT YOURSELF FIRST

Matthew 7:3
"And why beholdest thou the mote that is in thy brother's eye, but considerest not the beam that is in thine own eye?" (KJV)

I read a funny story about a serviceman who once wrote about a moment of comedy he had witnessed in the army. It happened during a company inspection at the Redstone Arsenal in Alabama. The inspection was being conducted by a full bird colonel. Everything had gone routinely until the esteemed officer came to a particular soldier. He stopped and gazed intently at him, looking up and down at him with eyes of steel. He then blasted forth forcefully, "Button up that pocket, soldier!" The soldier was mortified, and managed to finally reply, "Right now, sir?" "Of course, this moment!" the colonel snapped. Then to the shock and amazement of all present, the somewhat shaken soldier carefully reached out and buttoned the flap on the colonel's shirt pocket. The officer had been quick to notice the young soldier's uniform faux pas, but had not even taken notice of his own!

The Bible very distinctly warns us to be slow to see and pronounce the short-comings and flaws of those around us. Every time we do, we open up a door that, too often, invites even sharper criticism of our own selves! The Bible says the same judgment we impose on others will be used to judge us! If we are sharp and harsh to judge others, then we better be in a position to be judged just as sharply and harshly!

We should be sure to take an honest inventory of our own actions before we rush to point out the flaws in the lives of those around us. Somehow, when we look at ourselves first, it makes the weaknesses of others around us not seem as bad as we first believed!

Be sure to look at yourself carefully before you take on the role of the judge of others.

APPLICATION:
1. If you are presently judging anyone around you, turn them over to God instead, and look more closely at your own mistakes.
2. Instead of picking at the blemishes of others, point to what God has done through you, despite your own flaws!

PRAYER:
Lord, I choose to judge myself that I will not be judged! Amen.

FEBRUARY 9
DO YOU REALLY TRUST HIM?

Proverbs 3:9-10
"Honor the LORD by making him an offering from the best of all that your land produces. If you do, your barns will be filled with grain, and you will have too much wine to store it all." (TEV)

I heard a story of a missionary in Africa who received a knock on his hut's door one afternoon. He opened the door and saw a native boy holding a large fish in his hands. The boy said, "Reverend, you taught us what tithing is, so here. I have brought you my tithe." As the missionary gratefully took the fish, he questioned the boy, "If this is your tithe, where are your other nine fish?" The boy beamed and said, "Oh, they are still back in the river. I am going back to catch them now." Wow! What an expression of true faith and trust in God's Word!

In the passage of Proverbs shown above, honor means to give weight and importance to God. How? By giving Him your first fruits. It brings a twofold blessing with it. It brings the blessing on what you already have and what you are producing!

The word honor is a word that is often connected to money in the Bible. When it says the elder (poimen - pastor) is worthy of double honor, that word speaks specifically of money. (I Timothy 5:17)

When we give to God our first, and our best, it opens doors of financial possibilities that are far beyond our natural ability. Then, the "streams" will yield to us the increase. Because we have presented our best, we will harvest the very best possible!

This kind of trust places God in a position of responsibility to us, to meet every need in our lives. This is what trust and belief in God does; it transfers the responsibility of our success off our shoulders solely and places it on the shoulders of God's promises for our lives.

The question is not can or will God take care of the needs of His people, but rather will His people really trust and believe in Him enough to honor Him with their resources?

APPLICATION:
  1. Be sure you are not giving God "leftovers."
  2. Remember tithing is a door opener.

PRAYER:
Lord, forgive me for not offering you the first and the best. As you bring increase into my life, I will honor you. Amen.

FEBRUARY 10
GOD IS GOOD—ALL THE TIME

Exodus 34:6
"And the LORD passed by before him, and proclaimed, The LORD, The LORD
God, merciful and gracious, longsuffering, and abundant in
goodness and truth," (KJV)

What is goodness? Goodness is not a passive quality. It is the deliberate act of bringing into another's presence something that is lacking. It brings a definite improvement to what already exists.

God is not sometimes merciful, and sometimes just. He is infinitely merciful and just! God is infinitely and unchangeably good at all times.

Haddon Robinson says it best, "With Him the calf is always the fatted calf; the robe is always the best robe; the joy is always unspeakable; and the peace passes understanding. There is no grudging in God's goodness. He does not measure His goodness by drops like a druggist filling a prescription. It comes upon in floods. If only we recognize the lavish abundance of His gifts, what a difference it would make in our lives!"

He brings His goodness into the hardest and most needed moments of our lives. When everything around us is in disarray, everything is dark, everything is in extreme adversity, He comes on the scene with His goodness. He rescues us and reminds us His goodness is greater than any bad thing that may come against us!

We, too, should display His nature to those around us needing it most. Ralph Waldo Emerson wrote in his *Journals*, "It doesn't take great stature, prominence or finances to be great—It is very hard to be simple enough to be good!"

God is this way with us. He is ultimately powerful, ultimately supreme, yet, He understands that what we need Him to be most of all is good!

APPLICATION:
1. Thank God, today, for the goodness He has shown you this week.
2. Adjust your response to those around you in relationship to His goodness towards you.

PRAYER:
Lord, thank you, today, for the many times you have given me your goodness in times of hardships. Help me to show your goodness to others. Amen.

FEBRUARY 11
DO NOT BE FOOLED AGAIN

Proverbs 4:14-15
"Enter not into the path of the wicked, and go not in the way of evil men. Avoid it, pass not by it, turn from it, and pass away." (KJV)

Popular author, Isaac Asimov, shared his story of the first, and only, time he gambled in his life. Here is his true story:

"Shortly after I married, my wife left town to visit her folks. I was at loose ends, and I was lured into a poker game with the boys. When it was all over, my conscience smote me, for I had been brought up by a puritanical father to eschew gambling in all its forms (and I had never rebelled). All I could do was confess.

On my next trip home, I said with all the casualness I could manage, 'I played a game of poker with the boys, Papa, for money.' My father stared at me in astonishment and said, 'How did you make out?' I said, 'I lost 15 cents.'

He said, 'Thank goodness. You could have won 15 cents!'

He was probably right. Winning the first time out might have hooked me. As it was, I never played poker again!"

Sin has a sinister hook in it. It promises much and delivers little, but heartache. It often gives in the beginning, but always takes away, often all, in the end.

My good friend, and one of my spiritual fathers, the late, great man of God, Dr. Roy Hicks, had a saying he quoted often: "Sin will take you further than you want to go, keep you longer than you want to stay and make you pay more than you are able to pay!" He is right!

APPLICATION:
1. Lay down anything you are doing that will eventually lead you astray.
2. No matter what your weaknesses may be, avoid the things, people and places that cause you to stumble.

PRAYER:
Lord, forgive me for taking part in the things which bring me defeat and hurt. Strengthen my inner self that I might not give into sin's appeal. Amen.

FEBRUARY 12
GOD'S GRACE PERIOD

Romans 5:20-21

"The law was added so that the trespass might increase. But where sin increased, grace increased all the more, so that, just as sin reigned in death, so also grace might reign through righteousness to bring eternal life through Jesus Christ our Lord." (NIV)

My wife and I have carried a life insurance policy on her mother for over 15 years. I have always kept the premiums up to date and usually pay in advance. Recently, there was a mix-up. Somehow, the bill was misplaced. Then, one day I received a letter from the insurance company stating it had lapsed. I was shocked! At her age, it would have been nearly impossible to get her coverage again. Even if we could have, it would have been unaffordable. I immediately contacted the company to inquire if anything could be done to reinstate the policy. I knew it was my fault.

The representative responded with a letter explaining an error on their part in their prior correspondence. It had not lapsed. Instead, it had gone into a grace period. There was still time to rectify the policy, which we did!

We may not realize it, but we are so often in God's grace period. Are we guilty? Yes. Have we been negligent with our actions and deeds? Yes. However, He has been covering us with His grace.

Now, we should realize grace is not indefinite. There is a time of retribution if no action is eventually taken. We must repent and return to Him. It is not meant to be abused or tread under by careless and intentional acts of sin. There is a time for us to take responsibility for our actions and change. Thank God for His grace period until we do!

APPLICATION:
1. If you have been in a grace period over a sin lately, make the adjustments now and repent.
2. Do not sin without repentance! Give all of your life over to God, today!

PRAYER:
Lord, thank you for the many "grace periods" you have given me over the course of my life. Show me where I am over-extending your grace and give me the courage to repent. Amen.

FEBRUARY 13
CARRY SOMEONE

Mark 2:9-12

"Whether it is easier to say to the sick of palsy, Thy sins be forgiven thee; or to say, Arise, and take up thy bed, and walk? But that ye may know that the Son of man hath power on earth to forgive sins, (he saith to the sick of palsy,) I say unto thee, Arise, and take up thy bed, and go thy way into thine house. And immediately, he arose, took up the bed, and went forth before them all; insomuch that they were all amazed, and glorified God, saying, We never saw it on this fashion." (KJV)

At first glance of this story in the Bible, the healing seems to be the real story. Some might say the forgiveness of sins is the central thought. Both of these are good points, but, perhaps the most overlooked point is the friends who brought this young man to Jesus. They arrived and found a packed house, so they climbed to the roof. When they began to pull the roof off, they risked the wrath of those gathered inside. Still, they lowered the lame man down to Jesus.

Notice how without these good friends and their determination, this man would have remained disabled, despite Jesus being in his area!

Dr. J. Wilbur Chapman, famous evangelist, said the New Testament records tales of 40 people, each suffering from the same disease, who were healed by Jesus. Of this number, 34 were either brought to Jesus by friends, or He was taken to them. In only six cases out of 40, did the sufferers find the way to Jesus without assistance. Of the vast number of people who find their way to Jesus today, most of them reach Him because of their friends' concern for the welfare of their souls!

Look closely around you. There are lame people everywhere who have been crippled by the circumstances of life. Take the time to take them to the Healer!

APPLICATION:
   1. Take notice of those around you who need to be made whole.
   2. Be willing to take the time and make the effort to get them to Jesus.

PRAYER:
Lord, give me eyes to see and a heart to care for those I am around who are in need of what you have for them. Amen.

FEBRUARY 14
YOU ARE LOVED

Isaiah 49:16

"Behold, I have graven thee upon the palms of my hands;" (KJV)

Have you ever considered the depth of love God has for you? He has such a deep, undying love for you He carries the scars, which He received on the cross for you, into eternity.

After Jesus was raised from the dead, he told Thomas to put his fingers in the holes in the palms of His hands.

Every time Jesus stretches out His hands, they reflect the love He has for you! Every time He summons for the angels, His love for you is reflected. Every time He reaches for the things of Heaven around Him, His love for you is reflected!

I read a story about a young man who was very much in love with the girl of his dreams. He finally popped the question, but she turned him down. He was devastated! Yet, he persisted. Time passed and finally she moved away from him and left him broken-hearted. Every week, he wrote her at least one love letter, asking her to marry him. Forty years later, and hundreds of letters later, he received the first response from her since that fateful night. She finally said, "Yes!" Although they were well into their 60's, they were married and lived out the remainder of their lives very happily together!

It is the same way with us. All of our lives, God slips love letters under the door of our lives, until finally, we say, "Yes!" It is like the popular Christian recording artist, Michael W. Smith, sang in one of his many hit songs: "There may be a lot of things that you are not, but you are not unloved!"

No matter what is going on in your life, remember, you are loved!

APPLICATION:
1. Remember, today and always, you are truly loved by the Creator!
2. Do not buy into the idea your life is without meaning.
3. The next time you feel you are not loved, picture in your heart the scars of the love remaining on His hands because of His love for you.

PRAYER:

Lord, thank you so much for loving me throughout my life until I finally said, "Yes!" Amen.

FEBRUARY 15
HE IS THE HEALER

Hebrews 13:8
"Jesus Christ, the same, yesterday, today and forever." (KJV)

If you were to ask most any protestant believer if they believe Jesus Christ still saves today, they would say emphatically, "Yes!" They understand He has not changed. However, if you ask them if He still heals today, many would reply: "You never know what God will do!" "If it's not God's will...," or even, "That was for Biblical times." Yet, if He is the same today as He was yesterday, and He saved yesterday, and He still saves today, then He must still heal today because He does not change! This is not about being denominationally correct. It is about being spiritually correct. I have discovered over the years, much of what many Christians believe is based on their experiences and not on the Word of God.

Too often, the Word of God is the last place referenced when God's people get sick. We rely heavily on doctors and medicine to bring our healing. Thank God for modern medicine. God absolutely uses these methods to bring us help. However, too often, we do not even consult God or His Word for our lives along with the help physicians offer.

The truth is at some point in our lives, it is possible medicine alone will not be the answer. At those times, it is critical we know who our healer is and have confidence it is His will to heal our physical bodies, just as He always did when He was here on the earth. In this present world of advanced medicine and medical technology, it is too easy to reach for the doctor's number instead of the Bible. He is still the great physician! He is still Jehovah Rapha! He is the same today as He was yesterday!

May we reconsider where our first place of reference is and remember He said, "I am the Lord God that healeth thee!"

APPLICATION:
1. If you are presently suffering from a bodily affliction, speak the Word of God over your ailment, in addition to any medical treatment you may be under.
2. Begin to speak the Word over your body every day, even when you are well, and confess Jesus is your healer!

PRAYER:
Lord, I believe that by your stripes, I am healed. Forgive me for not calling on you first when I am feeling ill. Amen

FEBRUARY 16
HE MADE IT

Luke 3:22
"And the Holy Ghost descended in a bodily shape like a dove upon him, and a voice came from Heaven, which said, Thou art my beloved Son; in thee I am well pleased." (KJV)

In Gordon Brownville's, *Symbols of the Holy Spirit*, he recites a story about Roald Amundsen, the great Norwegian explorer. Amundsen was the first to discover the magnetic meridian of the North Pole and to discover the South Pole. Amundsen, on one of his trips, took a homing pigeon with him. When he finally reached the top of the world, he opened the bird's cage and set it free.

Imagine what Amundsen's wife must have felt, back in Norway, when she looked up from the porch of her home and saw the pigeon circling in the sky above. She must have shouted, "I know He's alive! I know my husband is still alive!"

After Jesus was raised from the dead, and later returned to Heaven, He promised the disciples the sure sign He made it to Heaven would be the Holy Spirit. As a result, just 10 days after his ascension, the Holy Spirit came upon those gathered in the upper room. (Acts 2) The most important thing about this moment was not that His people received the Holy Spirit, but it signaled to all mankind He is alive! Our Savior is alive!

The disciples had clung to His promise to send them the Holy Spirit. He fulfilled His promise. Now, every time the Spirit manifests, it confirms Jesus reached Heaven! He made it! Because He did, one day we will, too!

APPLICATION:
1. Ask God to fill or stir up within you the power of His Holy Spirit, today.
2. Think of the times you have been in the presence of the manifestation of His Spirit.

PRAYER:
Lord, stir up the Holy Spirit within me. Make me mindful you accomplished the mission set before you and you are forever alive! Amen.

FEBRUARY 17
WHERE IS YOUR HOPE?

Job 17:15
"And where is now my hope? As for my hope, who shall see it?" (KJV)

Have you ever recorded a televised football game because you had to be somewhere else when it was broadcasted? Then, you found out your team won before you were able to watch the game? Have you ever noticed how differently you react to circumstances when watching that game? Your team is down 35 points in the first half. Your team drives all the way down the field to the one yard line and fumbles the ball. Yet, you do not lose hope, do you? Why? Because you know in the end, your team wins!

We are given the assurance God has already worked out the finish for us. He has looked ahead and already pronounced Jesus is Lord, forever. He has pronounced we, who believe, will be reigning and ruling with Him for 1,000 years on the earth. He has already pronounced we will walk on streets of gold and never be sick or hurt again. He has already pronounced we will be reunited with our loved ones, forever! He has already pronounced Satan will eventually be thrown into the lake of fire.

No matter what you may be going through today, no matter how hopeless your situation may seem, always remember the end is NOT in question. You are destined to win! As long as you keep the heart of hope beating inside your spirit, you will be able to go on because you know the outcome is not in question!

Do not get discouraged if the present circumstances seem to suggest you are not going to make it. Remember, the game is "fixed" in your favor!

APPLICATION:
1. Reach intently towards Heaven, today. Ask God to restore the hope inside you.
2. Remind yourself of the finish God has in store for His people.
3. Remind yourself in hard times things will turn to your favor.

PRAYER:
Lord, give me hope to live, love and believe again. I know you have my future securely in your hands! Amen.

FEBRUARY 18
DRINK FROM THE RIGHT CUP

Proverbs 15:33
"Fear of the LORD teaches wisdom; humility precedes honor." (NLT)

A full cup cannot be filled. When you are filled with yourself and your needs, there is not room for more. Yet, when you empty yourself, you make a place for something greater than yourself to fill you up. Your capacity to receive will increase beyond your previously perceived limits.

When we drink from the cup of humility, we never become full of ourselves. Consider if you were to have a glass that is half full, an empty glass and a full glass. The empty one is no good because it does not have anything to give. The full one is no good because it does not have room for anymore. The half full one is able to do both give and receive.

In contrast, when we drink from the cup of pride, we become puffed up. We have no room left to receive and no desire to pour out, unless it suits us. We become a useless vessel to God and to others. God resists the proud.

When we humble ourselves, we always open up the door for more to be poured in, while we are pouring out. Your cup will never run dry when you operate in humility!

The more we empty our lives of our selfishness and pride, we make room for God to pour more into us and through us. We keep ourselves in a position of receiving constantly from Heaven's vast resources. We become a constantly flowing brook of fresh water supplying life to all who touch it!

All of this comes from drinking, daily, from the living water of His Word. It is dispensed by being in constant fellowship with Him and drinking in His presence.

Be sure you reject the cup of self and always choose the cup of His will. This cup is never full, but is always being filled with more!

APPLICATION:
1. Ask yourself, today, which cup have you been drinking from?
2. Purposely, resist pride and reach for the cup of humility, today.

PRAYER:
Lord, forgive me for having pride in my life, and being too full to receive and too full to give to others. Amen.

FEBRUARY 19
FUEL UP WITH JOY

Psalms 30:5
"For his anger endureth but a moment; in his favor is life: weeping may endure for a night, but joy cometh in the morning." (KJV)

Accomplished minister and author, Tony Campolo, said, "Most Christians I know have just enough of the Gospel to make them miserable, but not enough to make them joyful."

Sometimes I wonder what Christians are "fueling up" on. Too often, they are found on a road of unhappiness, making them discontent and empty, while the Word of God teaches us, *"...The joy of the Lord is our strength."* (Nehemiah 8:10 KJV)

Joy is a decision as much as it is a state of affairs. Real joy is revealed when times are uncertain. It promises something better than the present moment, regardless of the circumstances. It is not able to steal away the victory He has promised to us as believers.

Joy is not an emotion. It is not just mere happiness because happiness is always dependent on situations, emotions and contentment. There is an old story that probably says it best: "An old dog was watching a young dog chase his tail. The young dog stopped to rest, and told the older dog, 'I believe happiness is in my tail, and if I catch it, then I will have happiness!' The older, wiser dog said, 'I caught mine once... and I found that happiness is not in the catching, it's in the pursuit.'"

It may appear some people have always "caught" everything they were chasing; however, many times they have not found joy in it! Their "fuel" does not carry them very far. They run out of gas quickly!

The Word of God has a supply of joy built to last throughout every season of your life. It is there even when nothing suggests you should be experiencing any sense of peace and fulfillment. It is there when your dreams have suffered a setback.

Remember to "fuel up," daily, at the station of His Word and in your prayer closet. If you do, you will never run out of joy!

APPLICATION:
1. Meditate on the Word of God over your circumstances, today.
2. Speak God's promises out of your mouth, and not your circumstances.

PRAYER:
Lord, help me to purposely "fuel up," today, on joy! Amen.

FEBRUARY 20
LIBERTY IS PRECIOUS

Acts 22:28
"...with a great sum I obtained this freedom...!" (KJV)

There is no greater force on the earth than the force of freedom. It is the reason Jesus came to the earth. It is costly, yet priceless. It is attainable, yet elusive. It is desirable, yet disagreeable.

Here in America, fierce devotion to the cause of freedom is the driving force, for which men and women join the military. The late President Ronald Reagan said, "No arsenal, or no weapon in the arsenals of the world, is so formidable as the will and moral courage of free men and women."

For freedom to be attained and preserved, someone must do something heroic. There are some likely, and not so likely, heroes or heroines in God's Word for us to examine. Moses, Joshua, David, Naomi and Paul all became heroes of freedom for God's people.

Here in America, we have heroes of freedom in our precious military men and women. They are obvious heroes. However, there are also some "unusual heroes" as well. For example: the single mom who works two jobs to assure her children the best life possible, the young husband who works long hours and does not succumb to the temptations of other women, and the senior citizen who has given years and years of his/her life to hard work, raising a family and enduring losses and tragedies. Despite it all, these people maintain their faith and are an example to those who will come after them. These individuals take the failures of their lives and use them to help others who have fallen into the same pits of life.

Heroes are all around us. The cause is always the same—freedom. Thank God for living in a country where we have the opportunities to pursue our dreams and reach for the stars. Thank God for our heroes!

APPLICATION:
1. Consider the freedom and liberty you enjoy, today, and give thanks for it.
2. Do not squander your freedom on yourself, be a hero to someone, today!

PRAYER:
Lord, thank you so much for our precious liberty! Help me be an example of someone who has used this freedom with integrity. Amen.

FEBRUARY 21
YOUR LIFE IS A SEED

John 12:25
"He that loveth his life shall lose it; and he that hateth his life in this world shall keep it unto life eternal." (KJV)

The more we allow our lives to be planted, the greater the harvest will be from our lives. While it is a hard, yet simple process to plant things, it is very difficult to plant our lives, especially for others to harvest. However, the more we offer our lives as a seed to be sown for the sake of the Kingdom, the more we become fulfilled as believers.

A believer visiting a mission field said to one of the dedicated workers, "My, you certainly are buried out here!" The missionary quietly replied, "We were not buried—we were planted! We buried ourselves long before we ever arrived on this field."

When you share your life, you expand the potential of your life. There are hidden things deposited inside of you that only become discovered when you are willing to invest yourself in others. This is not to say we should give it all away to strangers and neglect our families. Our families deserve for us to reserve the best of ourselves for them. However, there is a portion of your life God desires for you to plant for the good of others. There are people who need what you have inside of you. Jesus reminds us we actually find our lives when we allow ourselves to lose them for the good and well-being of others around us!

Something eternal is birthed when we surrender a part of our natural lives. We become more alive. We become more productive. Somehow it even seems we have more time, instead of less, when we give some away. Just remember, as believers, it is more natural to "die out" to ourselves than to live for ourselves! Your life is greater than you know! It is a seed!

APPLICATION:
1. Be sure to find more ways to give yourself to others, while not excluding those you love.
2. Purposely, give of yourself to those who need you most.

PRAYER:
Lord, help me to see the needs of those around me and give my life to them. May my life be a seed that always produces. Amen.

FEBRUARY 22
TWO AS ONE OR ONE VS. ONE

Genesis 2:24

"Therefore shall a man leave his father and his mother, and shall cleave unto his wife: and they shall be one flesh." (KJV)

There was a husband and wife who arrived at church in the same car, yet they were miles apart. They had gotten into one of those spirited arguments before church that married couples so often do, and failed to get their problem resolved. God's sovereignty and humor was reflected in an innocent secretary's typographical error. As the wife sat still steaming in church over the argument, she happened to glance down at the church bulletin. She and her husband were scheduled to sing a duet during the worship service. She was at first startled when she read the word next to their names, which was supposed to explain their appearance. Typed next to their name was the word "duel." After she got over the initial shock, she began to smile at the miscue and then looked at her husband, who also flashed a grin as he had also discovered the misprint. The decision was now theirs to make it. A duet or a duel? Through the innocence of that miscue and the warmth of that Sunday service she reached for his hand and the duet began.

This story gives us a picture of the reality of having a successful marriage. We can make everything we do a duet or a duel. We can work through the misunderstandings or we can lash out and continue to poke at the infected wounds.

The Word reveals clearly to us God's intentions, from the garden forth, have always been for a union that compliments and brings help and relief to those who are joined together.

It is time for us to forsake and forgive the disagreements, and instead, find the common ground which brought us together in the first place! It is time for the Church to realize, once and for all, we are much stronger and much more effective when we join forces. When two become one, the enemy is done!

APPLICATION:
1. Rediscover the things you first found compatible in your spouse.
2. Accentuate the positive and minimize the negative.

PRAYER:
Lord, help me to see, once again, the good and complimentary things my spouse has brought into our marriage. Give me a heart to overlook those things that would divide us. Amen.

FEBRUARY 23
MEEKNESS IS FOR THE MIGHTY

Matthew 5:5
"Blessed are the meek, for they shall inherit the earth." (KJV)

What is Bible meekness? The Hebrew word, *aw-nawv*, means "to be voluntarily humble; to purposely lower yourself, even when you are objectively in a higher place of stature or position."

Meekness is a condition of the heart and not a sign of weakness. Real Bible meekness is a sign of strength. It cannot be demanded, but is in reality, a form of an offering.

Some of the greatest heroes of the Bible were considered meek including Jesus (Matthew 11:29) and Moses (Numbers 12). You may not include John the Baptist among the meek heroes of the Bible at first, but consider the following: He was such a powerful figure that Josephus, the great Jewish historian, who lived during the time well after John's death, stated when John's name was mentioned people still trembled at the thought of him. Jesus' eulogy of John expressed, *"[He was] greater than any man born of woman."* (Luke 7:28 KJV) Yet, when John saw Christ, instead of giving a speech about his own great accomplishments, he sent his disciples to Jesus telling them, *"He must increase but I must decrease."* (John 3:30 KJV) When asked who he was, he simply said, *"I am nobody. I am to be heard, not to be seen. I am just a voice."* (John 1:23 KJV)

Another great meek Biblical hero was David. Consider how David never describes his victory over Goliath in all of the Psalms. He was quick to mention the Lord was the Great Shepherd and he was merely a sheep in His pasture.

Presently, we are witnessing a time of great boasting, great self-exaltation and great self-promotion. It is a time of "divas" and entourages. Where is the meekness which makes us truly mighty?

APPLICATION:
1. Humble yourself, today. Choose to lower yourself in some places you are obviously higher in.
2. Read about the Bible heroes you consider the mightiest. Mirror the meekness that moved them to might.

PRAYER:
Lord, I desire the meekness that makes me mighty. Amen.

FEBRUARY 24
ANSWERING THE CALL TO MINISTRY

Psalms 139:13
"For thou has possessed my reins thou hast covered me in my mother's womb."
(KJV)

One night in a river town in southern Ohio, there was a fearful storm, which suddenly raised the river and sent a flood sweeping over the town. It was at the hour when residents were returning from Sunday evening church services. Friends were separated in the darkness and a number of lives were lost. A little girl, who had become separated from her friends, was saved in a way that seemed nearly miraculous. Her father, who had gone in search for her, wandered about, calling her, with little hope of making himself heard, even if she were near. Suddenly, he felt her little hands clasping his. She heard him calling, "Come this way! I am here!" Afterwards she was later questioned, "But how did you know it was your father calling you?" someone asked. "How did I know?" she returned, wonderingly. "I think I ought to know my father's voice. I've been with him enough!"

Do you believe He has called you to ministry? Paul said he was called from his mother's womb. It took him the first part of his life to hear and respond to that call. Once he accepted it, he never looked back. He finished his course.

Young Samuel was raised in the temple, but it took three times for God to call him before he realized it was not Eli. He became one of the most trustworthy prophets of his time because he answered the call.

What is the key to being able to remain firm in your commitment to God? It is simply "being with God." The more time you spend in His Word and in prayer before Him, the more acquainted you become with His voice and His will. Then, when you find yourself in peril, you will be able to discern His voice and be delivered!

It all begins when you say: "Yes," to what He is telling you to do today, telling you to do for Him in your church and accepting the relationship He has placed in your life. Answer the call!

APPLICATION:
1. Set aside at least a few minutes, today, and be still before God. He will speak to you about your life and the plan He has for you!
2. Increase your prayer time, even if it is just a few minutes.

PRAYER:
Lord, thank you for having a purpose for my life in your Kingdom. I desire to hear from you. When I do, I will be sure to obey. Amen.

FEBRUARY 25
BOWLING FOR UNITY

Psalms 133:1

"Behold, how good and how pleasant it is for brethren to dwell together in unity!" (KJV)

Robert D. Putnam writes, "Before October 29, 1997, John Lambert and Andy Boschma knew each other only through their local bowling league at Ypsi-Arbor Lanes in Ypsilanti, Michigan. Lambert, a 64-year-old, retired employee of the University of Michigan Hospital, had been on a kidney transplant waiting list for three years. When Boschma, a 33-year-old accountant, learned casually of Lambert's need he unexpectedly offered to donate one of his own kidneys. 'Andy saw something in me that others didn't,' remembers Lambert. 'When we were in the hospital, Andy said to me, 'John, I really like you and have a lot of respect for you. I wouldn't hesitate to do this all over again.' I got choked up.' Boschma returned the feeling: 'I obviously feel a kinship [with Lambert]. I cared about him before, but now I'm really rooting for him.'"

This moving story speaks for itself, but the photograph accompanying this report in the *Ann Arbor News* reveals that in addition to their differences in profession and generation, Boschma is Caucasian and Lambert is African American. The fact that they bowled together made all the difference!

Unity has a special effect for everyone involved. The word unity in Psalms 133 literally means "together." So the above verse could literally read this way: *"Behold, how good and how pleasant it is for brethren to dwell together, together!"* There is a big difference in being gathered in a room or space with others and being "together" with them.

Too often, we are with someone, but not really with them at all. We find points of disagreement, instead of points we are alike in. We let the differences become greater than the things we are in harmony with. It is time for us to be "together, together" with our brothers and sisters in the Lord!

APPLICATION:
1. Be sure you are "together, together" with those God has placed in your life!
2. Find the common need and ground in the lives of the people around you and accent that today.

PRAYER:
Lord, lead me into unity with those around me, today. I choose to be "together" with them and not be divisive. Amen.

FEBRUARY 26
THE PAYOFF IS COMING

Luke 8:15

"But that on the good ground are they, which in an honest and good heart, having heard the word, keep it, and bring forth fruit with patience." (KJV)

Pastor and author, Rick Warren, says, "As I wrote in the *Purpose Driven Life*, each of us comes into the world with a specific purpose that God has in mind for us. Our job is to find out what that purpose is. Toward the end of my time in seminary in the late 1970's, I went through a period of questioning. I knew I wanted to spend my life serving God, but I didn't know how. As part of that questioning, I wrote to 100 of the biggest churches in the country and asked what the secret to their growth was. I got a lot of different answers, but one of them stood out. That answer was 'stay put.'"

When we commit to something, we must give it an opportunity to grow! Not staying put is probably the greatest reason for failing in life or ministry.

An elder minister asked me how old I was when we first started our church. I replied, "30." He said to me, "Son, if you really want to see this church become something great, stay with it. Don't move around and 35 years from now, you'll be glad you did!" What did he mean? The payoff is coming! It has. It will.

Sometimes it seems that payday will never come. It seems all the effort and sacrifice has gone totally unnoticed. However, God is an excellent accountant! He has watched over every single seed you have sown and He is preparing a reward even at this moment!

Faithfulness means being patiently committed to something to see it to the end! It means having confidence that if you continue to do what is right, something good is inevitable.

If you are presently waiting on something to happen that you have placed before God, continue to be patient because the payoff is coming!

APPLICATION:
1. Be sure you are not getting "itchy" and restless in the things you are praying for.
2. Confess the payoff is coming your way!

PRAYER:
Lord, thank you for being patient with me when I have been impatient with you. Amen.

FEBRUARY 27
BE GROUNDED IN PEACE

Proverbs 14:30
"A heart at peace gives life to the body, but envy rots the bones." (NIV)

Dwight Lyman Moody once said, "A great many people are trying to make peace, but that has already been done. God has not left it for us to do; all we have to do is enter into it."

This statement is so true for the believer. Peace is very obtainable; however, we must make adjustments in our thinking to receive it because peace is the deliberate adjustment of our lives to the will of God.

Peace does not necessarily mean the lack of conflict. In fact, we have mistaken the lack of trouble as peace. If that is true, then one incident can take away our peace. If that is true, one bad experience in a relationship can take away our peace. The same is true if we are depending on finding it in our job, family, etc., it can quickly be taken away.

We must become grounded in our peace. We must understand we follow the Prince of Peace. He knows how to guide us through the uncertain times. He will always provide what we need to calm the storms and to bring us to the shoreline.

There is a story of a ship that was wrecked in a furious storm. During the height of the storm, a little boy was tossed overboard, but miraculously survived by riding a piece of the wreckage to the shore, where he clung to a rock all night. The next morning he was rescued and asked if he trembled during the night. He answered, "Yes, I did tremble, but the rock did not!" When you trust in the Rock, you have nothing to fear!

There is no doubt storms will come along. Sometimes we may even feel as though we have been thrown overboard. However, we must remember Jesus appears in stormy times! He comes just when we need Him most.

APPLICATION:
1. Examine yourself, today. Is your peace firmly grounded in Him or in circumstances?
2. Have you adjusted your will to His? Peace will come if you do.

PRAYER:
Lord, restore the peace of Heaven to my soul. I repent of allowing my circumstances to steal my peace from me. Amen.

FEBRUARY 28
GETTING BETTER ACQUAINTED

Job 22:21
"Acquaint now thyself with him, and be at peace: thereby good shall come unto thee." (KJV)

There is a story that recalls how one morning, in 1888, Alfred Nobel picked up the morning newspaper and was startled to read his own obituary. It was his brother who had actually passed away, but an overzealous reporter, who had failed to check to see if his story was indeed factual, wrote of the untimely death of the inventor of dynamite. Nobel, who was an armaments manufacturer merchant, was now a merchant of his own death. Because of this unusual chance to see his life as others saw it, Nobel resolved to make clear his true desire for peace and not destruction. He arranged for the income from all his fortunes to fund an award to be made to those persons who did the most for the cause of peace. So, today, we remember Alfred Nobel not as an arms merchant of destruction, but as the founder of the Nobel Prize for Peace.

Before we became Christians, our lives were on a certain collision course with destruction. Peace was always elusive, just out of our reach. However, when we opened our lives to Jesus Christ, we were introduced to the peace that passes all understanding. Because we became acquainted with Him, we now have access to a peace previously unknown to us.

When you first meet some people, you may really dislike them or not trust them. Yet, over time, you may find them to be one of your closest friends. The better acquainted you became with them, the better the relationship became.

It is this way with us, as believers. When we get to know Him better, we develop a greater sense of peace even in the worst of times. We discover we can trust Him with our very lives! This peace enables us to reach out to those around us who are in trouble. We, who were at one time merchants of turmoil and disillusionment, now bring the sweet presence of God to a world in disarray. Because we are better acquainted with Him, we have received our personal Prize for Peace!

APPLICATION:
1. Be sure to spread peace to those around you, today.
2. Avoid all strife and dissension and pursue peace, today.

PRAYER:
Lord, thank you for giving me peace in my life, today, and removing the paths of destruction. Amen.

Confessing that we are entering a season of promotion is meaningless without the confession built on prayer! Amen!

MARCH 1
USE YOUR PIPELINE
Job 22:27

"Thou shalt make thy prayer unto him, and he shall hear thee…" (KJV)

E.M. Bounds, known as one of the greatest prayer warriors, wrote: "Paul, Luther, Wesley—what would these chosen ones of God be without the distinguishing and controlling element of prayer? They were leaders for God because they were mighty in prayer. They were not leaders because of brilliancy in thought, nor because of their exhaustless resources, their magnificent culture or their natural endowment; but they were leaders because by the power of prayer, they could command the power of God. Praying men means much more than 'men who pray by habit.' It means 'men with whom prayer is a mighty force,' an energy that moves Heaven and pours untold treasures of good on earth."

People of real Bible faith are sticklers for our confession, but if we do not pray, all of the confessing in the world will not matter. Prayer sets the table for our confession. Confession by itself, is nothing more than positive thinking. We must pray to have a foundation for our confession to be built on.

Prayer is not a religious practice, but a powerful means of communication. It gives us access to Heaven and all of its resources while we are here on the earth. Prayer opens the door for the miraculous. It invites God to intervene in the affairs of mankind. It brings His will into the earth. Jesus told His disciples to pray: *"Thy will be done in earth as it is in Heaven."* (Matthew 6:10 KJV)

Someone wise in ministry once made this observation: "Most failures in the Christian life are prayer failures!" I have found this to be true in my own life. We have not because we ask not!

Prayer is the compass to your life. It aims your life in the direction God has planned for you. When you pray about the direction of your life, you arrive at the destination God has for you. We must keep the pipeline open if we are to find ourselves in the center of His will!

APPLICATION:
1. Pray, daily, not only about the things you desire, but the things God desires for you.
2. Let your prayer life speak for you!

PRAYER:
Lord, thank you for opening up the Heavens when I pray. Amen.

MARCH 2
ARE YOU PREPARED?

Proverbs 24:27
"Prepare thy work without, and make it fit for thyself in the field; and afterwards build thine house." (KJV)

A young man applied for a job as a farmhand. When asked for his qualifications, he said, "I can sleep when the wind blows." This puzzled the farmer, but he took a liking to the young man and hired him. A few days later, the farmer and his wife were awakened in the night by a violent storm. They quickly began to check things out to see if all was secure. They found the shutters of the farmhouse had been securely fastened. A good supply of logs had been set next to the fireplace. The farm implements had been placed in the storage shed, safe from the elements. The tractor had been moved into the garage. The barn had been properly locked. All was well. Even the animals were calm. It was at that moment the farmer grasped the meaning of the young man's words, "I can sleep when the wind blows." Because the farmhand had performed his work loyally and faithfully, when the skies were not clear, he was prepared for fear. He was able to sleep in peace.

For us to continue on to what God wants for us, there must be some preparation on our part. Acts 2 is a perfect example of those who prepared themselves for a greater move of God. Jesus appeared to over 500 people after His resurrection, but only 120 were prepared to receive the promise from the Spirit.

Every great athlete knows without preparation, there will be no performance. Their dedication to their future begins well before the time they finally step into the arena of competition.

The things you are doing today are merely steps of training for tomorrow. Remember, today's preparation determines tomorrow's achievement!

APPLICATION:
1. Assess your present behavior. Are your preparations enough to achieve your dream?
2. Be sure to begin to prepare for tomorrow, today!

PRAYER:
Lord, show me where I am lacking in preparation. I will make the necessary adjustments. Amen.

MARCH 3
DO NOT HIDE FROM HIS PRESENCE

Genesis 3:8

"And they heard the voice of the LORD God walking in the garden in the cool of the day: and Adam and his wife hid themselves from the presence of the LORD God amongst the trees of the garden." (KJV)

God intended for man to live in His presence. Satan drew them away from His presence. He distracted them by pointing out the only thing they were prohibited from, a single tree! When Eve succumbed to his deception and Adam joined her, they were at their most crucial moment. They should have turned to God, but instead, they turned away from His presence.

Every time someone in the Bible turned from His presence, something bad happened. Cain fled from His presence and became so miserable he sought death, but could not find it. He could have obtained mercy and remained in God's presence. David left the presence of God for the presence of a woman. He became not only an adulterer, but also a conspirator to a murderer. The sword never left his house. He could have had the greatest family and kingdom ever. Jonah fled from God's presence and almost caused the sinking of a ship and its passengers. He could have obeyed and possibly have been considered a great prophet.

The enemy does not want us to seek God's presence, especially after we have disobeyed God. He brings condemnation, guilt and shame. He wants us to stay off of the path we have strayed away from; however, that is when we need to quickly return to Him.

The presence of God is always good for us. It brings things that are out of order into light and sorts them out for us, thus empowering us to make changes. It heals the wounds of our past. It inspires us to follow the path, which is fitted just for our lives.

Like a young child who is anxious to see their parents after being separated because of work or daycare, we should have that same sense of excitement and anticipation when we prepare to enter His presence! Do not run away from His presence, run into it!

APPLICATION:
1. Decide to find His presence, and place yourself inside of it more often.
2. Even if you sin, do not run from God, run to Him!

PRAYER:
Lord, I desire to be in your presence. I will seek you at all times! Amen.

MARCH 4
BE ONE OF THOSE WHO OVERCOME

John 16:33
"I have told you all this so that you will have peace of heart and mind. Here on earth you will have many trials and sorrows; but cheer up, for I have overcome the world." (TLB)

A woman took her husband to the doctor's office. After his checkup, the doctor said, "Your husband is suffering from a very serious infection." The husband, who was hard of hearing said, "What did he say?" His wife said, "He says you're sick." The doctor went on, "But, there is hope. You just need to reduce his stress. Each morning, give him a healthy breakfast. Be pleasant, nice and kind. For lunch and dinner make him his favorite meal. Do not discuss your problems with him; it will only make his stress worse. Do not yell at him or argue with him. And most importantly, just cater to your husband's every whim. If you can do this for him for the next six months to a year, I think your husband will have a complete recovery." The husband said, "What did he say?" His wife said, "He says you're going to die!"

Have you ever noticed how closely knitted your life is with others? This can be a good thing, but it can also be a hard thing. Some people are helpers, while others are hinderers. We depend on others to overcome for us, when we should be overcoming for ourselves.

We, as Christians, have the ultimate example in Jesus! He has gone before us and paved a road for us to travel. He overcame every kind of betrayal and hardship that we could possibly face. The Bible also tells us in Hebrews 12:1-2 there are grandstands of the prophets and past saints who are watching us. Great heroes of faith dealt with every manner of persecution and trials as examples.

However, those people are gone now. It is time for us to overcome and not only hear of others who overcome.

No matter what you are facing today, remember you are able to overcome because of those who have gone before you. The road set before you is well paved with overcoming faith!

APPLICATION:
1. Reference those who have gone through some of the same tests you are facing at the present moment.
2. Be sure you are walking by faith and not by sight.

PRAYER:
Lord, I make a conscience effort to walk the road that has been proven before me. Amen.

MARCH 5
TRUTH OR CONSEQUENCES?

Proverbs 14:12
"There is a way which seemeth right unto a man, but the end thereof are the ways of death." (KJV)

A Sunday school class was discussing King Solomon. Students pointed out that though Solomon had been so wise, he made some foolish choices. Finally, the teacher asked, "Are we picking too much on Solomon?" One older student replied wryly, "Ah, with all those wives, he was used to it!"

It is true that while Solomon was known to be the wealthiest and wisest man alive, his choices still cost him. There were some consequences to his actions, he eventually had to deal with. God always has a better way for us to do things if our choices are based on His Word.

Someone said about choices, "There is good, better and best." In the Word of God, choice implies "best." We would say of an expensive garment of clothing, "It is made of choice fabrics." You could say we need to make choice, choices!

He has a higher way. It causes your life to bear fruit beyond logic. It replaces the unpredictability of life. It causes you to be fulfilled. Yet, all of these things are contingent on the choices we make, and with every choice, there is a consequence. When we make a wrong choice or decision, we will always suffer. What produces wrong decisions? A short list would probably include the following: being led by people (Joshua 1), being led by your senses (Genesis 3:1-6; 13:1), being led by wrong information (Psalms 1), being led by the moment, fads, trends, peer pressure (Proverbs 14:29) and being led by frustration (Cain – Genesis 4).

As you go along in life, take the time to ask God for help in your decision making. He is listening to you and eager to help you find the right path for your life. Be sure to make your decisions based on the truth of His Word. If you do, you will have no consequences to fear!

APPLICATION:
  1. Review the decisions you have made and ask the tough questions.
  2. When making all future decisions, consider the possible consequences.

PRAYER:
Lord, forgive me for the poor choices I have made. Guide me into the truth so that I might make the right decisions. Amen.

MARCH 6
FINDING GOD'S WILL

Psalms 32:8
"I will instruct you and teach you in the way you should go; I will guide you with My eye…" (NKJV)

One of the most inspiring truths in the entire Bible is the fact that God has a plan for every life. It matters where you work because God has a plan for your life. It matters where you go to college because God has a plan for your life. It matters who you marry because God has a plan for your life. It matters where you go to church because God has a plan for your life.

God does not only call preachers. His divine will applies to all of us. However, the question is, what is God's calling for your life? How do you find it? Does God's will materialize the same way for everyone? The truth is God made you autonomous. You have the right to decide what you want to do, who you want to marry, where you want to go, etc.

In the movie, *Bruce Almighty*, Bruce finally realizes and understands surrendering everything is not just about his plans, so he eventually surrenders to God in prayer. His prayer is a plea of desperation and a good example to consider. In the fateful moment he surrenders, he says emphatically, "You win! I'm done! Please, I don't wanna do this anymore! I don't wanna be God. I want you to decide what's right for me. I surrender to your will!"

The scriptures point out everything is not coincidental, but a product of our choices. When we humble ourselves and pray, God's will becomes clear to us and He "nudges" us towards His divine plan for us. It is up to us to listen and carry out His plan for our lives. When you make that decision, you begin to hear and understand His will better day by day. First, it is by doing the simple and obvious things God requires of us. Then, He gives us more detailed instructions, leads us and helps us chart an exciting and rewarding course.

As you begin each day, seek to find His will and to walk in it. Ask Him to clearly instruct you in the decisions lying before you for that particular day. When you do, you will become fulfilled.

APPLICATION:
1. Truthfully evaluate the uncertain areas of your life.
2. Be sure you are seeking God's will for your life and not your own.

PRAYER:
Lord, I desire to be in the center of your will. Please show me the path reserved for my life. Amen.

MARCH 7
THE VOICE OF GOD

John 1:1-2
"In the beginning was the Word, and the Word was with God, and the Word was God. The same was in the beginning with God." (KJV)

The Word of God is the voice of God. As Augustine said, "When the Word of God is spoken, God speaks!" God put the Word in human form, so He could have a voice to humanity.

The Church has many different functions taking place on Sundays, but the most important event is the preaching of the Word.

According to II Timothy 2:15, the Word of God rightly divides our lives. The Greek word used for rightly divide is *orthotomeo*, (or-thot-om-eh'-o) which means "to cut straight a way; hold a straight course, to doing right; to make the way smooth, to correct."

God's Word works like a GPS system. It is designed to guide us to some pre-destined moments for our lives. Just as the GPS systems talk to you by providing details keeping you on the right roads, God's Word will speak to your heart and mind. When you hear the voice of His Word and listen to what He is saying, He will route you to your destination.

A traveler was preparing for a long trip. A friend asked if he was all packed and he said, "Yup, just about. I've got my guidebook, a lamp, a mirror, a microscope, a volume of fine poetry, a package of old letters, a song book, a sword, a hammer and a set of books." "But," the friend said, "you can't get all of that in one suitcase." "Sure, I can," replied the traveler, "It doesn't take much room." He reached for his Bible, placed it in the suitcase and closed the lid.

We should place the highest value on God's Word. His voice will become easily discernable for us when we do. We will arise in the morning hearing His words and go to bed at night hearing His whispers!

APPLICATION:
   1. Spend additional time in His Word, today.
   2. Listen to a preaching CD on your way to and from work, today.

PRAYER:
Lord, I desire to hear your voice. I purposely cut off the noise around me and open my heart and mind to your voice. Amen.

MARCH 8
BUILD YOURSELF AN ALTAR

Genesis 8:20-21
"And Noah builded an altar unto the LORD; and took every clean beast, and of every clean fowl, and offered burnt offerings on the altar. And the LORD smelled a sweet savour; and the LORD said in his heart, I will not again curse the ground any more for man's sake..." (KJV)

The first altar built brought about a covenant with God. He promised to never destroy the earth by water again. Despite the condition of the world, the altar became a place of redemption for all future generations. The word *altar* means "slaughter place; high place." An altar is a structure used in worship and a place to offer sacrifices.

In the Bible, altars were not always necessarily in a temple. Altars imply an open structure. This reveals to us that we can worship God or offer a sacrifice anywhere, anytime.

Altars bring a sweet scent into the presence of God. Altars bring change. There are different types of altars in the Bible. There were earthen altars, which symbolized God's encounter with human beings. God talked with the people from Heaven, such as He did with Moses when He gave him the Ten Commandments. There were stone altars. These symbolized obedience, such as they did for Gideon. Angels were present at Gideon's altar and peace came at a time of great peril and distress. There were bronze altars. These symbolized putting God first. Praise to God by the bronze altar produced the glory of God. There were also gold altars designated as the altar of incense. A gold alter was located in the inner room of the sanctuary, just outside the Holy of Holies! It symbolized purification, surrender and acceptance.

We should always find a place to "build" an altar, from which to worship and approach God. When we do, He will come!

APPLICATION:
1. Stop, today, and "build" an altar before God. Find a quiet place where you can commune with Him.
2. Offer all of yourself, both the good and bad, and He will bless you.

PRAYER:
Lord, please accept the sacrifice of my worship, today, and transform me into what you would have me to be. Amen.

81

MARCH 9
HE IS ALL YOU NEED

Philippians 4:19
"And with all his abundant wealth through Christ Jesus, my God will supply all your needs." (TEV)

Everyone needs something. Some think it is the right person. They imagine, "If I can just find the right person, they will accept me." Some think it is more power or more money. They believe, "If I just had a little more money, people would respect me and take notice of me." However, power and money will never make you happy. Why? Because you can never get enough.

People continue to search for what they need, but often, they are searching for the wrong thing. The truth is we seldom know what we really need.

I saw an episode of the *Twilight Zone* once, in which an old peddler in a town was sought by everyone because he could see what they needed before they could. The peddler always seemed to have what they needed.

God is this way. He knows what is next. He knows what is further down the road. He knows how to position us to be in the right place at the right time. Remember, Joseph? He was exiled to Egypt, far from the family God predicted. However, God had what Joseph needed waiting for him in Egypt. Joseph confessed before his brothers that God had "sent" him ahead of them to preserve them in the great famine because he had what they needed!

We must realize it is not really a person, money, fame or power that will fulfill us human beings. It is not the success the world offers. The truth is we need more of Him. Before you got out of bed today, He had something prepared just for you. More of Him always translates into your daily life and demands. More of Him causes you to be content until better days come!

Do not worry about the economy or the stock market. Just remember, He supplies all of your needs!

APPLICATION:
1. Be sure you are trusting in Him for your fulfillment and not other things or people.
2. Confess Him as El Shaddai—The God who is more than enough!

PRAYER:
Lord, I confess you as my Lord, Savior and supplier of all my needs! You are all I need! Amen.

MARCH 10
THERE IS LIFE AT THE CROSS

Colossians 2:14

"...having canceled the written code, with its regulations, that was against us and that stood opposed to us; he took it away, nailing it to the cross." (NIV)

There was an officer patrolling on night duty in northern England some years ago when he heard a quivering sob. Turning towards the noise's direction, he saw a little boy sitting on a doorstep in the shadows. With tears rolling down his cheeks, the child whimpered, "I'm lost. Take me home." The policeman began naming street after street, trying to help him remember where he lived. When that failed, he repeated the names of the shops and hotels in the area, but all without success. Then, the officer remembered a well-known church with a large, white cross towering high above the city's center. He pointed to it and said, "Do you live anywhere near that?" The boy's face immediately brightened. "Yes! Take me to the cross! I can find my way home from there!"

The cross is probably the most enigmatic symbol in human history. It symbolized everything that was dark, dreary and dead. Yet, it is also the single most illuminated place in history because of the tremendous sacrifice of the Son of God on the cross.

It was the place where the greatest injustice of the ages was transacted. It was the place where the greatest abandonment took place. It was the place where the greatest betrayal took place. Yet, it is also the place where the greatest redemption, the greatest pardon and the greatest display of faithfulness took place.

People, centuries later, are still enamored by it. They wear it as jewelry around their neck. They hang it on their walls. They are drawn to it without knowing why. If we ever lose our way in life, there is a place we can turn to find our direction. The place is the cross of Christ.

APPLICATION:
1. Stop, today, and thank God for the cross of Calvary.
2. Take your cares, your sins and your hurts to the place of death and life!

PRAYER:
Lord, thank you for the unparalleled sacrifice you made at the cross for me. May I never forget what you did for me. Amen.

MARCH 11
PUT FIRST THINGS FIRST

Deuteronomy 14:23
"Bring this tithe to eat before the Lord your God at the place he shall choose as his sanctuary; this applies to your tithes of grain, new wine, olive oil, and the firstborn of your flocks and herds. The purpose of tithing is to teach you always to put God first in your lives." (TLB)

Someone once said, "You have to crawl out on the limb to get to the fruit!" In 1947, Chuck Yeager broke the sound barrier. He had flown missions before in the Air Force. He had experienced the exhilaration of soaring high into the skies at extreme speeds and altitudes. Yet, one experience proved to be different from any other flight before. He was in a special aircraft located inside of another plane. When the plane reached a certain altitude and speed, his aircraft was released from the plane. Because he was already going at a fast rate when he was released, it was not long before he reached the sound barrier, or Mach 1. Just as he approached the sound barrier, his aircraft began to shake so violently he thought it was going to break apart. As a result, his first thought was to back off. However, the pilot in him pushed to go ahead and speed up. The more he sped up, the more the shaking increased. Then, suddenly something amazing happened—the aircraft smoothed out! He had broken the barrier and now it was easier to fly.

I have noticed many people over the years approach the tithing barrier. They shake and quake in fear of losing their belongings or going broke. However, everyone who has pressed through the barrier discovers things smooth out.

We need to understand, as Christians, if we obey God, He will never let us go without. If we put first things first, we will surely see the best God has for our lives!

APPLICATION:
1. If you are not tithing, giving God 10 percent of your first fruits, then begin immediately.
2. Trust God to supply what you lack without fear or reservation.

PRAYER:
Lord, forgive me for not tithing, thereby not trusting you. I pledge to put first things first and go through the "tithing barrier." Amen.

MARCH 12
IT IS OKAY TO PLAY

Matthew 18:3

"...Except ye be converted, and become as little children, ye shall not enter the kingdom of Heaven." (KJV)

When I was a boy, we lived on Oak Street. It was not a bad place to live. It was a dead end street with just a few houses on it. Everyone knew each other and it was ordinary for people to borrow needed goods from each other and visit unannounced. There was a commonality about living there.

In warm weather, the big event at night was to play kickball in the street. Because there was little traffic, it was the perfect place. The unique thing was the adults could join the game. There were construction workers, factory workers, nurses and soldiers who laughed, jumped, screamed and shouted as the game was being played. They enjoyed the game even more than we did!

Too often, we make the Kingdom of God too complicated. We get too serious. We lose the joy we should be experiencing. God never intends for us to become so mature we cannot experience the thrill of being His children!

Most people, if asked, what part of life they would want to live over again, if only for a little while, would choose a time during their childhood. Why? It is because the serious things of life are still ahead. A child does not really have to deal with serious matters. Instead, they are able to enjoy the life they were given. They do not have great responsibilities. They are able to just be children!

Although we have been born-again, we must realize we will always be His children! While our responsibilities are much greater, we should still build time into our busy schedules to just enjoy the life He has given us!

APPLICATION:
1. Do something fun, today, something making you laugh.
2. If you have children, take some time to do something "childish" with them.

PRAYER:
Lord, thank you for giving me permission to enjoy the life you have given me. Amen.

85

MARCH 13
HE IS NOT HOLDING OUT ON YOU

Luke 12:32
"So don't be afraid, little flock. For it gives your Father great happiness to give you in the Kingdom." (TLB)

I was walking through downtown Washington, D.C., on one occasion, and noticed how many homeless people were lying on the sidewalks. As they saw people approach, many would hold their hands out, hoping for some change. I was reluctant to give them anything, thinking they would likely spend it on cigarettes or alcohol. However, on this occasion, something unexpected happened. A man approached me and asked if I had five dollars. I said, "I don't have five dollars to give you, but I do have some change." When I reached into my back pocket to get the change I was planning to give, a five dollar bill fell out! I was flabbergasted! I scooped up the five dollar bill and was going to put it back in my pocket until I realized he also saw it, so I reluctantly gave it to him. I do not know what he did with it, but later that evening God began to speak to me about what happened. He told me what I had done was a good example of how people think He treats His people. They believe He shows them blessings, but then puts them back in His pocket and gives them something else. He was, of course, right! How often do we settle for something other than what God has promised us? How often do we get discouraged and give up on walking in faith and believing God will fulfill our desires, as we obey and serve Him?

He does not find pleasure in withholding His blessings from us. His pleasure is dispersing them to us. He is looking for ways to get us to the breakthrough that we desire.

We must realize He does not "hold out" on us. There may be delays or hindrances preventing the good things of God from becoming ours, but it is never because He is "holding out" on us!

APPLICATION:
1. Be sure you are walking in faith over the things God has promised you, today.
2. Do not say God has passed you over!

PRAYER:
Lord, I repent of not trusting your Word for my life. I trust you to bring me every good thing I lack. Amen.

MARCH 14
USE THE HAMMER

Jeremiah 23:29

"Is not my word as a fire? saith the LORD; and like a hammer that breaketh the rock in pieces?" (KJV)

I was raised in a house where there was little honesty or integrity. When words were spoken, they were seldom backed up with corresponding action. Although I was only a child, I noticed we often had bad or discouraging things happening around us almost all of the time. It seemed we were just a family of bad luck. It was accepted and expected!

In 1976, I went to a little storefront church and received Jesus Christ as my Lord and Savior. Something more than just my spirit was reborn. I felt some things "break" on the inside of me in my thinking. I suddenly felt there was something greater in me than I had imagined. I did not fully realize then what that meant, but it provoked an insatiable appetite in me for God's Word.

The thing I noticed more and more as I read and studied was God actually meant what He said! His words came to pass! Then, as I got a better understanding, I realized, I needed to become a person of integrity, too. I needed to choose my words carefully and then be committed to following through in order for them to come to pass.

I discovered if I placed God's Word in my mouth, my life would begin to find its greater meaning. His Word became a "hammer" in my life that broke up the hard ground of disappointment. My luck changed! I found out when I spoke God's Word out of my mouth, He brought it to pass. Things that once seemed unmovable, were now being removed with very little resistance. For the first time in my life, I began to understand His Word was the most powerful thing in the universe. His Word is just as powerful today as it was then. We need to take this powerful tool out of our spiritual toolbox and use it, daily!

APPLICATION:
1. Cut off all distractions and read your Bible, today. Read Psalms 34, Ephesians 6 or your favorite passage.
2. Speak the Word of God out of your mouth, today, over the situation(s) pressing on you the most.

PRAYER:
Lord, your Word says I am an overcomer. I speak and believe you will cause me to triumph and win over all obstacles! Amen.

MARCH 15
LET THE FIRE BURN

Jeremiah 20:9
*"Then I said, I will not make mention of him, nor speak any more in his name.
But his word was in mine heart as a burning fire shut up in my bones, and I was
weary with forbearing, and I could not stay."* (KJV)

Jeremiah found himself in an environment of false prophets, apathy and even disgust for God's Word. Despite this negative environment, Jeremiah could not keep the Word of God bottled up inside of him. He spoke and preached it for over 40 years—without any results! Most people today would not even speak it for 40 days or even 40 hours if they did not see results. Yet, eventually God vindicated Jeremiah and all of His words came to pass!

I heard a story of a man marooned on an island. After a while of not being rescued, he accepted he would spend the remainder of his life there, alone. He adapted to his surroundings and learned how to live off of the island and its environment. He learned how to spark fire from rocks he found there. He became a great hunter with his homemade spear. He became an adept fisherman with his straw and vine made net. He even built a bamboo hut to keep warm at night and cool during the day. However, over time, he became bitter at God for his plight. Then, one night, he got so mad he put out the fire he had used to cook his fish, instead of letting it burn for warmth throughout the night. It just so happened, a reconnaissance plane flew over the island that night, but saw nothing because the fire had been put out. Although the man was eventually rescued 10 years later by the same flying reconnaissance plane, it cost him 10 years of his life!

Jeremiah said His Word was like a fire that was shut up in his bone! Even though there were no signs Israel would awaken out of its slumber, he continued to let the fire of the Word burn through him and eventually God intervened for His people.

APPLICATION:
1. Keep the fires of salvation burning in your heart.
2. Stay in the Word at all times.

PRAYER:
Lord, stir up the embers of your presence in me for all to see! Amen.

MARCH 16
YOU CAN PLEASE GOD

I Thessalonians 4:1

"Finally, brothers, we instructed you how to live in order to please God, as in fact you are living. Now we ask you and urge you in the Lord Jesus to do this more and more." (NIV)

God has special plans for those who please Him. The impossible things become possible. He opens the Heavens for those who seek His will.

When my children were younger, I intended to make sure they received everything I had missed in my childhood. I worked extra hours, including nights, weekends and any other time possible to ensure holidays were truly special. They had birthday parties with cake, ice cream and presents. At Christmas, we had presents that consumed our living room. It was a very special time of celebration.

Because our budget was limited, we were not able to do many special things very often during the rest of the year. However, when one of our children did something pleasing, we would find a way to do something special for them. On one occasion, our son received better grades on his report card than usual. It was not close to his birthday or Christmas, but I wanted to do something to reward him, so I painted his room the color he wanted—three walls black and one yellow (to symbolize the Christian rock band, Stryper). Being a house painter for 20 years certainly came in handy! My natural response to his willingness to accomplish something pleasing to his mother and me was to bless him.

We must realize God wants to bless us beyond the normal pattern of His blessings. He wants to reward us for our obedience. He wants you to go from glory to glory!

How do we please Him? First, we please Him through obedience. I Samuel 15:22 says, *"To obey is better than to sacrifice."* (KJV) When we make it a priority to obey God, He becomes more involved with our needs. The second way is to live a life of faith. Hebrews tells us plainly that without faith we cannot please God. To live in faith is very pleasing to Him!

APPLICATION:
1. Ask God what you could do to please Him, today.
2. Respond by acting now! Do not delay!

PRAYER:
Lord, it is my desire to do the things that are pleasing in your sight. Amen.

MARCH 17
YOU CANNOT PLEASE EVERYONE

I Thessalonians 2:4

"...but just as we have been approved by God to be entrusted with the gospel, so we speak, not as pleasing men, but God who examines our hearts." (NASV)

If you have ever been a leader of a group, you probably noticed it is hard to get everyone in the group in agreement and even harder to maintain it. Personalities emerge, opinions become protests and civility vanishes from the scene. This is when you, as a leader, must be willing to take charge. The purpose of the group must be protected. Decisions must be absolute. Of course, some will not agree, but the mission must become the focal point and not the dissension.

An old fable that has been passed down for generations tells about an elderly man who was traveling with a boy and a donkey. As they walked through a village, the man was leading the donkey and the boy was walking behind. The townspeople said the old man was a fool for not riding the donkey; so to please them, he climbed upon the animal's back. When they came to the next village, the townspeople said the old man was cruel for enjoying the ride, while the child followed behind on foot. So, to please them, he got off and set the boy on the animal's back and continued on his way. In the third village, people accused the child of being lazy for making the old man walk, and suggested they both ride the donkey. So, the man climbed on and they set off again. In the fourth village, the townspeople were indignant at the cruelty to the donkey because he was made to carry two people. The frustrated man was last seen carrying the donkey down the road.

We smile, but this story makes a good point, we cannot please everyone! If we are striving to please God and fulfill His will for our lives, then that must take precedence over everything else.

APPLICATION:
1. Examine the decisions you are making today. Are you being true to yourself and the vision inside of you?
2. Adjust your decision making to please God first and foremost.

PRAYER:
Lord, with your help, I will not be a man pleaser. Give me the courage to stand for what I know is right. Amen.

MARCH 18
THE VALUE OF PRAISE

Psalms 9:1-3
*"O Lord, I will praise you with all my heart and tell everyone about the
marvelous things you do. I will be glad, yes, filled with joy because of you. I will
sing your praises, O Lord God above all gods. My enemies will fall back and
perish in your presence;"* (TLB)

Praise comes from a Latin word meaning "value or price." To give praise to
God is to proclaim His merit or price. The way you praise Him is a reflection of
how much value you personally place on what He has done for you.

Praise is a response to a gift. A proper response to a gift is not, "How much
do I owe you?" It is, "Thank you!" The way we say thanks is with our praise and
worship. Praise is focusing our heart on God. There are seven Hebrew words for
praise with *Tchilliah* being the highest. The book of Psalms is a book of songs.
The title means "Hallelujah" or "Praise the Lord," and it literally means "a song
accompanied by music." The Levites were given the responsibility to sing praises
to God during the morning and evening offerings. They were considered the
lowest of the priestly sect. They were chosen by God. They were given as a gift to
Israel to maintain the glory.

Praise has always been linked to warfare in the Bible. Abraham was fed a
sacramental meal after defeating his enemies. Joshua took Jericho by encircling
the camp with a praise service. God promised to answer when two or three are
gathered together in His name. Matthew 18:20) When we offer praise to God, we
bring Him on the scene. I have always noticed after I praise God, I feel stronger.
It is because of His presence. God wants us to develop our own praise to Him. He
wants us to sing our own song. He wants us to speak the things He has done. If we
do, we will find praise is the most valuable thing we have access to!

APPLICATION:
1. Today, stop on several occasions and sing out praise for what God has
   done for you.
2. Sing a known song or make one up about your own life.

PRAYER:
*Lord, I make a decision, today, to sing praises out to you. I know my enemies will
fall by the wayside when I do. Amen.*

MARCH 19
CREATED ON PURPOSE WITH A PURPOSE

Acts 26:16
"But rise, and stand upon thy feet: for I have appeared unto thee for this purpose, to make thee a minister and a witness both of these things which thou hast seen, and of those things in the which I will appear unto thee;" (KJV)

Everything has a purpose. Every life has a purpose. The word *purpose* means "the reason that something was created." The purpose of something is determined by the Creator. Nothing determines its own purpose. It is determined by the Creator of it!

For example, a microphone stand can be used as a doorstop, but it is not the intended purpose for it. An airplane could be used as a permanent residence; however, the plane's creator did not design it to be a house. A bread toaster could be used for a paperweight, but it is not its function. The microphone stand, the airplane and the toaster are all made with the same substance, but they all have their own different, unique purpose.

You were created for a purpose. God did not hide His purpose for your life from you, but for you!

Most people are clueless about their purpose, and consequently, spend most of their time searching for it and becoming frustrated from not finding it. The best places to find your purpose are in prayer, the Word of God and church. As a matter of fact, one of the main reasons to attend church is to find your purpose.

While you are serving, praying, worshipping and listening to the Word of God, He is making deposits into your life to help you complete the divine mission you were placed here for.

Do not get discouraged if you have not found your purpose yet. E.V. Hill said, "I may not be what I ought to be, but I am not what I used to be!"

APPLICATION:
1. Purposely spend time asking God what you were created for.
2. Be willing to make necessary adjustments to walk in the purpose He has for your life.

PRAYER:
Lord, show me the purpose you had in mind when you created me, and guide me to that mission. Amen.

MARCH 20
BELONGING BECAUSE OF RIGHTEOUSNESS

Matthew 5:10
"Blessed are those who are persecuted because of righteousness, for theirs is the kingdom of Heaven." (NIV)

I was painting a house for a wealthy lady many years ago, when something humorous, and at the same time startling, happened. She left the house in the morning and told me she would return later. A co-worker and I were painting the outside of the house when we ran out of paint. I asked the young man working with me to get a couple of gallons of paint from the garage. A few seconds later, I heard a loud siren go off! When he had opened the garage door, the security alarm had been triggered. In just a matter of minutes, a man with a shotgun appeared from the woods behind the house. We decided inside the garage was the best place to wait until the authorities arrived. The man approached us with caution and asked us what we were doing. I explained we were hired house painters and we had unknowingly opened the armed door. He cautiously accepted our explanation, after we confirmed the name of the maid who worked for the family. We were relieved. Then, with the siren still howling, two police cars sped down the driveway. Officers jumped out of the cars with weapons drawn. They found us sitting in the garage. After a few minutes of reassuring the officers, they accepted our reason for the excitement and left.

The point is we had a right to be in the house. Although it was not our house, the owner had given us the right to be there. God has given His children the keys to His house. He has given us the "rights" to all that is His. We are not only "guests," but we are bone of His bone and flesh of His flesh. Righteousness gives us access to God's best!

The next time you feel a sense of unworthiness, just remember your name is written in Heaven! You belong!

APPLICATION:
1. Ask yourself if you are walking in the righteousness that has been provided for you.
2. Declare your righteousness.

PRAYER:
Lord, I thank you for your righteousness. I realize because of what you have done for me, I am not restricted from your very best. Amen.

MARCH 21
SERVING EXALTS

Joshua 24:15
"...but as for me and my house, we will serve the Lord." (KJV)

Someone once said, "If you wish to be a leader, you will be frustrated, for very few people wish to be led. If you aim to be a servant, you will never be frustrated because very few wish to serve!" This statement is regrettably accurate. Leading people can result in real frustration. Too many times, people want something when they serve. Regardless, if they are paid staff members or volunteers, they usually expect to be compensated in some way for their services.

The Word of God provides special rewards for those with a servant's heart. Joshua served Moses and became his replacement when he died. The widow woman served Elijah and had an endless supply of meal and oil. Rahab assisted Israelite spies, which resulted in her life and her family's lives being spared. Paul called himself, "Paul, a servant of Christ," and became the greatest apostle ever.

Jesus was the greatest servant who ever lived. He said, *"For even the Son of Man did not come to be served, but to serve, and to give His life as a ransom for many."* (Mark 10:45 ESV) He also pointed out, *"And whosoever will be chief among you, let him be your servant: Even as the Son of Man came not to be ministered unto, but to minister."* (Matthew 20:27-28 KJV) Jesus humbled Himself and washed the feet of the disciples, and became the King of Kings and Lord of Lords.

All of these examples show us service always comes before exaltation, recognition and notoriety. It precedes every great promotion and every great victory in the believer's life.

Are you looking to advance higher in the Kingdom of God? The process has always been the same. If we will humble ourselves and serve others, He will exalt us and reward us in a way possible only through Him.

APPLICATION:
1. Find someone to serve, today. Humble yourself and be willing to give away the gift inside of you.
2. Instead of looking to receive something, look to serve someone who is unable to serve themselves or others.

PRAYER:
Lord, lead me to someone who has a need I can supply, today. Amen.

MARCH 22
THROW YOUR HEART

Jeremiah 32:17
"Ah Lord GOD! Behold, thou hast made the Heaven and the earth by the great power and stretched out arm, and there is nothing too hard for thee:" (KJV)

A coach was training a prize winning athlete who was very gifted. He won the city competition, and if he won the state competition, he would be eligible for the Olympics. Prior to the competition, the athlete said, "I have a problem. There's one boy who can jump six inches higher than I can; I just can't break the barrier." The coach, a Christian, decided to use Philippians 4:13 to inspire the young athlete. "We are not only going to raise the bar six inches higher, but add an additional three inches. All you have to do is throw your heart over the bar, and your body will follow," said the coach. The very next time he got ready to jump, the coach's words resounded inside of him. He ran faster than before and jumped higher than ever. The young athlete won the state competition! We must realize the hardest hurdle for our success has already been cleared through the redemptive work of Jesus Christ, through His life, death and resurrection.

Our challenge is to have unshakable confidence nothing we come up against is bigger than the God we serve. When we surrender all to Christ and serve Him with all of our hearts, the impossible becomes possible!

I noticed the first few years of my ministry were mostly spent in frustration. I just did not seem to be able to reach the breakthrough I had been confessing. However, somewhere along the way, without consciously realizing it, I was giving more and more of my heart to the Lord and my trust was getting greater and greater. The hard things did not seem to affect me the same way they once did, nor did they seem to last as long.

We must be willing to accept the challenges before us, and not hold anything back from Him. If we will do this consistently, with all of our hearts, we will break through all barriers!

APPLICATION:
    1. Apply all of your heart to the things God tells you to do.
    2. Do not settle for "just about," "close" or "almost."

PRAYER:
Lord, I surrender all of my heart to your will and those you have sent to lead and guide me. Amen.

MARCH 23
THE SPIRIT GIVES LIFE

Job 33:4
"The Spirit of God hath made me, and the breath of the Almighty
hath given me life." (KJV)

Have you considered how differently you felt about your problems after spending time praying in the Spirit or being in an atmosphere where the Spirit of God was evident? You were probably much less worried, and even inspired, about a positive outcome. The reason is the spiritual realm is a higher realm than that of the flesh. It is a dimension superseding the natural!

In 1981, I went through a terrible season in my life. I lost everything, including my marriage, my vision, and for a season, I even lost my way. I was so depressed and became suicidal. I had very little support from my family, and only had a couple of Christian friends. (Thank God I had them!) I did not know what to do. I felt, in my flesh, pressure and hopelessness. However, I began to cry out to God. I prayed and fasted, day and night, in intervals over the next six months. I shut off all distractions. I concentrated on God, His Word and His Spirit.

Then, something changed. Nothing seemed different on the outside. My circumstances remained the same. Instead, something changed on the inside of me. I was transformed into another person! The presence of God's Spirit had saturated me. He not only renewed my body, but also my mind. My hopelessness lifted. My depression was replaced with joy. I was solidly back on the path God had laid out for my life. The Spirit of God had breathed inside of me. My courage and enthusiasm to fulfill the dream inside of me was refueled!

That was nearly 30 years ago, and I have never been empty since. His Spirit is ready to breathe a fresh breath into your life and situations, today. Are you ready to receive?

APPLICATION:
1. Spend a few extra minutes, today, in the Spirit of God.
2. Be still, cut off distractions and receive a renewing from Him.

PRAYER:
Lord, I open my life up to you, today. Breathe into my soul your Spirit. I receive a new breath of life from Heaven, today! Amen.

MARCH 24
THE POWER OF BECOMING ONE

Acts 2:44-45

*"And all that believed were together, and had all things in common; and sold
their possessions and goods, and parted them to all men,
as every man had need." (KJV)*

There is a wonderful, powerful commodity called synergy. The definition of *synergy* is "the interaction of parts that when combined produce a total effect that is greater than the sum of individual parts."

This power was demonstrated perfectly in the book of Acts. The new Church of Jesus Christ had been birthed. The people did not have a functioning church building at the beginning. They had to meet in houses, fields or wherever they could gather. It became apparent for them to survive, they had to come together in every way, including financially. Therefore, they brought their money and goods to the disciples, who in turn, found a way to distribute them to the people as needed. As a result, the church grew quickly and the power of God became even stronger than in the days of Jesus!

Even nature teaches us the power of synergy, the power of becoming one. When you see geese flying south for the winter, flying along in their distinguished "V formation," you might be interested to know what science has discovered concerning why they fly in such a way. As each bird flaps its wings, it creates an uplift for the bird immediately following. By flying in a "V formation," the whole flock adds at least 71% greater flying range than if each bird flew on its own. If a goose falls out of formation, it feels the drag and resistance of trying to go it alone, and quickly gets back into formation to take advantage of the lifting power of the bird immediately in front. When the lead goose gets tired, he rotates back in the wing and another goose flies point. The geese honk from behind to encourage those up front to keep up their speed. Finally, when a goose gets sick, or is wounded by a shot and falls, two geese fall out of formation and follow the distressed goose down to help and protect it. They stay with it until it is either able to fly or dies. Then, they launch out on their own or join another formation until they catch up with their original flock.

We need this synergy in today's Church—the power of becoming one!

APPLICATION:
  1. Today, give of yourself to help someone else in need.
  2. Keep yourself in contact with those who are in your life.

PRAYER:
Lord, remind me to give, today, of myself to others. Amen.

97

MARCH 25
ONE HEART FOR ALL

Acts 4:32-33

"And the multitude of them that believed were of one heart and of one soul: neither said any of them that ought of the things which he possessed was his own; but they had all things common. And with great power gave the apostles witness of the resurrection of the Lord Jesus: and great grace was upon them all." (KJV)

Two men were riding a bicycle built for two. They came to a big, steep hill. It took a great deal of struggle for the men to complete what proved to be a very stiff climb. When they got to the top, the man in front turned to the other and said, "My, that sure was a hard climb." The fellow in the back replied, "Yes, and if I hadn't kept the brakes on all the way, we would certainly have rolled down backwards!"

I often wonder why people pull so hard against each other. Even many Christians seem to have a difficult time joining forces and pulling together. Great churches have been split over people's inability to enter into agreement. The color of carpet or the type of light fixtures to install have been such points of contention over the years and caused good friends on committees to come to blows with each other.

On the other hand, enormous mountains have been moved when people found a way to get in agreement. When we share a common purpose, there is nothing beyond our reach. There are seven great things that come from community: 1. It helps you focus on the thing of importance. 2. It helps diminish pride. 3. It keeps you from becoming isolated. 4. It increases your productivity—two can accomplish more than one. 5. It helps invoke new relationships. 6. It helps you develop team spirit. 7. It helps expand your potential.

These things prove what is obvious; we need each other! We need to join together to fully accomplish the great commission. We must become one heart!

APPLICATION:
  1. Find common ground with those around you, today.
  2. Stay clear of strife and contention.

PRAYER:
Lord, steer my heart to those in need whom I can be of help to today. Help my heart to be joined with theirs! Amen.

MARCH 26
EVALUATE OR BE EVALUATED

Colossians 4:12

"Epaphras, from your city, a servant of Christ Jesus, sends you his greetings. He always prays earnestly for you, asking God to make you strong and perfect, fully confident of the whole will of God." (TLB)

During the days the legendary Knute Rockne was coaching Notre Dame, a sports columnist of a South Bend newspaper earned the reputation of the meanest, most cutting and critical writer in the country. The writer who remained anonymous apparently knew Notre Dame very well, and wrote mostly about the team's weaknesses and miscues. He wrote pointedly about the mistakes of individual players. He told about those who were lazy, those who were lax in their training and their lack of preparation. Predictably, when the players heard about this column, they became outraged. The players' egos were stung by the transparency of the column, and they went to Rockne and complained. He listened with concern, but told them there was nothing he could do to stop the writer. His advice was the only way the players could hope to soften the writer's reports was to go out and play with more intensity, so that the writer would have no choice, but to accentuate the positive.

This went on for quite awhile until later Rockne revealed he was the infamous columnist himself! Because he was the coach of the team, he was extensively familiar with their tendencies and weaknesses. He also knew how to motivate his team and bring out their best. This critical, public evaluation was his shrewd way of developing his team into a championship team, and it worked!

Sometimes, we need to be painfully truthful with our own imperfections and short-fallings. By being willing to self-evaluate, we can often avoid the inevitable, which is evaluation by someone else!

APPLICATION:
1. Stop for a few minutes and do a self-evaluation of the areas of your life needing improvement.
2. Make a list and find scripture to stand on that will help you change and improve your behavior.

PRAYER:
Lord, show me the things about myself needing improvement and give me the courage and strength to change them. Amen.

99

MARCH 27
OVERCOMING BETRAYAL

Psalms 55:12-14

"For it was not an enemy that reproached me; then I could have borne it: neither was it he that hated me that did magnify himself against me; then I would have hid myself from him: But it was thou, a man mine equal, my guide, and mine acquaintance. We took sweet counsel together, and walked unto the house of God in company." (KJV)

Of all the wounds we endure in our lifetimes, perhaps the most severe is the wound of betrayal. It cuts deep into the tenderest regions of our being and extracts something from the inside of us that may never be replaced. Betrayal can come in many forms. It may be in the form of infidelity in a marriage. It may be from a partnership in business. It may be from some formerly trusted confidant who makes confidential information public. It may come from trusting your children, only to discover they willingly disobeyed you. The damage is more amplified when it originates from someone calling him/herself a Christian.

This kind of wound is difficult to understand and even more difficult to recover from. It usually stems from some kind of jealousy, envy or expectation that resulted in some sort of disappointment.

Jesus knew what it was like. He was abandoned at a time when it seemed he was in greatest need. Judas was disappointed Jesus did not pursue an earthly throne in His day. His disappointment led him to betrayal.

What can you do if you have been betrayed? Re-evaluate where you place your faith. Human beings are apt to fail at some time and place. Enter into His healing arms. Be slow to take strangers into your confidence. Remember, no one should be Lord of your life, except Jesus!

APPLICATION:

1. Today, decide to forgive those who have betrayed you. Remember, forgiveness does not mean you have to allow them to be as close to you as they once were.
2. Let God be your closest confidant. He can be trusted.

PRAYER:

Lord, I decide, today, to forgive anyone who has betrayed me. Heal the hurt and restore peace to my life. Amen.

MARCH 28
LIFE ON THE INSIDE

Jeremiah 1:5
"Before I formed you in the womb I knew you, before you were born I set you apart; I appointed you as a prophet to the nations." (NIV)

What does God say about life in the womb? It is very clear human beings have worth even before they are born. God knew you, as He knew Jeremiah, long before you were born or even conceived. He knew you, thought about you and planned for you.

He had a plan mapped out which required your presence on the earth at a specific time among a specific group of people.

The truth is God is at work in a person's life even while in the womb. God's divine nature goes into the creation of every human being. Someone once said, "God doesn't make mistakes, people make mistakes." This truly resonates in my life. I was the last of nine birth children. My mother was unmarried and nearly 43 years old when I was born. In addition to these circumstances, it was 1958, a very conservative time in our country, during which unwed mothers were negatively scrutinized. Thankfully, abortion was not legal, and while available, it was more difficult to obtain one. Anyone looking on from the outside would have, and probably did say, "What is that older, poor, unwed mother going to do with another child? He probably will not amount to anything. There are just too many obstacles for a child born into that environment to overcome."

However, they were wrong. With the help of God, He has found a way to make something good out of something bad. That is what God can do when He has a life to work with. No one can, or should attempt to predict the future of another's life. Everyone deserves to live!

APPLICATION:
1. Treat all people with respect because God has a plan for them.
2. Remind yourself your own life is precious and defend those who cannot defend themselves—the unborn!

PRAYER:
Lord, I pray for every judge and elected official's heart to be softened to the cause for unborn life. Help me not to judge their views, but pray for your Spirit to speak to them. Amen.

MARCH 29
KNOWN WHILE UNKNOWN

Psalms 139:13-14
*"For you created my inmost being; you knit me together in my mother's womb.
I praise you because I am fearfully and wonderfully made; your works are
wonderful, I know that full well."* (NIV)

As I stated in yesterday's devotional, abortion is a very personal subject to me because of my own background. If abortions would have been more convenient in the late 50's, I probably would not have been born. I have often wondered if the person with the ability to cure AIDS, cancer, diabetes and every other debilitating and fatal disease was not already sent to this planet in the womb of an expecting mother, but was never given the opportunity to be born.

I realize this is a hot subject politically, but it should never be one morally. Common sense affirms that any living being, outside or inside of the womb, should be respected and given the opportunity to live and discover his/her destiny.

Tertullian said, "For us murder is once for all forbidden; so even the child in the womb... is not lawful for us to destroy. To forbid birth is only quicker murder... The fruit is always present in the seed." Joel Reiter said, "I believe this society will one day look back at the horror of abortion, and critics will ask, 'Where was the Church?' Instead of pointing the finger at scared and often abandoned young women or becoming violent in protests, we, the Church of Jesus Christ, must fight this fight in other ways. Foremost, we should pray for a change in heart for judges and politicians. We should encourage adoption. We should support local crisis pregnancy centers that offer not only alternatives to abortion, but also counsel to those women who have had abortions for any reason. Those women need and deserve the Church's acceptance and forgiveness. Not every person who gets an abortion is bad and not every person who is "pro-choice" is a murderer. Most people have been misled or uninformed."

Although the world may not desire to know the child in the womb, God knows each one of them. There are no unknown people in Christ!

APPLICATION:
1. Pray for the unborn, today.
2. If you, or someone you know is considering an abortion, lovingly speak to her about the sacredness and possibilities of life.

PRAYER:
Lord, speak to the hearts of those near me who are considering abortion, today, and heal those who have had one. Amen.

MARCH 30
INNOCENT UNTIL PROVEN GUILTY

Deuteronomy 27:25
*"Cursed be he that taketh reward to slay an innocent person. And all the people
shall say, Amen." (KJV)*

Something very unusual and eventually amusing happened to me when I was
19. I committed Grand Theft Auto—without knowing it! My story is (and I'm
sticking to it): I was on my way to the bank on a busy Friday afternoon to cash
my check before they closed, so I would have some money for the weekend.
Unfortunately, my car suddenly ran out of gas. I was still about five miles away
from the bank, and I knew I could never walk there and get my check cashed
before they closed. Just then, I noticed I was stranded directly across the street
from the place my father worked. I walked across the street, found him and asked
if I could use his truck to go to the bank and gas station to buy gas for my gas
container. He said "Yes," and pitched me his keys. I went out to the parking lot
and opened the door to the truck and drove off.

I went to the bank, filled my gas container and I returned to my car. I had
just begun pouring gas into my car's tank, when suddenly, I saw a van barreling
towards me with two police cars following. A man jumped out of the van and
started hollering, "He stole my truck! He stole my truck! That's my truck!"

I was shocked and explained he was mistaken. He vehemently declared he
was not mistaken, and assured the police the truck belonged to him. I told him my
father worked just across the street, which happened to be the same place this man
was employed. The police recommended we all go find my father, so we could
straighten out the facts. What we finally discovered was that both my father and
the man in the van, not only worked at the same place, but also had the same color,
model and make of truck. It just so happened that my father's keys opened and
started the wrong truck! I was guilty, yet I was innocent of Grand Theft Auto! We
all laughed and still laugh about it today.

It is the same way with us, as believers. We are all guilty of sin. Yet, we are
innocent because of what Jesus did for us!

APPLICATION:
1. Be sure you fairly assess those you come in contact with, today.
2. Remind yourself you have been declared innocent by the greatest Judge of
   all!

PRAYER:
Lord, thank you for professing me innocent when I am guilty. Amen.

MARCH 31
HE IS ALWAYS THERE!

Psalms 18:2
*"The LORD is my rock, and my fortress, and my deliverer; my God, my strength,
in whom I will trust; my buckler, and the horn of my salvation,
and my high tower."* (KJV)

Another story from my childhood, which reminds me of just how much the Lord has watched over me, occurred when I was about 11 years old. I was riding my bicycle in a local mall parking lot on a Sunday evening during the summer. The mall was closed, so I had the entire lot to myself. I had just installed a speedometer on my bike, so I was trying to see how fast I could go. I peddled as hard as I possibly could and was rounding a corner when something unexpected happened. A car seemed to come out of nowhere and the driver did not see me. It was moving too fast to stop. There was nothing I could do to stop it, so I closed my eyes and yelled out, "Jesus, help me!" I was not even a Christian in those days, but I did believe in God. The next thing I remember was hitting something and falling over. I heard screaming tires, and I thought I was dead. When I opened my eyes, I realized I was not in Heaven, or the other place! I was lying on the pavement with barely a scratch!

Even though I was not a Christian, God was already at work in my life. His grace was looking out for me when I was not even thinking of Him! He was beginning to place His presence in my life in ways that were totally unknown to me.

That is how God is. Even though we are not aware of His presence, He is always there! He is watching and waiting for just the right moment to bring His love and goodness to us in such a way, that we respond by giving our lives to Him.

I look back and realize although I had not answered the call of God for my life at that time, God was already looking out for me and protecting me. I found out He was always there!

APPLICATION:
1. Thank God for His past, present and future protection.
2. Consider how God has had His hand on your life before you even responded to Him.

PRAYER:
Lord, I thank you for your divine protection over my life. I praise you for being there for me when I did not even know it and being there for me in the future. Amen.

APRIL 1
DO NOT BE TRICKED

Proverbs 20:1
"Wine is a mocker and strong drink is raging, and whosoever is deceived thereby is not wise." (KJV)

I read a humorous story a few years ago about the effects of alcohol when you consider what it can do to rats. The story said that during the spring of 1999, in New Delhi, India, a couple of rats got into some confiscated moonshine in storage at the police station. The culprits were soon found inside a back alley trying to attack several cats!

Whether it is consumed by rats or people, alcohol can trick the consumer's thinking, and may potentially lead to deadly behavior. We have declared war on drugs, tobacco and teenage pregnancy, but you could probably go less than a half mile and someone will be glad to sell you all of the alcohol you can afford. It is ironic you do not see tobacco ads on television anymore, but you can be watching just about any program and see multi-million dollar beer ads. They even say, "Drink responsibly." Even worse, is the growing number of Christians who drink alcohol under the guise of "all things in moderation." The Church has gone from a position of opposing alcohol to a position of complicity.

As Christians, we must never forget our bodies are the temple of the Holy Spirit. We have been purchased for His use. You cannot be a mighty man or woman of God and use alcohol. John the Baptist did not drink wine or strong drink, and Jesus called him the greatest prophet who ever lived.

Alcohol deceives you and tries to convince you the next time will be different. It promises something it cannot deliver. We must not let the casualness of society trick us. Alcohol attracts trouble!

The enemy works in our lives this way: he offers us something that appears on the surface to be enjoyable, but hides the fact it is ultimately destructive.

Be sure you are not fooled by its attraction. Just look around at the effect it has had on others and the path of destruction it always seems leave. Do not be tricked!

APPLICATION:
1. Be sure you are not tricked into drinking alcohol.
2. Pray for those you know who are bound by alcohol.

PRAYER:
Lord, help me stay clear from the deception of alcohol. Deliver those around me who are tricked by its allure. Amen.

APRIL 2
WHEN A MAN LOVES A WOMAN

Ephesians 5:28
"That is how husbands should treat their wives, loving them as parts of themselves. For since a man and his wife are now one, a man is really doing himself a favor and loving himself when he loves his wife!" (TLB)

In these days of attacks on traditional families, there are some troubling statistics that deal with marriage. In a survey of senior pastors, the following stats came forth: 70 percent of all counseling sessions conducted by pastors are marriage related. Nine out of ten counseling sessions deal with family life. Only 10 percent are purely spiritual issues, and 20 percent deal with children. 90 percent of the husbands surveyed believe their marriages are at least marginally happy. Only 30 percent of the women surveyed believe the same thing. These statistics reveal something that must be addressed; men are still unskilled in what it takes to make their wives happy. I like the French proverb that says, "A deaf husband and a blind wife are always a happy couple." Herbert Samuel said, "It takes two to make a marriage a success, and only one to make it a failure."

The term "wearing the pants" in today's society generally means who is in charge. There is a great power struggle in today's marriages. There is an emergence of equality in all walks of life. Where does the Christian man stand?

Louis K. Anspacher said, "Marriage is that relation between man and woman in which the independence is equal, the dependence mutual, and the obligation reciprocal." This means men must learn how to respect the individualism of their wives, while maintaining their position as the head of the household. Husbands need to discover what it takes to bring fulfillment to their wives. When they do, the natural response of their wives will be to submit willingly in a loving, lasting relationship.

APPLICATION:
1. If you are married, purposely do something to please your spouse unconditionally, today.
2. Be sure you never demand submission. Help create an environment that is equally shared.

PRAYER:
Lord, show me how to do those things that bring out the best in my spouse. Help me to never be demanding, but caring and loving. Amen.

APRIL 3
BUILDING ON YOUR BLESSING

Psalms 115:14-15
"The LORD shall increase you more and more, you and your children. Ye are blessed of the LORD which made Heaven and earth." (KJV)

God desires for you to build on what He has given you, not to live on it! It is not enough to get off to a right start in building our marriage, career or church on God's principles. We must continuously build on what has been started.

I believe there are six basic principles that will help us continue building upon what God has already blessed: First, we must remain faithful to God to the end. Faithfulness can only be determined by time. (Mark 13:13) Second, God must be in control of our life from start to finish. We cannot deviate and go back to serving ourselves. (Matthew 16:24-26) Third, we must not allow ourselves to become stagnant spiritually, going from faith to faith, glory to glory. (II Corinthians 3:17-18) Fourth, we must seek His presence on a daily basis. God gives us His glory with the intention of it transforming us, not entertaining us! He wants us to take our spiritual experience to the next level. (Exodus 33:14-15) Fifth, we have to keep ourselves stirred up about what we have already received. Sometimes, we are the only one who will encourage ourselves! (I Samuel 20:6) Last, we must thank God, everyday, for what He has already done for us. By giving thanks, we remind not only God, but also ourselves! Gratitude reproduces and nurtures what was already started. (Psalms 103:1-6)

Robert Schuller said it well when he said, "God particularly pours out His blessings upon those who know how much they need Him." We are challenged to continue to grow up in Him in all things. So, no matter how long we may have been believers in Jesus Christ, it is time to put ourselves in position to build on our blessing!

APPLICATION:
1. Be sure to challenge yourself, today, in the six steps that are outlined above.
2. Give more of yourself to God, today, and open up your life for Him to build upon what He has started.

PRAYER:
Lord, I recommit myself to stay on the path you have given me to follow. I will not quit or lag behind, but continue on to the finish line. Amen.

APRIL 4
THANK GOD FOR PREVENTION

Isaiah 58:8-9

"If you do these things, God will shed his own glorious light upon you. He will heal you; your godliness will lead you forward, goodness will be a shield before you, and the glory of the Lord will protect you from behind. Then when you call, the Lord will answer. 'Yes, I am here,' he will quickly reply." (TLB)

An old, overused, but true, proverb is, "An ounce of prevention is worth a pound of cure." Oscar Wilde once said, "If you don't get everything you want, think of the things you don't get that you don't want." I was praying one day and was thanking God for what He had been doing in my life when I felt an interruption inside of my spirit. It was then, I heard that still, small voice say, "There are more things to be thankful for than you are aware of."

My interpretation of those words is God was attempting to tell me I do not notice all of the good things He is doing for me every day in my life. He also pointed out to me there are many things going on around me I am oblivious to that could be potentially destructive: possible problems, troubles and even tragedies. There are situations I never have to confront because they were dealt with by His presence, unknowingly to me.

What accident did I avoid today because I went a different route? What problem did not materialize today because I did not speak the wrong thing, or I did speak the right thing? What future curse was prevented from coming upon me because of a simple decision I made today to pray or read the Word of God? There is really no way to truly determine what my day might have been like instead of what it was.

One thing is for sure; our lives are much more involved and complex than we can imagine, and our God is in constant contact with our lives and our world!

APPLICATION:
1. Thank God, today, for the things that did not come upon you that otherwise might have.
2. Be sure to pray before you start your day.

PRAYER:
Lord, thank you so very much for not allowing the destroyer to bring his destruction to me and my household today. Keep me from the wrong path and lead me by your Spirit. Amen.

APRIL 5
WE HAVE ANGELS

Hebrews 13:2
"Be not forgetful to entertain strangers: for thereby some have entertained angels unawares." (KJV)

One of the most interesting and probably least understood subjects in the Word of God is the ministry of angels. I like the story of the little first grader who loved to sing. One day, while riding in the car, she sang along with a CD by Michael W. Smith. The song she was mimicking was *Angels Unaware*. When it got to the line, "Maybe we are entertaining angels unaware," she sang a different version. Little Jenny sang, "Maybe we are irritating angels unaware." Her rendition may be more truthful than Smith's.

I truly believe, we, as Christians, grossly under use the ministry of angels at our disposal. God has commissioned angels to respond to the believer. Many Christians are unaware or unbelieving where angels are concerned. Some believers even deny any possibility of supernatural intervention in today's times. They are convinced angelic activity was regulated to Bible days only. However, that is not the truth!

I personally have never physically seen an angel, but just because I have not seen one does not make them less real. I have had numerous inexplicable things happen in my life that were beyond human reasoning.

One day, I was painting on a roof, holding on with one hand and painting with the other hand. The hand I was holding on with slipped. It was a steep roof, and I was certainly going to fall off, when something grabbed my hand and fastened it back to the place it was before it slipped! I have had many similar things happen to me in times of danger. I am completely convinced they were supernatural. How do we get angels activated in our lives? We must believe they are sent for us and call on the name of Jesus. When we do, we will experience this great benefit of the believer!

APPLICATION:
1. Thank God for His angels who are encamped around you, daily.
2. Speak the name of Jesus over your life and around you, daily.

PRAYER:
Lord, thank you for the ministry of angels you sent to minister to me. I believe they are at work around me continuously. Amen.

APRIL 6
FACTS ABOUT ANGELS

Hebrews 1:13-14
"But to which of the angels said he at any time, Sit on my right hand, until I make thine enemies thy footstool? Are they not all ministering spirits, sent forth to minister for them who shall be heirs of salvation?" (KJV)

Are you born-again? If so, angels have been provided for you and your family's protection, provision and blessing. However, to fully grasp what they are designed for, we must investigate the Word of God for some important facts.

Angels are mentioned 300 times in the Bible. They are mentioned 100 times in the Old Testament in 17 books, and 200 times in the New Testament in 20 books. They appeared to people 104 times in the Bible.

Angels were in Jesus' arrival, ministry, resurrection, ascension and return. They are involved in all of God's works, provisions, healings and wars. Who are they and what are they doing? They were created before the earth was formed. (Psalms 104:1-4) They are innumerable. (Revelation 5:11) Some fell with Lucifer. (Isaiah 14, Ezekiel 28) Some are bound in chains. (Genesis 6:1-3; Jude 1:6, II Peter 2:4) Some are warring in the atmosphere. (Ephesians 6:12)

More facts about angels: They have bodies.(I Corinthians 15:40) They eat. (Psalms 78:24-25) Your angels do not leave you just because you grow up or get older. (Matthew 18:10; Psalms 34:7) Angels never die. (Luke 20:36)

I heard a great revelation regarding how angels are activated and moving in our lives. (Psalms 103:20) When we speak the Word of God, they are summoned to carry out the will of God for our lives on the earth! (Special thanks to Michael Jacobs for this insight.)

We can see by these facts that the ministry of the angels to God's people is underestimated and understated. We should continue to study this fascinating subject and be continuously thankful for their intervention!

APPLICATION:
1. Stop and think about the many times in your life when angels most likely intervened.
2. Speak the Word about your life and over your life, so that your angels may respond to it.

PRAYER:
Lord, thank you for the ministry of angels in my life today. I am grateful for the salvation delivered to me because of their ministry. Amen.

APRIL 7
WHAT IS YOUR STORY?

Psalms 90:9
"...we spend our years as a tale that is told." (KJV)

The age old question is "What is life?" The age old answer is usually "Life is what you make of it." As cliché as that may be, it is a reality. Our lives are mostly a collection of decisions we have made that have produced the outcome of our existence.

I have officiated many funeral services throughout the years. Psalms 90:9 is usually my lead scripture in most instances. Then, I read the obituary, which generally gives specific information about the deceased: what his/her profession was, where he/she was employed, what church he/she belonged to and who his/her surviving family members were.

Then, when I get to the actual memorial message, I include memorable traits, hobbies, tastes and achievements. My job is to paint as accurate of a picture as I possibly can about him/her, so that anyone who did not know him/her well gets a good sense of who he/she was.

Also, I am obligated to bring the person's memory to life again in a few short moments for those who knew him/her best. I remind them of the significant place the departed held in their lives and encourage them to embrace the good memories for their own lifetime.

This is the way it is with our own lives. Daily, new pages are being written about us. Our story is unfolding. Do you like what the chapters are presently saying? If not, there is still time for a new script. With God's forgiveness, there is also time for a rewrite of some previous chapters. Our lives are a tale that is told!

When your life is over and someone eulogizes you, what will be your story?

APPLICATION: *I would hope it's a story of redemption*

1. Be sure to review what is being written right now. Make any necessary changes to the script.
2. If you do not like the previous chapters, decide to make all remaining chapters so different that the first chapters fade away.

PRAYER:
Lord, my desire is to save the best of my life's story for the finish. Help me to forget the dark chapters and bring in some bright ones. Amen.

APRIL 8
CHANGE IS GOOD

Psalms 55:19
"God shall hear, and afflict them, even he that abideth of old. Selah. Because they have no changes, therefore they fear not God." (KJV)

Heraclitus said, "You cannot step twice into the same river; for other waters are continually flowing on." Equally true is the statement, "The president of today is the postage stamp of tomorrow."

Everything has a season. A *season* is defined as "enough or sufficient time; or appointed time." Every season brings about a change and with the change, something new is available that was not available in the previous season.

Our whole lives are about changes. We go from diapers to adolescence, from adolescence to adulthood, from adulthood to senior life and from senior life to the grave. Nothing can stop or even effectively slow down the inevitable!

However, change is also about new possibilities, new experiences, new relationships and new places. The truth is we need to change. Change is not bad. We need to be discerning about the changes God desires for our lives. Failure to change often brings calamity. Do we see the need for change when it comes? Bruce Fairfield said, "Keep changing. When you're through changing, you're through."

Do not resist the changes God orchestrates in your life. Joseph was a man who found his life in constant change. He was the family man, but went from the family favorite to the pit. He went from the pit to a stranger's house, which eventually caused him to be put in prison. Yet, he went from the prison to the palace!

If you are in a season of change, find God in it and follow Him. He will lead you from the pit to the palace! James Baldwin accurately observed, "People can cry much easier than they can change."

APPLICATION:
1. Take an inventory of your present circumstances. Are you in a season of change?
2. If you are, find God in the change and ask Him how you can make it the most positive season of your life.

PRAYER:
Lord, I will not resist the changes you present in my life. Help me to make the proper adjustments and receive everything you want for me. Amen.

APRIL 9
ARE YOU READY TO FORGIVE

Psalms 86:5

"For thou, Lord art good and ready to forgive; and plenteous in mercy unto all them that call upon thee." (KJV)

"Have you forgiven all your enemies?" inquired a minister. "Haven't got any," said the old man. "Remarkable!" replied the minister. "But how did a red-blooded, two fisted, old battler like you go through life without making any enemies?" asked the minister. The elderly grandfather remarked casually, "I shot 'em."

This conversation pretty much sums up the way we usually deal with relationships. If someone does something we disapprove of, we pull the trigger that shoots them out of our lives, instead of working to salvage them. If we see someone who is wounded, instead of hunting for bandages, we are hunting for another bullet!

After years of observation, I have often remarked you can do 999 things people agree with and do one thing they disagree with, and they will only remember the one thing. They will forget about the good things and good times you have spent together and refuse to forgive and start over. It is as if there were never any good days, history of good times or friendship.

Forgiveness for the believer is not optional. It is not a feeling. It is a choice we make. Like God, we must be willing to show mercy. Mercy always makes a way for forgiveness. Forgiving is a way of settling outstanding debts owed to you. Some debts can never be collected. The only way of settling these debts is to forgive them.

Another important result of forgiveness is it delivers us from evil. (Luke 11:4) Forgiveness thwarts the attacks of the Devil. (II Corinthians 2:10-11)

When we forgive, we "put to death" our attitudes and agendas. When they are laid to rest, then, and only then, something fresh and new can come forth!

APPLICATION:
1. If you are currently in un-forgiveness, be sure you release these grievances to God and forgive those people today, before the sun sets.
2. If you need to be forgiven by someone, pray for God to speak to their heart and soften it towards you.

PRAYER:
Lord, I choose today, to forgive those who have trespassed against me. I leave them in your hands and ask for all bitterness in my heart to be removed. Amen.

APRIL 10
ONCE A THIEF, ALWAYS A THIEF

John 10:10
"The thief cometh not, but for to steal, and to kill, and to destroy: I am come that they might have life, and that they might have it more abundantly." (KJV)

If I was asked to point out just one verse in the Bible that has had the greatest impact on my life, it would be John 10:10. I call it, "the great divide" scripture. This scripture accurately identifies the thief, robber and destroyer of our lives. It also tells us who the thief is not.

For years, even as a Christian, I believed God was my problem. I did not realize I had a sworn enemy antagonizing my family and me. It caused me to question God, my faith and the Word of God.

I found the Devil (Satan, Lucifer, etc.) is mentioned less than 20 times in the Old Testament, but over 60 times in the New Testament. When Jesus came, He exposed not only who Satan is, but also what he is. Satan is the troublemaker.

Jesus reminded the people He came, so that we might have life and life with abundance. He drew the line in the sand and shined the light on the Devil.

What is the Devil's personality? His personality is to rob the people of God of their faith. When you let the Devil come in, you are asking for trouble. Ephesians 4:27 says to give the Devil no place. The New English Bible translation of this verse says, *"Do not give the Devil and opportunity."* After all, to worm his way into our lives and minds, the Devil does not need much room at all—a little slit of a loophole will work just fine.

Satan is looking for a crack. The Puget Sound of Washington State, although very wet, occasionally cracks open as much as a mile and a half. Likewise, when we cannot absorb the Devil's attacks, a crack forms creating an entrance for him. It is through life's cracks and loopholes evil dynamics gain entrance. The Church must close these loopholes.

APPLICATION:
1. Be sure to place the blame of your troubles on the troublemaker and not God!
2. Submit yourself to God and resist the Devil. Satan will flee!

PRAYER:
Lord, I thank you for keeping the thief out of my life and giving me an abundant life. Amen.

APRIL 11
USE WHAT YOU HAVE

Romans 12:6
"Having then gifts according to the grace that is given to us..." (KJV)

Someone once said, "I don't know why I do what I do, but some of the things I do always bring comfort to those around me." This is a pretty good description of how God brings things to light that are deposited inside of us.

There are four different types of gifts God has given to His people listed in the Bible: 1. Ministerial gifts: apostles, prophets, evangelists, pastors and teachers. They are given to equip the saints to do the work of the ministry. (Ephesians 4:11) 2. Sign gifts: cast out Devils, speak with new tongues, take on serpents, purify deadly fluids and lay hands on the sick. They are available to every believer. (Mark 16:15-18) 3. Spiritual gifts: word of wisdom, word of knowledge, discerning of spirits, prophecy, diverse tongues, interpretation, working of miracles, faith and healings. (I Corinthians 12) 4. Motivational gifts. There are seven gifts (blessings) that motivate. A motivational gift is why you do what you do—what motivates you! Motivation flows through personality, gender, culture and ministry. Each one is unique and necessary. The first is prophecy. (Paul, Elijah, Jonah—I Kings 17-19) The second is serving. (Martha—Luke 10:38-42) The third is teaching. (Luke—Luke 1:1-4) The fourth is encouraging. (Barnabas—Acts 9:26-28; 15:39) The fifth is giving. (Widow Woman at the treasury—Luke 7:37; Mary with the Alabaster box) Administration is the sixth. (Jethro—Exodus 18:13-24) The last is mercy. (Jeremiah 1:4-12)

These gifts flow through us and when we understand how to use them, they become a great blessing to those around us. We must learn how to let our gifts flow out!

APPLICATION:
1. Discover the gifts you have inside of you. Learn how to let them flow out of you.
2. Learn how to identify the gifts inside of those around you, and allow them to be who they are.

PRAYER:
Lord, please show me how to use the gifts you have deposited in me. Amen.

APRIL 12
GOING FOR GREATNESS

Exodus 11:3
"And the LORD gave the people favour in the sight of the Egyptians. Moreover the man Moses was very great in the land of Egypt, in the sight of Pharaoh's servants, and in the sight of the people." (KJV)

One of the most amazing things about God is His ability to bring out greatness in very ordinary people. I know this personally. I am not calling myself great, but I understand where I came from and how God has commissioned very extraordinary things through my life. Only God could have known what was possible and how to bring it out. Henry Wadsworth Longfellow said, "Great men stand like solitary towers in the city of God."

How do we obtain the greatness God desires for us? I believe there are some steps, which will help lead us there. First of all, we must recognize what Jesus did for us. His work in us is still ongoing. The more we yield to His work, the more room for greatness there will be.

Second, we must continue to sow what we have. By serving others, we sow towards greatness. To become great, you must first serve. (Matthew 20:24-27) Dwight Lyman Moody observed, "The beginning of greatness is to be little; the increase of greatness is to be less; the perfection of greatness is to be nothing."

Third, we must realize the worst day as a Christian is still better than the best day as a sinner! As Christians, we should be filled with the hope of the Gospel. Sir Thomas Fuller said, "Great hopes make great men."

Fourth, we must do everything unto Him. Every time we lift up the Kingdom of God, we build a platform for our own greatness.

Finally, we must always remember, the Greater One is within us. Sir Walter Scott said it well, "All greatness is unconscious." We must always consider, "Great men never know they are great."

APPLICATION:
1. Be sure to humble yourself before God and allow Him to shine through you.
2. Use your gifts to benefit others today.

PRAYER:
Lord, I purposely devote my life to uplifting you. I trust you to lift me up as I do. Amen.

APRIL 13
GO AFTER THE LOST

Proverbs 14:25
"A witness who tells the truth saves good men from being sentenced to death,
but a false witness is a traitor." (TLB)

Have you ever lost something and then launched a relentless search until you found it? You probably turned every piece of furniture in your house upside down. You most likely looked in the same places several times. You cancelled appointments that, at the beginning of the day, seemed much more important. You had an urgency to recover that which was lost! Nothing mattered as much as finding the lost item.

God has the same urgency for lost souls. Nothing is as important to Him as recovering the crown of His creation—His people!

There are two classes of people. The first group includes those who have never been born-again. They have been on a journey leading to certain destruction. They do not know any other way. The second group is composed of those who have been in church, but have lost their way. They have been on the right path at some time in their lives, but have made a wrong turn. Each group will perish unless the body of Christ shows them the way.

Those who have been on the right road, but have left it, are most often referred to as Prodigals. They are everywhere! They are at work, the market and everywhere you go. They may have had a bad experience which caused them to stray. They might have even had a bad experience at a church or with God's people. However, regardless of their reason, without someone to intervene, they will be lost eternally.

John 3:16 tells us Jesus came, so every person can have access to the road leading to eternal life. We have been sent to reap His harvest. Let us ignite the urgency and pursue the lost!

APPLICATION:
1. Begin looking around you for the lost and be willing to lead them to the right road, today.
2. Let His love flow through you to them.

PRAYER:
Lord, ignite an urgency inside of me for those who are lost and on the wrong road. Your desire is my desire. Amen.

APRIL 14
MAKING MONEY YOUR SERVANT

Luke 16:11-13

"And if you are untrustworthy about worldly wealth, who will trust you with the true riches of Heaven? And if you are not faithful with other people's money, why should you be entrusted with money of your own? For neither you nor anyone else can serve two masters. You will hate one and show loyalty to the other, or else the other way around—you will be enthusiastic about one and despise the other. You cannot serve both God and money." (TLB)

How you handle finances reveals whether money serves you or if you serve money. People who depend on money allow themselves to become its servant. Over the many years I have been around church people, I have noticed a distinction between two different attitudes concerning money. There are those who constantly talk about money and repeatedly create schemes to get rich. They are always attempting to enlist you to join their "group." These people are so caught up in the pursuit of money, that even when they get it, they do not know what to do with it. They seldom spend much of it on their loved ones. They become "tight" with their pennies, trying to pile it up. If they give to the Kingdom of God at all, it is usually the minimum. Honestly, these people never seem to be very happy and content.

On the other hand, there are people who find a way to make money their servant. They are thoughtful to their family and those around them. They are generous and often out-give people with greater incomes. Yet, they seem to be content and very happy.

What is the difference? It is really a trust issue. The people serving money do not really trust God. They try to produce money themselves with their ingenuity and scheming. The people allowing money to serve them have discovered dependence on God, shifts the weight of their prosperity to Him. Be sure you are not serving money, but making it your servant!

APPLICATION:
1. Check your heart. Do you trust in money or God?
2. Identify the reason for your prosperity. It is to promote the Gospel and bless those around you.

PRAYER:
Lord, forgive me for serving money. Help me to be your servant only! Amen.

APRIL 15
RENDER UNTO GOD

Mark 12:15-17
"...Why tempt ye me? Bring me a penny, that I may see it. And they brought it. And he saith unto them, Whose is this image and superscription? And they said unto him, Caesar's. And Jesus answering said unto them, Render to Caesar the things that are Caesar's, and to God the things that are God's. And they marveled at him." (KJV)

Martin Luther astutely observed, "There are three conversions necessary: the conversion of the heart, mind and the purse." Of these three, today's generation seemingly finds the conversion of the purse the most difficult.

For most Americans, April 15th is a dreaded day. It is the last day for filing your income taxes. People stress over this for months, and often rush to the accountants or post office at the last possible moment. Their reasoning is they do not want to give the government any more of their money until they absolutely have to.

Many people have the same attitude towards giving to the Kingdom of God. They do not give anymore than they have to, and even then, usually do so because they feel guilty or pressured. Although often disregarded, God has established perimeters for giving. He has earmarked the tithe, 10 percent, as His. It is Holy. It is non-negotiable. If you keep it, you are cursed. It becomes stolen money.

I remember one time, when I was younger while working at Dairy Queen. A customer ran back into the dining room shouting, "It's just not worth it!" and handed me a dime. I inquired, "What's the dime was for?" He told me how just a week before, he was at another restaurant and was given ten dollars too much in change and kept it. As he was backing his car out of the parking lot of that restaurant, he hit another car, and it cost him over four hundred dollars to fix it! He explained he had just been in our store and was a few miles down the road, when he noticed he had been given ten cents too much, and it just was not worth the cost to keep it.

It is not worth it for us to keep what belongs to God!

APPLICATION:
1. Be sure you are rendering to God what is His.
2. Never negotiate with God over the tithe. It is already His! Do not disregard His giving perimeters.

PRAYER:
Lord, forgive me for not rendering to you what is already yours. Amen.

APRIL 16
WHAT CAN YOU DO TO BE A BLESSING?

Zechariah 8:13
"And it shall come to pass, that as ye were a curse among the heathen, O house of Judah, and house of Israel; so will I save you, and ye shall be a blessing: fear not, but let your hands be strong." (KJV)

Over 100 years ago, D.L. Moody lashed out as a loving critic to certain parts of the Church of his time for its misappropriation of energies. He said the Church reminded him of firemen straightening pictures on a wall of a burning house!

His point was not only for his day. Presently, we are surrounded by people God blesses in abundance, time after time, but many seldom seem to give back to others in any measure.

After you become a Christian, what is next for you? God's rule is once you become blessed, you are to become a blessing. Still, it is difficult sometimes to find a way to bless others on a consistent basis. We underestimate how God can use us to touch the lives of others.

There are six Bible attributes, which will help you be a blessing to God and to those He sends you to. The first is to be a worshipper. When you praise and worship, you help create an atmosphere where Jesus can appear. God always used the one closest to Him. The second way is to be wise hearted. God gives wisdom to those who ask Him. He uses people whose hearts are full of His wisdom. The next way is to be a worker. Dr. Mark T. Barclay said, "I want to work with God and not just for Him." When we offer to God what we have, He always breathes on it and it becomes blessed. The fourth way is to be a Word person. The more of the Word you have inside of you, the more it will pour out and bless others. The fifth way is to be a witness to others. Sheep beget sheep. Every time you tell your testimony, you bless others with hope. The final way is to be willing to use your abilities in the Kingdom. God has given you areas of unique ability, which are needed.

Always remember, you are God's hands and feet to those who cannot walk without help in life and those who cannot reach what God has for them without assistance.

APPLICATION:
1. Find someone today you can be a blessing to.
2. Apply the six principles to your life daily.

PRAYER:
Lord, increase my desire to bless those you place in my presence. Amen.

APRIL 17
OVERCOMING WEARINESS

II Samuel 21:15
"Now when the Philistines were at war again with Israel, David went down and his servants with him; and as they fought against the Philistines, David became weary." (NASV)

The Bible says even young men get weary. Sometimes we think weariness means to be weak, but that is not necessarily the case. Weariness often comes after making a stand against an attack!

Although David grew older, attacks still persisted. It seemed as if he could not keep up with the Philistines anymore. He was experiencing a prolonged series of setbacks, and he needed God to intervene. At this low moment in his life, David discovered something about warfare; our adversaries come again and again. When you win a battle, another one is around the corner!

II Samuel 21:19 says, *"Again a battle; yet a battle."* (KJV) David became exhausted. He had just lost a son, the nation was in famine and the Philistines were back. However, this time David had to find another way to fight, so he sang a song of praise. He rehearsed his victories. He thanked and praised God. David did not let his emotions rule his decision making. Instead, he reminded God of his love for Him and thanked Him for what He had already done in his life! This was familiar territory for him. What had worked before, would work again. David was mindful of these things: 1. God is a covenant keeping God. (Psalms 89:34-35) 2. God would not forsake him. (Psalms 27:10; 35:25) 3. It was God's will for him to win. (Psalms 37:23-34)

If you are experiencing a wave of weariness, just cry out to Him and He will answer you. You will overcome the weariness!

APPLICATION:
1. Place yourself into the presence of God and your weariness will turn into victory!
2. Reconsider your past victories and realize how you won because you did not quit when you were weary.

PRAYER:
Lord, I worship you in the middle of my weariness. I thank you for helping me win once again! Amen.

APRIL 18
OVERCOMING LIFE'S PRESSURES

Proverbs 24:10
"You are a poor specimen if you can't stand the pressure of adversity." (TLB)

The world we live in today is filled with daily pressures, which did not exist 100 years ago. We have crazy, over inflated schedules. We try to keep pace with those around us, so we will not fall back in the pack. We live in houses we cannot afford, drive cars we do not need and our credit is maxed out.

As real as some of these pressures may be, there is also pressure that comes in our spiritual lives. Temptations are everywhere luring us to do something other than follow God. Shakespeare said, "Tis one thing to be tempted, another thing to fall."

This is the constant war between the flesh and the spirit. The spirit is designed to stand up against the pressure. The flesh is designed to fall. Before we yield to the pressure of the flesh, we must consider the long term results of sin.

Esau gave in and lost his birthright. Lot's wife gave in and turned into a pillar of salt. Saul gave in and lost his kingdom and his life. There are always consequences, which accompany succumbing to temptations.

Adversity always reveals not only what we are made of, but also, who we really are. Are we the strong believer we portray to those around us? Or are we, in reality, living off the fumes of some past move of God in our lives?

Pressure will reveal the true position of our faith. The daily attacks on your faith will undoubtedly come. "Let us be like a bird for a moment, perched on a frail branch when he sings; though he feels it bend, yet he sings his song, knowing that he has wings." (Hugo)

So the question is not whether or not you will be under pressure, but what will you do when it comes?

APPLICATION:
1. Turn the pressure you feel, today, into faith by dealing with it in the Spirit through prayer.
2. Be sure to endure by not quitting, no matter how hard the trial may be.

PRAYER:
Lord, help me stay in the Spirit when the pressures come, and not to give into the weakness of the flesh. Amen.

APRIL 19
WHAT GOD REQUIRES OF YOU

Deuteronomy 10:12
*"And now, Israel, what does the Lord your God require of you except to
listen carefully to all he says to you, and to obey for your own good the
commandments I am giving you today, and to love him, and to
worship him with all your hearts and souls?"* (TLB)

I have always enjoyed the story of Oliver Cromwell, who reigned over the British government for a season. Someone brought it to the attention of Lord Cromwell that the British government was running low on silver for coins. Lord Cromwell sent his men to investigate the local cathedral to determine if there were precious metals there. After investigating, they reported, "The only silver we could find is in the radical soldier statues of the saints standing in the corners." To which Lord Cromwell and the statesman of England replied, "Good! We'll melt down the saints and put them into circulation." (Source Unknown)

Before one can go in and possess the land, one must first meet the requirements. The children of Israel did not know how to possess. They had forgotten in captivity. They were accustomed to following tyrant's orders, which only benefited him.

However, God was trying to help them go somewhere they had not ever been, and inherit something, which once was out of reach. They needed to qualify first! The requirements for qualification were simple: 1. They had to listen to His direction. 2. They had to love Him. 3. They had to worship only Him.

Today, those same requirements apply. If we will listen to Him, He will direct us to victory. If we love Him first, He will supply all our needs. If we worship Him, He will be our God and carry and defend us. Are you ready to get into circulation? Are you ready to apply?

APPLICATION:
1. Retain the requirements and be sure to adjust accordingly.
2. Be willing to modify your direction as He speaks to you.

PRAYER:
Lord, I willingly open my ears to hear you. I make a decision to love you with all my heart. I choose to worship only you. I am ready to be led. Amen.

APRIL 20
LEADING WITH INTEGRITY

Psalms 78:72
"So he shepherded them (led) according to the integrity of his heart, and guided them with his skillful hands." (NASV)

If you are a candidate for leadership, you must have integrity! Integrity is standing behind the things you say you believe. The Hebrew word is *tom* (tome) meaning "upright, complete and perfect, or mature." It means to be unbending in times of stress. It means maintaining a solid character when others compromise.

The Bible shows us what happens when God's people walk in integrity. Joseph was placed in a situation where he could have compromised, and given into the seductive wife of his master. However, he held his integrity fast, even though it caused him to be thrown into prison. In the short term, it looked like a bad decision, but later, paid great dividends. His integrity was rewarded by his promotion to the top leader in the land under only Pharaoh.

There are some things about integrity we should consider. First, Psalms 25:21 explains: integrity preserves, and maintains rightness. Integrity has a long lasting ability to preserve the beholder of it. Second, Psalms 7:8 says we are judged according to our integrity. Eventually, our integrity is the only true measuring stick of who we are. Third, Genesis 20 says integrity brings about the mercy of God in time of need. It can be a lifesaver. God is present where integrity is practiced. I Kings 9:1-5 explains that integrity brings His Holiness to the situation. Integrity creates a Holy environment for God's presence.

In our lives, we will have daily challenges against our integrity. We must understand God is looking for leaders. If we maintain our integrity, we will be the leading candidates. Integrity is always the slower way to victory, but is also the sure way to victory.

APPLICATION:
1. Check your heart for integrity.
2. Do not to compromise. Remember, God is looking for integrity in our lives.

PRAYER:
Lord, forgive me for not using integrity in all areas of my life. Give me the strength and grace to be a leader for your Kingdom. Amen.

APRIL 21
RUNNING THE RACE

Hebrews 12:1-2
"Since we have such a huge crowd of men of faith watching us from the grandstands, let us strip off anything that slows us down or holds us back, and especially those sins that wrap themselves tightly around our feet and trip us up; and let us run with patience the particular race that God has set before us."
(TLB)

Have you ever tried to run a race with a suitcase full of bricks? Many years ago, I preached a message using that illustration. I filled a suitcase with bricks and placed it on the stage before the congregation arrived. I started my sermon with Hebrews 12:1-2, and asked a congregational member to come up, take the suitcase and run with it. When he lifted the suitcase, he almost dropped it and could not even walk with it. I used this illustration to prove a point—we, too often, try to run the race of faith with baggage that should never be a part of our running gear.

There are things that we must rid ourselves of if we are going to be successful. Ten pieces of unnecessary baggage are: 1. Worry. Do not spend time worrying about things on earth. God has a master plan for this world and you. 2. Temptation. Separate yourself on purpose from temptation. Do not give place to the Devil. 3. Sexual Sins. Have nothing to do with sexual sin, impurity, lust and shameful desires. Cut off all possibility of sexual misconduct. 4. Idols. Do not worship material things in life. Do not pursue success, for the sake of success. 5. Anger. Cast off and throw away all rotten garments of anger. Anger is the forerunner of hatred. 6. Hatred. Cast off the rotten garment of hatred. Hatred is the result of anger that has not been dealt with. 7. Cursing. Cast off the rotten garment of cursing. The power of life and death are in the tongue. 8. Lying. Do not tell lies to others. Telling a lie is the foundation for all evil. 9. Vanity. Do not worry about making a good impression on others. Be yourself. God has accepted you and that is good enough. 10. Bitterness. Never hold grudges. The Greek word means "groan, as in pain or discomfort." As long as you hold a grudge, you are self-inflicting pain.

Unload the "bricks" keeping you from running freely today!

APPLICATION:
1. Check yourself for unnecessary baggage.
2. Cast off the things that are slowing you down!

PRAYER:
Lord, help me to unload the things slowing me down! Amen.

APRIL 22
RUNNING TO WIN

I Corinthians 9:24-25

"Know ye not that they which run in a race run all, but one receiveth the prize?
So run, that ye may obtain. And every man that striveth for the mastery is
temperate in all things. Now they do it to obtain a corruptible crown;
but we an incorruptible." (KJV)

Frank Harrington, pastor of the Peachtree Presbyterian Church in Atlanta, Georgia, says it always bothers him when the runners are running hurdles, and they knock down one or two of them. He says he thinks they should go back and straighten them up. If his mother were coaching, they would. It would be important to her that they leave things neat and in order for the next runners. "But then," Dr. Harrington states, "Hurdlers who win gold medals don't look back—they ignore the fallen hurdles and keep on running toward the finish line!"

No matter how fast you run or how hard you run, eventually there will be unexpected things that will cross your path. I was running one day in my neighborhood when suddenly a dog came seemingly from nowhere and ran right out in front of me. I did not hesitate or stop, I kept running. In fact, I ran faster!

There are always going to be things in the path of victory slowing you down, distracting you or making you weary. However, this is when you need to gain your second wind. A good runner will tell you this is not as much of a physical renewal of energy as it is mental. They purposely remind themselves what is at stake and use it as a focal point. This gives them incentive to reach deep inside and gain one more push of acceleration.

When you find yourself winded, it is important to remind yourself what is ahead. God has some preset rewards at the finish line. Remember, while winning is important, finishing is essential!

APPLICATION:
1. If you are winded, focus on the finish line.
2. Do not let the things of daily life slow you down or distract you from finishing.

PRAYER:
Lord, I purpose in my heart that I will keep my focus on you and finish the race as you place your Spirit upon me. Amen.

APRIL 23
DEALING WITH TRAGEDY

Job 10:19-22

"I should have been as though I had not been; I should have been carried from the womb to the grave. Are not my days few? Cease then, and let me alone, that I may take comfort a little, before I go whence I shall not return, even to the land of darkness itself and of the shadow of death; A land of darkness, as darkness itself; and of the shadow of death, without any order, and where the light is as darkness." (KJV)

Being a pastor, I have walked with people through some very dark moments of their lives. I have been there when families have dealt with suicides, murders and fatal car wrecks, among many other tragic events. It is always hard to understand why. Yet, as Christians, we must consider the following: When something bad happens to a Christian, it is either because they are doing something wrong, or they are doing something right.

There are reasons for each situation. Saphira and Ananias suffered a tragic ending for lying to the Holy Ghost. Stephen suffered a tragic ending for maintaining a Christian witness.

I have noticed most so called "Word people" have no concept of dealing with tragedy. They "confess" it will not happen to them, and if it does, they are not prepared to handle it. Something equally as disturbing is their quick judgment of people who are suffering from the effects of a tragic incident. They miss opportunities to give comfort and to be the arms of love, so desperately needed at those moments. They give "pat" answers to those who are hurting around them. Like John Henry Jowett said, "God does not comfort us to make us comfortable, but to make us comforters."

If you have suffered from tragedy, do not let grief get the best of you. Do not blame yourself for things that have happened to you. They may just have happened because you have done something right!

APPLICATION:
   1. Let God heal you if you are hurting from a past tragic event.
   2. Remember, bad things happen to good people.

PRAYER:
Lord, fill me with your love and healing. Help me understand the things I do not understand. Amen.

APRIL 24
SO WHAT DO YOU THINK?

Proverbs 23:7
"For as he thinketh in his heart, so is he..." (KJV)

William James said, "The greatest discovery of my generation is that human beings can alter their lives by altering their attitudes of mind."

Although this statement may borderline on Christian Science, it is still Biblically sound. God has installed inside of every human being the capability to reach higher, but it begins with what we think about our own life.

Unlike dianetics, Biblical transformation is based on human thought that comes as a result of meditating on God's Word. It is replacing human calculations and discernments with the creative power of the spoken Word. The same Word God used when He spoke the universe into existence in the book of Genesis.

In 1978, two years after my born-again experience, I found my life still in a downward spiral. I discovered being a Christian did not change my external circumstances at all. As a matter of fact, the next three years were some of my worst. I lost everything!

Yet, during that time I listened to a tape by Kenneth Copeland entitled, *The Power of the Tongue.* I soon discovered the secret to my success was under my nose. The secret was to speak His Word about my life out of my own mouth. I began to spend enormous amounts of time reading and listening to God's Word. During that time something happened inside of me—my thinking about myself changed. I began to see myself as an overcomer on the earth—not just when I got to Heaven. I started speaking the Word over and over, and it was not long until I recovered all I had lost in even greater measure. I changed what I thought and as a result, changed my life.

Emerson said, "A man is what he thinks about all day long." The Roman emperor, Marcus Aurelius, put it this way, "A man's life is what his thoughts make of it." So, what do you think?

APPLICATION:
1. Spend some time meditating on what God says about your life.
2. Use Jeremiah 29:11, *"For I know the thoughts that I think towards you... To give you a future and a hope."* (NKJV)

PRAYER:
Lord, I purposely flush the thoughts regarding my life that are counter-productive and speak what you say about me. I say your Word says I am saved, healed and delivered, and I am! Amen.

APRIL 25
ENTERING HIS PRESENCE

Psalms 16:11
"You have let me experience the joys of life and the exquisite pleasure of your own eternal presence." (TLB)

Have you ever had the opportunity to meet someone you either admired or had great respect for? Something inside of you becomes excited and even a bit fearful. You want to see and meet them, but you do not want to say or do something silly that will bring embarrassment to you.

Entering the presence of God is just the opposite! It calms all of your fears. It brings a peace and projects unexpected acceptance. It makes you, the sinner, feel welcome in the presence of pure holiness. It is the beginning of transformation. It produces unspeakable joy. It marks the will of God clearly for your life and gives direction. It produces the power of God.

The presence of God produces freshness in your life. You realize God is the only one who can bring true and lasting pleasure to your life. There is a sense of hope that becomes ignited inside of you, a sense that no matter how bleak your circumstances may be—you are going to make it!

Many years ago, I was at the Southwest Believer's Convention in Ft. Worth, Texas, in a worship service. The worship leader, Len Mink, began to minister prophetically in song. The words he sang really resonated inside of my spirit. He said, "The excitement you desire is in Me, saith the Lord. You won't find it any place else!"

I found these words to be very accurate. There are many things in this life that bring satisfaction, but it is always temporary. Yet, when we enter His presence, it is always new and refreshing! How can you enter in? With thanksgiving.

God is waiting for us to draw closer to Him. He has opened the door of His throne room and given us a standing invitation to enter even when we are in need of His help.

So, what are you waiting for? Enter His presence, today!

APPLICATION:
1. Stop and spend some time just thanking God and enter into His presence, today!
2. Leave all of your problems at His feet! Enjoy!

PRAYER:
Lord, I enter into your presence with great anticipation. Fill me with your glory! Amen.

APRIL 26
PASSING YOUR MANTLE

II Kings 2:12-14

"And Elisha saw it, and he cried, My father, my father, the chariot of Israel, and the horsemen thereof. And he saw him no more: and he took hold of his own clothes, and rent them into two pieces. He took up also the mantle of Elijah that fell from him, and went back, and stood by the bank of Jordan; And he took the mantle of Elijah that fell from him, and smote the waters, and said, Where is the LORD God of Elijah? And when he also had smitten the waters, they parted hither and thither: and Elisha went over." (KJV)

Webster defines a *mantle* as "something that covers, envelops, or conceals." The Hebrew word *addereth* means "glory, cloak and splendor; magnificence." Elisha saw the splendor within Elijah and equated it with the prophet's mantle he wore. He saw the evidence of God's power in Elijah's life and desired to carry that same anointing in his life. Jesus' mantle was so full of His anointing that the woman with the issue of blood touched the hem of if His garment and was instantly healed. (Luke 8:43-48)

The truth is everyone has a mantle. It is an apparent gift and touch from Heaven, which blesses people when they are exposed to it. It may be a gift to build things, to design things, to cook, to work with handicapped people or perhaps in the area of the arts. Some people are aware of it and some are not. Likewise, God's plan is for us to not only let the mantle flow through us to help others, but to also pass it on to those who can contain and disperse it.

What we have is meant to be passed on to those around us. Isaiah 38:19 says, *"...One generation makes known your faithfulness to the next."* (TLB) The mantle we possess is the result of someone else passing it on to us.

I liken it to the story of the guy who was called to fix a piece of machinery at a factory. He hit it twice with a hammer and sent a bill for 100 dollars. "What!?" asked the owner. "One dollar for hitting and 99 dollars for knowing where to hit!" replied a staff member.

If you know where to hit, then pass it on!

APPLICATION:
    1. Let the mantle that is on you flow out and pass it on.
    2. Remember, there is no success without a successor.

PRAYER:
Lord, help me to lead others, so that when I am done, I have found my own replacement! Amen.

APRIL 27
WHAT GOD WANTS FOR EVERY BELIEVER

III John 1:2

"Beloved, I wish above all things that thou mayest prosper and be in health,
even as thy soul prospereth." (KJV)

The above scripture was written to the elders. God's will was unquestioningly for every believer to excel. Because this verse was written to the elders, it was apparent not every believer was at the maturity level to handle God's blessings.

God promised financial prosperity. There can be no question God wants His people to prosper financially. God is a God of increase! (Leviticus 26:1-10) There certainly is no shortage on the earth. Gold is mentioned 361 times in the Bible, including just outside of the Garden of Eden. (Genesis 2:8-16) Someone calculated the present known wealth on the earth and what its value would be if it were divided among all believers. The result? About 10 million dollars for everyone! It is just in the wrong hands, for now.

The second promise listed is physical well being. In a time of uncertain health coverage and failing insurance companies, this is a great promise from God. Jesus' death was only after he had addressed our need for bodily health by receiving stripes on His back. (Isaiah 53:4-5) Even with the advancement of medicine, people are still dying all around us at alarming rates.

Both of these great promises are for the present, not in Heaven, as many preach and believe. There will be no need for financial blessings, nor will there be any sickness or diseases to be healed from in Heaven.

The most important thing to consider is both promises are contingent on spiritual prosperity first. There must be stability in character to handle money. There must be a full dependence on God, without wavering, to walk in divine health.

No matter what others may tell you God wants from you, do not look to them for your direction. Mature in your faith and these things will be yours!

APPLICATION:
1. Be sure you exercise your faith and "grow up" in Him in all things.
2. Do not pursue things—pursue Him!

PRAYER:
Lord, thank you for the promise of your blessing. By faith, I receive! Amen.

131

APRIL 28
THE GIFT OF CHILDREN

Psalms 127:3-5
"Children are a gift from God; they are his reward. Children born to a young man are like sharp arrows to defend him. Happy is the man who has his quiver full of them. That man shall have the help he needs when arguing with his enemies." (TLB)

Peter Collier said, "You're family is what you've got... It's your limit and your possibilities. Sometimes you'll get so far away from it you'll think you're outside its influence forever, then before you figure out what's happening, it will be right beside you, pulling the strings. Some people get crushed by their families. Others are saved by them." There is no doubt your family can be a great source of frustration, but it can be a great source of strength and love.

The great American entertainer Art Linkletter used to host a television program back in the 1950's entitled, *Kids Say the Darndest Things*. I like an episode, in which a little girl climbed up on the lap of her great grandmother and looked at her white hair and wrinkles and asked, "Did God make you?" "Yes," the grandmother replied. The little girl asked another question, "Did God make me, too?" To which the grandmother said, "Yes." The little girl questioned yet again, "Well, don't you think He's doing a better job now than he used to?"

Additionally, there was a little boy who wrote his pastor a letter and said, "Dear Preacher, I heard you say to love our enemies. I am only six and do not have any yet. I hope to have some when I am seven. Your friend, Jimmy."

If you are afraid of being embarrassed by something your children may say in public, rest easy—it will happen! Our children's church director has told me on several occasions that the children in her class innocently "tell" on their parents. She said one little boy after being asked if his parents read him a Bible story before bed had replied, "My daddy usually falls asleep in the living room in his chair right after he has had a few beers!" Another little girl said when asked if her daddy lived at home with her and her mommy, "I don't have a daddy around the house, but I do have a lot of uncles that come and stay all night with my mommy!"

APPLICATION:
1. Spend quality time with your children.
2. Be assured they are listening and repeating what you say and do!

PRAYER:
Lord, thank you for my family. Help me be the right example. Amen.

APRIL 29
LEFT OUT

Hebrews 8:12
"For I will be merciful to their unrighteousness, and their sins and their iniquities will I remember no more." (KJV)

Have you ever had someone tell you something about someone you knew, but you already knew what they were telling you? Yet, they left out part of the story? This is how it is with Satan and God in your life.

The enemy tells you God is unhappy with you, and you may as well go ahead and sin. However, if you have already gone to God and repented for that sin, then that sin has been "left out" of the story of your life.

I saw a movie about a criminal who had served his full term in prison and had finally been released. He went out into the world after years of incarceration and found himself missing his old cell and old life. He just could not seem to adjust to the fact that particular part of his life was gone. He struggled until finally one day, he intentionally committed a crime and had to return to prison. He just could not come to terms that his past had been forgiven. It had been cast out.

I see many Christians who are the same way. They just cannot seem to understand their old records of sin have been left out of their history. They just cannot grasp they have become new and their old man has died. They just keep digging him up.

We must come to grips with what has been done for us. We are not old sinners, saved by grace. We were old sinners. We were saved by grace. Now, we are born-again believers. We are *"created in Christ Jesus unto good works."* (Ephesians 2:10 KJV)

If God has chosen to "leave out" the past parts of your life of sin, then you should not keep putting them back in. Let us walk in the newness of life in Christ Jesus. Let us not fall to the old tactics of the Devil where our past is concerned. After all, our past has been left out of the story of our lives!

APPLICATION:
1. Do not bring your past up anymore unless it is to testify to others of God's forgiveness.
2. Walk as a born-again believer!

PRAYER:
Lord, I choose to forgive myself the way you have forgiven me. I will leave out what you have removed from my life. Amen.

APRIL 30
BREAKING THE SPIRIT OF POVERTY

Isaiah 41:17-19

"When the poor and needy seek water and there is none, and their tongues are parched from thirst, then I will answer when they cry to me. I, Israel's God, will not ever forsake them. I will open up rivers for them on high plateaus! I will give them fountains of water in the valleys! In the deserts will be pools of water, and rivers fed by springs shall flow across the dry, parched ground. I will plant trees—cedars, myrtle, olive trees, the cypress, fir and pine—on barren land." (TLB)

Poverty entered this planet as a result of sin. In the Garden of Eden, there was no lack of any good thing. As a matter of fact, gold was even plenteous nearby. It was a place of lush and lavish living.

When sin entered in, the curse entered. Man had to sweat and toil for menial things such as food, shelter and clothing. Instead of yielding without resistance, it took hard work to bring in a harvest.

There were things man could not control affecting his harvest: weather conditions, insects, thieves and animals.

While poverty will not keep you from the Kingdom of God, it will hinder your ability to fulfill the covenant to be a blessing. As Sydney Smith said, "Poverty is no disgrace to a man, but it is confoundedly inconvenient."

I was raised in object poverty. I saw the effects it had on our lives. We had winters with no heat in our home. We moved often because we were behind on rent. We seldom had groceries, except for the first of the month. I saw how poverty robbed us of hope. I saw how it caused us to be shunned and looked down on at school and in the community. There was nothing good about it.

The worst thing about it was it prevented us from having a positive affect on our friends and relatives. They were in the vicious grip of it as well.

From cover to cover, poverty is viewed as a result of the curse. How do we know this? You will not see any in Heaven when we get there!

APPLICATION:
1. Be sure you are being a blessing to those around you.
2. Do not "buy in" to the theology poverty is a blessing!

PRAYER:
Lord, thank you for all of your blessings. I rebuke the spirit of poverty away from me and my family. Amen.

134

MAY 1
BUT GOD

Hebrews 3:4
"For every house has a builder, but God is the one who made everything."
(NLT)

I cannot count how many times in my life I have seemingly come up against something that I could not overcome. Sometimes it has been financial, sometimes physical, sometimes spiritual and sometimes relational. I was at the end of my wits... BUT GOD came through! I was looking through the Word of God one day and decided to look at some "BUT GOD" scriptures. Here are just a few:

Genesis 31:7 says, *"And your father hath deceived me, and changed my wages ten times; BUT GOD suffered him not to hurt me."* (KJV)
Genesis 50:20 says, *"But as for you, ye thought evil against me; BUT GOD meant it unto good, to bring to pass, as it is this day, to save much people alive."* (KJV)
I Samuel 23:14 says, *"...And David abode in the wilderness in strong holds, and remained in a mountain in the wilderness of Ziph. And Saul sought him every day, BUT GOD delivered him not into his hand."* (KJV)
Psalms 73:26 says, *"My flesh and my heart faileth: BUT GOD is the strength of my heart, and my portion forever."* (KJV)
Acts 7:9 says, *"And the patriarchs, moved with envy, sold Joseph into Egypt: BUT GOD was with him,"* (KJV)
Acts 13:30 says, *"BUT GOD raised him from the dead:"* (KJV)
Romans 5:8 says, *"BUT GOD commendeth his love toward us, in that, while we were yet sinners, Christ died for us."* (KJV)
I Corinthians 2:9-10 says, *"...Eye hath not seen, nor ear heard, neither have entered into the heart of man, the things which God hath prepared for them that love him, BUT GOD hath revealed them unto us by his Spirit: for the Spirit searcheth all things, yea, the deep things of God."* (KJV)
I Corinthians 3:6 says, *"I have planted, Apollos watered; BUT GOD gave the increase."* (KJV)

APPLICATION:
1. Remember, whatever you are facing, you are not alone—BUT GOD!
2. Every time you feel you cannot overcome, shout, "BUT GOD!"

PRAYER:
Lord, I will remember that no matter what, you are with me—BUT GOD! Amen.

MAY 2
GOD IS FAITHFUL

I Corinthians 10:13
"There hath no temptation taken you but such as is common to man: but God is faithful, who will not suffer you to be tempted above that ye are able; but will with temptation also make a way to escape, that ye may be able to bear it."
(KJV)

God's faithfulness is immeasurable. It is best discovered when it is most needed. When everything comes crashing down around you, He makes a way for us to arrive on the other side.

Each day brings with it a different challenge for our lives. God has already made provisions for these challenges before we even need them. It is much like the hibiscus flower, whose blossoms come in a kaleidoscope of colors ranging from white, yellow, orange and deep red. Their shape and texture vary. They originate from the Philippines and can be seen commonly throughout the land. The most distinct aspect of this colorful flower is that it blooms every morning. However, the unusual thing is the bloom lasts only one day. This means if you were to have a bouquet, they would only last a single day.

God has something prepared for us every day. It is His faithfulness. It is what we need, when we need it. When things do not seem to make sense, His faithfulness can be counted on. When the pressure is beyond human coping ability, His faithfulness helps lift the weight and strain. When the walls of temptation surround you, His faithfulness opens an unseen door for you to walk through.

Faithfulness involves faith, for without it, it is impossible to please God. Sometimes we have to trust in the person we are being faithful to when there is no reason to trust them. We have to trust it is worth it to continue to have faith, and regardless of the problems, they will change. There are many things in life we cannot depend on. God's faithfulness is not one of them!

APPLICATION:
   1. Decide to trust Him with your temptations and the accompanying stress.
   2. Remind yourself God's faithfulness can be depended on.

PRAYER:
Lord, help me find the door of escape you have provided for me and remember that you are faithful! Amen.

MAY 3
GOOD DEEDS ARE GODLY

Ecclesiastes 3:11-12
"He hath made every thing beautiful in his time: also he hath set the world
in their heart, so that no man can find out the work that God maketh from the
beginning to the end. I know that there is no good in them, but for a man to
rejoice, and to do good in his life." (KJV)

Probably one for my favorite quotes is from Frederick Robertson, who said, "Do right and God's recompense to you will be the power to do more right!"

The Bible says in Acts 10:38, *"How God anointed Jesus Christ of Nazareth with the Holy Ghost and power: who went about doing good, and healing all that were oppressed with the Devil, for God was with him."* (KJV) Good deeds and being a good person is not enough to save the soul, but it should be a by-product of a transformed life.

I have noticed over my lifetime every time God promotes me, it is never just about me and my needs, but also about the needs of others. God positions me, so I can make an impact on the hurts and discouragements of those I am in contact with. When I carry out good works, I bring God on the scene. He unveils His goodness through me, while I care for those in need and distress.

This was true for Joseph's family. Joseph was sent ahead of them, so that when famine came, he was already in position to make a difference. This favor came with a high cost, but he had been steady to do the good and right thing, while in exile in Egypt.

The Church seems to have forgotten it is an institution of good works purposed for a lost and dying world. Thomas Skinner said, "The Church should be a model so that when the world says, 'Where can we find justice (healing, peace, acceptance and love)?' We can say, 'Over here!'"

APPLICATION:
1. Find someone, today, who is in need and do something good for them just because you can.
2. Tell someone who is hurting, or yourself if you are hurting, "Over here!"

PRAYER:
Lord, show me who I need to touch, today, with your goodness. Make an appointment I will know you have arranged and I will keep it! Amen.

MAY 4
GOD'S DISCOVERY ZONE

Deuteronomy 29:29
*"The secret things belong unto Jehovah our God; but the things that are
revealed belong unto us and to our children for ever, that we
may do all the words of this law."* (ASV)

The word *Jehovah* in the above verse is *Jehovah Galah* (Aramaic). It literally means "revealer of secrets." God has always desired to unveil Himself to us. He began with the life of His son, Jesus. Jesus said, *"Anyone who has seen me, has seen the Father."* (John 14:9 NLT)

We must remember we serve the God of the universe who holds all of the wisdom of the ages. He is the ancient of all days. There is nothing hidden from Him. However, there are things He has hidden for us.

We must discover the things belonging to us. We have a right to lay claim to those things we are taught. When we act on what we have been taught from God's Word about our lives, God produces what He has promised.

God has no shortages in Heaven. He has placed plenty of provision on the earth. However, we are told to ask, seek and knock. If we are passive, we will live a life of frustration with the knowledge God has the ability to keep us, protect us and provide for us. We will go without, when we could have so much more.

Now, is the time to discover what God has for you. He is not holding out on you. He wants more for you than you have discovered. Greek mythology portrays the image of time as a man with long hair in front, but bald in the back. The interpretation is you must catch time and opportunity as it is coming toward you because once it has passed, there is nothing left to grab. We have allowed time and opportunities to pass us by. However, we must be aware that God's time is always, now. Grab hold today! He is waiting to unveil things in your life, today. Search Him out for the answers that belong to you.

APPLICATION:
1. Spend time, today, reciting scriptures that promise provision for your life!
2. If you do not understand or are stumped about something going on in your life, ask God to reveal the answer to you.

PRAYER:
Lord, show me the hidden things of my life, today! Amen.

MAY 5
IS SICKNESS A FRIEND OR AN ENEMY

Psalms 107:20
"He sent his word, and healed them, and delivered them
from their destructions." (KJV)

If it were true God afflicts sickness on people to teach them a lesson, then why did we never see Jesus imposing sickness on people, while He was on earth? He was always removing it!

When we see Jesus before the cross, He was beaten for what purpose? It was not for sin; the blood was for the sin. According to Isaiah 53:4-5; Matthew 8:16-17; and I Peter 2:24, the stripes were for our healing. It was for the physical body—not the spirit.

Sickness is not a friend or the work of God in our lives. Consider the language surrounding sickness: "He's had a heart *attack*." (to set upon in a forceful or violent, aggressive manner) "They just had a hard *seizure*." (take by violence) "She had a *stroke*." (hit or blow) "They're *coming down* with the flu." (to lose ground) "He's *struggling* with his health." (contend vigorously with adverse conditions) "When they were in the hospital, they had a *brush* with death." (confrontation) "She's *combating* a virus." (combat; military action)

Given these words, do you think sickness is a friend or an enemy? Jesus healed all manner of sickness and disease. (Matthew 4:23)

If it is God's will for you to be sick, and it is a friend and an instrument of God for your life, then why did Jesus go about and undo God's will for people's life? Jesus said He did the works and will of God on the earth. He was a healer. It is not God's will to afflict His people with sickness.

I personally believe the doctrine "God makes people sick" is straight from the pits of Hell. Do not buy in to it. Sickness is not the friend of God, but of the enemy!

APPLICATION:
1. Confess Jesus is your healer, today!
2. Be sure you do not listen or receive the doctrine "God makes you sick" any longer.

PRAYER:
Lord, I confess you are my healer! I have no doubt you never make me sick, but always desire to make me well! Amen.

MAY 6
WHY ARE GOD'S PEOPLE UNWELL?

Hosea 4:6
"My people are destroyed for lack of knowledge: because thou hast rejected knowledge, I will also reject thee..." (KJV)

If it is God's will for His people to be well, then why are so many sick so often? This question is a very perplexing one indeed. I do not believe the answer is necessarily applicable in the case of someone who has lived a long life. Our bodies certainly do wear out. Sometimes the elderly do not respond to healing, and the person is tired and ready to let go and go to Heaven.

Medicine certainly has its place and should always be used along with our faith. Do not get into condemnation for going to the doctor.

What is the primary cause of people being sick and not being well? I believe there are five primary causes: 1. Lack of knowledge that healing is provided. (Mark 3:1-5) I was in church for awhile before I discovered it was God's will for me to be well. Consequently, when I got sick, I did not even pray to be well. 2. Lack of belief that it is the will of God. (Matthew 17:14-20) When I discovered God wanted me well, I changed what I believed, and God healed me. 3. Lack of time spent listening to God's Word. (Joshua 1:8) People want to be healed without meditating on the Word. 4. Lack of demand placed on their faith. (Matthew 9:29) Even after we discover we have a covenant of health, we still must use our faith to receive it. We do this by placing the Word of healing in our mouths. 5. Failure to properly take care of our bodies. I Timothy 4:8-9 says, *"For bodily exercise profiteth little: but Godliness is profitable unto all things, having promise of the life that now is, and of that which is to come. This is a faithful saying and worthy of all acceptation."* (KJV)

While this list certainly is not all inclusive, I believe it is a good starting guide to help you discover God's will for your health. If you follow it, you will be a person who is healed!

APPLICATION:
1. Speak the Word of healing over your body, today!
2. Go to God whenever you begin feeling sick and make a decision to walk in faith.

PRAYER:
Lord, I believe it is your will for me to be well. I confess you are my source of healing! Amen.

MAY 7
WHAT WAS SO SPECIAL ABOUT DANIEL?

Daniel 1:9
"Now God had brought Daniel into favour and tender love with the prince of the eunuchs." (KJV)

Daniel is accurately considered one of the most heroic people in the Bible. He stood up to the king, slept fearlessly in a den of lions and provoked a sweeping change in the enemy's kingdom.

To understand what set Daniel apart from his contemporaries, we should consider Daniel's early life. Daniel and his friends had been kidnapped and brought to a foreign land from their homes in Judah. Their futures would have seemed hopeless, but each of them possessed personal traits and abilities qualifying them for jobs as servants in the king's palace. For some, this might have seemed like a dead end to their dreams. Yet, they brought something unseen with them to the palace; they brought their faith in the God of Abraham, Isaac and Jacob.

When interrogated to surrender his convictions, Daniel resisted. He also continued in the same manner of life, even his eating habits! This proved to be an attribute of great importance. Daniel was given access to the table of the king, but he chose a menial menu and proved it was a healthy choice. This choice was a springboard of his faith, which eventually gave him an opportunity to prove the realness of his God.

After refusing to bow to the graven image and continuing to pray to his God, he and his friends were eventually delivered from a fiery furnace and he was delivered from the lion's den.

Do you cling tightly to your convictions when distressing situations arise? Do you continue to stand for what you believe, or do you bend when faced with adversity?

Look deep inside and find your convictions once again. When you do, decide to live by them in every type of season!

APPLICATION:
1. Review what convictions you possess and reaffirm them.
2. Do not compromise when adversity comes. Stand strong and allow God to cause your convictions to be vindicated!

PRAYER:
Lord, forgive me for bowing to pressure and adversity instead of bowing in prayer. Amen.

far better than I used to be but so far to go!

MAY 8
GUILTY BY ASSOCIATION

I Corinthians 15:33
"Be not deceived: Evil companionships corrupt good morals." (ASV)

Many years ago a contemporary Christian artist, Steve Taylor, had a song on one of his albums entitled *Guilty by Association*. The song satirically described people who could not function without doing business with Christians. The problem is the Christians being characterized were hypocrites.

The word *associate* means "frequently in the company of another; connected with another; joined with another in common pursuit; to unite or combine resources for a common goal. To hang out with, or are tight with."

There is much truth regarding our willingness to associate with people who are placing a stamp of approval or disapproval on others' actions. Even worse, these traits begin to induce this behavior in us. With those thoughts in mind, I want to point out five things we should remember when we are frequently in the presence of others: 1. Everyone you spend time with will either add something to your life or take something away. They will either influence you or you will influence them. (Hebrews 7:7) 2. Do not allow sinners to influence you. You cannot get in the garbage without stinking. An old proverb says, "Do not eat garlic and you will not smell of garlic." (I Corinthians 15:32-34 TLB) 3. If you believe in something, it will show. The more you listen to those things around you, the more they change your thinking. (Matthew 6:21) 4. What you wear and what you say shows who you have spent time with the most. Sports gear always has a team logo on it and announces to others what team you support when you wear it. We should "wear" our Godly lifestyle, so others can see it, and not be influenced to "wear" sin. (Acts 4:13) 5. If you hang out with God and His people, you will do the impossible! (John 14:12-14) It only takes one other believer to agree with you.

God has a plan for you. You are someone, with something, going somewhere. Be careful who you associate with.

APPLICATION:
1. Ask yourself if you are influencing those around you.
2. If not, are they influencing you?

PRAYER:
Lord, show me the people I should be with and those I should not! Amen.

142

MAY 9
OH, BEHAVE

I Timothy 3:15
*"But if I tarry long, that thou mayest know how thou oughtest to behave thyself
in the house of God, which is the church of the living God,
the pillar and ground of the truth."* (KJV)

The saying, "Oh, Behave!" became popular a few years back when it was used in a couple of movies. When we were children, we probably heard our mothers say it to us hundreds of time. Surprisingly, I have discovered people do not know how to behave in the house of God.

People come to church often unprepared to be in the presence of God. They come in with bad attitudes and are preoccupied with their work or problems. Consequently, they leave just as frustrated as when they arrived.

In modern America, we have become so casual we do not understand the significance of being in His presence. We dress like we are going to the beach and not like we are entering His throne room. I am not preaching the clothes line, but we should at least think about whose presence we will be in before selecting our attire and appearance.

There are some things that happen in church, which do not happen anywhere else. Church is the place where you grow your relationship with the Father. It is your place of introduction to the Creator of all. It is a place where you can hear from God. This does not mean you do not ever receive these things away from church, but God designed the gathering of His people because some things need corporate faith and not just individual faith. Paul Tournier was correct when he said, "There are two things that we cannot do alone. The first is marriage, the other is to be a Christian."

We need to get a better understanding of how we should behave in the house of God. We should enter His gates with thanksgiving and His courts with praise. We should present ourselves in a respectful, thoughtful manner. When we approach Him with honor and reverence, there is nothing that He will withhold from our lives!

APPLICATION:
1. If you are not preparing yourself properly to go before Him, make the needed adjustments.
2. Pray and prepare yourself before you arrive at church.

PRAYER:
Lord, forgive me for not coming to your house with my heart and life in order. Amen.

MAY 10
13 REASONS TO BE A CHURCH MEMBER

Matthew 16:18
"And I say also unto thee, That thou art Peter, and upon this rock I will build my church; and the gates of Hell shall not prevail against it." (KJV)

Being a church member will not assure you a place in Heaven. It does not guarantee your prayers will be answered. It will not stop the enemy from coming against you. If these things are true, and they are, then what are the benefits of being a committed church member?

Here is a list of 13 good reasons you need to be a member of a church:

1. You learn the ways of Christ by being in an environment that encourages His life to come through you. (I Corinthians 4:17; Ephesians 1:22)
2. You learn how to be in harmony with others. Romans 14:19 says, *"In this way aim for harmony in the church, and try to build each other up."* (TLB) We are members of His body and need to be in contact with each other.
3. You learn how to be a Christian. (Acts 11:26) It is impossible to be a doctor without going to medical school. We need to be taught Christianity.
4. You hear things the world cannot hear. (Acts 11:22) The Word is always being spoken, but not being heard. Faith will come when you are in church.
5. You learn how to pray. (Acts 12:5) Prayer that brings power!
6. You are given to wise leaders. (Acts 14:23) Everyone needs to be led.
7. Prophetic ministry is placed in your life. (Acts 13:1; I Corinthians 12:28)
8. You learn how to walk in peace and comfort. (Acts 9:31)
9. You are fed well! (Acts 20:28) The Manna from Heaven is given.
10. You learn the principles of giving and receiving. (Philippians 4:15)
11. You learn how to worship God. (Hebrews 2:12)
12. You are given the opportunity to help others. (III John 1:6)
13. You have a place to get healed. (James 5:14)

APPLICATION:
1. If you are a member of a church, then become the best member you can be!
2. The effort you put into your church will determine what you are able to receive back.

PRAYER:
Lord, I desire to be a great church member. Forgive me for not giving more of myself to my church. Amen.

MAY 11
WHEN HE COMES, HE BLESSES

Exodus 20:24
"Wherever I cause my name to be honored, I will come to you and bless you."
(NIV)

I remember when I was a young boy my Uncle Henry would come over and visit occasionally. He was one of my favorite uncles. He was a rather large man in stature, and he always had a funny story or a joke to tell. Whenever he visited our house, he would usually give me some money: a quarter, a half dollar or sometimes even a dollar! It was a big deal to me back then. I used to hope he would come over often, because aside from the money, he made us all feel better. He was that kind of person.

God wants to visit our lives more often. He desires to pour out more than you have ever dreamed of. He wants to open up His Heavens over your life. When the Heavens open, there is a down pour. He wants to bless you in such a way that your life will be much better than it ever was before! Our biggest problem is we are, too often, so short-sighted and place unnecessary limits on God. As a result, we do not receive the blessings He really desires for us.

I was walking on the beach early one morning while on vacation and stared out over the ocean. It was a crystal clear morning, so you could see for miles. The thought came to me, "God is just like the ocean, His blessings go as far as you can see." Then, I heard the voice of God say inside of me, "You can only see so far out over the ocean, but the ocean goes much farther than you can see. I am the same way. My blessings go much further than you can see!"

We must guard ourselves from limiting God and His blessings over our lives. Even when things are difficult, God can be trusted! When you get to a place and say, "I do not see how God is going to do this or that," remember, God is much more than you can see. Do not limit Him. Do not be short-sighted. He has much, much more for you than you can imagine. If you dare to trust and believe in Him, then He will come and He will bless you!

APPLICATION:
1. Lift the limits off of your faith.
2. Expect God to bless you.

PRAYER:
Lord, I trust when you come upon the situations of my life, you will bring your blessings with you! Amen.

MAY 12
ARMED FOR SERVICE

James 4:7
*"Submit yourselves therefore to God. Resist the Devil,
and he will flee from you."* (KJV)

I visited Washington, D.C., for the first time in 1991, and was able to take a tour of the White House. The first thing I noticed was the guards posted at the gates. They looked harmless enough until they walked out to open the gates. Then, I spotted their weapons. They were armed for service. If someone was foolish enough to try to force their way through, they would have been dealt with quickly.

God has armed His people. He has not left us defenseless. We have been issued powerful weapons through Him to pull down strongholds. He knows when you have a strong defense, the enemy cannot break through.

Before you are issued weapons, you are sworn to use them in defense of that which you have been given to guard. The armament is given to protect you in case of engagement with the enemy. The purpose of the Devil's attack is to get us to lose trust in our armor.

We have been deputized to carry out the Gospel. To be *deputized* means "to be delegated with the same authority as the one who delegated it." It also means "to act as a substitute with the authority to act." It means "to be second in command; one who takes charge when his superior is absent."

There are five critical things that will help you use your weapons with power. The first is you must be able to take orders. (Luke 6:46) The second is you must be familiar with the enemy. (II Corinthians 2:11) The third is you must be familiar with the handbook. (Isaiah 34:16) Fourth, you must trust your fellow soldiers. (Ephesians 4:3-4) Last, you must believe in the cause. (I Samuel 17:29)

Although we do not seem to use our weapons often enough, God has given them to us to enforce the laws of the Kingdom now, on this earth, until He returns. Be sure to check your weapons and get them ready to fire. God wants you to win!

APPLICATION:
   1. Be alert and check your armor according to Ephesians 6.
   2. Enforce your position of authority with God by submitting yourself to God and resisting the Devil.

PRAYER:
Lord, I take the authority you have given me and choose to use the weapons at my disposal. Amen.

MAY 13
TURN TEMPTATION INTO TRIUMPH

James 1:12
"Let no man say when he is tempted, I am tempted of God:
for God cannot be tempted with evil, neither tempteth he any man: But every
man is tempted, when he is drawn away of his own lust, and enticed. Then, when
lust hath conceived, it bringeth forth sin: and sin when it is finished,
bringeth forth death. Do not err, my beloved brethren." (KJV)

Erwin Lutzer said, "Temptation is not sin, it is a call to battle!" Shakespeare said, "Things sweet to the taste prove in digestion sour!"

Giving into temptation is trading God's way of life for Satan's. The common, everyday temptations are the most dangerous because they are constantly around us and in pursuit of us. God will always provide the means for you to withstand temptation's pressure.

Billy Graham said, "The most important thing for us to remember is that God never tempts any man. That is Satan's business."

Mark 1:13; I Thessalonians 3:5; Luke 4:2, 13; I Corinthians 7:5; and Revelation 2:10, all refer to Satan as the tempter. God only tests His people with good things, opportunities or loyalty.

How do you take the upper-hand over this life's temptations? Allow God to speak to you through the inner man first, and then resist the tempting things using God's Word and God's Spirit. What can we do to finally triumph over temptation? First, we must be people of prayer. (Matthew 26:41) Second, we must confront our temptation by seeking the face of Jesus. (Hebrews 4:12-16) Third, we must attend to the words of God. (Proverbs 4:20-23) Last, we must cast down imaginations. (Psalms 119:113)

If we are determined to pass the tests of the flesh, then God will help us and we will overcome them. Do not forget: temptation is not a sin—giving in to it is.

APPLICATION:
  1. Do not accuse God of the trials you are experiencing.
  2. Do not give in to the things that are bringing temptation into your life.

PRAYER:
Lord, I resist the temptations and trials trying to overtake me. Help me to trust in you only. Amen.

147

MAY 14
GOD SEES WHO YOU ARE

I Samuel 16:7
"Man looketh on outward appearance, but God looketh on the heart." (KJV)

Jesse had seven sons who seemed to be much more qualified than David. In fact, the "other" son was not even brought to Samuel for evaluation. Yet, one by one, the seven were passed over. That left only one—David!

Surely, it could not be David. He was too young. He was a lowly shepherd. He was soft-looking, "ruddy" or sun-burned and had never been considered as a soldier. The closest he had been to the "action" was to deliver cheese sandwiches to his brothers, the "real warriors."

Yet, Samuel knew God must have seen something the others had overlooked. When David came before Samuel, he was confirmed as the one who should be anointed. God saw something in David, which qualified him, something unseen by others.

God sees some things in you, you do not see! He looks deeper than the obvious. He considers the heart. Everything that may seem to disqualify you is of much less importance, than the condition of your heart.

In my own life, I have come to realize there are many more preachers who are better than me. There are many more pastors who are better pastors than I am. Many have natural gifts and talent, which I do not possess. There is nothing I can do about that. However, I can do something about the condition of my heart. I have noticed God has covered me even when I did not make the best possible choices. Yet, because my heart was right and my motive was to please God, God turned those choices into the best choices.

Do not get discouraged about being overlooked. Remember, God knows who you are!

APPLICATION:
1. Check the condition of your heart.
2. Be patient. God knows who you are and when to use you in His Kingdom.

PRAYER:
Lord, check my heart and show me where I lack. Amen.

MAY 15
THE POWER OF AGREEMENT

Matthew 18:19-20
"Again I say unto you, that if two of you shall agree on earth as touching any thing that they shall ask, it shall be done for them my Father which is in Heaven. For where two or three are gathered together in my name, there am I in the midst of them." (KJV)

I like the story of the Pastor who is speaking to the Bishop on the phone discussing the new church that is being started. The conversation went something like this, "Bad news, Bishop. Our church planning team is divided on whether to call the new congregation 'First United Church' or 'United First Church!'"

For true agreement, there must be a way to unite and not divide. The power of agreement is the most powerful force on the earth today. Being in agreement does not mean being the same. It means understanding the differences, placing your differences aside and finding a way to join your part with someone else's.

This is probably best illustrated in a good marriage. It is true that opposites attract. We search out people who have what we lack. This is not only a good thing, but also intelligent. However, the thing that attracts you can be a point of contention if you lack an understanding of how to come into agreement. Agreement produces peace. Peace is coming to a mutual agreement. It literally means "to bind together."

Jesus gave a pointed lesson about the need for agreement to His disciples. (John 13:1-17) Jesus washed their feet knowing the division existing between them. He was providing them an example that the Kingdom is not about greatness, but about being in agreement for the task.

We should always seek agreement when possible. When we do, we can be sure God's presence will seek us out!

APPLICATION:
1. If you are in disagreement with someone valuable in your life, find a way to get in agreement.
2. This may require you to say you are sorry, forgive him/her, ask for forgiveness or compromise.

PRAYER:
Lord, it is my desire to be in agreement with those you have sent to be a blessing in my life. Please forgive my stubbornness and pride. Amen.

MAY 16
GOD'S WAITING ROOM

Hebrews 10:36
"For ye have need of patience, that, after ye have done the will of God, ye might receive the promise." (KJV)

How many times have you been at a doctor, dentist or lawyer's office, and had to wait… and wait… and wait, even though you had an appointment and were on time for it? I believe this is one of the most annoying things we are required to do in our lives!

Sometimes it is the same with God. It just seems like He keeps us waiting… and waiting… and waiting, even though we feel we have done everything that can be done.

Bible patience is different from natural patience. Bible patience involves God's plan for our lives and His continued attempts to help us find it.

What is Bible patience? According to Unger's Bible Dictionary, it is "to bear long, suffer long, be long-suffering, patiently endure; be of long spirit, not to lose heart; to preserve patiently and bravely enduring misfortunes and troubles." I would add it is to trust God completely in times of uncertainty while maintaining your faith.

A great Bible example of patience is Mordecai. Haman devised an evil plan to place Mordecai on the gallows he had prepared for him. However, Mordecai had exposed a plot to assassinate Xerxes—thus he had saved the king's life. Although his good deed was recorded in the history books, Mordecai had gone unnoticed and unrewarded. God had saved Mordecai's reward for the right time. Just as Haman was about to hang Mordecai unjustly, the king was ready to give the reward. God had swung things in Mordecai's favor and exposed the deception Haman had propagated.

Sometimes God's promises to reward our obedience seem to be forgotten or far away. Yet, for every moment we continue to walk in patience, we are being prepared for our breakthrough. Be patient. God steps in when it will do the most good. Besides, patience is developed in God's waiting room!

APPLICATION:
1. Be sure you are being patient in your life right now.
2. Do not murmur or complain—Trust God!

PRAYER:
Lord, I thank you for preparing blessings in my life right now. Forgive me for not fully trusting you. Amen.

MAY 17
HURRY UP AND WAIT

James 1:3-4
*"Knowing this, that the trying of your faith worketh patience. But let patience
have her perfect work, that ye may be perfect and entire,
wanting nothing."* (KJV)

I took my teenage daughter and one of her friends to meet the band Hanson
several years ago in Memphis, Tennessee. Hanson was appearing at a mall and
was going to meet, greet and sign autographs. Their appearance was scheduled
for 2:00 p.m. in the afternoon. My daughter was emphatic that we should be at
the mall when it opened at 10:00 a.m. Internally, I thought, "That's way too early!
They're not as big now as they were a few years ago. There probably won't be that
many people there." I was wrong.

When we arrived at the mall, there were teenage girls everywhere. When
we got inside, we discovered the band would only be there for a certain amount
of time. This meant when we got in line, we might or might not see them. My
daughter was borderline hysterical. The good news was that we just made the cut.
We were close to the last ones to make it to their table. Our hurriedness to wait
had paid off!

In light of our scripture, patience could mean the ability to see the end of a situation before arriving at it. (Job 5:7-11) A Persian proverb states, "Have patience!
All things are difficult before they become easy!"

Genesis 29 tells us of the patient love that Jacob had for Rachel. We can learn
things from his life that we need to do to develop our patience.

First, we need to keep our eyes on the prize. Jacob spent seven years working
to pay for Rachel because he was so much in love with her. However, those seven
years seemed like only a few days. Secondly, we must not get impatient trying to
acquire the greatly desired prize. Lastly, we must occupy our time with the things
of God. When in the midst of a hardship, the secret of patience is doing something
else in the meanwhile.

A Canadian proverb explains, "Patience is a tree whose root is bitter, but its
fruit is very sweet." Patience pays in the long run, so hurry up and wait!

APPLICATION:
1. Do not get frustrated while you are waiting—God is moving!
2. Remind yourself good things come to those who wait.

PRAYER:
*Lord, forgive me for my impatience. I will wait on you and trust the plan you have
for my life. Amen.*

151

MAY 18
THE SLOW POISON OF SIN

Genesis 2:16-17
"And the LORD God commanded the man, saying, Of every tree
of the garden thou mayest freely eat: But of the tree of the knowledge of good
and evil, thou shalt not eat of it: for in the day that thou eatest
thereof thou shalt surely die." (KJV)

A Frankfort, Kentucky, woman was the victim of a strange accident. She arose in the night to get a drink of water. While drinking the water she unknowingly swallowed a small, black spider, which had fallen off of the faucet of her kitchen sink and into her drinking glass. She felt the spider going down her throat, but did not know what it was. Within a couple of hours, she became nauseated and ejected the spider, but not until it had bitten her internally. The poison from the bite soon spread through her system, and her condition became life-threatening. Her flesh puffed up in rolls and ridges, her ears swelled so tightly that blood oozed through the skin and her tongue swelled until she almost suffocated. Emergency Room physicians worked for several hours administering all the antidotes known to medical science and finally saved her life. The little spider that had such a venomous bite was no larger than a pea, possessed the ability to roll itself up into a complete ball and float on the water like a piece of cork. This story gives us insight into how sin can seem so small, and yet, be so destructive.

When Adam disobeyed God after He had spoken the words found in Genesis 2, one might anticipate Adam's death. However, most theologians believe Adam actually lived several hundred more years after his disobedience. Although it appeared to have little effect on the outside, it had poisoned the inside. As a result, those sins were present in his spiritual bloodstream upon his death.

We must not be deceived by the slowness of the process. Sin is a slow poison, but it is a poison, nonetheless. The only remedy for it is repentance in the blood of Christ.

APPLICATION:
   1. Clear your life of the poison of sin.
   2. If you have already ingested sin, ask God for the remedy of His forgiveness.

PRAYER:
Lord, heal and cleanse me from the poison of sin. Amen.

MAY 19
WHY WORRY?

Philippians 4:6
"Don't worry about anything; instead, pray about everything; tell God your needs, and don't forget to thank him for his answers!" (TLB)

O.F. Gober said, "Life's too short for worrying. Yes, that's what worries me." Some studies suggest 70 percent of all patients who go to physicians could cure themselves, if they only got rid of their fears, worries and bad eating habits.

According to the National Bureau of Standards, a dense fog covering seven city blocks to a depth of 100 feet is composed of less than one glass of water. This means the moisture found in a fog covering such a large area of land would not even fill a single glass. This can be compared to the things we worry about.

I grew up with a professional worrier–my mother. She would worry about everything. If there was not anything to worry about, then she would worry about not worrying. I saw how it kept her from really enjoying her life. It paralyzed her. She was afraid to travel and even more afraid for me and my siblings to travel.

Later in her life, she became ill and her worry kept her from receiving her healing. It caused me to see how destructive worry can be. However, she was a Christian. Thankfully, she is well and in Heaven now.

The Bible tells us how to deal with worry. We have to thank God and praise him in everything. We are to meditate on the Word of God and not the word of the world. We must speak God's promise for our lives when we are facing adversity. We must focus on things that are good, pure, honest, virtuous and praiseworthy.

When we get our minds off of the things we are worrying about and place our focus on the things of God, then worry will lose its grip. After all, *"Who is he that will harm you, if ye be followers of that which is good?"* (I Peter 3:13 KJV) Today, ask yourself, "Why worry?"

APPLICATION:
1. Do not let worry drive the decisions of your life.
2. Speak the Word of God over the things that bring you worry.

PRAYER:
Lord, forgive me for worrying over things that I have already trusted you for. Amen.

MAY 20
THE DEFEATING NATURE OF WORRY

Luke 12:26
"And if worry can't even do such little things as that, what's the use of worrying over bigger things?" (TLB)

Worry always brings defeat. According to John MacArthur, many years ago the Mayo Clinic stated that statistically 80 percent to 85 percent of their total case load of patients were ill, either in reality, or artificially, due directly to mental stress. MacArthur also noted a fairly recent article in a leading medical journal entitled, *Is Stress the Cause of All Diseases?* The article stated at the beginning of the century, bacteria were considered to be the primary cause of illness. Today, mental stress has replaced bacteria!

I have listed 10 defeating attributes of worry:

1. Worry brings distractions. (John 11) Martha lost sight of why Jesus was present. She could have focused on the Word to empower her to pray for Lazarus.
2. Worry invites trouble. It prepares the heart for what the head has already accepted as truth. It believes for the worst.
3. Anxiety, or worry, often probes people to blame others for their situations. Martha blamed Mary. Those who worry believe everyone is against them.
4. Worry negates trust. Trusting with your heart means not being swayed by your own emotions. (Proverbs 3:5-6)
5. Worry invites defeat. It opens the door for the enemy. It closes the door for deliverance.
6. Worry produces anger. Psalms 37:8 says, *"Stop your anger! Turn off your wrath. Don't fret and worry—it only leads to harm!"* (TLB) The word *fret* means "to express or verbalize worry over something."
7. Worry negates our faith in what we know from God's Word. It takes the place of the truth of God's Word. It reduces our faith to wishful thinking.
8. Worry paralyzes positive decision-making. There is a difference in worry and concern. Concern moves you to a positive action; worry immobilizes you.
9. Worry causes us to truly seek God's help as a last result and not a first. (Matthew 6:25-31)
10. Worry interferes with our relationship with God. (Hebrews 11:6) It removes the "all things are possible" from our lives.

Do not let worry defeat you. Keep your trust in the Lord!

APPLICATION:
1. Do not worry about the things God is in charge of.
2. Keep your faith in God and do not lean to your own understanding.

PRAYER:
Lord, help me to not worry, but to keep my eyes on you. Amen.

MAY 21
POSITIONED FOR SUCCESS

Psalms 62:7-8
"My protection and success come from God alone. He is my refuge, a Rock where no enemy can reach me. O my people, trust him all the time. Pour out your longings before him, for he can help!" (TLB)

Every time you turn on the television, there is someone promising to show you how to become successful. They assure the viewers, if they follow their plan and pay a fee, they too, will have plenty of extra money and be successful.

However, the Bible is the most trustworthy manual to follow if your desire is to find lasting success. God has a plan for our lives, which will take us from failure to success. Booker T. Washington said it this way, "A measure of a man's success is not what he achieves, but what he overcomes."

I like the example given in the following true account:

In August, 1978, the first successful transatlantic balloon flight became reality when Double Eagle II touched ground in a barley field in the small village of Miserey, France. Yet, success in this accomplishment did not come easy. During the years from 1873 through 1978, 13 attempts had been made—all ending in failure. After an unsuccessful attempt in 1977, in which Double Eagle ended up in Iceland, Double Eagle II was successful in making that historic six day trip from Presque Isle, Maine, to Miserey, France.

What made the difference between the unsuccessful trip and the successful one? One difference was the addition of another man. A second difference was experience. Maxie Anderson, one of the crew, put it this way, "I don't think that you can fly the Atlantic without experience, and that's one reason it hadn't been flown before. Success in any venture is just the intelligent application of failure." (Cited in the National Geographic, December 1978, pp. 858-882)

If you have failed before, do not give up! You have gained valuable experience, and now you just may be ready to succeed. If you continue to trust God, He will position you for success!

APPLICATION:
   1. Place all of your failures before Him.
   2. Ask God to place people in your life who will help you succeed.

PRAYER:
Lord, thank you for helping me be successful your way. Amen.

MAY 22
CASTING AWAY YOUR CRUTCHES

Hebrews 12:12-13

"Wherefore lift up the hands which hang down, and the feeble knees; And make straight paths for your feet, lest that which is lame be turned out of the way; but let it rather be healed." (KJV)

What is a crutch? According to Webster's Dictionary, it is "a staff or support to assist a lame or infirmed person in walking; anything that serves as a temporary support, prop: the use of liquor as psychological crutch." In other words, it is something that supports an impaired object. It is intended to be temporary.

There are three primary types of crutches. The first are physical crutches. (Mark 10:46-52; Acts 3) The second are psychological crutches. (Numbers 13:29-33; Proverbs 23:7) The third are spiritual crutches. (Luke 4:16; Psalms 137:1-6)

Crutches serve a useful purpose. They support weaker limbs. They prevent further damage. They help to hide the limp a person has. They are meant to be a part of the healing process, but not the entirety of it. They can also be destructive if overused.

We have a lot of limping people in the body of Christ. People become afraid to attempt to use the injured area. They place their dependence on the crutch and not on the Word of God. They sometimes become accustomed to the attention the "limp" brings them and do not pursue their healing.

What is your crutch? As long as you hold onto your crutch, you will always be restricted in how far you can go, how fast you can get there and how much you can do when you arrive.

Although it is easy to use our hurts and scars as excuses, only when we become determined to be well will we really begin to live again. Our crutches become unnecessary as we focus on the needs of others.

We must remember that Jesus healed them all. He carried our grief and sorrows, and paid the price for our sins. We do not have to walk with a limp the rest of our lives. We can get well and cast away our crutches!

APPLICATION:
1. Take all of your heartaches and wounds, and place them before His cross.
2. Do not use your hurts as an excuse to keep yourself down.

PRAYER:
Lord, please heal the wounds of my past. Make me whole that I might glorify your name. Amen.

MAY 23
REAR-VIEW MIRROR

Philippians 3:13-14
"Brothers, I do not consider myself yet to have taken hold of it. But one thing
I do: Forgetting what is behind and straining toward what is ahead, I press on
toward the goal to win the prize for which God has called me
Heavenward in Christ Jesus." (NIV)

Have you ever driven past something that was noticeable, and then gazed in your rear-view mirror and watched it fade away as you continued on? The distance eventually caused you to lose total sight of the things previously present.

Sometimes, our past is a little harder to shake than the scenery on a highway. We think we are past it, but it appears right in our rear-view mirror, reminding us where we have been and who we have been. Just about the time you think you are free from the past, someone will come along who does not realize you are not the same person they remembered you to be, and remind you of whom you were.

We have to be sure we keep ourselves moving toward what He has for our lives and away from the things that we used to be. We may have to cut off some relationships. We may have to stay away from some former hangouts. When we see past things trying to close back in on us, we may have to purposely keep ourselves in the Word more than normal.

The thing that will help us keep the distance more than ever is found in II Corinthians 8:10-12, *"And herein I give my advice: for this is expedient for you, who have begun before, not only to do, but also to be forward a year ago. Now therefore perform the doing of it; that as there was a readiness to will, so there may be a performance also out of that which ye have. For if there be first a willing mind, it is accepted according to that a man hath, and not according to that he hath not."* (KJV)

Keep going forward and do not look back. There is nothing for you in your rear-view mirror.

APPLICATION:
1. Do no look back—Keep moving forward!
2. Separate yourself from the things or people attempting to take you backwards.

PRAYER:
Lord, thank you for delivering me from my past. Help me to always go forward and never be caught looking behind. Amen.

MAY 24
RIGHT THINKING

Philippians 2:5
"Let this mind be in you, which was also in Christ Jesus: Who, being in the right form of God..." (KJV)

I heard a preacher on the radio tell a story of a guy who went around saying Jesus appeared to him regularly. Once, he told John MacArthur that Jesus had appeared to him one morning while he was shaving. MacArthur asked, "What did you do?" He said, "I just kept on shaving." "Then that wasn't Jesus!" MacArthur replied.

Every time Jesus came in contact with people something happened. He moved people. What was it that caused Jesus to change the landscape of His people? Have you ever wondered, "What did Jesus think?" According to the Bible, in Philippians, there were five things Christ considered: 1. *"He thought it not robbery to be equal with God: 2. But made himself of no reputation, 3. And took upon him the form of a servant and was made in the likeness of men: And being found in fashion as a man, 4. He humbled himself, 5. And became obedient unto death, even the death of the cross. Wherefore God also hath highly exalted him, and given him a name which is above every name:"*

God's desire is for us to think like Christ and change our behavior. We must change what we think. We are created in His image. We need to have our minds renewed.

How can we do that? We must keep in mind what Christ did. His purpose was given by God. His power was greater than Satan's. His needs were met by His Father. The Word of God is settled forever. He had the deep desire to do the will of God.

What does God expect for us? He expects us to keep our thoughts on Godly virtues. (Philippians 4:6-8) He expects us to keep our minds on the things of Heaven and not earth. (Colossians 3:3) He expects us not to speak every thought. (Matthew 6:31) He expects us not to fellowship with darkness. (I Corinthians 11) He expects us to pray in the Spirit.

Our minds can cause unfruitfulness. If we think like Christ and fulfill God's expectations, wrong thinking will change into right thinking. It all starts or stops according to what we allow our minds to focus on!

APPLICATION:
1. Purge your mind of things that are not Christ centered.
2. Think according to the scriptures about your own life.

PRAYER:
Lord, please help me to think the way you do. I believe it is your will for me to be like you. Amen.

MAY 25
GOD'S SUPPLY ROOM

Philippians 1:19
"For I know that this shall turn to my salvation through your prayer, and the supply of the Spirit of Jesus Christ." (KJV)

When I was very young we lived in a rural area, where the general store also served as the post office, feed store and hardware store. It was an old building and was rather crowded with stuff. There was a door in the back of the building called the "supply room." Whatever was not found on the store room floor could almost always be found in the supply room.

God has a supply room with the things we need, things that we cannot get on our own. He brings them to us through the supply of the Spirit. Whenever we choose to open our lives to the Spirit of God, we move beyond the natural and move into the supernatural. We invite God's provision to become a reality.

What are the keys that open the door to our supply? First of all, to be in the supply room, we must be among God's people. There are things just out of our reach requiring the help of others. Then, we must memorize the inventory of God's Word. There is no substitute for time spent in the Word. It opens up things previously closed to us. Finally, we must trust that what we are lacking has already been purchased through the payment of Christ at the cross. Our account was set up the day we accepted Him. We must realize we are considered worthy of His favors, not because of our merits, but because He placed such a high value on us.

If you find yourself without, then take the time to go to Him. He will lead you to the place where your supply is already waiting, His supply room!

APPLICATION:
    1. Take the time to enter into His presence and ask for your provision.
    2. Keep yourself in the midst of His people and spend time in His Word.

PRAYER:
Lord, thank you for providing the necessary things for me to become what you would have me be. Amen.

MAY 26
AFTER THE STORM

Ecclesiastes 7:8
*"Better is the end of a thing than the beginning thereof: and the patient in spirit
is better than the proud in the spirit. Say not thou, What is the cause that the
former days were better than these? For thou dost not inquire wisely concerning
this.* (KJV) *Finishing is better than starting! Patience
is better than pride!"* (TLB)

In January of 1999, my hometown of Clarksville, Tennessee, was hit by an
F-4 tornado. My wife and I were in Ft. Worth, Texas, at a ministerial convention
when we received the news. We quickly changed our plans and flew home immediately. The next morning, we were allowed access to the damaged downtown
area, which was extremely close to our church. The damage was incredible.

The sight was so destructive; it seemed unimaginable it would ever look
the same again. However, over 10 years have passed since then, and recently an
updated picture of then and now was published. The downtown area does not look
the same as it did before the tornado—it looks much, much better. The reconstruction was completely successful.

After a storm of any kind, including divorce, death or loss, what takes place?
The first thing must be damage assessment. What was taken? What was left?
Then, plans have to be re-evaluated. Rebuilding must be considered. Do you
really want things to be like they were before, or do you want a complete redesign
and reconstruction?

With every storm, there is an opening. JFK said, "When written in Chinese
the word crisis is composed of two characters. One represents danger and the
other represents opportunity."

There are six things you must do. First, you must remember that the Word
is your blueprints. Secondly, you need to hire an architect—the Spirit of God!
(Psalms 107:29-32) Thirdly, you have to sow into someone else's project.
(Ecclesiastes 11:1-6) Fourthly, you must consider what has been built from the
dust before. (Isaiah 26:15-19) Fifthly, you must allow God to be the contractor.
(Isaiah 64:5-9) Lastly, do not use cheap materials. (Proverbs 10:25)

Remember, there is not only life after the storm, but a better life!

APPLICATION:
1. Be willing to rebuild.
2. Make plans beyond the storms of your life.

PRAYER:
Lord, thank you for helping me rebuild my life. Amen.

MAY 27
A NEW DAY FOR A NEW MAN

II Corinthians 5:17-18
"Now the Lord is that Spirit: and where the Spirit of the Lord is, there is freedom. And we, who with unveiled faces all reflect the Lord's glory are being transformed into his likeness with ever-increasing glory, which comes from the Lord, who is the Spirit." (NIV)

When you become a Christian, God changes everything about what makes you who you are. Your life has now been rerouted to the purpose you were created for. The past becomes nothing more than a reference point of where you have been and what God has done to bring you into His Kingdom.

Paul knew this better than anyone. The same Paul, who once was a terrorist towards God's people, became their champion. Galatians 1:21-24 says, *"Afterwards I came into the regions of Syria and Cilicia; And was unknown by face unto the churches of Judaea which were in Christ: But they had heard only, That he which persecuted us in times past now preacheth the faith which once he destroyed. And they glorified God in me!"* (KJV)

Augustine was approached by a lady of the evening he had formerly known. She said, "It is I." He replied, "Yes, but it is not I." There is more to life than what we have known.

I live near Nashville, Tennessee, so when I heard the following story, I believed it. A man bought an AM radio, tuned it to WSM 650 for the Grand Ole' Opry. Then, he tore off the knobs and threw them away because he had already tuned into everything he ever wanted or expected to hear. We should tune into God this way!

Sometimes we lose sight of the fact we are truly new creations in Christ. We try to serve Him with our old mentality instead of our new position as sons and daughters of God.

The truth is God has so much more for your life. There are no longer any limits. Now, anything is possible and everything is in reach. You are new and this is a new day!

APPLICATION:
  1. Remind yourself you are a new creation in Christ!
  2. Reach forth to become the things you were created to be.

PRAYER:
Lord, show me what you want me to be and reveal how to be it. Amen.

MAY 28
CHANGING YOUR REPUTATION

Ecclesiastes 7:1
"A good reputation is more valuable than the most expensive perfume." (TLB)

Sometimes it is so hard to shake off the reputation we have built over our lifetimes. Some people just cannot seem to grasp that you are not the same person they remember. So how then, can you change your reputation?

It takes time. People are slow to be convinced, especially if you have supposedly "changed" in the past. It takes having a record to stand on. You have to have a season of consistent behavior. It takes developing character. There must be a period of tests, and passing the tests we have formerly failed. There is a Japanese proverb stating, "The reputation of a thousand years may be determined by the conduct of one hour."

The most important ingredient is our relationship with God. We now operate under a different set of laws. We are not operating in the laws of self. Deuteronomy 4:5-6 says, *"These are the laws for you to obey when you arrive in the land where you will live. They are from the Lord our God. He has given them to me to pass on to you. If you obey them, they will give you a reputation for wisdom and intelligence. When the surrounding nations hear these laws, they will exclaim, 'What other nation is as wise and prudent as Israel!'"* (TLB) Changing your reputation requires listening to God.

How do you maintain a good reputation once you have established it? Look into a different mirror. (James 1:26) Find yourself some new models. (Hebrews 12:2) Continually sow good things. (Jeremiah 14:7) Abandon the former life, acquaintances and connections. (I Corinthians 15:33) Do not worry about what people think. (I Corinthians 9:2) Realize you are His now. (II Corinthians 6:18)

So, what do you want your present reputation to be? It is up to you!

APPLICATION:
1. Go to the Word and find yourself in Him.
2. Break from the old reputation and walk in the newness of life because it is who you really are.

PRAYER:
Lord, help me to develop the reputation that glorifies you. Give me the strength to walk free from my past reputation. Amen.

MAY 29
FAITH THAT TAKES YOU ACROSS
THE FINISH LINE

II Timothy 4:7
"I have fought a good fight, I have finished my course,
I have kept the faith:" (KJV)

I read a story about a marathon runner who was considered the best in the world. He ran the best race, but did not win. He easily out-distanced all of his competitors. He had a huge lead and coasted towards the finish line. As he approached the finish, he stumbled and fell just yards away from the end. He broke his ankle and could not even drag himself to the finish. He was almost there, but almost was not good enough.

I have watched a lot of people over the years do some really great things... for a season. They would easily be the best in their field, but in the end, they lost everything. They just could not finish.

So, what will help you make it all the way to the finish line? It will take faith. There are different degrees of faith. There is "little faith" which is found four times in Matthew and once in Luke. There is "strong faith" which is found in Romans 4:20. There is "temporary faith" found when Peter walked on the water. (Matthew 14:29) Then, there is "lasting faith." Paul had lasting faith, which took him through every challenge and hardship. His faith helped him "outlast" his problems.

How do we get increase and keep our faith to the finish? We must have the God kind of faith found in Mark 11:22—faith in God, which believes the impossible. We must live by faith. Faith living is recorded four times in scripture. (Habakkuk 2:4; Romans 1:17; Galatians 3:11; Hebrews 10:38) We must walk by faith and not by sight. (II Corinthians 5:7) We must spend time listening to the Word. (Romans 10:17)

Remember, I John 5:4 says, *"This is the victory that over come the world, even our faith!"* (KJV) Our faith will help us make it to the finish line!

APPLICATION:
1. Check your faith level, today. Be sure you are operating in Bible faith.
2. Feed your faith and starve your fears!

PRAYER:
Lord, help me to walk in, live by and stay in faith, so that I can finish. Amen.

MAY 30
FALLING FORWARD

Psalms 18:28-29
"You, O LORD, keep my lamp burning; my God turns my darkness into light. With your help I can advance against a troop; with my God I can scale a wall."
(NIV)

No matter how perfect our lives may seem to be, at some point, we are surely going to take a fall. It is part of life. Our first steps in our lives were most likely followed by a series of falls. Yet, how can we take advantage of the falls? How can we gain from the scars?

God wants us to transform our defeats into victory. The Latin phrase is *Spolia Optima*; the trophies of our conflicts. The scars we have born are a trophy of our battles. Jesus still had scars after the resurrection, but they did not symbolize defeat; they symbolized victory.

What we do with failure is our decision. Everyone fails. There is no such thing as a born loser. Michael Jordan missed half of his shots. Babe Ruth is the all time strikeout king. Edison had 32,000 failed experiments before he conducted light.

Failure is the test of success. Failure is temporary. Failure is not determined by one incident or one event. It is a person's response to the failure that matters. Failure can be countered by preparation. Most of the time when you fail a test in school, it is not graded on how you performed the day you tested, instead your grade reflects how you prepared for the test.

Basketball coach, Rick Pitino, said, "Failure is good. It's like fertilizer. (Stinks at first, but brings forth fruit afterwards) Everything I've learned about coaching, I've learned from making mistakes."

We must learn from our failures. If we learn how to, we can take advantage of the mistakes, use our scars as trophies earned from overcoming failures and fall forward!

APPLICATION:
1. Consider your failures as trophies earned from overcoming.
2. Use the mistakes you have made to your advantage to measure how far you have come.

PRAYER:
Lord, I thank you for not giving up on me. I thank you that every time I have fallen, you have been there. I have not fallen backwards, but forward. Amen.

MAY 31
GOING THE RIGHT WAY

Proverbs 14:12
"Before every man there is a wide and pleasant road that seems right but ends in death." (TLB)

I worked construction for nearly 20 years as a house painter. One day, I was on my way to a job site by a lake. I was supposed to paint a cabin, and it was my first time to this particular area. The cabin was located on a gravel road, of which there were many. The scenery was beautiful. Green trees surrounded either side of the road and each road seemed to lead down to the lakeside. I approached a hill expecting a road to follow, which would overlook and lead to the lake, as all of the others did. When I topped the hill, I was surprised at what I almost did—I almost drove off a cliff above the lake.

There are many things we do in this life, which seem to be leading us to a great destination, but some lead us to despair and destruction. It is so important that we choose the right road. Going the wrong direction can cost us in ways we may never recover from.

Still, it is understandable when we go the wrong way if we are in new territories or on unfamiliar paths. The signs may seem right; however, they may be misleading. Some experiences, although harmful in the short term, can be useful later. Some, in time, help us gain experience. Job 8:8-10 says, *"Read the history books and see—for we were born but yesterday and know so little; our days here on earth are as transient as shadows. But the wisdom of the past will teach you. The experience of others will speak to you, reminding you that those who forget God have no hope."* (TLB) It is critical we use the map of God's Word to navigate the places we have never traveled before. When we follow the route He has laid out for us, we will never find ourselves going the wrong way!

APPLICATION:
1. Check the direction you are going in and be sure you are following His instructions.
2. If you are following His plan, do not let anything cause you to go the wrong way.

PRAYER:
Lord, please direct me in the way I should go. Help me to be able to distinguish the signs you are placing before me. Amen.

JUNE 1
LET HIS WORD COME NOW

Jeremiah 17:14-15
"Heal me, O LORD, and I shall be healed; save me, and I shall be saved: for thou art my praise. Behold, they say unto me, Where is the word of the LORD? Let it come now." (KJV)

There are times when you cannot seem to find the answers you seek. There are times when you have exhausted every possible solution and still cannot come to a hopeful conclusion. It is during these times, we need His Word to come forth.

The Jewish nation had rebelled against God in Jeremiah's day. They were in captivity again. God continued to speak to them about their plight through His servant, Jeremiah, but they would not listen to him. It was even beginning to affect Jeremiah. He had been proclaiming God's Word to a nation of people and it was falling on deaf ears. Jeremiah had already begged God to use someone else and told God how under qualified he was. He had decided not to preach the Word, but he could not contain himself. It was like a fire shut up in his bones. It took over 40 years for God to begin the process of redemption for His people. It was not because His Word had lost power, but because the children of Israel had lost sight of the validity and value the Word possesses.

Although there was redemption ahead, it was never sustained until Jesus came. According to John 1, *"The Word became flesh and dwelt among men."* (KJV) Over 400 years had passed since the last significant prophet had lived and brought the Word of God to His people.

The Bible is clear about the value of God's Word. It produces healing, salvation, deliverance, peace, joy, hope, faith and provision among many other things. The Bible tells us Heaven and earth will pass away, but His Word will never pass away.

If you presently find yourself in need of something more, something now, look no further than His Word.

APPLICATION:
1. Set aside some quality time in today's schedule to spend time in His Word.
2. If it has been a while since you have seen a significant breakthrough, keep your confidence in His Word.

PRAYER:
Lord, give me an appetite for your Word, so that I might wait for it. Amen.

JUNE 2
HEAVEN IS A LONG HELLO

John 14:1-3
*"Let not you heart be troubled: ye believe in God, believe also in me. In my
Father's house are many mansions: if it were not so, I would have told you. I go
to prepare a place for you. And if I go and prepare a place for you, I will come
again, and receive you unto myself; that where I am,
there ye may also be."* (KJV)

There was a popular contemporary Christian song by Billy Sprague back
in the early 90's entitled, *Heaven Is a Long Hello*. My understanding is Sprague
wrote it after someone close to him passed away. God reminded him the end was
really just the beginning. Heaven really is a long, "Hello!"

That song made me think more about what Heaven must be like. I began to
study the scriptures on the subject. I discovered, while the Word does not have
very many details about Heaven, it does give us some insight. The most important
thing we should realize is Heaven is a real place. According to Hebrews 11:8-16,
Heaven is much like a planet. According to Psalms 102:16-21, it contains a city.
Revelation 21:21 says it has streets. There are also people in Heaven according
to Revelation. Ezekiel 2 tells us it has a throne room and also gives a detailed
description of it. Psalms 78:24 and Revelation 21:23 speak of the fact there is
food in Heaven. Revelation 5:8 mentions music. Revelation 22 reveals there are
trees there as well. Although we are not sure if our pets will be there, animals are
definitely there according to II Kings 2:11 and Psalms 36:6.

These are just a few things we know will be waiting on us when we get to
Heaven. The best thing about Heaven is what is missing there: tears, fears, dying
and crying, according to Revelations 21:1-4.

If someone you loved has passed and was a Christian, then they are now
enjoying the splendor of Heaven. Heaven is a long, "Hello!"

APPLICATION:
1. If you have someone in Heaven, do not grieve—just be sure to join them
later.
2. Every time you feel sad for a loved one who has gone on before you,
remind yourself they are alive and in Heaven.

PRAYER:
Lord, thank you for Heaven. Help me to keep myself right before you. Amen.

JUNE 3
SOMEDAY I'M GONNA MOVE UP TO HEAVEN

Hebrews 9:24
"For Christ is not entered into the Holy places made with hands, which are the figures of the true; but into Heaven itself, now to appear in the presence of God for us:" (KJV)

Before my mother passed in 1993, she called me to her bedside to tell me something very startling—she had written a song! In her younger days of good health, she was an accomplished banjo player. I recall childhood memories of cars pulling into the driveway and people with guitar cases getting out. In a matter of minutes, we would have a mini-concert in our living room. However, in all of my mother's 77 years, she had never written even one song—until the last couple of weeks of her life. The song was entitled, *Someday I'm Gonna Move Up to Heaven.* When she passed, my wife wrote an additional chorus for it and my sister-in-law, April, sang it at her memorial service. Below are the lyrics to the first verse my mother wrote:

Someday, I'm gonna move up to Heaven; someday, some glorious day. Where the flowers bloom forever and never fade away. Someday I'm gonna be with my Jesus; up there with that glorious throne. Where He's prepared a mansion for me and praise God; I'm going home.

As I stated in yesterday's devotional, Heaven is a real place with real things. The scriptures say Heaven contains jewels and gold in Revelation 21. Revelation also states angels are there. Matthew 6:9 and Psalms 33:13-14 proclaim God is there. Jesus is also there, according to Hebrews 9:24 and Acts 1:8. Luke 19 tells us the prophets are there. Perhaps, on the most personal note, our loved ones who were Christians are there. (I Thessalonians)

If we continue to follow the Lord, then my mother's song will be true for us one day. Because, someday I'm gonna move up to Heaven!

APPLICATION:
1. Pray for your family members who are lost.
2. Be sure to ready yourself for your future in Heaven.

PRAYER:
Lord, please teach me to be patient and wait on you. I do believe in Heaven and I want to go there. Amen.

JUNE 4
WHO DO YOU HONOR?

Romans 13:7
"Render therefore to all their dues: tribute to whom tribute is due; custom to whom custom; fear to whom fear; honour to whom honour." (KJV)

Calvin Coolidge once said, "No person was ever honored for what he received; honor has been the reward for what he gave." We honor people for many reasons in America. We honor them for their athletic achievements, their acting abilities, their singing or instrument expertise, their breakthroughs in science or medicine and the list could continue. These are all noteworthy achievements and they certainly have their place. Yet, there is an honor all of us should have as believers. We should honor our God by how we live and how we treat the important people He has placed in our lives.

The word *honor* means "to place value on; to dearly prize; to put the highest value on; to stand for and defend with fervor." The Bible is a book of honor.

Honor is not just a feeling. It has certain attributes. It causes you to believe in something, to place a high value on it. It causes you to put yourself second and not be concerned with your own agenda. Romans 12:10 says, *"Be kindly affectionate one to another with brotherly love; in honor preferring one another."* (KJV) It causes you to do the right thing, no matter what. The cause becomes greater than the personal loss it may bring you. It causes you to defend something with the utmost loyalty.

We should show deference and preference to certain people God places in our lives. There are seven people in our lives who should be honored: God, authorities, spouses, parents, employers, elders and pastors. They deserve our respect, honor and recognition while they are with us. We owe them for the good things they have done for us. Pay the debt of honor. You owe it!

APPLICATION:
1. Are you giving honor to those who have positively affected your life?
2. Be sure to do something, today, to show your honor for someone special in your life.

PRAYER:
Lord, forgive me for not giving honor to those you have blessed my life with. I know when I honor them, I am honoring you. Amen.

JUNE 5
HOW DEEP DO YOU WANT TO GO?

Ezekiel 47:1-5

"...I saw a stream flowing eastward from beneath the Temple and passing to the right of the altar, that is, on the south side...where I saw the stream flowing along... Measuring as he went...he took me 1,500 feet and told me to cross again. This time the water was up to my knees. Fifteen hundred feet after that it was up to my waist. Another 1,500 feet it had become a river so deep I wouldn't be able to get across unless I were to swim. It was too deep to cross on foot." (TLB)

In 1999, I took a trip to Korea to minister. While preparing to preach to several thousand people in a stadium in downtown Seoul, God gave me this message. I had already been there for several days and was rather tired from the travel, the change in cuisine and from preaching multiple messages. God revealed to me that people go as deep as they want to go with Him. There are levels or degrees of depths available, but it is up to each of us to decide how deep we will go.

First of all, some are only ankle deep. I call them "splashers." They are just testing the waters. They are spectators, but not participators, much like the rich, young ruler. He kept some of the Commandments, but was unwilling to take the plunge. Some are knee deep. I call them "waders." They are more dry than wet. They never experience full commitment. They are similar to Aaron. He stood up against Pharaoh, but did not stand up against the people. Then, there are those who are waist deep. I call them, "floaters." They are half wet and half dry. They are like Peter before Pentecost. He glorified Jesus and walked on water, but when he doubted Jesus, he almost went under. "Floaters" are in the most danger because they could swim, but they could also drown. Then, there are those who have water over their head. I call them "swimmers." They are submersed in water, head to toe with no dry places, like Paul. He was sold out, fully persuaded and fully committed.

How deep are you? How deep are you willing to go?

APPLICATION:

1. Be sure to check your depth. Be honest. Go deeper!

PRAYER:

Lord, it is my desire to go deeper with you. Help me to swim! Amen.

JUNE 6
READY TO LAUNCH

Luke 5:4-7
*"Now when he had left speaking, he said unto Simon, Launch out into the deep,
and let down your nets for a draught. And Simon answering said unto him,
Master, we have toiled all the night, and have taken nothing: nevertheless at thy
word I will let down the net. And when they had this done, they enclosed a great
multitude of fishes: and their net brake. And they beckoned unto their partners,
which were in the other ship, that they should come and help them. And they
came, and filled both the ships, so that they began to sink."* (KJV)

I was staying at a resort in Florida a few years ago, enjoying the beach and sunshine, when I saw something spectacular. Down the coast at Cape Canaveral, they had just launched a space satellite. The sight was stunning! It was a crystal clear day and everyone paused to take in the wondrous sight.

God is ready to "launch" your life. He has plans to raise you up for others to see. He has plans for your life, which will cause you to be blessed and be a blessing. Yet, how will He do this?

The first thing we must do is to act on His Word. After the disciples acted on His Word, they thrust into the deep. This was where they found the real catch! They had to overcome their natural doubt. After all, Peter was a professional fisherman and he had determined the conditions were not right for fishing on that occasion. However, when he disregarded his experience and reason, and trusted the Word of Jesus, he received a catch greater than ever before.

We must be willing to take the risk of acting on His Word. We must be willing to take the dive and take the plunge. God will always give you more than you can handle. He will always give you more than enough for yourself, so that others around you will be blessed as well.

The disciples were better fishermen after they sold out to Jesus. Do not doubt His command to go out into the deep. He is ready to launch you today!

APPLICATION:
1. Listen to what He is telling you to do and launch out!
2. Do not let doubt stop you from receiving your "boat load."

PRAYER:
Lord, forgive me for playing it safe. I am ready for you to launch me. Amen.

JUNE 7
WHAT DO YOU BELIEVE?

Romans 1:25
"Instead of believing what they knew was the truth about God, they deliberately chose to believe lies. So they prayed to the things God made, but wouldn't obey the blessed God who made these things." (TLB)

Jesus said over 80 times, "I tell you the truth." He also said 20 times, "Now you've heard it said, but I say unto you." Everyone, everywhere, proclaims they have the truth, the real answers and the real solutions. However, as believers, our source of truth can only be found in scripture.

Our beliefs are fashioned by what we hear, experience and practice. Our beliefs determine our actions. They guide us and help us make decisions, and the consequences are always a result of our beliefs. The truth is we do not really know what we believe until a time of stress or challenge comes upon us. People think they are unmovable about something they stand for until a test or storm blows through. Then, our beliefs are truly revealed.

If we do not have God's truth buried deep in our hearts, we will be moved by our feelings, and feelings are a terrible leader. Proverbs 4:23 states, *"Above all else, guard your affections. For they influence everything else in your life."* (TLB)

The Word of God is stable, dependable and consistent. It works in all types of situations, all types of trouble and all types of hardships. It has been proven, tried and tested. It has not changed. It has no need of modification.

If you choose to trust the world, you will become like them and change beliefs again and again. Dr. Spock's theory changed. The average lifespan of a science book is only 18 months because of new discoveries.

Someone once said, "The beliefs that you hold today are yours—you can continue to believe them or change!" Luke 21:33 proclaims, *"Though Heaven and earth pass away, but my word shall not pass away."* (KJV) So, the question is, what do you believe?

APPLICATION:
   1. Check your beliefs. Are they solidly founded on His Word?
   2. Do not let the world's truth replace God's truth.

PRAYER:
Lord, I choose to trust in you and your truth. I believe you! Amen.

JUNE 8
MAKING THE RIGHT DECISION

Mark 11:2-4

"And saith unto them, Go your way into the village over against you: and as soon as ye be entered into it, ye shall find a colt tied, whereon never man sat: loose him, and bring him. And if any man say unto you, Why do ye this? Say ye that the Lord hath need of him; and straightway he will send him hither. And they went their way, and found the colt tied by the door without in a place where two ways met; and they loose him." (KJV)

Have you ever traveled on a road you have never been on, when the path leads you to a fork in the roadway? Without any signs or directions, you are left to guess which way is the right way.

It is the same with life. There are many things we face that we have never faced before. When we face these things, we are likely to make the wrong decision, if we do not get good directions.

The word *decision* means "to determine a course of action; to remove all but one option; unquestionable, definite direction." It is derived from a word that means "to cut." Every decision cuts a clear path for us. Then, we are left to walk it out.

We can recover from some bad decisions, but there are some bad decisions we may have to pay for—for the rest of our lives.

God wants to help us make the right decisions. Psalms 46:1-2 says, *"God is our refuge and strength, a very present help in trouble. Therefore will not we fear, though the earth be removed, and though the mountains be carried into the midst of the sea;"* (KJV) God is an ever present help in time of need. If this is true, why do we not seek Him?

If we are confused about what decision is right, we must ask. My associate pastor and I went to a neighboring city several times to visit a parishioner's son, who had repeatedly been jailed. Every single time we traveled to visit him, we got lost. Although it was a very tiny city, we continually lost our way. You know what we never did? We never asked anyone for help.

There is a Jewish proverb, which says, "It is better to ask the way 10 times than to take the wrong road once." Let us ask and make the right decisions!

APPLICATION:
1. Stop and ask for direction and help, if you are facing and important decision.
2. Make sure the decisions you are making have been presented to God first.

PRAYER:
Lord, it is my desire to make right decisions. I need help! Amen.

JUNE 9
TAKING GOD'S GUIDANCE

Psalms 25:9
"He guides the humble in what is right and teaches them his way." (NIV)

Leonard Ravenhill said, "Men give advice; God gives guidance." Abraham did not know the way, but he knew the Guide. God is a terrific guide.

My wife, Ginger, and I went to a tourist sight in Israel with my pastor and a group of church people recently. We had never been there before. Although we watched a documentary about the Holy Lands before we left, we really did not know much about what we would see. I was hopeful we would have a good guide when we arrived there, and we did. His name was Nir. He was a Hebrew scholar and spoke terrific English. He had been a guide for several years. When we arrived at certain sites along our tour, he would spend about 10 minutes explaining what we were about to see. He gave us background and history, relating it to our lives as Christians. Before we left each site, he would allow us to ask him questions. I sat behind him on the tour bus and must have asked him dozens of questions. He was very gracious and I learned more about the land of Israel in a few days during this trip, than I had in over 30 years of my personal Biblical studies.

God wants to help guide us into good decision-making. Prayer can help God's people make good decisions. Prayer is an essential resource in good decision-making. The Bible also provides resources for resolving life's dilemmas, making right decisions and distinguishing true values from worldly banalities. Wise decisions result from seeking information, and God's Word is a place of accurate information.

God has promised to give us wisdom if we ask. In the Living Bible, James 1:6 says, *"When you ask him, be sure that you really expect him to tell you, for a doubtful mind will be as unsettled as a wave of the sea that is driven and tossed by the wind."* James is referring not only to knowledge, but the ability to make wise decisions in difficult circumstances. If we allow God to guide us by His Holy Spirit, He will always direct us to the right path. Take God's guidance and you will never be lost!

APPLICATION:
1. Ask God to guide you.
2. Be willing to re-route, if you are going in the wrong direction.

PRAYER:
Lord, if I am on the wrong path, please guide me to the right place! Amen.

175

JUNE 10
THE PORTRAIT OF A SPIRITUAL FATHER

Proverbs 19:26
"He that waseth his father, and chaseth away his mother, is a son that causeth shame, and bringeth reproach." (KJV)

I grew up without a natural father in my life for the most part. My mother and father were never married, and my father was not around throughout the years. I did not think I needed a father until I became a Christian. Then, I realized what I had been missing. I finally had a real father in God Almighty!

Still, time passed and I realized God wanted me to have a natural father figure in my life to guide me in my spiritual life. It took several years for me to find the right one. Yet, when I did, my life changed. The next several years were exceptional and I give credit to that particular spiritual father. I now have several very wise, experienced men who speak into my life and a pastor who really pastors me.

According to the Word of God, there are certain qualities of a spiritual father. Paul gives us a good illustration in I Corinthians 4:14-21. First, not everyone can father you. Second, spiritual fathers are selected by their children. It is not the father who looks for the child. The child must come back, as in the prodigal son. Third, some people can instruct salvation, but cannot father. A natural father can help conceive, but may not help in the upbringing. Fourth, fathers can ask for fellowship, instructors cannot. Fifth, instructors teach, fathers teach and lead. Sixth, instructors give information, fathers give impartation. Lastly, fathers must be mature and seasoned.

When God brings the right spiritual father into your life, be sure to be submissive and teachable. They are not there to dictate over you, but rather be a loving example of who the Heavenly Father is. They are Heaven sent.

Everyone needs a father and a spiritual father. Be sure you identify who your spiritual father is and let him lead you!

APPLICATION:
1. Be sure you give way for a spiritual father in your life.
2. Let God speak into your life through your spiritual father and follow his lead.

PRAYER:
Lord, help me pay the right respect to my spiritual father. I know my life will be blessed through my association with him. Amen.

JUNE 11
PRAYING WITH A PURPOSE

Matthew 6:5-8

"And now about prayer. When you pray, don't be like the hypocrites who pretended piety by praying publicly on street corners and in all the synagogues where everyone can see them. Truly, that is all the reward they will ever get. But when you pray, go away by yourself, all alone, and shut the door behind you and pray to your Father secretly, and your Father, who knows your secrets, will reward you. Don't recite the same prayer over and over as the heathen do, who think prayers are answered only by repeating them again and again. Remember, your Father knows exactly what you need even before you ask him!" (TLB)

Justin Cornwall said, "Prayer is more than a polite interview with God, at which, we have our picture taken with Him, so we can prove our posterity that we once had an audience with Him."

Prayer is certainly more than just having a "Kodak moment" with God. It is our time to place our hearts, lives and needs at His feet. Prayer opens up our possibilities. God is ready to do what He has already promised for us, but prayer is a catalyst, which brings His promises to reality.

In the Bible, there are some good examples of those who prayed with a purpose. Abraham prayed for Abimelech to be healed in Genesis 20. Moses prayed for the fire to be quenched in Numbers 11:1. In Deuteronomy 9, Moses prayed for the people to be spared. Hannah prayed for a son in I Samuel 1:10. Samuel prayed for direction in I Samuel 8:6. Elisha prayed for a child to be revived in II Kings 4:33. Hezekiah prayed for a longer life in II Kings 20:2. Nehemiah prayed for provision in Nehemiah 2:4. Job prayed for his friends in Job 42:10. Daniel prayed, despite the king's decree in Daniel 6:10.

These are just some Old Testament examples of praying with a purpose. Be sure when you go before Him in prayer, you pray with a purpose!

APPLICATION:
1. Before you pray the next time, find a purpose to accompany your prayer.
2. Be sure you always pray and believe!

PRAYER:
Lord, I decide to pray with a purpose and wait on you. Amen.

2018 I pray for the division and gossip to be eradicated between Wayne, Devon, Nick and myself. Enough! I pray that God continue to open doors at Faith Tabernacle if it be HIS will. I pray for health & prosperity in Jesus name

177

JUNE 12
BREAKTHROUGHS COME THROUGH FASTING

Joel 2:12-13

"'But even now,' says the LORD, 'repent sincerely and return to me with fasting and weeping and mourning. Let your broken heart show your sorrow...'" (TEV)

I heard of someone who asked their pastor, "Why do they call it fasting when it goes so slow?" Fasting is certainly not the most pleasant of spiritual practices. Yet, it is not supposed to be. It is a time to rend the heart and fine tune the spirit. Fasting is dying out to the flesh.

Jesus best represented the principle in John 12:23-24, *"And Jesus answered them saying, The hour is come, that the Son of man should be glorified. Verily, verily I say unto you, Except a corn of wheat fall into the ground and die, it abideth alone: but if it die, it bringeth forth much fruit..."* (KJV)

Fasting places the focus off of self and onto the most urgent task at hand. Every time the people of God were about to go up against a bigger opponent and inherit, they called for a fast. God required them to look to Him for guidance. Fasting turned the attention away from the problem and onto Him. It brought their breakthrough. What are you seeking a breakthrough in?

There are some things all Christians should seek a breakthrough for: First, we should seek to save people in our churches and families. Second, we should seek a greater anointing in our churches and in our lives. Third, we should seek breakthroughs in personal issues and things pressing in our lives. Fourth, we need breakthroughs with our young people. We must stand in the gap for our children. And fifth, we should seek to see our enemies fall. When someone opposes you, he/she opposes God.

If you are in a place, today, where you need Heavenly help and guidance, consider calling a personal fast. Your breakthrough is just ahead!

APPLICATION:
1. Make a decision to set aside some meals and time with God in the next few days.
2. Be sure to pray and study the Word as much as possible during your fast.

PRAYER:
Lord, show me the things you desire through my life when I fast. I do believe you will bring my breakthrough. Amen.

JUNE 13
THE REWARDS OF FASTING

Isaiah 58:6
"Is not this the fast that I have chosen? To loose the bands of wickedness, to undo the heavy burdens, and to let the oppressed go free, and that ye break every yoke?" (KJV)

What is fasting? It is abstinence from food: a religious mortification. The Hebrew word *tsuwm* means to abstain from eating. It is voluntary and deliberate abstinence from food. Fasting does not change God or His Word, but it changes us and our position to receive what His Word has already said. It is abstinence from earthly food, and instead, dining on Heavenly food. Fasting is a form of discipline.

There are 20 rewards mentioned in Isaiah 58 connected to fasting. Each one results from placing Heaven and God above earthly and natural desires. Consider the rewards when you fast.

1. It loosens the bands of wickedness.
2. It undoes the heavy burdens.
3. It releases the oppressed.
4. It breaks every yoke.
5. Light increases.
6. Your health springs forward speedily.
7. You become aware of your righteousness in Him.
8. You cut off the sneak attacks of the Devil.
9. Your prayers become energized.
10. It causes hope to spring up in a hopeless situation.
11. It brings guidance and direction.
12. It waters your spirit.
13. It re-energizes your physical strength.
14. It makes you like a watered garden.
15. You regain lost spiritual blessings.
16. Your Godly heritage is rediscovered.
17. A hedge is built to fill up the broken areas.
18. You take your streets back.
19. You ride on the high places of the earth.
20. You receive the heritage of Jacob (Israel). (Deuteronomy 32:9-14)

God and His amazing ways. I turned to this on 7/12 - completely wrong day but just yesterday spoke w/ Wells Fargo about the possibility of Rick and I owning 8313 Old Town Dr. again - my home for ten years. Still in disbelief. I am motivated to fast and give God the Glory! 2018

Although we do not fast to gain a reward, God always releases His favor on those who do!

179

APPLICATION:
1. Consider the great rewards resulting from fasting and prayer.
2. Purposely, set aside some time to spend with God and fast, and then expect His rewards!

PRAYER:
Lord, help me to hear your voice when I fast. I believe you and all you want for my life. Amen.

JUNE 14
SUCCESS THE RIGHT WAY

Joshua 1:8
"This book of the law shall not depart out of thy mouth; but thou shalt meditate therein day and night, that thou mayest observe to do according to all that is written therein: for then thou shalt make thy way prosperous, and then thou shalt have good success." (KJV)

What is the definition of success? It means "to reach a goal; accomplishing things that were not previously accomplished." Success is not about how much you have, but how much you achieve. If you achieve something others have failed, and you were committed to it, then you are successful.

God's Word is the source of our success. The Word of God is our manual. It is a stimulator. It contains examples of people who were faced with the same types of situations we face today, and shows us how some of them received desired results and success.

God also places us in an environment that takes us to success. This environment includes others whom God has designated to be part of our success.

When I met my wife, Ginger, I did not have anything: no credit, no assets, no money and a stalled job due to the economy of the late 70's and early 80's. She did not have much either, but she was a hard worker and handled money well (a weakness I inherited from my family). In the next few years, we bought our first home and began to see success as pastors. Without her, there is no way I could have been a success on any level. There is no doubt about it; our success is tied to others.

Your success or failure is always tied to others. Any lasting success is because of hard work. The average millionaire works 14 hours a day. Success also comes from overcoming obstacles, suffering discomfort without quitting and standing up for what is right. With God, all things are possible. Losers make excuses; winners make progress!

APPLICATION:
1. Be sure to meditate in God's Word and you will be successful.
2. Let God place people in your life who will be a part of your success. Be sure to thank those who already are.

PRAYER:
Lord, thank you for helping me be successful the right way. Amen.

JUNE 15
BE SUPPORTIVE OF YOUR LEADERS

Exodus 17:11-12

"And it came to pass, when Moses held up his hand, that Israel prevailed: and when he let down his hand, Amalek prevailed. But Moses' hands were heavy; and they took a stone, and put it under him, and he sat thereon; and Aaron and Hur stayed up his hands, the one on the one side, and the other on the other side; and his hands were steady until the going down of the sun." (KJV)

When you support your leaders, their anointing works for you. God has a way of blessing your life through those who lead you.

Leadership is not nearly as glamorous as it seems. Moses discovered this. He had barely led the people of Egypt before they turned on him, when Pharaoh pursued them to the Red Sea. David discovered the same when he had returned from the battlefield to discover the enemy had attacked his hometown and brought destruction. Some of the same people, who cheered for David when he conquered Goliath, were ready to stone him.

Yet, there is a Biblical precedence that God always protects and keeps His people when they follow and support those who lead them. God places gifts inside of men and women, which are meant to benefit the rest of the body. They come in the form of apostles, prophets, evangelists, pastors and teachers. God flows His anointing through them.

However, be mindful, when you rise against God's leaders, you are rising against His anointing. It is dangerous to threaten His anointing!

Be sure to respect and honor your Godly leaders. If you do, you will be blessed. If their arms are heavy, help lift them up and God will lift you up!

APPLICATION:
1. Thank God for the Godly leaders He has placed around you.
2. Do something to honor or support them, today.

PRAYER:
Lord, thank you for the leaders you have placed in my life. May you richly bless their lives because they are a blessing to me and others. Amen.

JUNE 16
ONLY YOU CAN PREVENT FOREST FIRES

James 3:4-5
*"And a tiny rudder makes a huge ship turn wherever the pilot wants it to go,
even though the winds are strong. So also the tongue is a small thing, but what
enormous damage it can do. A great forest can be set on fire by one tiny spark."*
(TLB)

Many years ago, there was a national campaign to stop the needless forest
fires, which were often caused by careless people. The slogan was, "Only you can
prevent forest fires." The campaign illustrated someone throwing a lit cigarette
out of a window. Although the cigarette only had a small spark, it often caused
great, uncontrollable, untamed forest fires.

However, the small spark which causes the greatest destruction for a human
being is our tongues. There is power in the tongue according to Proverbs 18:21. In
fact, it has enough power to cause death or life. If you do not control your words,
they can start a series of events in your life, which will be difficult to overcome.

Psalms 45:1 reveals that the tongue writes the script of your life. We cannot
be reckless with our language. Job 6:24 says, *"Teach me, and I will hold my
tongue: and cause me to understand wherein I have erred."* (KJV)

If you pay close attention to the words spoken by people who seem to always
be struggling, you will discover most of their words are negative and usually to
come to pass.

However, just as the tongue produces "fires," it also produces success. Your
tongue has the power to uproot all of your problems. Luke 17:6 states, *" 'If your
faith were only the size of a mustard seed,' Jesus answered, 'it would be large
enough to uproot that mulberry tree over there and send it hurling into the sea!
Your command would bring immediate results!' "* (TLB)

Either way, negative or positive, one thing is certain; the tongue is the spark
of our fortunes. Be sure you are not starting any needless forest fires in your life
with careless words!

APPLICATION:
1. Check the words spoken from your mouth carefully.
2. If you are "starting fires," put them out with the right words—God's Word!

PRAYER:
*Lord, please forgive the words I have wrongfully spoken and let them fall to the
ground. Amen.*

JUNE 17
THE LAW OF FAITH

Romans 3:26-28
"To declare, I say, at this time his righteousness: that he might be just, and the justifier of him which believeth in Jesus. Where is boasting then? It is excluded. By what law? Of works? Nay: but by the law of faith. Therefore we conclude that a man is justified by faith without the deeds of the law." (KJV)

There is a law of faith. It operates the same every time you enforce it. Faith is not a fantasy; it is based on the Word. It always lines up with the will of God. However, it must be understood for it to work for you.

The Wright brothers created the airplane in the early 1900's, but man could have flown centuries before, even in the Garden of Eden because the laws governing aerodynamics were the same then as they are now. Today, we can fly faster, better and more safely than early pilots because of a better understanding of those laws—not because the laws have changed.

When you operate in the law of faith, it makes a demand on the resources of God, including the promises of His Word and His anointing. In Luke 8:43, the woman with the issue of blood made a demand on the anointing by operating in faith. Why did Jesus say to her, "Your faith has made you whole," instead of, "My anointing has made you whole?" The reason she was healed is she correctly operated in the laws, which govern faith.

Faith operates when the laws are followed, not because of hardships, but in hardships. If hardships brought faith, then everyone would be a faith giant. Hardships may build character, but they do not build faith!

Be sure you are following the law of faith. Do not expect it to work for you if you are "breaking the law."

APPLICATION:
1. Consider the things you are doing spiritually, now.
2. Are you operating in faith?

PRAYER:
Lord, I choose to operate in faith. Teach me to operate in the law of faith and not break the law. Amen.

JUNE 18
TRAINING UP OUR CHILDREN

Proverbs 22:6
"Train up a child in the way that he should go and when he is old (mature) he will not depart from it." (KJV)

A little boy made it clear he did not want to go to kindergarten. So, his mother was prepared for the worst day when he came home from his first day at school. "So, how did you enjoy kindergarten?" she asked. "Well," he admitted, "I enjoyed it more than I wanted to!"

It is up to us to train our children. Although they are not always going to agree with the discipline they are given, without it, they are sure to fail. Discipline and punishment are not the same. Discipline is teaching them what is right. Punishment is correcting wrong behavior as witnessed in the scriptures in Proverbs 13:24; 23:13 and 29:15. Dr. Ross Campbell said, "The better disciplined a child is the less punishment will be required."

How do we discipline and train most effectively? We must communicate our love. There are 10 different ways to communicate it:

1. The marital relationship is critical to bring about love and stability. Discipline is always easier when two are involved.
2. Make eye contact with your children. Eye contact is a way to direct a behavior and communicate affection.
3. Make physical contact. Sometimes a firm touch is just as effective.
4. Give them your full attention.
5. Do not try to live your life vicariously through your children. Allow them to be themselves. Encourage them to be unique.
6. Allow them to be angry, but not sin. Do not suppress anger. Jesus was angry at times.
7. Do not be afraid to apologize when you are wrong. It teaches them forgiveness.
8. Always inject love into their moments of failure. Children need to be reassured even when they are wrong, they are still loved. Love never fails!
9. Tell them your testimony. They want to know about your spirituality. Tell them God is the best thing ever in your life.
10. Do not panic.

Remember, they are children. Trust the training!

185

APPLICATION:
   1. If you are a parent, remember everyday you are training your children.
   2. Be sure all training has love involved.

PRAYER:
Lord, thank you for my children, or my future children. Help me teach and train them as you would have me to. Amen.

JUNE 19
SEVEN WAYS TO DEFEAT THE DEVIL

I John 3:8

"...For this purpose the Son of God was manifested, (appear, visible or known what has been hidden or unknown), that he might destroy the works of the Devil." (KJV)

The Devil is our enemy! We are in for a fight. He is goes about as a roaring lion seeking whom he may devour.

We also have the commission to destroy the works of the Devil. God has "deputized" us to arrest the works of darkness. According to the Bible, there are things we can do to defeat the Devil. Below is a list of seven things we can do:

1. We can defeat the Devil by the Word of God. In Luke 4, Jesus used the Word of God to combat the Devil when He was tempted.
2. We can defeat the Devil by submitting ourselves fully unto God. The definition of *submit* is "to arrange under, to subordinate, to yield to one's admonition or advice."
3. We can defeat the Devil by resisting him. James 4:7 says, *"...Resist the Devil, and he will flee from you."* (KJV) *Resist* means "to withstand the action or effect of; to refrain or abstain from, with difficulty."
4. We can defeat the Devil by drawing nigh unto God. The closer you get to God, the more His glory gets on you. Since the time Jesus defeated Satan at Calvary and the grave, Satan does not have access to God or His throne. His glory destroys Satan's works! Become joined to God with no disconnection, much like the fingers to the hand.
5. We can defeat the Devil if we speak no evil. James 4:11 says, *"Speak not evil one of another, brethren. He that speaketh evil of his brother, and judgeth his brother, speaketh evil of the law, and judgeth the law: but if thou judge the law, thou art not a doer of the law, but a judge. There is one lawgiver who is able to save and to destroy: who art thou that judgest another?"* (KJV)
6. We can defeat the Devil if we give him no place. Ephesians 4:27 says, *"Neither give place to the Devil."* (KJV)
7. We can defeat the Devil if we put on the whole armor of God. Ephesians 6:10-18 explains when you have your full armor in place, there is no doubt, it is possible to defeat the Devil!

APPLICATION:
1. Be sure to use the above checklist.
2. Remember, you can only defeat the Devil today. You still have to face him tomorrow. Be consistent, and you will win!

PRAYER:
Lord, I choose to submit fully unto you and resist the enemy. With your help and your Word, I am confident I can defeat him, today! Amen.

JUNE 20
WHAT KIND OF SOLDIER ARE YOU?

II Timothy 2:3-4

"Thou therefore endure hardness, as a good soldier of Jesus Christ. No man that warreth entangleth himself with the affairs of this life; that he may please him who hath chosen him to be a soldier." (KJV)

I am privileged to live in a military town. Our city is just miles away from Fort Campbell, Kentucky, the home of the Screaming Eagles 101st Airborne Division. It is a prolific division, which has been in the center of every modern war.

Although I have never personally served in the military, I have hundreds of active and retired military personnel in my church. I have watched them deploy numerous times and be separated from their families. They have returned from wars and military actions with scars, both physical and emotional. There is no group on earth I have any greater respect for.

However, we must realize we are soldiers in the army of the Lord. We have been sworn in under the banner of the blood stained cross of Jesus Christ. We have been commissioned to fight the fight of faith. We have been armed with His armor and been given our marching orders to take the message of liberty through Christ to the world.

In order to be the kind of soldier who brings honor to our Commander, there are five things we must do. First, we must be able to take orders. Luke 6:46 says, *"And why call ye me, Lord, Lord and do not the things which I say?"* (KJV) Second, you must be familiar with the enemy. II Corinthians 2:11 says, *"Lest Satan should get an advantage of us: for we are not ignorant of his devices."* (KJV) Third, we must be familiar with the handbook. Isaiah 34:16 says, *"Search the book of the Lord and see all that he will do..."* (TLB) Fourth, we must trust our fellow soldiers. Ephesians 4:3 says, *"Try always to be led along together by the Holy Spirit and so be at peace with one another."* (TLB) Finally, we must believe in the cause. I Samuel 17:29 says, *"And David said, What have I now done? Is there not a cause?"* (KJV)

We are all soldiers under His charge. The question is: what kind of soldier are you?

APPLICATION:
1. Check your demeanor as a soldier. Report for duty, daily!

PRAYER:
Lord, I am reporting for duty, today. I will follow you! Amen.

JUNE 21
THE KINGDOM IS YOURS

Luke 12:32
"Fear not, little flock; for it is your Father's good pleasure to give you the kingdom." (KJV)

One of the hardest things we must learn as Christians is to accept what God has purchased for us through His Son, Jesus Christ. We struggle to "get" God to do something for us. We think we have to manufacture something to move the favor of God over our lives. However, nothing could be further from the truth. God has already blessed us all with spiritual blessings. We have access to the very Spirit of God. He was sent to those gathered in the upper room. He is here today!

The hardest obstacle we face is receiving those things God desires for us. We have heard theological preaching for so long; we somehow think everything good can only be obtained when we get to Heaven or we think we are not worthy to receive it. We have accepted the belief that if it is available now, it is always for someone else, somewhere else.

Jesus spent three and a half years of His ministry showing people what was rightfully theirs. He healed people everywhere. He healed people who differed from one another and were suffering from many types of diseases. He freed people everywhere. Many different people with differing devils were freed. He fed multitudes and turned water into wine.

His entire ministry was to reveal to God's people that He was a great provider. He showed them nothing was impossible with Him. He stirred their faith to the level that even the dead were raised, not in Heaven, not after the resurrection, but in that present moment.

We know scripture teaches us in Hebrews 13:8, *"Jesus Christ, the same yesterday, today and forever."* (KJV) This includes right now.

He is a now God. Whatever you are facing today, He has already made a provision for you. He has already put in place the things you need to live a full life. He has already given you everything you can imagine. Will you receive? The Kingdom is yours!

APPLICATION:
1. Make the decision, today, to receive what God has for your life.
2. Remind yourself what you are worth because of His blood.

PRAYER:
Lord, thank you for giving me your Kingdom. I am grateful for your provision! Amen.

JUNE 22
THE LAYING ON OF HANDS

Hebrews 6:1-2
"Therefore leaving the principles of the doctrine of Christ, let us go unto perfection; not laying again the foundation of repentance from dead works, and of faith toward God, Of the doctrine of baptisms, and of laying on of hands..."
(KJV)

The laying on of hands is a Bible doctrine. The laying on of hands symbolized a transfer: transfer of power, anointing, healing, privileges, favor or a blessing bestowed. It always meant empowerment, which did not previously exist.

In the Old Testament the laying on of hands is primarily associated with the sacrifices prescribed in the Law. An Israelite making a burnt offering was to lay his hands on the animal's head, so that it might be an acceptable sacrifice for his atonement.

During the Passover, it meant taking the penalty for someone else's crimes. In Leviticus 16, the hands were laid on the "scapegoat" symbolizing atonement.

Without question, the laying on of hands is very significant. Throughout the Bible, there are occasions of a charge for the laying on of hands. Here is a short list:

1. A blessing bestowed. In Matthew 19:13-15, Jesus corrected His disciples for not allowing the children to have hands laid on them.
2. The transferring of authority. In Acts 6:5-8; 13:2-5, the church grew mightily as the disciples laid hands on people.
3. Anointing. In Acts 8:14-20; 9:16-19; 19:5-7, 11; I Timothy 4:14; II Timothy 1:6-7, the anointing was released into those who needed it most when hands were laid on them.
4. Signs and wonders. In Acts 5:12; 14:1-3, every time the early church leaders laid hands on people, signs and wonders manifested.
5. Healing. In Mark 5:23; 6:2-3; 6:12-13; 8:23-25; Acts 28:6-9, Jesus laid hands on people at times. He demonstrated the significance of it.

APPLICATION:
1. Take the time to study the times people had hands laid on them in the Bible.
2. If you are sick, call on the elders of the church for prayer and the laying on of hands.

PRAYER:
Lord, give me the understanding of the laying on of hands. Amen.

JUNE 23
WHO IS THIS MAN?

Mark 4:35-41

"As evening fell, Jesus said to his disciples, 'Let's cross to the other side of the lake.' ... But soon a terrible storm arose. High waves began to break into the boat until it was nearly full of water and about to sink. Jesus was asleep at the back of the boat with his head on a cushion. Frantically they wakened him, shouting, 'Teacher, don't you even care that we are all about to drown?' Then he rebuked the wind and said to the sea, 'Quiet down!' And the wind fell, and there was a great calm! ... And they were filled with awe and said among themselves, 'Who is this man, that even the winds and seas obey him?'" (TLB)

When Jesus appeared, He unveiled to humanity who the living God really was. Jesus showed He cared. He brought hope, joy and life back to God's people. He bewildered the religious people by being "among" the people and He fulfilled the Abrahamic Covenant.

Everywhere He went, people asked the question, "Who is this man?" Luke 9:9 says, *"'I beheaded John,' Herod said, 'so who is this man about whom I hear such strange stories?' And he tried to see him."* (TLB) Matthew 21:9-10 says, *"Then the crowds surged on ahead and pressing along behind, shouting, 'God bless King David's Son! God's Man is here!' ... 'Bless him, Lord! Praise God in highest Heaven!' The entire city of Jerusalem was stirred as he entered. 'Who is this?' they asked"* (TLB)

Luke 7:48 in the NIV says, *"Then Jesus said to her, 'Your sins are forgiven.' The other guests began to say among themselves, 'Who is this who even forgives sins?'"* Then in John 5:10 we see, *"...and so the Jews said to the man who had been healed, 'It is the Sabbath; the law forbids you to carry your mat.' But he replied, 'The man who made me well said to me, 'Pick up your mat and walk' So they asked him, 'Who is this fellow who told you to pick it up and walk?'"* (TLB)

So, who is this man to you?

APPLICATION:
1. Do you consider who died for you? Who is the man to you?
2. Make His will your will.

PRAYER:
Lord, help me to understand who Jesus really is. Amen.

JUNE 24
WHO IS THIS MAN IN THE OLD TESTAMENT?

Psalms 89:6
"For who in the Heaven can be compared unto the LORD? Who among the songs of the mighty can be likened unto the LORD?" (KJV)

I do not pretend the following revelation originated with me. I received it from Jerry Savelle, who obtained it from Oral Roberts, who received it from E.W. Kenyon. I know Jesus is in every book of the Bible, thus answering: Who is this man? I will tell you who He is!

In Genesis, He is the one Creator of all, the ark of safety and the ram in the thicket. In Exodus, He is the burning bush, the rod that parted the Red Sea and the sacrifice that brought atonement. In Leviticus, He is the blood on the altar, the giver of the law, and the glory that appeared. In Numbers, He is the cloud by day, the fire by night, the provider and protector of Israel. In Deuteronomy, He is the giver of the Covenant, the one who gives wealth and the one who overtakes you with blessings. In Joshua, He is the scarlet cord of Rehab, the presence in the Ark, the one who parted the Jordan River and the one who caused the walls of Jericho to fall. In Judges, He is the lamp in the army of Gideon's pitchers and the one who restored Samson's strength, so that he slew more Philistines in the end than in the beginning. In Ruth, He is the one who gave Ruth the husband she desired, and gave her a son, who would become David's grandfather. In I Samuel, He is the stone that slew Goliath (no ordinary stone). He is the presence in the ark that caused the Philistines to tremble when it entered their camp. In II Samuel, He is David's rock, fortress, shield, high tower and refuge. In I Kings, He is Solomon's wisdom and understanding. He is the fire that consumed Elijah's sacrifice. In II Kings, He is the mantle of Elijah and the double anointing of Elisha. In I Chronicles, He is the Father God of the children of Israel. He is the spirit that drove David's mighty men. In II Chronicles, He is the glory in the temple that was so strong that even the priests received. He is the ambush set for the enemy. In Ezra, He is the one who stirred the king and provoked him to finance the rebuilding of the wall. In Nehemiah, He is the Lord of joy and strength. He is the wall Nehemiah built. In Esther, He is the light, gladness, joy and honor of the Jews. In Job, He is the one who blessed Job and gave him double, so his latter end was better. Job lived 140 years and saw four generations. In Psalms, He is the song of David and the great shepherd who prophesied the king is coming again. In Proverbs, He is the Word that produces health and gives favor. He is the one who makes you rich and adds no sorrow to it. In Ecclesiastes, He is the one who gives man his portion and brings bread in on every wave. In Song of Solomon, He is the one who gives romance to lovers. In Isaiah, He is the redeemer to come, the Lord crucified and the one who bore stripes for our healing today. In Jeremiah, He is the fire shut up in your bones and the one who gives you the expected end.

In Lamentations, He is the Lord of new mercies every morning and the one who is good to those who wait for Him. In Ezekiel, He is the coming rain and the one who brought dry bones to life (You). In Daniel, He is the fourth man (miracle times 7). He is the one who shut the Lion's mouth (The Devil). In Hosea, He is the one who feeds Israel. He is the former and latter rain. In Joel, He is the Holy Ghost Baptizer to come, the one who will save anyone who will call on His name. In Amos, He is the plumb line of His people, the one who reveals secrets to His people. In Obadiah, He is the deliverer of the house of Jacob (yours too). In Jonah, He is the great fish that swallowed Jonah. He is the one who spared the city and gave Jonah another chance (you, too). In Micah, He is the God who pardons iniquity and delights in mercy. In Nahum, He is the God who reserves wrath for His enemies. In Habakkuk, He is the Lord who makes you ride on the high places of the earth and the one who gives you vision. In Zephaniah, He is the judge of all nations and the one who will take away all evil. In Zechariah, He is the rescuer of our children. He is the one who signals for them and takes them into the bright clouds of Heaven and the coming King. In Malachi, He is the priest of our tithe. He is the one who rebukes the devourer and the Son of righteousness.

Jesus was in the Old Testament and not just in the New Testament! Who is this man?

APPLICATION:
1. Memorize the books of the Old Testament
2. Do it by learning the first five, and then add the second five, and so on until you can recite all thirty-nine books in order.

PRAYER:
Lord, thank you for showing Jesus throughout the Word of God! Amen.

JUNE 25
WHO IS THIS MAN IN THE NEW TESTAMENT

Luke 5:21
"The Pharisees and the teachers of the law began thinking to themselves, 'Who is this fellow who speaks blasphemy? Who can forgive sins but God alone?'"
(NIV)

Who is this man in the New Testament? I will tell you who He is! In Matthew, Mark, Luke and John, He was born of a virgin, healed the sick, raised the dead, cast out devils, walked on water, fed 4,000, fed 5,000, cursed the fig tree, cleansed the temple, reproved religion, prayed until blood came out, washed the disciples feet, was crucified on Calvary, spent three days and three nights in Hell, preached to the spirits in prison, led the captive free, rose from the grave, appeared to over 500 people, ascended to the Father and sat down at His right hand. In Acts, He is the baptizer in the Holy Ghost and fire. He is the one who stood up to welcome Stephen home to Heaven. He is the one who spoke to Saul on the road to Damascus and transformed him into Paul. In Romans, He is the one who makes us more than a conqueror and the one who renews our minds. In I Corinthians, He is the head of the Church, the one who gives hope and love and the one who orchestrates the gifts. In II Corinthians, He is the one who always causes us to triumph and the one who makes us a new creature. In Galatians, He is the one who justifies by faith and redeems us from the curse. In Ephesians, He is the chief cornerstone, the one who raised us up together with Him in Heavenly places and the giver of gifts to the Church. In Philippians, He is the one who gives us strength to accomplish all things and supplies all needs. In Colossians, He is the one who is all in all, the rewarder of the inheritance. In I Thessalonians, He is the Lord coming again. In II Thessalonians, He is the Lord of grace and the giver of peace. In I Timothy, He is our Savior and Lord. In II Timothy, He is the judge of the dead. He is the one who gives us power, love and a sound mind. In Titus, He is the one who brings salvation to all men and redeems us from sin and iniquity. In Philemon, He is the one who provides every good thing. In Hebrews, He is the high priest of His people and the one who makes intercession, the same yesterday, today and forever. In James, He is the giver of the crown of life, the Lord of glory. In I Peter, He is the one who suffered for our sins. By His stripes, we are healed. In II Peter, He is the one who gives all things that pertain to life and Godliness. In I John, He is the Lord of light and love. In II John, He is the Son of the Father God. In III John, He is the one who desires for you to prosper and be in health, even as your soul prospers. In Jude, He is the one who preserves you and multiplies mercy. In Revelation, He is the Alpha, Omega—first, last, beginning and end. He is the first begotten from the dead, the one who was dead and is now alive, the one who has the keys of death and Hell and who stands at the door and knocks. He is the first rider of white horses with the armies of Heaven and the one who breaks the seal of the book. He is the one the angels, the elders and the beasts in Heaven cried to, "Holy Holy, Worthy." He is the one who cast Satan and his allies into Hell–then into the lake of fire. He is the one who lights up the great city of Heaven—where there is no sickness, death, pain or tears. He is the ruler forever, the Prince of Peace, the King of Kings, the Lord of Lords, the Son of God and my Savior!

We know Jesus lived. He was a man in history, as well as a man for all times!

APPLICATION:
1. Memorize all of the books in the New Testament.
2. Use the same formula as the Old Testament: five in order, etc.

PRAYER:
Lord, thank you, Jesus is found in every book of the New Testament. Amen.

JUNE 26
WHERE ARE THE MIRACLES?

Judges 6:13
"...Gideon replied, 'if the Lord is with us, why has all this happened to us? And where are all the miracles our ancestors have told us about—such as when God brought them out of Egypt? Now the Lord has thrown us away and has let the Midianites ruin us.'" (TLB)

I have been in church for well over 30 years and I have seen God do some amazing things. Yet, I cannot say I have seen consistently, the miracles witnessed in the early Church. I believe we should.

So the question is, "Where are the miracles?" Webster's Dictionary defines a *miracle* as "an extraordinary occurrence that surpasses all known human powers or natural forces and is ascribed to a divine or supernatural cause, especially to God; a superb or surpassing example of something; wonder; marvel."

Fred Craddock tells the following story: "A young pastor goes to pray with an older woman. She's near death; she's in the hospital lying on the pillow gasping for breath. He visits with her and then says, 'I need to go, but would you like to have prayer first?' The old woman says, 'Yes.' He says, 'Well, what would you like us to pray for today?' And she says, 'I'd like to pray I'll be healed.' The young pastor gasps, but goes on, 'Lord, we pray for you to sustain this sick sister. And if it be thy will, we pray that she will be restored to health and to service. But if it's not thy will, we accept the circumstance.' Suddenly, the old woman opens her eyes and sits up in bed. She throws her feet over the side of the bed. She stands up. She says, 'I think I'm healed!' The pastor goes down the steps, and out to the parking lot. Before he opens the door of his car, he looks up and says, 'Don't you ever do that to me again!'"

There is no doubt we must begin to believe God will do the things among us, which man cannot do, and the things belonging solely to Him and to no one else. We must not accept that miracles are not for today.

I think the modern day Church knows miracles are possible, but we are scratching our heads and asking, "Where are the miracles?"

APPLICATION:
1. Resolve miracles are for today and for your life.
2. Resist unbelief and doubt no matter what.

PRAYER:
Lord, help me to believe miracles are for me. Amen.

JUNE 27
SEVEN THINGS, WHICH CREATE AN ATMOSPHERE FOR A MIRACLE

John 11:47
"Then gathered the chief priests and the Pharisees a council, and said, What do we? For this man doeth miracles." (KJV)

Miracles are mentioned throughout scripture. God's divine nature is to do those things man cannot produce. It is to set things right that have been damaged or destroyed. However, miracles are not automatic. There are things which create the right atmosphere for miracles to manifest in our lives.

Consider seven things which create an atmosphere for a miracle. Each one increases the potential for a miracle to come forth.

1. Testimonies. The Woman with the issue of blood testifies of her healing in front of Jairus in Mark 5:25. The result? A miracle for Jairus' daughter.
2. Faith. Faith makes a demand on the anointing. In Mark 10:52, blind Bartimaeus made a demand on the anointing by casting his garment aside by faith.
3. Praise. By centering your thoughts on the Lord, you leave little room for doubt to enter in. In Acts 16, Paul and Silas praised at midnight and a miracle caused their prison cells to spring open.
4. Prayer. By asking God, you open the doorway from Heaven to earth. James 5:17 confirms only those people who pray fervently bring the miraculous into existence.
5. Giving. By presenting a memorial before the Lord, you take all of the importance off of earthly provision and rely totally upon the Heavenly provision. Acts 10:2-4 illustrates how God does supernatural things through our giving.
6. Promoting the Gospel. When you have the desire to do God's work on the behalf of others, you give God an opportunity to move. Matthew 10:1-2; 10:5-10 states when the disciples went forth to preach, the same miracles in Jesus' ministry manifested through them.
7. Obeying the Word. God has a divine reason for prompting you to do the things He asks or tells His servant(s) to ask. Matthew 8:1-11 reveals when the centurion approached Jesus, he had confidence in the spoken Word and the result was a miracle for his servant.

We need to position ourselves for God's intervention. When we do, miracles will become reality!

APPLICATION:
1. Be sure you are in a position to receive a miracle.
2. Pray for those around you who are in need of a miracle.

PRAYER:
Lord, please give miracles to those who need them most in my life. Amen.

love this 6/27/18

JUNE 28
THE MIRACLES OF JESUS

John 6:2
"And a great multitude followed him, because they saw his miracles which he did on them that were diseased." (KJV)

Medical science is an instrument of God. Jesus never once spoke against doctors. He chose one to be a disciple. However, He recognized the limitations of man and He intervened many times to perform miracles for those He was in contact with. Jesus did not have to touch lepers. He could have been just as effective from 100 yards away, but He touched them.

There is a distinct difference between healing and miracles. Many times when people come up for healing, they really desire a miracle. Healing is a process, and miracles are spontaneous. God is not obligated to do miracles; they are sovereign acts. He is bound to His Word, however. He is bound to someone who believes in faith. Faith can, and does, cause miracles, but it also calls for the gift of supernatural faith for miracles to happen.

Let us look at a list of His miracles:

1. Turning water into wine. (John 2:1-11)
2. The calming of the wind. (Mark 4:36-39)
3. Healing of the Nobleman's son. (John 4:46-54)
4. Deliverance of the demoniac in the Synagogue. (Luke 4:31-37)
5. Healing of Peter's mother-in-law. (Matthew 8:14-15)
6. The first draught of fishes. (Luke 5:4-11)
7. Cleansing the leper. (Matthew 8:2-3)
8. Healing the paralytic. (Matthew 9:2-6)
9. He walked through a crowd that intended to push Him over the cliff. (Luke 4:29-30)
10. Healing of the man at Bethesda. (John 5:1-9)
11. Healing the man with the withered hand. (Matthew 12:10-14)
12. Healing of the centurion's servant. (Matthew 8:5-13)
13. Raising the widow's son from the Nain. (Luke 7:11-15)
14. Casting out of the dumb and blind spirit. (Matthew 12:22)
15. Stilling the storm. (Matthew 8:23-27)
16. Healing the demoniac at Gadara. (Mark 5:1-11)
17. Healing the woman with the issue of blood. (Matthew 9:20)
18. The raising of Jairus' daughter. (Matthew 9:23-25)
19. Healing of the two blind men. (Matthew 20:30-34)
20. Casting out the speech impaired spirit. (Luke 11:14)

When you say the name, "Jesus," you say, "Miracle Man!"

APPLICATION:
    1. Study the miracles of Jesus carefully.
    2. Ask for the things you need or the things someone you know needs.

PRAYER:
Lord, thank you for being a miracle worker–yesterday, today and forever. Amen.

JUNE 29
THE MIRACLES OF JESUS, PART TWO

John 12:37
"But though he had done so many miracles before them,
yet they believed not on him." (KJV)

Here is the continuation of the miracles of Jesus in the New Testament.

21. Feeding of the 5,000. (Matthew 14:15-21)
22. Walking on the water. (Matthew 14:25-30; Mark 6:46)
23. Delivering the syrophoenician's daughter. (Matthew 15:22-28)
24. Healing the deaf and dumb man. (Mark 9:25)
25. Feeding the 4,000 plus. (Matthew 15:32-39)
26. Healing the blind man of Bethsaida. (Mark 8:22-25)
27. Casting the demon out of the lunatic boy. (Luke 4:31-37)
28. The coin in the fish's mouth. (Matthew 17:24-27)
29. Healing of the man born blind. (John 9:1-6)
30. Healing of the woman with 18 years infirmity. (Luke 13:11-13)
31. Healing the man with dropsy. (Matthew 9:1-8)
32. The raising of Lazarus. (John 11:25-44)
33. Cleansing of the 10 lepers. (Luke 17:11-19)
34. Healing of blind Bartimaeus. (Mark 10:46-50)
35. Cursing of the fig tree. (Mark 11:14-24)
36. Healing of Malchus' ear. (Luke 22:49-52)
37. Second draught of fishes. (John 21:3-11)
38. Jesus resurrected walked through doors. (John 20:19-21)
39. More miracles. (Matthew 15:30; 4:24; 8:16-17; 12:15; 14:14; Mark 7:37)

These are recorded miracles only. John 21:25 says, *"And there are also many other things which Jesus did, the which, if they should be written every one, I suppose that even the world itself could not contain the books that should be written. Amen."* (KJV) Then, there are the things He continues to do today. He is the same yesterday, today and forever. He is the sea walking, devil casting out, tomb raiding, great physician! He is the blood washing, sin forgiving, second-chance giving, Lord of glory! He is the Lamb of God and He has a miracle for you today!

APPLICATION:
1. Deal with any unbelief, which may have been placed in your heart concerning miracles.
2. Begin to meditate on God's Word for the miracles needed in the world you live in and seek God for a breakthrough.

PRAYER:
Lord, I act in faith, today, for a miracle. Amen.

Rick and I sowed $400 into the Shunemite offering @ Holy Spirit Conference last night. We are believing that God has supernaturally provided us with provision; miracle provision and opportunity. Yes, Lord, I act in faith, today, for our financial miracle. Amen 2018

JUNE 30
10 WAYS TO KEEP A HEALTHY MARRIAGE

Psalms 101:2
"I will try to walk a blameless path, but how I need your help, especially in my own home, where I long to act as I should." (TLB)

H. Norman Wright said, "Every person who comes into marriage is an amateur, and no couple who marries is ever compatible. It is a lifelong process of becoming compatible."

There is no doubt marriage is a work in progress. I have been married to my beautiful wife for nearly 30 years. Some days it is bliss. Some days it is... (Oh, well, my wife is probably going to read this).

Here are some helpful tips to keep a marriage healthy:

1. A healthy marriage is about surrender. When you realize you are in love with someone, their desires will be more important than your own.
2. A healthy marriage is about trust. Keeping your word proves over and over that when you say, "I love you," you really mean it.
3. A healthy marriage is about helping. When you do the little things to help the person you love, you benefit in the long run. Opening a car door, taking out the trash, etc. goes a long way.
4. A healthy marriage is about caring. When you love someone, you take their hurt upon yourself. Be sensitive to the hurts your spouse may have, both physically and emotionally.
5. A healthy marriage is about appreciation. Look for ways to show how much you appreciate your spouse. Cards, candy and flowers are good, but compliments are the most valued.
6. A healthy marriage is about giving your best. Make sure no one else gets what your spouse deserves.
7. A healthy marriage is about commitment. There is no such thing as a successful marriage. There are marriages that give up and marriages that keep trying. That is the only difference.
8. A healthy marriage is about spending time together. There is no substitute for time spent with a loved one.
9. Marriage is about learning to change. Making adjustments is the key to longevity in marriage.
10. Marriage is about sexual fulfillment. Be sure your spouse receives every consideration physically. This keeps lust for others from manifesting.

You can have a healthy marriage!

APPLICATION:
1. Do the things that are helpful for maintaining your marriage.
2. Put the needs of your spouse first, as you did when you dated.

PRAYER:
Lord, forgive me for not keeping my marriage healthy and help me to do so from this point forward. Amen.

JULY 1
HURRY UP AND WAIT

Habakkuk 2:1-4

*"I will climb up to my watchtower and stand at my guardpost. There I will wait
to see what the Lord says and how he will answer my complaint. Then the Lord
said to me, 'Write my answer plainly on tablets, so that a runner can carry the
correct message to others. This vision is for a future time. It describes the end,
and it will be fulfilled. If it seems slow in coming, wait patiently,
for it will surely take place. It will not be delayed.'"* (NLT)

Have you ever gone to the doctor sick and wanting relief? Then, when you
arrive, you are seated in the waiting room for what seems like a short eternity?
Then, when you see the doctor, he finds your problem, prescribes medication and
you get well. Although the waiting was not pleasant, you received the desired
result.

A waiting room can become a discovery room—a discovery of self. In I
Samuel 17:20, David discovered while he was waiting he would become more
than a shepherd of animals; he would be King. God makes the waiting well worth
it.

God's timetable is only realized by those who are patient. Bible patience is
listening until you hear what God is saying. When you listen, others can benefit
from what you hear. Light always comes when we wait on the Lord.

Are we afraid if we sit still for a few minutes, God might speak to us? Bill
Gothard said, "Patience is accepting a difficult situation without giving God a
deadline to remove it."

Some other insightful proverbs about waiting include: "Hasty climbers have
sudden falls," "A delay is better than a disaster," and "Have patience! All things
are difficult before they become easy."

When you are patient, God brings out the best. Patience is the bearer of lasting
things. It is the fruit producer of your life. Be patient when you find yourself in
God's waiting room.

APPLICATION:
1. If you have been impatient, place yourself in God's presence.
2. Use the time you are waiting to discover something about yourself.

PRAYER:
*Lord, forgive me for being impatient. Help me learn the things about me that I
need to learn. Amen.*

JULY 2
TIMING IS EVERYTHING

Psalms 37:7
"Be still before the LORD and wait patiently for him; do not fret when men succeed in their ways, when they carry out their wicked schemes." (NIV)

A young Christian man asked an older believer for prayer. "Will you please pray for me to become more patient?" he asked. The aged saint agreed. They knelt together and the elder man began to pray, "Lord, send this young man tribulation in the morning; send this young man tribulation in the afternoon; send this young man…" At that point the young Christian blurted out, "No, no! I didn't ask you to pray for tribulation! I wanted you to pray for patience!" "Ah," responded the wise Christian, "it's through tribulation that we learn patience."

Tribulation does not necessarily teach patience, but it does reveal whether we have it or not. Israel would not wait for the right leader, so they settled for Saul. We are all waiting for different things in our lives. However, God's delivery time can be trusted. Even if we seem to suffer a loss, it is only temporary. God has something better just ahead.

How can we stay patient while we are waiting for His timing? The secret is simple; we must find something else to do while waiting. Jesus took advantage of every moment of His life by welcoming opportunities. He never wasted His time. John the Baptist knew that he could not deliver Israel. He knew he did not have the whole answer. So, what could he do? He could make the way for Jesus to come. He did his part.

Patience is an aggressive posture and not a positive one. Someone said, "With patience, a well can be dug with a spoon." One of the most famous telegrams in all of history is the one sent by the French General, Marshall Foch, to headquarters. He telegraphed, "My right flank is crumbling; my left is totally blocked. Situation excellent. I attack!"

Patience takes you to the end. (Ecclesiastes 7:8-9) Trust God's timing!

APPLICATION:
1. Stay faithful in times of waiting.
2. Remind yourself God will bring something better.

PRAYER:
Lord, I will wait on you and trust your timing. Amen.

JULY 3
LAYING IT ON THE LINE

Romans 8:31-34
"So, what do you think? With God on our side like this, how can we lose? If God didn't hesitate to put everything on the line for us, embracing our condition and exposing himself to the worst by sending his own Son, is there anything else he wouldn't gladly and freely do for us? And who would dare tangle with God by messing with one of God's chosen?" (The Message)

Jesus laid everything He had on the line for us. He risked the throne of Heaven and even His eternal soul. He fully trusted the Father would keep His promise to raise Him from the dead, and save His people through Him. John 15:13 says, *"Greater love hath no man than this, that a man lay down his life for his friends."* (KJV)

We have to lay it all down. Your attitude should be the kind shown to us by Jesus Christ. (Philippians 2:6) Obedience is the key. Obedience means to willingly and entirely follow without any deviation. Judges 12 reveals 42,000 people lost their lives all because they failed to pronounce the letter, "H."

Sacrifice is always a part of service. The early Christians of Rome were slaughtered unmercifully, and yet, the Word went forward. Constantine adopted Christianity as the official religion. Because the early Christians were willing to give their lives, it transformed a nation for the cause of Christianity.

Additionally, we must pass the test of discipleship. A *disciple* is defined as a pupil or learner. A disciple is expected to study, learn, live and pass on the teachings of his master. Discipleship is following, constantly. It is devotion to the teachings and leadership of the teacher. There are four necessary steps of discipleship. The first is continuing in the Word. (John 8:31) The second is continuing in His love. (John 15:9) The third is continuing after Jesus' example. (Luke 14:27) The final step is continuing in faith. (Acts 14:22)

If we are to be convincing as believers, we must be willing to lay everything down for the cause of Christ. Are you willing?

APPLICATION:
1. Are you being completely obedient to Christ? If not, begin today!
2. As a believer in Christ, be willing to make necessary sacrifices.

PRAYER:
Lord, I submit to you and will lay down my life for you. Amen.

JULY 4
THE HEROES OF FREEDOM

Acts 22:28
"And the chief captain answered, With a great sum obtained I this freedom..."
(KJV)

As I have previously stated, I live in a military town. The prolific 101st Airborne Division is located just outside of our city, at Fort Campbell, Kentucky. I have a church full of past and present heroes. These heroes, and those who have gone before them, paid a high price for the freedom we enjoy.

There is no greater force on the earth than the force of freedom. It is costly, yet priceless. It is attainable, yet elusive. It is desirable, yet disagreeable.

In America, the thing driving young men and women to join the military is fierce devotion to the cause of freedom. Ronald Reagan said, "No arsenal, or no weapon in the arsenals of the world, is so formidable as the will and moral courage of free men and women."

For freedom to be attained and preserved, someone must do something heroic. Below is an actual letter sent to me from one of my members deployed overseas:

Pastor William, Greetings from sunny Iraq. As I sit here, I can only ponder on how good GOD is, and how HIS protection is endless. I fly to different camps within Iraq, and every time we take off, I thank HIM for HIS angels, HIS protection and HIS mercy. I am a firm believer that Psalms 91 is the ultimate scripture; it has not failed me because we have had several mortar attacks to our base, but it has not come near me. They usually detonate on the airfield, which is close to us, but they have not landed near my living quarters.

I give HIM all the glory! Praise HIS Holy name! Give my best to all, and continue to pray for all our service members, whether here or getting ready to deploy. Have a safe and Happy Fourth of July... Prayers to all.

Today, we should thank God for those who give away precious time with their families to assure our families will be able to taste freedom for generations to come.

APPLICATION:
1. Pray for those who are protecting the freedom we enjoy.
2. Do something good for a military family. Buy their meal, etc.

PRAYER:
Lord, thank you for this country and its many heroes! Guide and protect them. Amen.

JULY 5
MONEY, JESUS AND THE DISCIPLES

III John 1:2-3

"Beloved, I wish above all things that thou mayest prosper and be in health, even as thy soul prospereth. For I rejoice greatly when the brethren came and testified of the truth that is in thee, even as thou walkest in the truth." (KJV)

God is ready to do something big in your finances. You must change the way you think about finances before God can bring about a breakthrough. True Bible prosperity is when the whole man prospers. Part of that prosperity is definitely in our finances.

We have had extreme teaching about money in the modern Church for years. For the first 50 years of the 20th century, the teaching was poverty driven. The belief was God did not intend for us to have anything while we are on earth, only in Heaven. Then, the second half shifted to a prosperity gospel, which was, for the most part, self-centered and self-indulging. The belief was the more wealth and possessions a person had, then the more it boasted God's favor in his/her life. Both have error in them.

Still, it is what you see that determines what you get. It is similar to the rooster who had the hens follow him out behind the hen house, where he showed them an ostrich egg. He said, "I don't want to put any pressure on you, but I want to show you what others are doing!"

To get an accurate picture of what God wants for us, we do not need to look any further than His disciples. We have been taught Jesus and the disciples were poor, but were they? James and John had a shipping business with hired hands. (Mark 1:19-21) Peter and Andrew were successful fishermen. (Matthew 4:18) Matthew was a tax collector. (Matthew 9:9) Luke was a physician. (Colossians 4:14) The disciples had to be told not to take any money or valuables with them. (Luke 9:1-3, 6) The disciples went to buy meat. (John 4:8) Jesus had a traveling ministry with wealth and contributors. (Luke 8:1-2) Jesus had a house. (Luke 9:51-58; John 1:35-39) He had so much in the treasury that Matthew, a money expert, did not suspect Judas was stealing from it. (John 12:5-6) The disciples were amazed when told it was difficult for rich men to enter Heaven and asked, "Who then can be saved?" (Mark 10:21-31)

APPLICATION:
1. Consider the kind of prosperity God desires for you.
2. Do not let traditional teaching rob you of the truth.

PRAYER:
Lord, I receive the kind of prosperity you want for my life. Amen.

JULY 6
THE CALL TO OUR CULTURE

Mark 16:15-16
"And he said unto them, Go ye into all the world, and preach the gospel to every creature. He that believeth and is baptized shall be saved; but he that believeth not shall be damned." (KJV)

Jesus was giving a commission to His Church in Mark 16, not only the Church of that day, but also the Church of today. Many things have changed since Jesus' time on earth. However, one thing remains the same. Man still needs the Savior!

Jesus always used the surrounding culture to relate His message. He spoke of current events, customs and traditions to help people connect with the Gospel. He reached the lost by recognizing their culture. Culture gives us a point of contact with the lost. When Paul spoke to the Athenians at the Aeropagus, he found two points of contact with them based on popular culture. The first was a reference to "an unknown god." The second was a quote from one of their poets. (Acts 17) Christians who avoid popular culture lose valuable tools for building bridges with non-Christians. (I Corinthians 9:19-23)

Real excellence is recognized in any culture. Daniel and his friends learned all they could about their new culture, so they could do their work with excellence. Yet, while they learned, they maintained steadfast allegiance to God, and God gave them skill and wisdom. Daniel (Belteshazzar), Hananiah (Shadrach), Mishael (Meshach) and Azariah (Abednego) were selected and used by God to touch a king because of their understanding and cunningness for their day. (Daniel 1)

The world is not impressed with spiritual things, but carnal. They are respectful of natural abilities and knowledge. These things open them up to the spiritual. They will become more receptive to a person who couples natural skill with spiritual genius. They will grow to recognize how invaluable such a person can become in their own lives.

Culture is a gift from God. It sets each person apart and gives them an opportunity to be used by God. Whatever you do, recognize and highlight the uniqueness of those around you. When you do, the Gospel can be preached!

APPLICATION:
1. Become better acquainted with the interests of those you are witnessing to.
2. Spread the Gospel by connecting to the culture around you.

PRAYER:
Lord, reveal to me the things I need to know that will open up greater opportunities for me to witness for your Kingdom. Amen.

JULY 7
YOUR MONEY AND YOU

Proverbs 10:4
"He becometh poor that dealeth with a slack hand;
but the hand of the diligent maketh rich."
(KJV)

Money can, and should, be a blessing! Ecclesiastes 7:12 reveals money can be a defense. *"For wisdom is a defense, and money is a defense: but the excellency of knowledge is, that wisdom giveth life to them that have it."* (KJV) Ecclesiastes 10:18-20 says, *"By much slothfulness the building decayeth; and through idleness of the hands the house droppeth through. A feast is made for laughter, and wine maketh merry: but money answereth all things. Curse not the king, no not in thy thought; and curse not the rich in thy bedchamber: for a bird of the air shall carry the voice, and that which hath wings shall tell the matter."* (KJV)

Your money is also a blabbermouth. It reveals what your real priorities are. Matthew 6:20-24 says, *"But lay up for yourselves treasures in Heaven, where neither moth nor rust doth corrupt, and where thieves do not break through nor steal: For where your treasure is, there will your heart be also...No man can serve two masters: for either he will hate the one, and love the other; or else he will hold to the one, and despise the other. Ye cannot serve God and mammon (money)."* (KJV)

Once, on the popular 1970's and 1980's series, *Dallas*, J.R. Ewing said to his rival, Cliff Barnes, "I can outlast anything you throw at me because I have money and a lot of it!" While his arrogance and pride were way off, his point was valid. In this present world money is a necessity, albeit sometimes an evil thing.

However, money does not have to be evil. It takes on the personality of the person who has it. Twenty dollars can be spent on alcohol and pornography, or it can be given to a missionary or used to buy an article of clothing for a child. The unfortunate truth is we need money to live.

For far too long Christians have been hesitant to talk about money, and too often, ignorant of how to handle it. We need to understand God will help us handle our money, so it is a blessing and not a curse!

APPLICATION:
1. Let the Word of God teach you how to handle your money and finances.
2. Use your money to be a blessing.

PRAYER:
Lord, give me wisdom about my money and how to use it. Amen.

JULY 8
ATTITUDE CHECK

Ezekiel 38:10
"Thus saith the Lord GOD; It shall also come to pass, that at the same time shall things come into thy mind, and thou shalt think an evil thought:" (KJV)

Your attitude is your most important asset. Without a good attitude, you will never reach your full potential. Your attitude is the "and then some," which gives you the little, extra edge over those whose thinking is wrong. Walt Emerson said, "What lies behind us and what lies before us are tiny matters compared to what lies within us."

The 1983 Cos Report on American Business reported 94 percent of all Fortune 500 executives attributed his/her success more to attitude than to any other basic ingredient.

Robert Half International, a San Francisco consulting firm, recently asked vice-presidents and personnel directors at 100 of America's largest companies to name the single greatest reason for firing an employee. The responses were very interesting and underscore the importance of attitude in the business world. Thirty percent of the cases were due to incompetence. Seventeen percent were attributed to the inability to get along with others. Dishonesty or lying consisted of 12 percent. Ten percent were due to negative attitudes. Seven percent could be blamed for the failure or refusal to follow instruction. Another seven percent were due to the lack of motivation. Additional reasons made up the remaining eight percent. Notice, although incompetence ranked first on the list, the next five were all attitude problems!

When your attitude is under control, according to God's Word, nothing is beyond your reach. Joseph maintained a good attitude even though he was betrayed, lied on and entrapped. The result was his exaltation to the second most powerful person in the world.

Your attitude determines what you see and how you handle your feelings. These two factors greatly determine your success. Your destinies in life will never be determined by your complaining spirits or high expectations. Life is full of surprises and the adjustment of your attitudes is a life-long project.

APPLICATION:
1. Check your attitude.
2. Place your attitude before God.

PRAYER:
Lord, help me to keep my attitude in check. Amen.

213

JULY 9
ATTITUDE DETERMINES ALTITUDE

Proverbs 15:13
"A merry heart maketh a cheerful countenance: but by sorrow of the heart the spirit is broken." (KJV)

Renewal of the mind is changing your attitude to God's will for you. Norman Vincent Peale relates this story in his book *Power of the Plus Factor*: "Once walking through the twisted little streets of Hong Kong, I came upon a tattoo studio. In the window were displayed samples of the tattoos available. On the chest or arms you could have tattooed an anchor or flag or mermaid or whatever. But what struck me with force was three words that could be tattooed on one's flesh, 'Born to lose.' I asked the Chinese tattoo artist, 'Does anyone really have that terrible phrase, *Born to lose*, tattooed on his body?' He replied, 'Yes, sometimes.' 'But,' I said, 'I just can't believe that anyone in his right mind would do that.' The Chinese man simply tapped his forehead and in broken English said, 'Before tattoo on body, tattoo on mind!'"

An airplane is navigated by its attitude. As a matter of fact, the altitude of a plane is determined by its attitude. Its height is capped off when the attitude is adjusted downward.

It is the attitude, which makes the difference. People with negative thinking may start well, have a few good days and win a match. However, sooner or later, and it is usually sooner, their attitudes will pull them down.

We are responsible for our attitudes. Our destinies in life will never be determined by our complaining spirits or high expectations. Life is full of surprises and the adjustment of our attitude is a life-long project. John Maxwell, speaking of his father, Melvin Maxwell, said, "He has always been my hero. He is a leader's leader. One of his strengths is his positive attitude. Recently, Dad and Mom spent some time with my family. As he opened his briefcase, I noticed a couple of motivational attitude books. I said, 'Dad, you're 70 years old. You've always had a great attitude. Are you still reading that stuff?' He looked me in the eye and said, 'Son, I have to keep working on my thought life. I am responsible to have a great attitude and maintain it. My attitude does not run on automatic.'"

APPLICATION:
1. Be sure your attitude reflects your desires.
2. Protect what you think at all costs!

PRAYER:
Lord, forgive me for harboring a wrong attitude. Amen.

JULY 10
MODESTY IS THE BEST POLICY

Romans 12:3
"For I say, through the grace given unto me, to every man that is among you,
not to think of himself more highly than he ought to think;
but to think soberly…" (KJV)

I heard a story of Christian Herter, who was running hard for reelection as governor of Massachusetts. One day he arrived late at a barbeque. He had not eaten all day and was famished. He joined the others in the serving line, eagerly receiving the succulent spread of tasty food. When he got to the place where the chicken was being served, he held out his plate and received one piece of chicken. The governor graciously spoke to the server and said, "Excuse me, do you mind if I get another piece of chicken? I am very hungry." The woman replied, "Sorry, I'm supposed to give one piece to each person." He repeated, "But I am starved," and again she said, "Only one to a customer." Herter, who was known by most as a normally modest man, decided this was the time to use the weight of his office and title, and said, "Madam, do you know who I am? I am the governor of this state." She replied, "Do you know who I am? I am the lady in charge of the chicken. Move along, mister!"

Sometimes, we need to be reminded we are not any better than those around us. When we begin to enjoy a little success, it is easy to lose sight of where we have come from. We can become demanding of others in ways that we formerly despised. We can forget what it was once like to be looked down upon and stepped on.

Jesus was a prime example of someone who had a right to demand special attention and comforts. Instead, He chose to make His life a one of consideration for others. He even humbled Himself and demonstrated to the disciples the way to gain favor in God's Kingdom by washing their feet, including Judas, just a short time before His betrayal, denial and crucifixion.

The next time you have the opportunity to flex your credentials, choose the road of modesty. It may be a seldom traveled road, but remember Jesus once walked there.

APPLICATION:
1. Be sure you choose modesty over being preferred.
2. Find someone "lower" than you and find a way to exalt them.

PRAYER:
Lord, I choose to walk the road of modesty that you have walked before me. Teach me honor and how to prefer others before myself. Amen.

JULY 11
BACK TO THE FUTURE

Ecclesiastes 1:9-10
"The thing that hath been, it is that which shall be; and that which is done is
that which shall be done: and there is no new thing under the sun. Is there any
thing whereof it may be said, See, this is new? It hath been already
of old time, which was before us." (KJV)

The ultra popular movie trilogy of the late 1980's, *Back to the Future*, was based on the premise of a young man, Marty McFly, played by Michael J. Fox, and a wacky professor, Doc Brown, played by Christopher Lloyd, who found a way to travel back in time in a DeLorean. They were able to go back in time and altar some events, thus changing the future. However, they discovered altering the past did not always help the future.

What would happen if we could go back in time? What would we change? The truth is if we were to alter even some of the bad things in our past, we would severely cripple ourselves from being formed and molded into the person we need to be.

Our past, good or bad, is a critical part of who we are. From it, we have emerged to be who we are today. God accepted us in the state we were in, fallen, broken and weak. He forgave us for our past, but encouraged us to use it as a testimony of His greatness.

Our testimony is one of the most powerful weapons we have as believers. Revelation 12:11 says, *"And they overcame him by the blood of the Lamb, and by the word of their testimony..."* (KJV) I see an equation in this scripture. His blood, plus our testimony, equals Satan's defeat! The enemy has no defense against our testimony because it always glorifies God. Then, we can always point to our future. Our future is sealed in Him. We have a rendezvous with destiny. We will be received into Heaven when our bodies wear out. We will rule and reign with Him on the earth for 1,000 years. We will spend eternity with Him.

There is no question; our future is bright. So, the next time Satan tries to discourage you, remind him about his future compared to yours! Go back to the future!

APPLICATION:
1. Consider your future in Heaven with Christ.
2. Use your past to testify of His greatness.

PRAYER:
Lord, I know you have a great future for me. Thank you! Amen.

JULY 12
ARE YOU BEARING FRUIT?

John 15:8
"Herein is my Father glorified, that ye bear much fruit; so shall ye be my disciples." (KJV)

Jesus held membership in the world's "oldest profession." No, not what you are thinking! The oldest profession was declared by God in Genesis 2:15, when the first human being was put in the garden and ordered to "tend and till the garden." What is the world's oldest profession? Gardening. Jesus' parables were drenched in gardening parallels.

What is real Bible fruit? According to John 15:16, it is fruit that remains. When everyone else around you falters in their walk with God, you continue to produce what He has called you to do. You keep multiplying what God places in your hand. It is fruit for others. Kenneth Copeland once said, "It's only what you do for others that really matters." He was right. Fruit trees do not bear fruit to sustain their own lives, but to sustain others.

There are byproducts of those who are fruit-bearers. Their prayers are answered. If your prayers are not being answered over a prolonged time, then you are not being a fruit-bearer. Do not follow people who do not get answers to their prayers. Fruit-bearers keep bearing fruit even when the season is hot and dry. When tests and trials come, they do not stop or cut off the supplier of their strength. They keep themselves nourished in the Word of God. The way they keep His Word alive in them is to constantly feed themselves with the Word. They continuously bask in the glow of His Spirit. By doing this, they are abiding in Him. The branch cannot live over a sustained time without being attached to the vine.

What will God do to help you bear fruit? He will prune you back by taking off all dead, decaying and unproductive pieces, so you will bear more fruit. God desires for you to be a fruit filled tree with plenty to give away and plenty to enjoy!

APPLICATION:
1. Be sure you are bearing fruit in all seasons.
2. Keep yourself in His presence, today and everyday, by being an extension of who He is.

PRAYER:
Lord, I desire to bear much fruit. Thank you for using me. Amen.

JULY 13
THE STORY OF SACRIFICE

Psalms 50:5-6
"Gather my saints together unto me; thou that have made a covenant with me by sacrifice. And the Heavens shall declare his righteousness: for God is judge himself. Selah." (KJV)

People who pay the price have a story to tell. There is a place in the Swiss Alps called the Halfway House. It is located halfway up the mountains. It is a place where those who decide to climb to the top can stop and make a decision to either go for it, or rest and go back down. Many who arrive there see the fireplace, food and comfort, and think, "We will just stay here." The rest put on the gear and get ready to make the sacrifice. The ones left behind make fun of those continuing the climb for a little while. Then, they look at the top of the mountain. They can see in the distance those who have gone on. They begin to feel badly about not continuing. The next day the ones who made it to the top, come back and pick up their friends who were left behind. They are so excited to go back down to tell their story of sacrifice and victory. The others are ashamed to go back and tell their story. What story do you tell?

Without sacrifice there is no lasting success. What you sow is what you reap. There is a decision we must make, either, "I'll pay now, or I'll play now." The "I'll play now" attitude says, "I'll play now" and later in life, look back and wonder, "What happened?" It looks for success without sacrifice. The "I'll pay now" attitude looks around later in life and says, "I'm grateful I paid the price." It realizes that with real sacrifice comes lasting success.

For the journey to be memorable and significant there must be sacrifice. The degree of sacrifice determines the degree of success and the sweetness thereof. When Olympians win, they have an exhilarating reaction. Why? Because they have sacrificed all of their life. The greatest joy comes from those who have made the great sacrifice.

You can play it safe or you can go to the top, if you are willing to sacrifice. So, what will your story be?

APPLICATION:
1. Do not get discouraged by the sacrifices you make.
2. Remember, the prize is for those who dare to climb to the top.

PRAYER:
Lord, I will sacrifice what is required of me with your help. Amen.

218

Wisdom is knowing when God wants us to retract and when He wants us to go back down the mountain and to forge ahead. 2018

JULY 14
BUILDING GOD'S HOUSE

II Samuel 7:5
"Go and tell my servant David, 'This is what the LORD says: Are you the one to build me a house to dwell in?'" (NIV)

An elderly couple willed a considerable amount of money to a church. Their lawyer said, "Why you could take a nice trip around the world instead." The elderly woman replied, "Yes, but we've seen all of this world that we want to see. That church is the place where our kids were taught, loved, prayed for, baptized, married and met Jesus in. Even though we may not live to see it, we want other children, like ours, to have the same opportunity."

I can remember when our church built its first building. It was such a time of joy, accomplishment and hard work. We had rented or leased buildings for the first 12 years of our existence. The buildings we occupied were old, worn and never intended to be houses of worship. In addition, they never really felt like home because we knew we did not own them. When the time and place were right, God opened the doors for us to finally buy instead of lease.

We discovered some truths about buying when we built. First, projects do not have a meaning; people have meaning. We were investing in lives, not things. Second, this was a defining moment in our lives. This edifice would outlast all of us and stand as a testimony of faith to our heirs. Third, our hearts focused on the Lord. David's project was the temple, but his heart was on ministering unto the Lord. David never even saw the temple built (Solomon, his son, did). Yet, David dedicated himself fully to the building of it. Fourth, it was a divine mission. It did not come out of a man driven idea, but was God driven to build up God. It is not for the pastor or staff, but for God. Fifth, we benefit more from ownership. God entrusts us with a church and His ministry, not only because of what we do for His Kingdom, but because of what it does for us. Finally, it becomes your church, not the church.

If you rent something, you do not treat it the same as if you own it. Are you more observing, caring and protective of your children or someone else's? Of course, the answer is your children. They are yours. If you are ever invited to help build God's house where you attend, be committed and understand you are building God a house!

APPLICATION:
1. If you have made a vow to a building program, keep it!
2. Support the leadership when a building program is ongoing.

PRAYER:
Lord, I will do my part in building you a house when asked. Amen.

219

JULY 15
DEVELOPING A GREAT LOVE FOR GOD

Psalms 40:16
"Let all those that seek thee rejoice and be glad in thee: let such as love thy salvation say continually, The LORD be magnified." (KJV)

God is looking for love from you. He has already acted first by offering you His unconditional love. He took His love to the level of providing a blood covenant. He spoke first. He acted first. He loved first. He is waiting for you to respond. He is listening. He is watching. How you respond in love is paramount. The power of God is hidden in the covenant of His love to you and your love to Him. The degree of success you enjoy is dependent on your understanding and response. Love is only truly enjoyed and appreciated when it is reciprocated. Love must be put on display. Love is not ashamed to make a public proclamation. The amount of love you have determines how intimate you become.

For us, as believers, it comes down to what we desire. The secret is in the desire to love Him and to know Him. The degree of our desire will determine how far our love for Him will take us.

When you examine scripture, there were varying degrees of love shown to God by His people. The children of Israel were in love with God, as long as things were going good. When things became unsettled, so did their love.

Jesus also experienced inconsistent displays of love. There were 70 appointed disciples, but we hear very little from them. Apparently, they were not willing to make the sacrifice to sit, surrender and serve. The 12 were willing to follow until Jesus needed them most at the cross. Only John was there.

The most revealing question Jesus asked after His resurrection was directed at Peter. Three times he asked, "Peter, do you love me?" "Are you willing to risk everything to show your love for me?" He is asking you the same question, today. He is asking, "Do you love me?"

APPLICATION:
1. Ask yourself honestly, today, "How is my love life for God?"
2. If you are lacking, check your desire for God and adjust.

PRAYER:
Lord, I desire to fall in love with you again. Stir that desire in me. Amen.

JULY 16
DON'T WORRY, BE HAPPY

Psalms 84:4-5
"How happy are those who can live in your Temple, singing your praises. Happy are those who are strong in the LORD, who want above all else to follow your footsteps. When they walk through the Valley of Weeping, it will become a place of springs where pools of blessing and refreshment collect after rains!" (TLB)

Happiness is much more than a feeling. Each Beatitude (the blessings listed by Jesus in the Sermon on the Mount in Matthew 5:3-11) tells how to be blessed and not necessarily happy. To be blessed means more than happiness. It implies the fortunate or enviable state of those who are in God's Kingdom. In both the Old and New Testaments, the word *blessed* is the same as the word *happy*. In Psalms 144:12-15, *happy* is Hebrew of *esher*, which means blessed and to progress.

There is a difference in striving for excellence and striving for perfection. It does not take long for us to learn things will not necessarily make us happy. Below are seven things, which cannot make you happy:

1. The pursuit of money. I Timothy 6:6 says, *"But godliness with contentment is great gain."* (NIV)
2. Pursuit of another person. John Powell said, "One of the most persistent and widely believed delusions is that one person can make another happy. You cannot confer on me the fullness of life. That has to be my choice."
3. Fame. Saul wanted popularity, but his character was not strong enough to handle the responsibilities accompanying it.
4. Personal achievement, such as passing a test, etc. There will always be another test.
5. Things. Things also bring with them emptiness.
6. Power. Power comes with responsibilities, which can be overwhelming and steal away precious time with family and friends.
7. Praise of other people. People's praise often has a string attached to it. It can turn from praise to criticism in just a moment's time.

Happiness, the Bible way, involves the willingness to accept God's Word and to alter our lifestyles to its statutes. Happiness held is the seed; happiness shared is the flower.

APPLICATION:
1. Consider what makes you happy.
2. Thank God for what you have and help those who have not.

221

PRAYER:
Lord, I will not worry. Instead, I will trust your Word and be happy! Amen.

July 17, 2018. Enjoying a little vacation in Orlando. Church mergers and phone loan modifications and my official job offer from tutoring all hung in the balance. Yet I will be joyful in all circumstances! All circumstances!

JULY 17
FILLED WITH JOY

John 16:22, 24
"And ye now therefore have sorrow: but I will see you again, and your heart shall rejoice, and your joy no man taketh from you...Hitherto have ye asked nothing in my name: ask, and ye shall receive, that your joy may be full." (KJV)

There were two very elderly ladies who were out for a drive. The lady driving the car came to a stop sign and sped right through it without stopping. The passenger did not say anything, but thought to herself, "She must not have seen that stop sign." They came to the next stop sign, and the lady driving did the same thing. She sped right through the stop sign again without stopping. The passenger lady once again did not say anything and thought to herself, "She must need better glasses." They came to yet another stop sign, and the driver did the same thing. She sped through the stop sign without stopping. This time, the passenger lady had enough and said, "Do you not realize you have run the last three stop signs?" The driver responded, "Oh! Am I driving?"

How is your joy today? The words joy and rejoice are used over 400 times in the Bible. The Hebrew language has more words for it than any other. There are 13 Hebrew root words. They are all tied to participation in religious expression. Unlike other Eastern religions, which call for solemness and self-debasement, Bible joy comes from the Greek word, *sim-kaw*, which means "delight, gladness, relief, blithersomeness; rejoice, festivity, elation, satisfaction and ecstacy," in other words, party!

The world today is crying out for joy, but they do not know where to look for it. There are more comedy clubs, comedians and whole television networks devoted to cartoons and comedy than ever. However, people go home from the clubs in the same, sad condition and turn off the TV with the same, hopeless situations.

The truth is when you become a born-again believer, joy is infused into your spirit. It is more than worldly happiness. It is the state of being secure in God with knowledge He is looking out for you in all circumstances. So, is it not time to fill up with joy?

APPLICATION:
1. Remind yourself, joy is already in your heart.
2. Decide to "bring it out" by meditating on His love and His Word.

PRAYER:
Lord, I purposely stir up the joy within me! Amen.

JULY 18
REAL AND LASTING JOY

Psalms 126:4-5
"Turn again our captivity, O LORD, as the streams in the south. They that sow in tears shall reap in joy." (KJV)

What is real and lasting joy? It is the happy state which results from knowing and serving God. When you find God, joy comes rushing in. It is not dependent on external circumstances. Philippians 4:4 says, *"Rejoice in the Lord always, and again I say rejoice!"* (KJV) Paul wrote this verse from jail. When you live in the joy of the Lord, you are fulfilled and are always fulfilling His desire for your life!

Why is it so important for God's people to be in joy? First, it is your strength. (Nehemiah 8:10) In the Hebrew it means safety or harbor. It maintains you securely. Second, it is the key to winning others. Psalms 51:12-13 says, *"Restore unto me the joy of my salvation; and uphold me with thy free (generous) spirit. Then I will teach transgressors thy ways; and sinners shall be converted unto thee."* (KJV) Third, it brings the answers of God. Ecclesiastes 5:20 says, *"For he shall not much remember the days of his life; because God answereth him in the joy of his heart."* (KJV) Fourth, your harvest is dependent on your joy. Joel 1:11 says, *"Be ye ashamed, O ye husbandmen; howl, O ye vinedressers, for the wheat and for the barley; because the harvest of the field is perished. The vine is dried up, and the fig tree languisheth...even all the trees of the field, are withered: because joy is withered away from the sons of men."* (KJV) Last, joy works when you are in trouble. James 1:2 says, *"Count it all joy when you fall into divers temptations."* (KJV)

The best part of joy is it will help you finish. Let Hebrews 12:2 show you the way, *"Looking unto Jesus, the author and finisher of our faith who for the joy that was set before Him endured the cross, despising the shame, and is set down at the right hand of the throne of God. For consider him that endured such contradiction of sinners against himself, lest ye be wearied and faint in your minds."* (KJV)

Jesus used joy to finish strong, and so can you! That is real and lasting joy!

APPLICATION:
1. Be sure you do not let your circumstances steal your joy.
2. When things are bad, you need to find a way to rejoice anyway.

PRAYER:
Lord, I will rejoice in you at all times! I will start the day and finish the day with joy! Amen.

JULY 19
DO NOT LOSE YOUR JOY

Isaiah 12:3
"Therefore with joy shall ye draw water out of the wells of salvation." (KJV)

Jerry Savelle wrote a great book many years ago entitled, *If the Devil Can't Steal Your Joy, He Can't Get Your Goods.* This book opened my eyes to a startling revelation. As long as I maintained my joy, I was able to stop the assaults of Satan. However, when I got into pity and depression, I lost ground.

If joy was placed in us at the moment of salvation, why do we not keep it? How do we lose our joy? There are a few things that will steal your joy away. The first is our circumstances. We can be joyful in spite of our circumstances. If we fix our hearts on who we belong to and serve, then despite the troubles, we will discover joy. Joy is looking ahead and believing in a good end, just as Jesus did at the cross. (Hebrews 12:2) The next way is the inability to cope with life. Suicide rates during the Great Depression increased from 14 to 17 per 100 thousand people. Depression paints a dark picture that shows no way of becoming bright. We must remember He is Light and the Light of men. The next way is stress. When people get stressed, they turn to anything giving them release. They try drugs, alcohol or anything that will sedate the problem. We, as believers, can get answers. The fourth way is the lack of relationship with God. No man backslides suddenly. Someone may say, "Yes, I did!" No. The thoughts were already there, but were not dealt with. Do not be fooled by Satan, your God will make a way. The next way is sin. David said, *"Restore unto me the joy of thy salvation."* (Psalms 51:12 KJV) The next way is the hardening of the heart. It will cause you to be unreceptive to the Word of God, which is life. You will turn to philosophical attitudes. Someone said, "Philosophy is a stud which enables a man to be unhappy more intelligently."

How do we get our joy back if we have lost it? The first way is by being around someone who has it. Reach out to someone else. Marilyn Monroe was clinching a phone when she died. The next way is by being in God's presence. Psalms 16:11 says, *"In thy presence is fullness of joy!"* (KJV) Focus on the good things of God. Acts 27:22 says, *"I exhort you to be of good cheer."* (KJV) Do not lose your joy!

APPLICATION:
1. If you are hurting, reach out to God for joy, today.
2. Keep your focus on Him and not your circumstances.

PRAYER:
Lord, I will rejoice in you always, and again I say rejoice! Amen.

JULY 20
GOD'S GLORY IN YOU

Haggai 2:9
"The glory of this latter house shall be greater than the former, saith the LORD of hosts: and in this place will I give peace, saith the LORD of hosts." (KJV)

God has always desired to dwell with His creation. However, in the Garden of Eden man lost that close intimacy. Consequently, God's glory was removed from man and was placed in objects until Pentecost.

The Tabernacle was God's presence with people. (Moses) The temple was God's people in His presence. (Solomon) When the Spirit came, it became God's presence in the temple of the people. (Jesus and us) The tabernacle is no longer horizontal, but vertical.

We need His glory manifesting in our lives. The glory brings His presence. In II Chronicles 5:13, the cloud filled the house when the glory came. The cloud was the container of the glory. It manifested as a cloud by day and fire by night. The cloud and fire were significant symbols. The cloud represented a shelter from the heat. According to I Corinthians 10:1-2, the cloud also provided moisture. It served as a guide to lead the way. (Numbers 10:33-36) Failure to follow could be drastic. (Numbers 14:39-45) The fire was present at night for protection. It was also present for light. They did not move until the pillar did. (Numbers 9:15-23) It should be the same with us today.

God knows our journey is filled with uncertainty and danger. This is why He has given us His glory in the latter days in the form of His Holy Spirit. We are the containers of His glory now. (II Corinthians 4:1-7) The same glory, which produced light in darkness, has illuminated us, so that we may walk in the presence of God at all times.

When His glory is present, so are His blessings. His glory contains our supply. The word *kaw-bawd* is translated as glory, meaning wealth, fame and supply! Not only do we experience His rich presence, He breaks the hold of the curse on our lives when His glory is present. We must be sure to cut our ties with this world more often and invite Him into our world. Then, we will have this wonderful glory in our house!

APPLICATION:
1. Find a few minutes, today, to invite His glory into you.
2. Let His glory transform you!

PRAYER:
Lord, activate the glory in me and surround me as well. Amen.

JULY 21
WHAT HAPPENS WHEN THE SPIRIT MOVES

Acts 4:31

"And when they had prayed, the place was shaken where they were assembled together; and they were all filled with the Holy Ghost, and they spake the Word of God with boldness." (KJV)

When God's Spirit moves, tremendous things happen, which do not occur at other times. God speaks when the Spirit moves! In the Garden, God spoke after the Spirit moved on the face of the deep. The result was light. In Matthew 3, God spoke from Heaven about Jesus, after the Spirit moved in the form of a dove.

The Spirit of the Lord brings wisdom, understanding, knowledge and the fear of the Lord. A.W. Tozer said, "God's thoughts belong to the world of spirit, man's to the world of intellect, and while spirit can embrace intellect, the human intellect can never comprehend spirit."

The Book of Isaiah gives some wonderful insight into what happens when the Spirit of God moves or is present. Isaiah 32:15 shows the Spirit of the Lord brings abundance. Isaiah 34:16 shows us the Spirit of the Lord carries out God's Word. Isaiah 40:13 reveals the Spirit of the Lord is the Master Counselor. Isaiah 44:3-5 reveals through the Spirit, God's true children will thrive. Isaiah 48:16 tells us the Spirit of the Lord sent Isaiah to prophesy. Isaiah 61:1 tells us God's servants (Isaiah and Jesus) were appointed by the Spirit to proclaim the Good News. Isaiah 63:10-11 says the Spirit of the Lord was grieved because of God's people. Isaiah 63:14 says the Spirit of the Lord gives rest.

When the Spirit of God moves, everyone is affected. (Jeremiah 31:12-15) When the Spirit flows, the enemy loses his grip. The moving of the Spirit removes sorrow. The moving of the Spirit causes prophetic things to happen. (II Peter 1:21)

We must place ourselves more in an atmosphere where God's Spirit is free to move. *"...where the Spirit of the Lord is, there is liberty."* (II Corinthians 3:17 KJV)

APPLICATION:
1. Ask God for the moving of His Spirit more in your life and your daily affairs.
2. Shut off other distractions and place yourself in His presence.

PRAYER:
Lord, fill me with your Spirit and show me what you want me to see. Amen.

JULY 22
HOW TO HEAR FROM GOD

Jeremiah 29:11-13

"I alone know the plans I have for you, plans to bring you prosperity and not disaster, plans to bring about the future you hope for. Then you will call to me. You will come and pray to me, and I will answer you. You will seek me, and you will find me because you will seek me with all your heart." (TEV)

After being in ministry well over 30 years, the number one question people ask me by far is, "How can I hear from God and know it is God?" God desires to reveal His plan for your life to you. God wants to speak to you. You want to listen.

Mary discovered it was necessary to sit and listen at His feet. (Luke 10:41-42) There is a difference between hearing and listening. Listening is wanting to hear!

I noticed in my own life, when I made it a priority to desire to listen and learn from God, He began to reveal Himself to me. It was not long before I heard His voice clearly, made some changes in my plans and my life, and His blessings manifested.

However, there are hindrances to hearing from God. First of all, there is neglect. (Hebrews 1:1-14) We are "too busy." We just do not set aside time for God to speak to us. If you are a young Christian, there is inexperience. (I Samuel 3:1-9) Samuel did not yet know the voice of the Lord. This is why we must spend more time in His presence. Then, there is sin. Sin separates, always! It causes a disconnect from God's voice. Isaiah 59:1-2 says, *"Behold the LORD'S hand is not shortened, that it cannot save; neither his ear heavy that it cannot hear: But your iniquities have separated between you and your God, and your sins have hid his face from you, that he will not hear."* (KJV) Then, there is bad company. People, who do not know God, cannot hear what He says. (I Corinthians 15:33) Also, not trusting what God has already done for you in the past. (Romans 15:4) Pay attention to patterns. Finally, and most importantly, there is no time spent in the Word. God and His Word are one. (John 1) God wants to speak to you. Be sure you are listening!

APPLICATION:
1. Ask God to speak to you.
2. Be alert and ready to hear what He is saying and obey Him!

PRAYER:
Lord, I desire to hear from you. Speak into my life! Amen.

JULY 23
ANSWER THE CALL

Jeremiah 33:3
*"Call unto me, and I will answer thee, and shew thee great and mighty things,
which thou knowest not."* (KJV)

God is speaking. The question is, are we listening? If we call on God in faith, He always returns the call. We must position ourselves where we can hear what He is saying, but how do we do this? I believe there are at least seven ways to listen and hear from God.

1. By ministering unto Him. (I Samuel 3:1-9) Through praise, worship and thanksgiving. Samuel waited in the presence of God in the temple and God began to speak. When we worship, we condition our hearts to be sensitive to God's voice.
2. Through other mature Christians. (I Samuel 3:5-6, 8) Eli had to explain to Samuel who was speaking to him. Being around other Christians who walk with God helps to sharpen our listening skills.
3. By testing the Spirit. (I John 4:1) What are the motives behind what you see and hear around you? Is it consistent? What is God doing? Is it persistent? Will this bless God and His people? Be sensitive to Him only.
4. You must submit to His Lordship: spirit, mind and body. Samuel said, "Here am I," over and over. (I Samuel 1-3) When you make Him Lord and not just Savior, your heart becomes His.
5. Having faith in God will speak to you. (Romans 10:9-13) When you operate in faith, God responds in a way, which is easily discernable.
6. Obey when God speaks. (Luke 5:1-8) When Peter obeyed Jesus, he received his greatest catch ever. God will speak. The more you obey what He says, the more often He will speak.
7. Prayer. There is no substitute for prayer. (John 15:7) Prayer is speaking God's Word back to Him. He responds by removing the obstacles in your life and confirms who He is inside of you.

We are in a time of mass communication. More than ever, we need to hear from Heaven. We need to get the mind of God over our lives. He is calling to us. We need to answer the call!

APPLICATION:
1. Ask God to speak to you in a way you can hear. *YES!*
2. Fine tune your listening skills by shutting off all distractions.

PRAYER:

Lord, I want to hear and obey your voice. Show me the way! Amen.

JULY 24
HOW MUCH FAITH DO YOU HAVE?

Deuteronomy 32:20
*"And he said, I will hide my face from them, I will see what their end shall be:
for they are a very forward (Perverse) generation, children in whom is no faith."*
(KJV)

It seems like everywhere you look, people are in a panic. Presently, as I am writing this, the stock market is bouncing up and down, unemployment is mounting and corporations are folding. No one seems to know what to do. The politicians even admit they are not sure what the next move should be. There seems to be little faith in the future.

It is times like these our faith is revealed. There is one stable, unchanging force we have at our disposal, the Word of God! Job outlined the perils, but also the remedy in Job 23:8-12, *"Behold, I go forward, but he is not there; and backward, but I cannot perceive him: On the left hand, where he doth work, but I cannot behold him: he hideth himself on the right hand, that I cannot behold him...But he knoweth the way that I take: when he hath tried me, I shall come forth as gold. My foot hath held his steps, his way have I kept, and not declined... Neither have I gone back from the commandment of his lips; I have esteemed the words of his mouth more than my necessary food."* (KJV)

The word *necessary* is *khoke*, which means "prescribed portion." Until the Word of God becomes your necessary food, you will never put it in your mouth at a time of need in faith. Faith speaks only what the Word says. The pressure is on the Word, not you.

The reality is the Word is already settled. (Psalms 89) If we base our faith on His Word, we will see it fade away.

"Faith is the substance of things hoped for..." (Hebrews 11:1 KJV) It is driven by things, which are not yet visible, but counted as done. Abraham was the father of faith. He believed without evidence which was deemed righteous. No matter what the outside conditions may be, faith is able to see through the storm and see the safety on the other side. So, how does your faith measure up?

APPLICATION:
1. Spend more time this week in the Word and meditate on what God can do.
2. Fast some meals. Decide to feast on His Word and make it your necessary food!

PRAYER:
Lord, I purposely feast on your Word and see my faith increase! Amen.

231

JULY 25
NEW BEGINNINGS

Psalms 77:11-12
"I will remember the works of the LORD: surely I will remember thy wonders of old. I will meditate also of all thy work, and talk of thy doings." (KJV)

I remember the last service we held in our old building downtown, which we occupied for eight years. The building was an old, abandoned police building. We had finally built a new building on our property on the edge of the city on Interstate 24. It marked a new beginning for our congregation. Still, it was a little bittersweet.

When God moves us to something new, it is time for reflection. There are three things we need to do: First, we need to look at the beginning. Job 8:7 says, *"Though thy beginning was small, yet thy latter end should greatly increase."* (KJV) It is so important to reflect on the beginning days. When we started the church, we had eight members. When we moved into the old police building, we had 70. When we moved eight years later, we had 1,200! Those early days were hard, but they were precious. God built something inside of us, which could not have been built any other way. Second, look at how far we have come: the accomplishments, the victories, the memories and the distance we have traveled. II Corinthians 8:10 says, *"And herein I give my advice: for this is expedient for you, who have begun before, not only to do, but also be forward a year ago."* (KJV) We must consider the lessons we have learned. Third, we must look at where we are going. What does the future hold? What is our vision, our hopes, dreams, goals and purpose? Hebrews 12:1 says, *"Wherefore seeing we also are compassed about with so great a cloud of witnesses, let us lay aside every weight, and the sin which doth so easily beset us, and let us run with patience the race that is set before us..."* (KJV) We are stronger because of what we have overcome. We are thankful for what we have enjoyed. We are humbled by the things entrusted to us. We are excited for the things He has laid before us. We are ready for a new beginning.

APPLICATION:
1. Before you move on, be sure to reflect on where you have been.
2. Carry the lessons from the past into your future.

PRAYER:
Lord, thank you for my history. Lead me into my destiny. Amen.

232

JULY 26
SURVIVOR OR OVERCOMER

I John 5:4-5

"For whatsoever is born of God overcometh the world: and this is the victory that overcometh the world, even our faith. Who is he that overcometh the world, but he that believeth that Jesus is the Son of God." (KJV)

The vast majority of Christians are survivors and not overcomers. They barely get by and seem to always fall for the same old tricks of the Devil. Yet, God has declared we should be overcomers.

To *survive* means "keep alive, continue to live, subsist, last, hang on, extant, exist." While there are many seasons of our lives, during which we have to do what we can just to survive, it is not how God wants us to live.

There are certain characteristics of people who are survivors. First, survivors would rather compromise than maintain a conviction. They will not take the heat for what they believe. They make acceptable decisions rather than God decisions. Next, survivors would rather take a poll than take a stand. They are trendy. They are afraid of being cut off from the crowd. Third, survivors would rather be luke-warm than hot. Hot people burn people. Lukewarm feels good to everybody and does not stir others. Fourth, survivors are faithful to dead causes instead of being fruitful to God's causes. Only what you do for the Kingdom will stand. If it is not bearing fruit, cut it off. Next, survivors are only into the things of God for the blessing and not the sacrifice. They are takers. As long as things are good, they serve God, but when things become hard they cave in. Finally, survivors would rather appear religious than move in the Spirit. There is a cost to moving in the Spirit. Yet, whatever you compromise to keep, you will lose.

However, an overcomer is someone who dedicates him/herself to doing things God's way. They are not concerned with short-lived victories. They are determined to be transformed into something new. Overcomers achieve and keep the upper hand on their flesh to win in Christ. Are you a survivor or an overcomer?

APPLICATION:
1. Be certain you have the mentality of an overcomer.
2. Do not settle for existence. Live!

PRAYER:
Lord, I confess I am an overcomer. I am not just a survivor. Amen.

233

JULY 27
T.G.I.F.

Ephesians 5:15-16
"Look therefore carefully how ye walk, not as unwise, but as wise; redeeming the time because the days are evil." (ASV)

It seems everyone gets excited about one day of the week—Friday! We start looking ahead on Monday and making plans on Tuesday. Friday represents being finished with work and being able to rest, relax or celebrate on the weekends. Friday means we have come to the end of our work. However, what have we done?

By the time you reach the age of 75, the clocks and watches of this world will have ticked away a total of nearly 2.5 billion seconds! Our precious time on earth is ticking away. Yet, how do we value it?

Bernard Berenson, an internationally famous art critic, had a zest for life. Even when he was in ill health, he cherished every moment. Shortly before he died at age 94, he said to a friend, "I would willingly stand at the street corners, hat in hand, asking the passersby to drop their unused minutes into it." We need to appreciate the value of time.

We have to make the most of the time we are given. We are living in the most prophetic time period in history. Everything that needs to be in place before the return of the Lord is either in place or in a position to be in place in a short time. Time in this present age is running out. The daylight is beginning to fade to dusk. It is almost night.

It is time to get the harvest in. It is time for bringing in the lost, hurt, discouraged and disillusioned. When Jesus said, *"Go into the world and preach the Gospel,"* there were 500 people present and only 12 preachers. (Mark 16:15 NKJV) The laymen were to do the work of the ministry. It is time for all of the "farmhands" to get into the fields and harvest before the crop is lost forever. We must focus on the lost. In Luke 15, there are three parables: the lost coin, the lost sheep and the lost son. The parables focus on each one's value becoming misplaced or lost. There was a search and a patrol for each lost item. There was great rejoicing when each was found!

APPLICATION:
1. Will you go to the fields, today?
2. Will you help others get ready for "Friday?"

PRAYER:
Lord, I will remind those around me the time is at hand! Amen.

JULY 28
BIGGER THAN YOU

Ephesians 3:20
"Now glory be to God, who by his mighty power at work within us, is able to do far more than we would ever dare to ask...or hope." (TLB)

There was a pastor who said, "Oh Lord, give me more power, give me more power!" God replied, "With plans no bigger than yours, you do not need more power!"

If we are to see bigger things than what we currently see, then we must make a bigger plan than we can handle. A miracle can only happen if the people do their part first.

Noah had to build the ark first, before the rain came. Abraham had to take Isaac to the mountain first, before the sacrifice was given to him. The people had to march around Jericho first, before the walls fell down. Gideon and his 300 men had to blow their horns and light the torches first, before God delivered them from their enemies. Naaman had to dip seven times in the Jordan River first, before his flesh was cleansed. David had to run at the Giant first, before he threw the stone that killed him. The three Hebrew children had to make a stand first, before the fourth man showed up. The disciples had to pour water first, before the miracle of the wine took place. The little boy had to give all he had first, before he received the 12 baskets. Jesus had to go to the cross first, before you could be saved.

Sacrifice produces the miracle. After the sacrifice, the miracle comes. There is a spiritual principle at work stating, "There is always more for you when you have fed others first." (John 6:1-12)

Everything God has told me to do, has been bigger than me. I have had to believe God for the resources, the personnel and the support.

If we are to move into the things God wants for us, it will take more than we can produce. We will have to stretch our faith. We will have to depend on God in ways we have not depended on Him before. It will take some courage to walk out the mission God has for you. It will be something bigger than you! *2018 Yes!*
Believing in the funds

APPLICATION:
  1. Are you believing God for something you cannot do without Him? *to*
  2. Be sure you do something first! *renovate NLCST*

We signed the lease! and grow it to

PRAYER:
Lord, I will believe you for something bigger than me! Amen. *Capacity and more!*

235

JULY 29
TRY A LITTLE KINDNESS

Isaiah 54:8-10
"In a little wrath I hid my face from thee for a moment; but with everlasting kindness will I have mercy on thee, saith the LORD thy Redeemer. For this is as the waters of Noah unto me: for I have sworn that the waters of Noah should no more go over the earth; so have I sworn that I would not be wroth with thee, nor rebuke thee. For the mountains shall depart, and the hills be removed; but my kindness shall not depart from thee, neither shall the covenant of my peace be removed, saith the LORD that hath mercy on thee." (KJV)

What is Bible kindness? According to Nelson's Bible Dictionary, it is "loving-kindness." In the Hebrew it is *chesed*, meaning God's loyal love and favor toward His people. In the Old Testament, the word translated as kindness or loving-kindness refers to God's long-suffering love. It is His determination to keep His promises to His chosen people in spite of their sin and rebellion. It is His steadfast love.

Kindness is a word about relationships. Kindness is about making new relationships. It is a covenant word. Rahab expected kindness in return for the kindness she showed the spies. (Joshua 2:12-14) David and Jonathan's friendship included kindness. (I Samuel 20:6) We should use the kindness God has shown us to touch the lives of others. God's grace is given, so you can share it with others.

When we show kindness, we are revealing who God really is. Henry Drummond said, "The greatest thing a man can do for his Heavenly Father is to be kind to some of His other children."

Someone once quipped, "Money will buy a fine dog, but only kindness will make him wag his tail." There is something about kindness which brings out the best in a person. It causes those who have been belligerent to take a hard look at themselves. It melts the hardest of hearts. It turns the gravest of circumstances into a time of healing. No matter what is going on, there is one thing we can always do. We can try a little kindness!

APPLICATION:
1. Find someone who is hurting and try a little kindness out on them.
2. If someone has been harsh, try a little kindness out on them.

PRAYER:
Lord, help me to show the kind of kindness to others you have shown me. Amen.

JULY 30
KEEP ON DOING GOOD

Romans 2:6-7
"Who will render to every man according to his deeds: To them who by patient continuance in well doing seek for glory and honour and ~~immorality~~, eternal life..." (KJV)   *"IMMORTALITY"*

A man was driving on a lonely road one summer day. He saw a car with a flat tire sitting on the shoulder of the road. A woman was standing next to the car looking down at the flat tire. The man decided to pull over and play the Good Samaritan. He grew hot, sweaty and dirty in the hot sun as he changed the tire. The woman was watching him and when he finished, she said, "Be sure and let the jack down easily because my husband is sleeping in the back seat of the car!"

Sometimes you do things for people who do not appreciate it. It can cause you to become callous. It can make you hesitate and think twice. There is always a reward for helping people, even if it does not seem like it.

A well-worn proverb says there are, "Ten rules for getting rid of the blues. Go out and do something for someone else, and repeat it nine times." It is true. It is hard to stay down when you are lifting others up.

I went through a season of very difficult challenges. Nothing I did seemed to be able to get me out of the near depression I was in. I prayed. I spent time in the Word. I fasted. I did everything I knew to do, but the cloud just would not lift. Then, I remembered the last time I faced the same kind of challenge. What did I do to get through? I started going more often to the place I went to then—the nursing home. I connected with some of the patients who did not have any remaining family members. The result was I found my purpose again. I looked at the pain and suffering they had and forgot about my own. By hearing a part of their healing, I discovered my own.

If you are in a place in your life where you just cannot seem to be lifted up, then you can find your way back by pulling those around you up. Just keep on doing good!

APPLICATION:
1. Find someone who is in greater need than you and do something good for them.
2. Do not get weary in well-doing.

PRAYER:
Lord, I purpose in my heart to do something good for those you place in my path. Amen.

JULY 31
WHAT DO YOU SEE?

Numbers 13:33
"And there we saw the giants, the sons of Anak, which come of the giants: and we were in our own sight as grasshoppers, and so we were in their sight." (KJV)

Helen Keller was once asked, "What would be worse than being blind?" Keller replied, "To have sight and have no vision." She was right. So many people have natural sight, but no spiritual vision.

How you see something depends on how you respond. The 10 Spies had eyes of fear. They underestimated what God could do. (Numbers 13:25-29) They returned from their reconnaissance mission and made no mention of God. They talked about how big the people were, the walls and the problems. How soon they had forgotten. Moses, without any weapons or armor, procured the most powerful man in the world to release them after 430 years of slavery with all of the spoils of Egypt. They had allowed the miracle of their release to become nothing more than a fading memory.

They underestimated what they could do through God. They underestimated what their decision would do to those around them. Their perception affected people. (Numbers 14:22-23) The people had always dreamed of the land of milk and honey, but they extinguished their vision. It brought discouragement, discontentment and defeat. (Numbers 14:1-4)

Joshua and Caleb also went into Canaan. They saw something else. They saw the potential of their God. They saw the bountifulness of the land. They saw the promise of their forefathers coming to pass. They saw with spiritual eyes. They had eyes of faith. Faith produced courage. Faith gave them confidence. Faith gave them Canaan. All of the spies had the same experiences and saw the same things in the natural. However, only two saw the possibilities before them. Only two saw through the eyes of faith.

APPLICATION:
1. When you are considering the things challenging you, be sure you are looking through eyes of faith.
2. God always backs up those who refuse to accept defeat.

PRAYER:
Lord, I will take another look at my life through the eyes of faith. Amen.

AUGUST 1
STILL

Habakkuk 3:17-18
*"Even though the fig trees have no fruit, and no grapes grow on the vines,
even though the olive crop fails and the fields produce no grain, even though
the sheep all die and the cattle stalls are empty, I will still be joyful and glad,
because the LORD God is my savior."* (TEV)

The typical Christians in today's age are for the most part "conditional Christians." They serve and worship God as long as the conditions of their life are favorable. However, we need to be Christians who still love, serve and worship God, even when everything around us is in distress.

We need to praise God, no matter what! *Habakkuk* means "to embrace." Real praise is praising God, no matter what. The word *embrace* in the Bible means "to accept joyfully." Sometimes you have to embrace things you do not want to embrace.

Sometimes you have to work a job you do not want to work. I received the call to ministry within the first year of my conversion in 1976. However, I did not have a place to preach, except at the local nursing homes. Needless to say, I had to continue to work my job painting houses. I did that for 19 more years before I was able to step into full time ministry.

For a while, I hated my job. I wanted so desperately to spend my time helping people and studying. Then, one day the Lord spoke to me and said, "How long do you want to be out here?" I said, "Not another day!" He said, "Then, quit complaining and embrace this season. I am training you and teaching you as you work." I began to look at my job differently. Soon, people on my job site began to ask me about my faith. I was able to share God with them and invite them to church. It was only a few short years later when I was able to step into full time ministry.

What are some of the unfavorable things you are involved in right now? No matter what, we must learn to embrace the moment. We must praise God even when everything seems to be going against us. Then, God will exalt us when we praise Him...Still!

APPLICATION:
1. Be sure you praise God today.
2. Be sure you still serve God even if things are presently bad.

PRAYER:
Lord, I will still praise you today and forever. Amen.

AUGUST 2
A LIFE OF PRAISE

Psalms 33:1
"...Praise is comely for the upright." (KJV)

We have learned praise means to take your present circumstances and no matter what, embrace God. Present situations may include living in a house you do not want to live in, staying in a marriage you do not want to stay in, etc.

Something happens when you praise God; you begin to expect things to get better! Praise is the winning response when trouble comes. Paul and Silas discovered this in prison at midnight. (Acts 16:25-26) Jehoshaphat discovered this when the armies of the enemies were about to attack the children of Israel. (II Chronicles 20:21-22) They discovered a powerful truth; praise stops the advances of the enemy. (Psalms 8, 18:2) Satan expects us to turn on God when trouble comes. It was his strategy for Job. However, Job said, *"Though he slay me, yet I will trust in him."* (Job 13:15 KJV) Job found a way to hold onto his faith and was greatly rewarded for it.

Praise is a military response. It is proclaiming the goodness, the power and the faithfulness of God. It invites God's intervention into our lives and circumstances. It brings about an atmosphere whereby the promises of God become a reality.

Psalms 100:4 instructs us to enter His gates with thanksgiving and His courts with praise. Without praise, we do not even get the attention of God. Praise is the password to the promises.

Praise reaches into the Heavens and activates the angels. There are countless scripture examples detailing how when praise was offered, the angels of Heaven came onto the scene.

Despite the hardships of life and Devil's attacks, we have access to God's presence. We must become warriors of praise. This not only includes praising God in the day, but also praising Him in the night. When we learn this lesson, our lives will become filled with His glory and His help!

APPLICATION:
1. Take some time, today, to praise God.
2. You do not have to praise Him for the hard circumstances of your life, but you can praise Him in the midst of them!

PRAYER:
Lord, I praise you with all of my being. You are my God and I will live a life of praise! Amen.

Praise God, I have a home to live in. We have a church building. We have 2 vehicles and income. 240 *We have health. children and Grandchildren!*

AUGUST 3
TURNING THINGS AROUND

Philippians 1:19
"For I know that through your prayers and the help given by the Spirit of Jesus Christ, what has happened to me will turn out for my deliverance." (NIV)

Grantland Rice, the legendary coach, said, "Failure wouldn't be so bad if it didn't attack the heart." This is so true. Failure rips things out of our lives from the inside out. Yet, failure does not have to be permanent.

John Maxwell said, "You can fail at something and not be a failure." There is a way to learn from failure and to turn things around. All we need is a breakthrough.

Everybody desires a breakthrough. There are key turning points in every battle fought. God desires to guide you into the center of His will. The word *turn* in Philippians 1:19, is derived from the Greek word, *Apobiano*, which means "as a ship that can be steered into a desired direction or destination. To change the outcome; the end result." Paul knew this very well. The more Paul was persecuted, the larger his audience became. More people wanted to get on board with the message. God turned his circumstances into his advantage.

What will turn your circumstances? First, prayer. Get connected with people who know how to pray. Prayer opens the door to the supply. Second, the supply of the Spirit. We must spend time in His presence to see our circumstances turn. Third, raising your expectation. Hope is connected to your expectation and faith is the substance of things hoped for! Fourth, changing your language. Your tongue is the rudder of your life. If a small rudder can turn an enormous ship, your tongue is the key to turning testing times into breakthroughs. Last, you must repent. Repentance places us back in the will of God and brings His intervention into our circumstances. John, Jesus and the disciples preached repentance. When you return to God, your situations begin to turn in your favor.

If you do these things, your next turn is just ahead, a turn into a breakthrough!

APPLICATION:
1. Check the five things listed. Are you ready for the next turn?
2. Trust God for a breakthrough.

PRAYER:
Lord, I will not accept failure! I trust you will turn things around for me. Amen.

AUGUST 4
A HEAVENLY CONNECTION

Ecclesiastes 4:12
"And one standing alone can be attacked and defeated, but two can stand back-to-back and conquer; three is even better, for a triple-braided cord is not easily broken." (TLB)

You may remember the following story previously referenced in this book. You will remember the two men riding a bicycle built for two when they came to a big, steep hill. It took a great deal of struggle for the men to complete what proved to be a very stiff climb. When they reached the top, the man in the front turned to the other and said, "Boy, that sure was a hard climb." The fellow in the back replied, "Yes, and if I hadn't kept the brakes on all the way, we would certainly have rolled back downwards!"

Too often, this is the picture of our lives. We pull against each other and hinder the work God desires to do in our lives. However, if we are going to accomplish what we were created to do, we must be able to walk together, work together and worship together.

The word *united* is defined as "joined, or linked; having a connection; joined together in sequence; linked coherently: attached, fastened; hinged, combined, merged." We must find a way to merge our lives with those around us.

When we face the disappointments of life alone, we often become weakened and lose hope. It takes having someone to stand with us, someone to lift us up and at times, carry us. Sometimes it takes trusting someone else's faith more than we do our own until we recover and regain our senses.

I believe we are all inept and lacking in particular areas of our lives. Alone, our weaknesses are exposed. Yet, when you find someone who is committed to your success, they will cover your weakness with their strength.

We are always more successful when we have had the assistance of others. Jesus was adamant about sending forth His disciples in pairs. He also reminded us it took two to agree to bring faith. It is a Heavenly connection!

APPLICATION:
1. Be sure to be in agreement with those God has placed in your life.
2. Find someone who has your best interest at heart.

PRAYER:
Lord, I repent for not allowing the people you have directed to me to speak into my life. Amen.

AUGUST 5
WHAT WILL BE YOUR STORY?

Hebrews 6:9

"But, beloved, we are persuaded better things of you, and things that accompany salvation, though we thus speak" (KJV)

Colonel Sanders retired at the age of 65 as a postal worker. He said, "Is this all I will do for the rest of my life? Sit on the porch and rock and wait for my Social Security check to come in?" He became the cook at a local restaurant and used his mother's recipe for fried chicken. The rest is history—his story! What will your story be?

Most great battles are won by those who press on a little longer than the assaults of their adversaries. They refuse to let their story end in defeat. Joshua asked for the sun to stand still, so he could fight and win. As one person said, "Just because you miss one train doesn't mean you have to cancel the whole vacation!"

We are prone to quit, too quickly, and give up on the ending. We accept our circumstances as final and do not consider God's capability to help us change the storyline. If something bad or disruptive happens to us, we accept there is nothing we can do about it. We concede it is just our fate, instead of making a stand and proclaiming, *"...If God be for us, who can be against us?"* (Romans 8:31 KJV)

Some people find themselves victims of divorce. They are left on life's roadside to wither and die. Divorce is a very difficult thing to overcome. However, if they decide to continue on with God, their story can change and even become something better than they would have had without the divorce.

There will always be another giant that we will have to face or another setback attempting to altar our lives. Yet, we still have the final word in our own lives as long as we follow the Lord. So, consider for your own life, "What will your story be?"

APPLICATION:
1. Do not get discouraged if your life is not unfolding the way you thought it would.
2. Do not accept defeat. Ask God for His help, so you can rewrite your story.

PRAYER:
Lord, I will not quit or give in to life's pressure. Give me strength to go on. Amen.

AUGUST 6
THE READING OF THE WILL

Hebrews 11:3
"Through faith, we understand that the worlds were framed by the Word of God, so that things which are seen were not made of things which do appear." (KJV)

The Bible is more than a book of words. It is a book of the last will and testament of Jesus to His disciples. It is not a book of words about Him, it is His words! It is His will and testament to His heirs; those who are born-again. Jesus bought and paid for our redemption, but He went beyond that. He opened the riches in glory up to those who would be the heirs of salvation.

The will must be read before you can know what is in it. You must have a representative before you who knows how to explain it, tell you your rights and how to receive everything written in it. The Holy Spirit is our representative who reveals what rightfully belongs to us through His Word.

The Word is available to us. If we choose not to take advantage of it, it is our own fault. It is like the couple who were checking out of their hotel room. The charges included 150 dollars for fruit. The man angrily stated, "We never ate any of the fruit! How can you charge us for it?" "It was there. It is not my fault you didn't take advantage of it," the clerk replied. The man took the bill and subtracted five dollars from each day. "What are you doing that for?" the clerk questioned. "For kissing my wife!" The clerk retorted, "I never kissed your wife!" The husband sneered, "It's not my fault! She was there everyday!"

God has provided everything needed in His Word for us to become successful. Our part is to study the will and accept what is written about us and to us. Then, when we finish our time here, we must be ready to face Him there.

APPLICATION:
1. Study the Word of God and underline every time you see the words, "in Him."
2. Do not let anyone mislead you concerning those things willed to you through His Word.

PRAYER:
Lord, thank you for including me in your will. I am ready to read what you say about me. Amen.

AUGUST 7
THE CONSEQUENCES OF SIN

Hebrews 11:24-25

"By faith, Moses, when he was come to years, refused to be called the son of Pharaoh's daughter; Choosing rather to suffer affliction with the people of God, than to enjoy the pleasures of sin for a season." (KJV)

If you listen to the voices of the world, then you would believe there is no consequence to unrepentant sin. As a matter of fact, many would say there is no such thing as sin, only choices. However, the truth is the Bible says when sin is finished, it brings forth death!

According to the Bible, there are sins unto death and sins that are not unto death. (I John 5:14-16) If you get caught in sins unto death, you will probably die early, if you do not repent. The first sin unto death is adultery, fornication and sexual sin. (I Corinthians 5:1) The second sin is the intrusion into ministry when you are not called. It will kill you or somebody around you. It is the same if you do have a call, and do not answer. The third sin is coming against God's anointed leaders. This is not to say you cannot get repentance, but you may not. The fourth sin is robbing God of His rightful tithe, as in the case with Saphira and Ananias. The tithe never belongs to us; it is always God's. We are thieves if we do not return it unto Him!

We must actively oppose sin and keep ourselves in the presence of God. We cannot keep making excuses for our sin. "It's the church's fault. It's my father or mother's fault." You must be brutally honest. It is our responsibility to walk in the salvation we have received from God, to take responsibility for our own sin and repent!

We must also realize it is only through the blood of Jesus we are able to be freed from the law of sin and death. There are not enough burnt offerings on this planet to take care of our sin problem. We must recognize God alone can forgive us and give us the victory over sin. However, we are charged to maintain that forgiveness. Do not let the enemy fool you. There are consequences to sin!

APPLICATION:
1. If you are harboring sin in your life, quit now!
2. Do not be deceived by sin. There are consequences, which accompany unrepentant sin.

PRAYER:
Lord, I repent of harboring sin in my life. Forgive me and help me to change. Amen.

AUGUST 8
REUNITED

II Samuel 12:22-24
"And he said, While the child was yet alive, I fasted and wept: for I said, Who can tell whether GOD will be gracious to me, that the child may live? But now he is dead, wherefore should I fast? Can I bring him back again? I shall go to him, but he shall not return to me. And David comforted Bath-sheba, his wife…" (KJV)

My wife, Ginger, is easily the strongest person I have ever met. Before we were married, her toddler son from a previous marriage tragically lost his life. He was hit and ran over by the driver of a car and killed. Most people never recover from this kind of tragic event. Yet, she has found a way!

Ginger and I met in 1981. She was coming out of an abusive marriage with the hurt of this event still fresh in her life. I did not know how to minister to her, so I gave her these scriptures. David was faced with a cold reality; his son was not going to live. However, David knew his God well enough to know it was not the end. Psalms 126:5-6 says, *"They that sow in tears shall reap in joy. He that goeth forth and weepeth, bearing precious seed, shall doubtless come again with rejoicing, bringing his sheaves with him!"* (KJV)

As hard as it is to lose someone you love to the harshness of death, the truth is there is a reunion coming—a reunion like no other! It will be a reunion that will not be interrupted by sickness, hurt, fear or death. The reunion will be unaffected by time. It will be a reunion that does not yield in separation.

Can you imagine how it will be when we get to Heaven? We will see the people we have led to Christ along the way. We may be surprised to see others there who made Jesus their Lord without our knowledge. We will see the precious loved ones who have passed in our families and who were covered by His blood. What a reunion that will be! Then, we will see Jesus. He made the great reunion possible by the willing sacrifice of His blood on the cross. The one who took on a flesh body and suffered like we do! No matter how hard today may be, no matter how much it hurts to miss those who have gone before us, we must have the faith of David. They may not return to us, but we can go to them! Be ready for the reunion!

APPLICATION:
1. Look to Heaven for hope.
2. Be ready!

PRAYER:
Lord, thank you for the day of the great reunion just ahead! Amen.

AUGUST 9
THE BLESSING OF CORRECTION

Proverbs 3:11-12
"My son, despise not the chastening of the LORD; neither be weary of his correction: For whom the LORD loveth he correcteth; even as a father the son in whom he delighteth." (KJV)

Most of the time, correction is looked on in a negative light. It seems like we consider it to be harsh or unnecessary. However, according to scripture, nothing could be further from the truth.

The word *correction* is the Hebrew word, *epimorphosis*, which means "straightening up again." Correction is putting things back into place that have been out of order. God corrects you to get you back on the right track.

Correction is the sum total of your success or failure in God. How you handle correction is crucial to your Christian walk, not just from evil. Miguel de Cervantes said, "It is one thing to praise discipline; another to submit to it." Erwin Lutzer said, "Discipline is a proof of our sonship." You are a legitimate son/daughter—God has the right to correct you as a father would a son or daughter. God chastens us the way we would our own children. To chasten means to correct. God corrects us to keep us out of harm's way. We do not correct our children by doing something harmful to them. God is not going to chasten you with something you have been redeemed from.

A business man, well known for his ruthless behavior, once told Mark Twain, "Before I die, I mean to make a pilgrimage to the Holy Land. I will climb Mount Sinai and read the Ten Commandments along at the top." Mark Twain said, "I have a better idea. You could stay in Boston and keep them."

The easiest way to avoid correction is to obey God in our daily walk with Him. When sin goes unchecked, it brings in judgment. However, when it is checked and correction is received, it brings in the glory.

If we are to become mature, fruitful believers, then we must receive correction. When we receive it and make the necessary changes, we will receive the blessing of correction!

APPLICATION:
1. If you need correction, receive it with humility.
2. Let God bring the blessing to you.

PRAYER:
Lord, I humbly accept the correction you desire for me. Amen.

247

AUGUST 10
WINNING THE WAR OF THE MIND

Isaiah 26:3
*"You will guard him and keep him in perfect and constant peace whose mind
(both its inclination and its character) is stayed on You because he commits
himself to You, leans on You and hopes confidently in You."* (Amplified Bible)

Startling statistics show that at any given time in America, there are between
15 and 20 million people suffering from depression. Of these depressed individuals, 15 percent will commit suicide. Each year, some 28 thousand Americans take
their own lives. A high percentage occurs around the Christmas holiday season.

In San Francisco, the Golden Gate Bridge is not only the city's trademark,
but it is also the final point of life for many people. Since the bridge opened in
1937, there have been nearly 1,000 confirmed suicides there. The bridge accounts
for about 10 percent of all suicides in San Francisco. The side of the bridge from
which so many people jump is significant. Reports indicate almost every person
has jumped off looking at the city rather than the ocean. Their final gaze at the city
seems to suggest each one was taking one last look for hope!

The greatest war a Christian will fight is the war of the mind. Roman 12:2
informs us we can only *"be transformed by the entire renewal of your mind by its
new ideals and its new attitude."* (Amplified Bible)

It is not a sin to suffer from, or battle, depression. Many great men in the
Bible suffered from it. David, Job and Elijah all had times of tremendous anxiety
and even depression. Even Jesus battled against it. He suffered mental anguish in
the wilderness, in the Garden of Gethsemane and on the cross. These were spiritual events, which manifested in the natural soul and mind.

Jesus combated and overcame depression by doing these three things: First,
He overcame through powerful, effectual prayer. Second, through faith. He
trusted the will of the Father. Jesus believed the Father would see Him through
all, including death. Third, through the Spirit. He knew as long as He fought in
the Spirit, He would prevail. We, too, can prevail and overcome. With His help,
we can win the war of the mind!

APPLICATION:
1. Look to God's Word when depression comes.
2. Let His Spirit come upon you to comfort and sustain you.

PRAYER:
Lord, with your help, I will not be depressed, but overcome! Amen.

AUGUST 11
DO NOT GIVE IN TO DEPRESSION

Isaiah 60:1-3

*"Arise (from the depression and prostration in which your
circumstances have kept you—rise to new life)! Shine (be radiant with the glory
of the Lord), for your light has come, and the glory of the Lord has risen upon
you! For behold, darkness shall cover the earth, and dense darkness all peoples,
but the Lord shall arise upon you...and His glory shall be seen on you! And
nations shall come to your light, and kings to the brightness of your rising..."*
(Amplified Bible)

Depression is best defined as "a sunken place; an area lower than the sur-rounding surface; sadness; gloom." In Psychiatry, it is considered, "a condition of general emotional dejection and withdrawal; sadness greater and more prolonged than that warranted by any objective reason."

I have fought against depression in my life. On at least two occasions, I have found myself sinking into depression. I lost hope, vision and desire. I could not see how things could ever improve or return to normalcy. I was miserable, with-drawn and despondent. I found myself questioning God. What is the objective of depression? It is to cause you to doubt God's plan for your life. It is driven by fear and panic. Depression causes you to lose sight of God's presence in your life. It places you in a weakened state emotionally and spiritually. When not dealt with, it causes you to lose your will to fight the good fight. It causes you to think it is not worth it to go on.

Depression is a thief, which will take you out of the hands of God and place you in the hands of the enemy. The enemy gets you to begin to buy into depres-sion by condemning you and pointing out your mistakes. The Devil causes you to blame yourself, others and God. Satan's purpose is to get you to give in until you are oppressed.

However, you can resist him. You can overcome his tactics. Remind yourself God is for you. He is not your enemy! He wants the best for you. He will help you to pursue, overtake and recover. Do not give in to depression!

APPLICATION:
1. Fight against depression by reminding yourself who you are in Christ Jesus.
2. Focus on what God has done for you before. He will do it again!

PRAYER:
Lord, I confess you are Lord. I will live and not die. Amen.

AUGUST 12
GET FREE, STAY FREE

Galatians 5:1
"Stand fast therefore in the liberty wherewith Christ hath made us free, and be not entangled again with the yoke of bondage." (KJV)

I read an article which stated over 50 percent of all incarcerated offenders commit another offence after they are released. It was startling. It seems when they were finally freed, they did not appreciate their freedom, nor value it enough to stay clean.

Often, we are the same way with God. We go to God with all kinds of habits, addictions and sins, and ask Him to deliver us. Then, after He does, too often, we go back to those things we have been freed from. It seems we have not learned how valuable our freedom is. To understand how much something is worth, we must first understand how much it cost.

Our freedom was purchased through the legal system God instituted. For sin, according to scripture, there must first be a shedding of blood. (Hebrews 9:22) Blood is required as the expression of a sacrifice and atonement. II Corinthians 5:21 states, *"For he hath made him to be sin for us, who knew no sin; that we might be made the righteousness of God in him."* (KJV)

Although Jesus was sinless, a payment was required which we could not and would not pay. Jesus purchased us with His own blood and freed us from the law of sin and death. (Romans 8:2) We are now exonerated from the penalty rightfully against us. It has been removed and now we stand pronounced, "Not guilty!"

You must stand in that freedom. How? First, you must remove yourself from the trappings of your former sin. Do not hang out where you became hung up. Second, remind yourself the old person is deceased. Do not try to resurrect what God has laid to rest. Do not allow yourself to get tangled up in your old life. Finally, take on the newness of Christ. We have been recreated in Him. Do not live like the old man/woman after you have been made a new one. If you have been made free, stay free!

APPLICATION:
1. Avoid your former hang outs and the people you hung out with.
2. When you feel the old man/woman trying to stir, remind yourself you are born-again!

PRAYER:
Lord, I will not get tangled up again! I am staying free! Amen.

AUGUST 13
LEGALISM OR LIFE?

Luke 11:46
"And he said, Woe unto you also, ye lawyers! For ye lade men with burdens, grievous to be borne, and ye yourselves touch not the burdens with one of your fingers." (KJV)

Joseph Fletcher said, "He who makes the law his standard is obligated to perform all its precepts, for to break one Commandment is to break the law. He who lives by faith and love is not judged on that basis, but by a standard infinitely higher and at the same time more attainable."

While the Bible certainly requires us to live a Holy life, it is based on God's love for us and our love for Him. It is never to be based on an unfeeling sense of duty alone.

You can get into a depth of legalism, which will cause you to miss the genuine move of God. Legalism takes your joy. It takes away your ability to have a genuine relationship with God. It will make you become robotic. Legalism is based only on an action or duty that you think is right to please God. It is not out of an expression of appreciation and thankfulness.

You can never please legalism. It brings condemnation. According to Romans 12:1, if we walk with Him, we are not condemned. You can never satisfy legalism. As soon as you do, it expands to something else. Legalists pressure a person to have the answers to everything, but offer no freedom.

When I was a young man I was in a particular church with so many rules, I wondered if anyone would be "good enough" to be saved. You could not wear this. You could not listen to that. You could not go here. You could not stop there. Yet, there was something missing—relationship. You were encouraged more to perform and conform, than to get closer to God. God knows how to convict us when we are walking out of line. When you are in a place of strict legalism, you become a man-pleaser and not a God-pleaser. You imitate the convictions of the person you are following and miss hearing, understanding and obeying God's voice for your own life. Keep His Commandments, but do not become a legalist!

APPLICATION:
1. Check your life. Have you become a legalist?
2. Do not pressure people to have your convictions. They are for you to follow!

PRAYER:
Lord, I will obey you out of love and thankfulness. Amen.

AUGUST 14
WOMEN AND THEIR PLACE

Psalms 68:11
"The Lord gave the command, and many women carried the news..." (TEV)

It is an age old argument, "What is the role of women in the Church?" While both sides always put up a good argument, which is truly more Biblical? What is a woman to do? Can she teach? Can she be involved at all in the business of the Church?

These questions are complex and the answers are not necessarily clear. However, we know God used many women in the Bible in critical roles who produced victories.

The first verse undoubtedly discussed is I Corinthians 14:34-35, *"Let your women keep silence in the churches: for it is not permitted unto them to speak; but they are commanded to be under obedience, as also saith the law. And if they will learn anything, let them ask their husbands at home: for it is a shame for women to speak in church."* (KJV) If you accept this verse literally, then women cannot teach the children, take care of the nursery, sing or even bake because they will most certainly speak while interacting with the male members. No church believes that! Verse 36 further reveals men and women were not seated together. Why were women not allowed to speak or sit with the men in church? Because women were not as educated during that time. Therefore, they were told not to interrupt the services by asking questions, but rather to ask their husbands at home. Also, the word *woman* in Greek means "wife." So, the verses' references to women did not mean every single woman. These verses were more about the wife being submissive, rather than the demand of women and their role in the church.

The next controversial verse is found in I Timothy 2:11-13, *"Let the woman learn in silence with all subjection. But I suffer not a woman to teach, nor to usurp authority over the man, but to be in silence. For Adam was first formed, then Eve."* (KJV) Again, these verses clearly explain the ignorance women in Bible days possessed. All education had to come from their husbands. Once again, the word, *woman* is *wife.* Therefore, theses verses did not apply to all women, just those who were married.

For too long, women have been suppressed by this errant doctrine! It is time to be bold enough to believe the Bible and not church doctrine.

APPLICATION:
1. Let God renew your mind concerning His place for women.
2. Give the women in your church the same respect God does.

PRAYER:
Lord, show me the truth about this subject. Amen.

252

AUGUST 15
WHAT IS A WOMAN TO DO?

Luke 1:38
*"And Mary said, Behold the handmaid of the Lord; be it unto
me according to thy word..."* (KJV)

A thorough and careful study of the Bible reveals women have a very important place in the Kingdom of God. Just gazing at the scriptures you will discover there were 14 prophetesses in the Bible. A *prophetess* is defined as, "A woman who speaks forth the oracles of God publicly to direct, correct and encourage God's people."

In II Kings 22:13-20, prophetess Huldah spoke the Word! Deborah was the greatest judge of all. She judged men and women of God. (Judges 4:4) In Luke 1:39-46, Elisabeth prophesied about the most important event ever, the birth of Jesus. Then, Mary prophesied. In Luke 2:36, Anna was named as a prophetess.

What about Acts 2:17-18? It says sons and daughters shall prophesy. There was no discrimination. The Civil Rights Movement was correct and successful because it was based on Christianity, which says all men and women are equal!

Verses 19-21 reveal the results of the sons and daughters prophesying are signs, wonders and salvation. The word *prophesy* in the New Testament means "to preach, proclaim, publish, and sing the Gospel."

What about women in the ministry? Romans 16:1-11 speaks of servants, deaconesses, helper of many, possibly a minister or a pastor. Phoebe is mentioned. Priscilla taught Apollos. Aquila and Priscilla co-pastored in their house. Junia was an apostle, one of the five-fold ministries.

I Corinthians 11:3-5 says, *"But every woman that prayeth or prophesieth with her head uncovered..."* (KJV) If women were not to ever prophesy, then why did the Bible tell them how to wear their hair when they did?

In conclusion, Psalms 68:9 states, *"The Lord gives the command; The women who proclaim good tidings are good hosts:"* (NASV) No wonder the Devil would push so hard to keep women from the pulpit. The body of Christ is comprised of over 50 percent women.

APPLICATION:
1. Study the Word about women and allow God to show you His will for them.
2. If you are a woman, be free from religious teaching!

PRAYER:
Lord, I will follow your lead as a woman of God. Amen.

AUGUST 16
HOW LONG?

Deuteronomy 2:3
"Ye have compassed this mountain long enough: turn you northward." (KJV)

For 40 long years the children of Israel had compassed the mountain just miles away from the Promised Land. God had not prevented them from entering in, but their own stubbornness and rebellion had. If they would have followed the Lord, they could have been in the land of milk and honey.

The same question is asked many times in the Bible, "How long?" Numbers 14:11 asks, *"How long will these people despise me?"* (TLB) How long before you believe? Joshua 18:3 asks, *"How long will you neglect to go and possess the land which the Lord God of your fathers has given you?"* (KJV) I Kings 18:21 asks, *"How long will you falter between two opinions?"* (NKJV) Job 8:2 asks, *"How long will you speak these wrong things?"* (NKJV) Proverbs 6:9 asks, *"How long will you sleep oh sluggard?"* (Amplified Bible)

We must ask ourselves these questions: "How long will we continue to go in circles? How long will we keep covering the same territory? How long will we be delayed from being in His perfect will? How long will we disobey God? How long will we live below the privileges bought and paid for on our behalf? How long will we allow the enemy to steal, kill and destroy our families and lives?"

The answer is it will continue as long as we allow it to. It is up to us to place ourselves in the will of God. It is up to us to walk in faith before God. It is up to us to resist the Devil and put him to flight. Place yourself in God's will and do not allow the Devil's attacks any longer!

APPLICATION:
1. Make a stand, today, against the Devil and his attacks on your life and family.
2. Decide to move into the things God has for you and do not delay!

PRAYER:
Lord, I repent of going in circles for too long. I am moving on to what you have for my life. Amen.

AUGUST 17
BLOOMING IN THE DESERT

Isaiah 35:6-7

"...for in the wilderness shall waters break out, and streams in the desert. And the parched ground shall become a pool, and the thirsty land springs of water."
(KJV)

You have to learn to bloom where you are planted. Joseph found himself in a foreign land, but because he kept his faith in God, he prospered and became powerful and successful.

Elijah was beside the Brook Cherith for a season. *Cherith* means "to be cut off or separated." However, God used the crows (unclean) to sustain him. After a while, the brook dried up! Yet, by then, the famine was over.

Because I live in a military town, many of the people who move to this area do not come by choice; they are assigned here. It is different than their hometown. The people are different. The surroundings are different. The culture is different. Many of them become homesick and do not like the area. They "dry" out. I have to encourage them to embrace the city, speak well of it and to seize the time they have here. When they do, an amazing thing happens. They begin to like the area and begin to flourish. They begin to "bloom" in the desert.

It is the same for us spiritually. We get into some very "dry" seasons. It seems that we will never be fruitful again. What should we do if we are in a season of dryness and there seems to be no breakthrough in sight? First of all, we must remember God knows where we are. (Deuteronomy 32:9) Second, we can build in the desert. (II Chronicles 26:10) Third, Psalms 78:40 tells us the deserts are turning points in our life. Fourth, Isaiah 40:1-5 states that deserts are a place you can straighten things out. Fifth, Isaiah 41:19 and Matthew 14:15 say deserts are places of unmistakable miracles! Sixth, Isaiah 43:19 states deserts are places where the old dies out. Finally, we must remember God shows up in the desert. (Mark 1:45; Luke 9:10)

No matter where you may be, remember you can bloom in the desert!

APPLICATION:
1. Do not curse the place you are in.
2. Speak well of your surroundings and embrace the moment.

PRAYER:
Lord, I will not denounce the place you have put me. I will embrace and flourish in it. Amen.

255

AUGUST 18
LEARNING TO ABOUND

Philippians 4:12
"I know both how to be abased, and I know how to abound: every where and in all things I am instructed both to be full and to be hungry, both to abound and to suffer need." (KJV)

I heard a story about a couple who brought a jar of money to their pastor. They said, "Pastor, there must be 1,000 dollars in there and it is all for the church." After counting the money, they discovered the amount was nearly 12,000 dollars! The husband uttered, "We must have brought the wrong jar!"

Somehow, we do not fully understand how God wants us to abound in His blessings. Most people know how to be abased, to go without and to accept seconds. Yet, few in the Kingdom ever truly understand how to receive and handle abundance.

It is similar to what happened in one elementary class. The teacher told the students to go home and count the stars they saw that night. A little boy who was in the class only counted 40. All of the others counted between 400 and 800. He said, "I guess they have a bigger back yard than I do!"

You must believe God has something more for you. There are seven necessary steps to abundance. The first is you must abound in your personal relationship with God. It is found in private fellowship and time spent with God. Second, you must abound in God's way of prospering. You must distance yourself from the temptations and lusts of this world. God's way of prospering is better than the deceit of quick riches. Third, you must abound in the Word. The Word must be implanted in your heart. Your heart produces what is in it. The Word brings abundance. Fourth, you must abound in your love life. Love never fails. Love is the magnet of abundance. Fifth, you must abound in your sowing. Look for ways to sow. Let God show you where the good ground is. It produces 30, 60 and even 100 fold! Sixth, you must abound in faithfulness. Faithfulness brings abundance. It is a slow, but certain path to God's best. Seventh, you must abound in thanksgiving. Thanksgiving releases the promises of His Word. It opens the door for more. Do not be fooled. God wants you to abound!

APPLICATION:
    1. Allow yourself to believe and receive God's abundance.
    2. Plan for God to place you in an environment where you can abound!

PRAYER:
Lord, teach me to abound that I might glorify your name. Amen.

AUGUST 19
DO THE WORK OF AN EVANGELIST

II Timothy 4:5
"But watch thou in all things, endure afflictions, do the work of an evangelist,
make full proof of thy ministry." (KJV)

There has never been a greater need for the Gospel than now. The word *evangelism* comes from the Greek word, *evangelion*, which means "the presentation of glad tidings to those without Christ accompanied with the demonstration of God's power; to declare and show glad tidings."

When we use the word *evangelist*, we generally think of a Hell, fire and brimstone preacher who comes through town and scares people to repentance, prays for the sick and has some miracles. There is a critical, five-fold ministry office of the evangelist for sure. Yet, the truth is every member of the body of Christ, although not being in the five-fold office of an evangelist, is called to do the work of an evangelist—to spread the Good News of Jesus Christ and to turn the lost to Christ.

Apostle Paul was also a great soul winner. His missionary trips were not only for the establishing of the Church, but for the redemption of the lost. Paul wrote to Timothy, "Do the work of an evangelist." Timothy was a pastor, not an evangelist. Yet, Paul did not want him to get so busy with the sheep that he did not try to reach the lost.

What should motivate us to evangelism? Love. Evangelism is about spreading God's love. (John 3:16) The Teltzal Indians of South Mexico have a word for love which means to hurt in the heart. We have to "hurt in the heart" for the lost. We have to see their need for salvation and be moved to reach them.

You may recall the story of the young man who asked a young woman to marry him. She turned down his proposal. They parted ways, but he would not give up. For the next 40 years, he sent her a love letter every week asking her to marry him. Her answer remained the same. Then, one day he received a letter from her. It said, "Yes!" They were married at the age of 60 and spent the next 30 years happy and fulfilled.

We must be someone who "slips love letters under the doors" of the lost. They may not say, "Yes," today, but they may tomorrow. Do the work of an evangelist!

APPLICATION:
1. Begin to pray for a desire to reach the lost.
2. Witness to someone today. Slip God's "love letter" to them!

PRAYER:
Lord, give me a burning desire to reach the lost! Amen.

AUGUST 20
LOOKING FOR THE LOST

Luke 19:5-10

"And when Jesus came to the place, he looked up, and saw him, and said unto him, Zacchaeus, make haste, and come down; for today I must abide at thy house. And he made haste, and came down, and received him joyfully…And Jesus said unto him, This day is salvation come to this house, forsomuch as he also is a son of Abraham. For the Son of man is come to seek and to save that which was lost." (KJV)

If you lose something of value, you will not rest until you find it! You will keep on looking and looking and looking! You will not rest until it is recovered.

We are called to be servants and witnesses to those who are lost and bring them to Christ, so they can be "found." However, a witness is of no value if he/she withholds evidence. The evidence is critical. Proverbs 14:25 says, *"A witness who tells the truth saves good men from being sentenced to death, but a false witness is a traitor."* (TLB)

We must offer the evidence of the transformation of our own lives to a lost and dying world. We must convince them there is another way other than the way of the world. We must prove to them Jesus is the Christ, the Son of the Living God! We must show them the love that first drew us to the cross. We must share His forgiveness, which has given us all a second chance.

The world is in need of exposure to the amazing grace, which was lovingly and generously offered for our redemption. Grace attracts those who have been hurt, forgotten and lost their way. It is our commission to show them the way. Like an ant who finds a piece of candy; he goes back after the colony!

As we go about our daily lives, it is crucial we do not get so busy with our daily tasks and lives, that we overlook those around us who are lost and undone. We should take on the love, grace and heart of the Master, and help others find their way home to Christ!

APPLICATION:
1. Make a conscience decision to look around you. Are there lost people in your path?
2. Ask God to show you who they are. Ask Him to give you the right words to speak to them.

PRAYER:
Lord, I will be a servant and witness for you, today. Amen.

AUGUST 21
GOING ON AND NOT GOING BACK

Exodus 14:12

"Is not this the word that we did tell thee in Egypt, saying, Let us alone, that we may serve the Egyptians? For it had been better for us to serve the Egyptians, than that we should die in the wilderness." (KJV)

Have you ever gotten excited about a trip, only to find the conditions along the way were not what you thought they would be? Did you long to go back home? That is what the children of Israel did.

They had just been delivered from 430 years of tyranny, slavery, starvation and mistreatment. They had even watched as Pharaoh's men slaughtered their children at birth! There was certainly no worse place on earth, than to be a slave in Egypt!

However, they forgot about the long, harsh days behind them, and instead became frustrated, angry and discontent with where God was leading them. They cried out for yesterday. They doubted whether the God who had so miraculously delivered them, could even feed and protect them. They wanted to go back.

This is the picture of many of God's people. God has brought them out of the darkness of drugs, alcohol, pornography, hurt, deceit and mistreatment. He has redeemed them with a mighty hand and given them a second chance. He has forgiven their pasts and promised them glorious futures. Then, when the journey gets hard and presents times of challenge, they long for the past. What did they really leave back there? They left a hopeless life leading to death.

We must make the decision to go on with God. We must make the decision to go on with salvation. We must make the decision to go on with our walk with Christ. We must make a decision to go on to the life He has planned for us. We must make the decision to go on to a life as a believer. There is nothing behind us worth going back to. Let us go on!

APPLICATION:
1. If you have found yourself longing for your past life, repent and look ahead to what God has for you.
2. Remind yourself of what you were delivered from.

PRAYER:
Lord, I want nothing I have left behind. I am going on! Amen.

AUGUST 22
LOOK NOW

Genesis 15:5-6
"And he brought him forth abroad, and said, Look now toward Heaven, and tell the stars, if thou be able to number them: and he said unto him, So shall thy seed be. And he believed in the LORD; and he counted it to him for righteousness."
(KJV)

Everybody needs vision. Vision breathes life into the moment and sparks hope. Sometimes we need to be reminded of the vision that has already been revealed to us.

Abraham had a vision problem. He had already been told God was going to cause him to be the father of many nations. He was told by the Lord to step outside and look. God said, "Look now!" even when there was no evidence.

God had to awaken, quicken and energize him by stirring up his vision. Vision is always now, even though it inspires and speaks of the future. If we do not have vision now, we will have no realized dreams tomorrow.

You must be able to see with your spirit. You cannot be limited only to what your natural eyes or senses reveal to you. Vision is a matter of your heart. If your heart is dull to the things of God, then you will not see what God has for you. As a result, if you cannot see it, you cannot have it.

We have to do things that fuel, help or ignite our vision. It is like the man with the seeing eye dog. The dog would stop at inopportune times. Once in the middle of a busy intersection with traffic everywhere, the dog stopped and the blind man froze in fear. Someone eventually helped them safely to the other side. Then, the blind man retrieved something from his pouch, searched for the dog's mouth and gave the dog a doggy treat. Bewildered, the rescuer asked, "What did you do that for? He almost got you killed!" The blind man retorted, "I did it so I could locate his mouth and know where his tail is, so I could kick it!"

We need to stop where we are and take a good look, now!

APPLICATION:
1. Whatever you have been told before about your vision, remind yourself of it.
2. Look, now!

PRAYER:
Lord, I will be stirred again in the vision you have placed in me. Amen.

AUGUST 23
GOD WILL DIRECT YOUR VISION

Job 33:15-16

"In a dream, in a vision of the night, when deep sleep falleth upon men, in slumberings upon the bed; then he openeth the ears of men, and sealeth their instruction." (KJV)

God places His vision inside of His people to bring about His will. God uses the situations we find ourselves in to bring forth things, which can only be accomplished with His help.

Not everybody will be excited about your vision. Joseph was a man with vision. Joseph's brothers envied him because of his dream and resented it. Yet, his vision would be important later, not only for himself, but for his family as well. God placed the vision in him. Even though it seemed the vision would never be realized, the vision came to pass.

Joseph's vision cost him everything including the love and support of his family. Yet, the vision was from God, and God was responsible for helping Joseph walk in the reality of it.

Every person has a vision from Heaven inside of him/her just waiting for them to find and pursue it. Vision breeds excitement. It stirs up the insides of a person and causes them to alter things to help accomplish the vision. It causes one to understand the larger picture of his/her life and destiny.

Here are some important facts about vision. First, people get mad when you have vision and they do not. They resent that you have heard from God and have a direction for your life. Second, you have to be where there is a vision to keep a vision. It is very difficult to maintain a vision in an environment that does not recognize vision. You have to be around people who have vision. Third, you have to do things that help position yourself to capture your vision. Put yourself in places, which will educate, train and develop you in the area of the vision you have. God has always given vision to His people. His vision is inside of you!

APPLICATION:
1. Take some time to pray over and consider the vision God has given you.
2. Fuel your vision with the Word of God by finding and quoting scripture relative to your vision.

PRAYER:
Lord, your vision is in my heart and I will pursue it. Amen.

My vision - to write and to speak

AUGUST 24
A SPECIAL GOD FOR A SPECIAL PEOPLE

Deuteronomy 7:6-7
"For thou art an Holy people unto the LORD thy God: the LORD thy God hath chosen thee to be special people unto himself, above all people that are upon the face of the earth. The LORD did not set his love upon you, nor choose you, because ye were more in number than any people; for ye were the fewest of all people:" (KJV)

The Bible is really a true romance story. It is a story of how God loved His people so much, He endured their rejection, their rebellion and their unbelief. It is a story of how God called them "special" and "married" Himself to them.

God has called you special! The Hebrew word for special is *c'gullah* (seg-ool-law), which means "shut up or stored up; treasure; stored up treasure." God considers you to be a stored up treasure. He has confidence in you when you do not have confidence in yourself. According to Matthew 13:44-46, you are like a treasure hidden in the field. You are a pearl of great price. You are the sum total of all that is lovely. You have been found. You have been purchased.

God has made some special promises for you. First of all, He has a special plan for a special people. Jeremiah 29:11-14 says He has a special plan for your life and future, which is good. Second, He has a special praise for a special people. Our praise summons the forces of Heaven and stops the forces of darkness. According to I Peter 2:4-9, we are the original rolling stones! Third, He has a special peace for a special people. The word *peace* in the New Testament is *eirene* (I-ray-nay). It means "to join, to set again in rest and quietness." He gives His people peace even when Hell is trying to close in on every side. Fourth, He has a special passion for a special people. Passion equals love. Ephesians 3:15-20 talks about His great love. In the Greek translation, love has many expressions and is large and ever expanding. Finally, He has a special place for a special people. Heaven in Hebrews 11:13-16 is defined as, *"the heights, His eternal abiding place!"* (KJV) We serve a special God. He has called you special!

APPLICATION:
1. Remind yourself, today, of how special you are to Him.
2. See yourself the way He does. You are His prized possession!

PRAYER:
Lord, thank you for considering me to be special! Amen.

AUGUST 25
HE WILL NOT FORGET YOU

Isaiah 49:15-16

*"Can a woman forget her sucking child, that she should not have compassion
on the son of her womb? Yea, they may forget, yet will I not forget thee. Behold I
have graven thee upon the palms of my hands; thy walls
are continually before me."* (KJV)

As a parent, there are so many things which remind me of our children. Even
when they are grown, it seems everywhere we look in our house we are reminded
of them. There are pictures everywhere of special moments, holidays and events.
We captured these moments, so we would always be reminded of them. It is the
same way with our Lord. We are graven in His hands. Even after He was raised
from the dead, He still had the holes in His hands that reminded Him of us. This
scripture in Isaiah was prophetic of Jesus taking the nails in His hands. The
same hands He showed Thomas after His resurrection when Thomas doubted.
Whenever we doubt whether He is reminded of us, we have to look again at the
nail prints in His hands. Jeremiah 31:3 says He loves us with an everlasting love,
which cannot be exhausted. Tony Campolo said, "God carries your picture in His
wallet." He shows it to His angels in Heaven. He is proud to be your Father!

The true measure of the depth of your faith is directly tied to the depth of your
comprehension of God's love for you. John 19:26 speaks of the disciple Jesus
loved! John had such a revelation of Jesus' great love for him that he was the only
disciple at the cross! Tradition reveals John was the only disciple who was not
martyred for his faith. Galatians 5:6 reveals faith worketh, or is energized, by how
much we understand God loves us. Saint Augustine of Hippo said, "God loves
each of us as if there were only one of us."

John 3:16 really shows us we are always on His mind. Psalms 17:8 says, *"You
are the apple of His eye."* (KJV) When you start thinking He has forgotten you,
remember the scars in His hands!

APPLICATION:
   1. Stop and think about the scars in His hands.
   2. When you feel unloved or unappreciated, remember the great love He has
      for you!

PRAYER:
Lord, thank you for not forgetting me! Amen.

AUGUST 26
WHAT WILL YOU DO WITH YOUR DREAM?

Daniel 4:9

"O Belteshazzar, master of the magicians, because I know that the spirit of the Holy gods is in thee, and no secret troubleth thee, tell me the visions of my dream that I have seen, and the interpretation thereof." (KJV)

We have to decide what we will do with the dream inside of us. We cannot let the critics define who we are. Critics are nothing more than dream killers most of the time.

Fred Astaire was given a memo after his first screen test, which read, "Can't act. Slightly bald. Can dance a little." He kept the memo over his Beverly Hills fireplace, alongside his numerous awards.

Everyday of your life is a day you should be moving towards the purpose you have been born for. As Alexander Wolcott said "There is no such thing in anyone's life as an unimportant day." This is the day the Lord has made!

To move towards your dream it only takes a little momentum to get you moving that direction. Sometimes you have to make your own momentum. An old proverb says, "If there is no wind when you sail, ROW!"

There was a man who had an older brother who was killed in World War II. He missed him so much. He withdrew into a shell. He started listening to the radio to soothe his pain. He dreamed of hosting his own radio show. That man was *American Bandstand's*, Dick Clark!

You cannot always trust other people's evaluation of your ability. God knows what you are capable of when others doubt. Walt Disney was fired by a newspaper when he was younger because he lacked imagination and ideas!

When people try to take your dream away or try to get you to abandon it, be sure you do not let go. If God has placed it in your heart, then it will come to pass. What will you do with your dream?

APPLICATION:
1. Guard the dream God has placed in your life.
2. As long as you know it is a God-given, God-driven dream, do not abandon it for any reason!

PRAYER:
Lord, thank you for the dream in my life. I will not let it die. Amen.

AUGUST 27
THE SAME JESUS

Hebrews 13:8
"Jesus Christ, the same yesterday, today and forever." (KJV)

Jesus is the same. He is the same one and true living God who came in the flesh for a lost and dying world. Matthew 21:42 tells us the same is the head of the corner. A cornerstone is the critical stone stabilizing the foundation. You can rely on Him!

Acts 2:33-36 reveals the same is at the right hand of God. He is waiting for two things: for us to walk in His grace and for the Church to use its authority to bring the works of darkness down.

John 1:1 tells us He is the same Jesus who was in the beginning. He created everything we see and became flesh for all of mankind to identify with. His power has not diminished. He is still the Lion of the Tribe of Judah!

John 1:29-34 says He is the same one who takes away the sin of the world— your yesterday. He erased your past sins and transgressions.

John 5:1-4 states He is the same Jesus who does something about your today. He is ready, willing and able to step into your troubles and struggles. He helps you overcome adversity and causes you to rise above it and become victorious.

Acts 1:11 says, *"Why stand ye gazing up into Heaven? This same Jesus, which is taken up from you into Heaven, shall so come in like manner as ye have seen him go into Heaven."* (KJV) He is your tomorrow. He has already prepared your future and provided everything you will need along life's way to find your way to the finish line. As a believer in Jesus Christ, you have an eternal life ahead, which will be far beyond anything you have ever dared to dream.

The Lord we serve is still the King of Kings and the Lord of Lords! He is the same yesterday, today and tomorrow!

APPLICATION:
1. Remind yourself the Lord you serve is still the same one who turned the world upside down at just 31 ½ years old!
2. Do not let the world you live in deceive you. Jesus is still alive and well, and full of grace and power!

PRAYER:
Lord, I do believe you are the same yesterday, today and forever. I know there is nothing too hard for you! Amen.

AUGUST 28
THE VALUE OF ENCOURAGEMENT

Isaiah 41:6-7

"They helped every one his neighbour; and every one said to his brother, Be of good courage. So the carpenter encouraged the goldsmith, and he that smootheth with the hammer him that smote the anvil, saying, It is ready for the sodering: and he fastened it with nails, that it should not be moved." (KJV)

More people fail because of lack of encouragement than for any other reason. Without encouragement along life's way, fear, distress and boredom set in. Everybody needs encouragement. Even those you think have it together, need some encouragement.

I remember a particular service at church where I was led to have an open forum and do a Q&A with the children. I asked each child what they wanted to be. When I spoke a word of encouragement about their possible choices, they began to glow and you could see the courage come up in them. We should speak encouraging words.

What is encouragement? It is "to comment, to inspire with courage, spirit or confidence; to stimulate by guidance, approval, etc." It also means "to promote; foster; inspire, give confidence to, inspirit, embolden, induce, give hope to, hearten, rally, egg on; spur, exhort, impel, sway, reassure, hearten, cheer, boost forward."

Proverbs 18:4 says, *"Wise words are like deep waters; wisdom flows from the wise like a bubbling brook."* (NLT)

We need encouraging people in our lives. Paul had Barnabas, whose very name means "Son of Encouragement." (Acts 4:36; Acts 11:22-25) Barnabas played a major role in encouraging and assisting Paul into the next level of his ministry. Additionally, Jesus was an encourager. (Luke 21:31-32) He offered His wisdom and guidance to many.

Of all things provoking us not to quit, encouragement is extremely valuable.

APPLICATION:

    1. Are you encouraged in the life God has given you?

    2. Be sure to encourage those around you everyday!

PRAYER:

Lord, I will be encouraged in you and I will encourage others! Amen.

AUGUST 29
BE COMPLIMENTARY

Proverbs 25:11
"A word fitly spoken is like apples of gold in settings of silver." (NKJV)

Sometimes we have to encourage ourselves. I Samuel 30:6 says David did when others were ready to stone him. Sometimes, no matter how bleak the situation may be, you have to accentuate the positive. It is like the little league pitcher who pitched a no hitter and lost 13-0 (he walked 18 batters)! His father calmed him by saying, "At least they didn't get a hit off of you!"

Sometimes we have to be able to see another possibility. It is like the little boy with the bat and baseball. The boy kept throwing the ball up in the air trying to hit it while saying, "I'm the greatest hitter in the world!" After several times of missing the ball, he came to a realization. He said, "Hey! I'm the greatest pitcher in the world!"

There was a boxer who was knocked out in the 12th round. His trainer was an eternal optimist who excelled in finding ways to encourage this young contender. When the boxer regained consciousness, his trainer smiled and said, "Hey kid! You came in second!"

The legendary UCLA basketball coach, John Wooden, understood the importance of giving compliments and his players applied it. Wooden instructed his players that whenever a basket was made, the scoring player was required to smile, wink or nod at the player who passed him the ball. When Coach Wooden gave these instructions to the team, one new player asked, "But Coach, what if he's not looking?" Wooden replied, "I guarantee he'll look." He was right. Everyone is looking for encouragement and affirmation.

When the Duke of Wellington was asked near the end of his life what one thing would he change, if he could live his life again? He replied, "I would give more praise."

If we will be sensitive to those we come in contact with and be willing to be complimentary, then God will surely send someone to us to encourage us when we need it most!

APPLICATION:
1. Today, look for people you are around and encourage them by positively complimenting them.
2. Start with those you love.

PRAYER:
Lord, lead me to those who need encouragement, today. Amen.

AUGUST 30
LIVING A FEARLESS LIFE

Psalms 118:6
"The Lord is on my side; I will not fear. What can man do unto me?" (KJV)

Fear is believing the lies of the Devil. It is the expectation of unwanted events. Fear is the natural feeling of alarm caused by the expectation of imminent danger, pain or disaster. The Old Testament word for fear is *yare'* (yaw-ray') which means "terrify, dreadful." The New Testament word is *phobos* or phobia. It means "dark anticipation of." Fear, not dealt with, will affect every area of your life. Fear drives the courage out of people and replaces it with timidity and cowardice.

According to II Timothy 1:7, fear is a spirit. This verse tells us the counter to fear is power: spiritual plane (spirit), love—emotional plane (soul) and sound mind/mental—(body).

Paul had a revelation of God's love for him and it caused him to live a fearless life. He counted everything as a loss except Christ! Paul knew the young pastor, Timothy, had a battle with the spirit of fear. Timothy was fearful when he heard Stephen had been stoned, the disciples had been beaten and Paul had been ship-wrecked. Timothy must have been unsure if the ministry was his best move!

Max Lucado said, "Fear. His modus operandi is to manipulate you with the mysterious, to taunt you with the unknown: fear of death, fear of failure, fear of God and fear of tomorrow. His arsenal is vast. His goal? To create cowardly, joyless souls. He doesn't want you to make the journey to the mountain. He figures if he can rattle you enough, you will take your eyes off the peaks and settle for a dull existence in the flatlands."

However, according to II Timothy 1:7, God has not given us the Spirit of fear. Fear is the work of darkness! God has given us the necessary weapons we need to resist fear and to walk in faith. We can live a fearless life!

APPLICATION:
1. Do not let the phobias of this life keep you from enjoying the life God has given you.
2. Remember, God is on your side! You are not alone in your life!

PRAYER:
Lord, help me to stand in faith and not be terrorized by the fear the enemy tries to get me to give into. Amen.

AUGUST 31
NO NEED TO FEAR

Isaiah 43:1-5

"But now thus saith the LORD that created thee, O Jacob, and he that formed thee, O Israel, Fear not: for I have redeemed thee, I have called thee by name; thou art mine. When thou passest through the waters, I will be with thee; and through the rivers, they shall not overflow thee: when thou walkest through the fire, thou shalt not be burned; neither shall the flame kindle upon thee. For I am the LORD thy God, the Holy One of Israel, thy Savior: I gave Egypt for thy ransom, Ethiopia and Seba for thee. Since thou wast precious in my sight, thou hast been honourable, and I have loved thee: therefore will I give men for thee, and people for thy life. Fear not: for I am with thee: I will bring thy seed from the east, and gather thee from the west;" (KJV)

Do you know the facts surrounding the construction of the Golden Gate Bridge of San Francisco? When it was being built, workers developed a great fear of falling. Bridge builders had a superstition that one man would die for every one million dollars spent on the project. The bridge was budgeted for 35 million dollars, so the fear was pervasive. The chief engineer, Joseph Strauss, also believed three dozen men could fall to their deaths. The impact of falling from the bridge to the water below is equivalent to hitting a brick wall at 80 miles per hour. To counter the sure fear the workers would face, Strauss made an unprecedented move and ordered a large trapeze net to be placed under the workers. Bridge builders had never enjoyed such a luxury, and the added security made them feel as though they could, as one worker said, "dance on the steel." The result, not even one man fell into the net! When the element of fear was removed, the workers excelled.

We must realize God has promised us He would defend us, keep us and preserve us. We have the "net" of His love, the "net" of His Spirit and the "net" of His angels to catch us whenever we are in a state of peril. Whenever an ominous presence comes on you, remember, you have been redeemed from fear!

APPLICATION:
  1. Do not accept the spirit of fear!
  2. Trust God for your peace and protection.

PRAYER:
Lord, help me stand in your peace and not fear! Amen.

SEPTEMBER 1
LOVE, THE ANSWER TO FEAR

I John 4:18
"There is no fear in love; but perfect love casteth out fear: because fear hath torment. He that feareth is not made perfect in love." (KJV)

Perfect love casts out fear. This thought is best illustrated in a story I heard about a Spanish father and his estranged son. The son left home, and the father later set out to find him. He searched for months, with no success. Desperate, the father turned to the newspaper for help. His ad simply read, "Dear Paco, meet me in front of the newspaper office at noon on Saturday. All is forgiven. I love you, Your Father." Saturday, 800 men named Paco showed up looking for forgiveness from their estranged fathers! Once these young men discovered their supposed father had forgiven them and still loves them, the fear separating them lost its power!

The world is filled with people who have been separated by fear. The antidote for that kind of fear is love. When we really get a revelation of God's love for us, we will not fear. When we realize we are covered in a love that is forgiving, understanding, patient and longsuffering, fear has no place in our lives. When we remind ourselves we are protected by a love that has gone the distance for us by taking our punishment and securing our lives eternally, fear has no space in our hearts.

We have been made alive in an endless love; a love whose thread runs throughout everything pertaining to our lives. Joy is tied to the love of God. He who fears death cannot enjoy life. Faith is tied to the love of God. (John 13:1-4, 23; 19:25-27; 20:2-4; 21:7; I John 5:3-4) Evangelism is tied to the love of God! (Matthew 28:19) The Gospel is simply—God loves you.

We need to show others His love. A revelation of God's love for us is the answer to fear.

APPLICATION:
1. When fear tries to grip your heart, remind yourself of God's love for you.
2. The more you meditate on His love for you, the more perfect it becomes.

PRAYER:
Lord, I confess your great love for me and I have no fear. Amen.

SEPTEMBER 2
EIGHT QUESTIONS ABOUT YESTERDAY

Luke 2:46
"And it came to pass, that after three days they found him in the temple, sitting in the midst of the doctors, both hearing them, and asking them questions."
(KJV)

Jesus was very inquisitive. Even as a young man, he was found in the temple asking hard questions of the priests. Yet, are we willing to ask hard questions of ourselves?

What was yesterday like for you? Was it a hard day? Were there things you could have used God's help with? By examining some hard questions about yesterday, we can see how things might have been better.

Did you look to Heaven for help? In Matthew 14:15-21, Jesus looked unto Heaven, prayed and a miracle took place. Psalms 121:1 says, *"I will lift up mine eyes unto the hills, whence cometh my help."* (KJV)

Did you believe God for the impossible? In Mark 10:27, we read, *"...with men this is impossible, but with God all things are possible."* (KJV) Hebrews 11:6 says we must *"...believe that He is and is a rewarder of them who diligently seek Him."* (KJV)

Did you stretch yourself? In Luke 6:10, Jesus told the man with the withered hand to stretch it forth. When he stretched it forth, it was healed. Did you do something that was beyond your ability?

Did you make excuses instead of pressing on? Luke 9:58-62 says, *"...no man putting forth his hand to the plow and looking back is fit for the kingdom of God."* (KJV) Complaining or not accepting responsibility keeps you from the miraculous.

Did you let fear get the best of you? Luke 21:26 states, *"Men's hearts failing them for fear..."* (KJV) In the novel *Robinson Crusoe* the good man, Friday, asks Robinson, "Why doesn't God destroy the Devil?" Robinson Crusoe gave him the right answer, the only answer, the great answer. He said, "God will destroy him."

Did you recognize and proclaim Jesus as Lord? In John 1:36, John said, *"Behold the Lamb of God..."* (KJV)

Did you live as though you were ready for His return? Titus 2:13 says we should be looking for His appearance. Jesus is coming!

Did you walk in love with others? Jude 1:21 reveals that walking in love keeps you in the mercy of God.

If you had answered, "Yes," to all eight questions, what would yesterday have been like?

271

APPLICATION:
1. Be sure to ask yourself hard questions.
2. Make adjustments to position yourself for improvement.

PRAYER:
Lord, forgive me for not asking myself the hard questions. Amen.

SEPTEMBER 3
THE BELIEVER'S CROWNS

II Chronicles 23:11
"Then they brought out the king's son, and put upon him the crown, and gave him the testimony, and made him king." (KJV)

According to the Bible, there are different types of crowns we may obtain. These are Heavenly crowns God will present to us when we stand before Him in Heaven.

First, there is the incorruptible crown. I Corinthians 9:24 says, *"Know ye not that they which run in a race run all, but one receiveth the prize? So run, that ye may obtain. And every man that striveth for the mastery is temperate in all things. Now they do it to obtain a corruptible crown; but we an incorruptible."* (KJV) This crown is presented to those who have lived a truly disciplined life. Self must be conquered. Second, there is the crown of rejoicing. I Thessalonians 2:19-20 says, *"For what is our hope, or joy, or crown of rejoicing?"* (KJV) This crown is for those who have been soul winners. The angels rejoice over one sinner who repents! Third, there is the crown of life. James 1:12 says, *"Blessed is the man that endureth temptation: for when he is tried, he shall receive the crown of life, which the Lord hath promised to them that love him."* (KJV) This crown is not given to every believer who is tried, but to every believer who endures! Fourth, there is the crown of glory. I Peter 5:4 says, *"And when the chief Shepherd shall appear, ye shall receive a crown of glory that fadeth not away."* (KJV) This crown is especially for those who lead and shepherd God's people. It entails caring for God's people through unselfish and willing service. Last, there is the crown of righteousness. II Timothy 4:8 says, *"Henceforth there is laid up for me a crown of righteousness, which the Lord, the righteous judge, shall give me at that day: and not to me only, but unto all them also that love his appearing."* (KJV) This crown is for those looking for His appearance and return with love.

So, remember, everything we go through and do as believers does not just affect today, but also our life to come. We will be eligible for the believer's crowns!

APPLICATION:
1. Consider the things you are doing and how they affect the crowns God has for you.
2. Thank God for the rewards of today and tomorrow.

PRAYER:
Lord, I am thankful for the crowns ahead. Amen.

SEPTEMBER 4
TAKING THE RIGHT ROAD

Deuteronomy 30:19
"I call Heaven and earth to record this day against you, that I have set before you life and death, blessing and cursing: therefore choose life, that both thou and thy seed may live." (KJV)

What is a crossroad? It is "a road that crosses another road or one that runs transversely to main roads; an intersection; a point at which a vital decision must be made."

Everyday, we face a multitude of decisions. Psychologists estimate we make about 1,200 decisions per day, when everyday minor decisions are calculated into the equation!

There is no doubt, the power to choose is the greatest power we possess. Our choices take us either closer to our desired destination or remove us further from it.

God desires to give us guidance for our lives. The Hebrew word for guide is *daw-rak*. It means "to bend, lead or direct towards something specific." We must let Him lead us. There is a right way that will take us to the right place. He will teach us how to make the right decisions at the right time. If you do not learn to make good decisions when you are at a crossroad, decisions will be made for you.

Ronald Reagan told of a shoemaker who was making a pair of shoes for him when he was a lad. The cobbler asked Ronald if he wanted a square or round toe. Ronald was unsure, so the cobbler told him to return in a day or two and let him know what he had decided. Ronald was still undecided. The cobbler told him the shoes would be ready the next day. When Ronald picked up the shoes, one had a round toe and one had a square toe. As an adult, Reagan commented, "Looking at those shoes taught me a lesson. If you don't make your own decisions, somebody else makes them for you."

Are you at a crossroad in your life today? Be sure to get His guidance before you go any further.

APPLICATION:
1. Ask God, today, to direct your decisions.
2. Follow His lead.

PRAYER:
Lord, I will follow your lead and choose the right road. Amen.

SEPTEMBER 5
EVERYBODY NEEDS A DREAM

Job 33:14-16

"For God speaketh once, yea twice, yet man perceiveth it not. In a dream, in a vision of the night, when deep sleep falleth upon men, in slumberings upon the bed; Then he openeth the ears of men and sealeth their instruction." (KJV)

Someone once wrote, "The poorest of all men is not the man without a cent, but the man without a dream." God will help you find, follow and finish your dream.

We need to be dream builders. We have been given a supernatural future by a supernatural God. All we need to realize our dreams is to have His light. He gives us the Word for our future before we can even conceive it.

Abraham was given a focal point. Noah was given a mandate. David was given a challenge. Joseph was given a prophecy. All were given something to dream about that was impossible, except through God. Each one became a reality. Michelangelo said, "Lord, grant that I may always desire more than I can accomplish."

Every dream must be cultivated. The Wall Street Journal had a full-page message entitled, *It's What You Do, Not When You Do It*. The message contained a listing of many eagle-like people who soared at various ages in their lives. Ted Williams, at age 42, slammed a home run in his last official time at bat. Mickey Mantle, at age 20, hit 23 home runs his first full year in the major leagues. Golda Meir was 71 when she became the Prime Minister of Israel. William Pitt II was 24 when he became the Prime Minister of Great Britain. George Bernard Shaw was 94 when one of his plays was first produced. Mozart was just seven when his first composition was published. Benjamin Franklin was a newspaper columnist at 16 and a framer of the United States Constitution when he was 81.

You are never too young, or too old, if you have a dream. Just ask Joash. He began to reign at seven years old! Just ask Noah. He was 500 years old when he built the ark!

Everyone needs a dream. Do you have one?

APPLICATION:
   1. Place the dream of your heart before God.
   2. Remember, He makes the impossible, possible!

PRAYER:
Lord, stir up the God given dream of my heart. Amen.

SEPTEMBER 6
BEHOLD, HERE COMES THE DREAMER

Ecclesiastes 5:3
"For a dream cometh through the multitude of business…" (KJV)

How do you find your dream? Sometimes it comes in everyday affairs of life. You may be doing the required, daily things and in the midst of them, discover your dream.

God speaks repetitiously. He leads us to our dreams, many times through our desires. By our natural inclination towards something, God brings us to a place where it becomes more than just our occupation. The whole time David was tending sheep and fighting off predators, he was being groomed to tend to a nation and fight off its enemies. The whole time Saul (Paul) was becoming politically popular and terrorizing Christians, he was being groomed to go before kings and leaders, and speak for Christianity.

Sometimes your dream comes through Godly men and women. Jeremiah 23:28 says, *"The prophet that hath a dream, let him tell a dream; and he that hath my word, let him speak my word faithfully."* (KJV) God will send trustworthy people into your life to validate what He has already placed in your heart. Not just anyone is qualified to interpret the dream God has given you. Only God appointed men and women should be given that place in your life.

Rick →

It is like the story of Uncle Irve and Aunt Harriet. After Aunt Harriet woke up, she told Uncle Irve, "I just dreamed you gave me a pearl necklace for Valentine's Day. What do you think that means?" "You'll find out tonight," he said. That evening, Uncle Irve came home with a package and gave it to his wife. Delighted, she opened it to find a book entitled, *The Meaning of Dreams*!

You cannot always share your dreams with everyone. After Joseph told his brothers about his dream, they tried to kill him and sold him away as a slave. They said, *"Here comes that dreamer. Then we'll see what becomes of his dreams."* (Genesis 37:19-20 NIV)

So, what will bring you into your destiny? What will they say about you? Behold, here comes the dreamer!

APPLICATION:
Writing
1. Write down the dream God has placed in your heart.
2. Find someone who is trusted and ask them to pray for you and speak into your life concerning your dream.

PRAYER:
Lord, I will pursue the dream you have given me with faith. Amen.

I've begun the blog and have seen it speak into the few followers of the page. Bigger - deeper - thank you, Lord

276

SEPTEMBER 7
DREAM KILLERS

Judges 7:15

*"When Gideon heard about man's dream and what it meant, he fell to his knees
and worshipped the LORD. Then he went back to the Israelite camp and said,
"Get up! The LORD is giving you victory over the Midianite army!"* (TEV)

It would be great if everyone who came along in your life was a dream builder.
Yet, many people are dream killers. David's brothers scoffed the notion of him
being able to enter the battle against the Philistines and Goliath. Noah could not
convince anyone, except family, to enter the ark. It is critical we understand there
are people who are dream killers.

Additionally, there are also things we do to kill our dreams. Here are some
dream killers: First, failing to forgive. Philippians 4:2 says, *"I beseech Euodias,
and beseech Syntyche, that they be the same mind in the Lord."* (KJV) This was
the only time they were mentioned. Do not let your failure to forgive others be
your legacy. The second is listening to hopeless people. Job 2:9 says, *"Then said
his (Job's) wife unto him, Dost thou still retain thine integrity? Curse God, and
die?"* (KJV) The third way is failure to have confidence in your faith. Hebrews
10:35 says, *"Cast not away therefore your confidence, which hath great recompense of reward."* (KJV) The fourth is becoming impatient with the process or
procrastination. Hebrews 10:36-37 says, *"For ye have need of patience, that,
after ye have done the will of God, ye might receive the promise. For yet a little
while, and he that shall come will come, and will not tarry."* (KJV) If you wait
for perfect conditions, you will never get anything done. The fifth factor is giving
in to adversity. Proverbs 24:10 says, *"If thou faint in the day of adversity, thy
strength is small."* (KJV) George Santayana said, "The difficult is that which can
be done immediately; the impossible is that which takes a little longer!" The sixth
is distancing oneself from the leader. Acts 27:11 says, *"Nevertheless the centurion
believed the master and the owner of the ship, more than those things which were
spoken by Paul."* (KJV) Leadership helps people accomplish what they would
not have accomplished alone. The final way is not plugging into someone else's
dream. By assisting others in the accomplishment of their dream, you will propel
towards your own!

APPLICATION:
1. Do not let anyone or anything kill your dream.
2. Keep your dream alive by following the right people.

PRAYER:
Lord, I will protect my dream from the dream killers. Amen.

277

SEPTEMBER 8
WINNING YOUR FAMILY TO GOD

Psalms 68:6
"He gives families to the lonely, and releases prisoners from jail, singing with joy! But for rebels there is famine and distress." (TLB)

God has commissioned the family. Family is before church in the Bible. In the Garden of Eden, He brought the first family together. He instituted the importance of the family structure. However, the enemy came and attacked immediately and has continued to assault the family unit ever since.

When you become a Christian, God had more in His mind than just saving you. God saved you to make a doorway to get the rest of your family to Heaven.

We should have a burden for our family's salvation. It seems we esteem strangers sometimes more than we do our own families. Ella Wheeler Wilcox wrote, "We flatter those we scarcely know. We please the fleeting guest, and deal full many a thoughtless blow to those who love us best. I sought my soul, but my soul eluded me; I sought my God; but my God eluded me; I sought my brother, and found all three."

A twelve year old boy carrying a smaller boy all over a playground was asked by a man, "Don't you get tired from carrying such a heavy, little boy around?" He replied, "Heck no, mister! He ain't heavy; he's my brother!"

When God saw the wickedness of man in Genesis 6, He ensured that before the destruction came forth on the earth, He spared the family. The preservation of the family was preeminent over everything else.

Acts 2:17 says the Spirit will be poured out on sons and daughters. Jesus also showed us the importance of looking out for family in the worse moment of His life. Jesus passed the care of his mother to John while on the cross. (John 19:25-28) All things were not accomplished until he arranged for His mother's care. We also see after Andrew heard Jesus for the first time, he went to his brother first. He told him the Good News. He brought him to Jesus.

As we become soul winners, we must place our own families at the top of that list.

APPLICATION:
1. Be sure to reach out to your own family.
2. Use your faith to get them to Christ.

PRAYER:
Lord, I pray for my family and believe for their salvation. Amen.

SEPTEMBER 9
SAVING YOUR HOUSE

Acts 16:31-32

"And they said, Believe on the Lord Jesus Christ, and thou shalt be saved, and thy house. And they spake unto him the word of the Lord, and to all that were in his house." (KJV)

We should all believe God for the salvation of our families. We have a responsibility to teach our children about Jesus and God. However, sometimes winning your family to God is harder than winning the world! There is an order that brings about a harvest in your family. This begins with someone believing and seeing their entire household saved. Yet, how do we convince people in our own house to become believers?

First of all, there must be a move of God in your life. You cannot tell them how to live if you do not show them. Second, you must be a person who consistently praises God. If you only praise God in the good times, and not the bad, you show your own lack of faith. Third, you must ask for light. It takes God revealing the hidden things to you that will make a difference in your witness to them. Fourth, you must ask for their salvation. Daily, place their names before Heaven. Persistence is the key! Fifth, you must believe for them. You cannot let the negative things you see in them cause doubt inside of you. Sixth, you must invite the presence of God into your house. When God's presence invades a house, the heaviness is lifted off. Seventh, you must give an offering to the Lord's ministry. Alms giving is a back breaker to the Devil. Let God lead you in what you should do. Eighth, you must rejoice! Begin rejoicing, daily, as if they are already serving God. This establishes your faith. Ninth, you must share your testimony and faith with your family. Be selective about the time and the content. Your testimony is your strongest evidence of God's grace. People in your family know you better than anyone else, and your transformation! Your family needs to see the Christ in you.

God will give you the grace you need to win your family to Him. Pray daily over their lives with the confidence He is already at work in their lives, and that it is only a matter of time before they respond to His call!

APPLICATION:
1. Place your families on the altar, daily.
2. Do not let anything discourage you. You have His promise!

PRAYER:
Lord, I believe you for every one of my family members. I believe not one will be lost! Amen.

SEPTEMBER 10
OUR HOUSE WILL SERVE THE LORD

Joshua 24:15
"And if it seem evil unto you to serve the LORD, choose you this day whom ye will serve; whether the gods which your fathers served that were on the other side of the flood, or the gods of the Amorites, in whose land ye dwell: but as for me and my house, we will serve the LORD." (KJV)

In his autobiography, Jonny Cash tells the story of his older brother, Jack, who was only 14 when he died. Jack worked at the high school agricultural shop, where he had a job cutting oak trees into fence posts. The money he earned helped support their family, who was struggling to survive by working in the cotton fields in rural Arkansas. A terrible accident occurred one day. A table saw severely cut Jack, resulting in his death a few days later. Sometime before his death, Jack had announced to his family and the community that he intended to be a preacher. Everyone agreed he would make a fine preacher, for his strong Christian character was already well known.

Johnny Cash looked up to his older brother and Jack's example, which influenced him until he died. Cash wrote, "Jack isn't really gone, anyway, any more than anyone is. For one thing, his influence on me is profound. When we were kids, he tried to turn me away from the way of death to the way of life, to steer me toward the light, and since he died his words and his example have been like signposts for me. The most important question in many of the conundrums and crises of my life has been, 'Which is Jack's way? Which direction would he have taken?' I haven't always gone that way, of course, but at least I've known where it was."

The direction of your house towards God is certain when you follow these things. First, you must be patient with your family. Second, you must be willing to listen to their problems. Third, you must be willing to forgive. Fourth, you must stand in the gap for them and pray. Fifth, you must fast for them. Sixth, you must trust the Word of God to come to pass. Seventh, you must speak life over them. Eighth, you must not judge them; you must love them! If you do these things, the day will come when your family will serve the Lord!

APPLICATION:
1. Start believing for your family, today.
2. Proclaim your family is saved!

PRAYER:
Lord, as for me and my house, we will serve you! Amen.

SEPTEMBER 11
IS THERE NOT A CAUSE?

I Samuel 17:29
"And David said, What have I now done? Is there not a cause?" (KJV)

I am not sure what the news headlines would have been on September 11, 2001, had there been no attacks on the United States, but whatever they would have been became irrelevant after the events that bright, sunny September morning. In fact, I do not think I remember any other news being broadcast. The news that day reminded everyone we live in a sadly fallen world. All of America, and most of the world found a common thread to wrap itself around that day—the fight against terrorism.

For people to come together, there must be a common cause. There must be a common interest, which provokes people to lay aside their differences to rally around something more important. The scene on Capitol Hill in the days following September 11th showed the Republican President, George W. Bush, hugging the Democratic Majority Leader, Tom Daschle. The Senators from both sides were sitting side by side; the congressmen and congresswomen were standing side by side. America, at least for a season, was truly united. It should not have taken a September 11th type of event to cause God's people to come together. We still have the same common enemy—Satan. He always comes to steal, kill and destroy. We certainly should be shoulder to shoulder in the fight everyday and not just in times of conflict!

We have common reasons, which should cause us to come together for the building of God's Kingdom. The results for standing together for a cause include:

1. Jesus speaks when we come together. (Luke 8:4)
2. It brings safety to us. (Proverbs 24:5)
3. It brings the Spirit of God to us. (Acts 2:1-4)
4. It provides us with a time to learn of others and to become servants to those around us. There is a time to stand together. (Isaiah 50:8)
5. There is freedom when you stand together. (Ezra 8:11)
6. There is peace when you stand together. (Philippians 1:27)
7. There is power when you stand together. (Acts 1:15)

How prophetic were the words of J.B. Priestley, 18th century scientist, "We are members of one body. We are responsible for each other. And the time will soon come when, if men will not learn that lesson, then they will be thought it in fire and blood and anguish."

Is there not a cause, today?

APPLICATION:
1. Find common ground, today, to stand with someone.
2. Eliminate disagreements.

PRAYER:
Lord, I will stand for the righteous cause of my faith! Amen.

SEPTEMBER 12
BE CONSISTENT

Ecclesiastes 9:11
"I returned, and saw under the sun, that the race is not to the swift, nor the battle to the strong, neither yet bread to the wise, nor yet riches to men of understanding, nor yet favour to men of skill; but time and change happeneth to them all." (KJV)

Joseph Joubert said, "Chance generally favors the prudent." In other words, people who are wise and follow right things consistently seem to have better "chances" than those who are careless and lazy!

What is consistency? Consistency is "the steadfast adherence to the same principles, course; believing in and being dedicated to a cause with the confidence that it will turn out well."

You are in training for the contests of life. Without being consistent in your pursuits, you will not be successful in the long term. In baseball, for instance, a good ball player must prove himself by being consistent throughout the season, and also throughout his career, to be considered one of the greatest. Cal Ripkin, Jr. was the epitome of consistency. He holds the record for consecutive starts at nearly 3,000 games. He is not in the top 10 in RBI's. He is not in the top 10 for homeruns in one's career. He is not in the top 10 in batting average. However, his greatness is he could be counted on everyday to play! If our Christian walk was more consistent, we would see far more wins for the cause of Christ. Consistency is learning to continue to do every day what you know will work tomorrow!

There are seven traits of consistency: constant performance, undeviating behavior, steady effort, uniform standards, persistence, steadfastness and faithfulness.

Consistency makes up for the deficiencies! It is not dependent on circumstances, but dependent on character. My wife Ginger and I were seriously lacking in numerous ways from being successful pastors for years, but we were consistent. God always rewards consistency! So, no matter how much you may lack in talent, ability or even opportunity, if you are consistent, your time will come!

APPLICATION:
1. Stay on a steady track and do not get weary.
2. Trust that your consistency will bring you the right "chances."

PRAYER:
Lord, I will be consistent in my walk with you! Amen.

SEPTEMBER 13
A FEW GOOD MEN

Isaiah 5:13
"Therefore my people are gone into captivity because they have no knowledge; and their honorable men are famished, and their multitude dried up with thirst."
(KJV)

In the movie, *A Few Good Men*, the defendant was charged with conduct unbecoming of a marine and was discharged. Before he left the courtroom, he saluted the Lieutenant and said, "You don't have to wear a patch on your arm to possess honor."

The Bible is a book of honor. It represents the honor of God to be true and faithful, and His honorable sacrifice to give all for the cause of humanity. Honor is not just a feeling. It has certain attributes. The word *honor* means "to place the highest value on; to dearly prize; to stand for and defend with fervor, be just; fairness and straightforwardness of conduct."

There are two kinds of honor. The first is the honor given to others. Calvin Coolidge said, "No person was ever honored for what he received. Honor has been the reward for what he gave." The second honor is determined by the way you choose to live. Samuel Taylor Coleridge said, "Our own heart, and not other men's opinions, form true honor."

There are many honorable people in the Bible. The following is a list I composed I like to call the "Dandy Dozen."

1. Noah was just a man. His honor was to his God and not man. (Genesis 6:9)
2. Lot could have listened to his wife and longed for Sodom, but he honored God's direction. (Genesis 19)
3. Samuel was pressured to give false prophecies, but he did not. (I Samuel 9:6)
4. David had numerous opportunities to slay Saul, but he honored his position and the anointing placed on him. (I Samuel 22:14)
5. Jabez did not let his name define him. (I Chronicles 4:9)
6. Joseph, Mary's husband, chose not to shame Mary with divorce. (Matthew 1:19)
7. Simeon waited patiently for the arrival of Jesus in the temple. (Luke 2:25)
8. John the Baptist held fast in front of Herod. (Mark 6:20)
9. Joseph of Arimathea sought Jesus' body. (Mark 15:43)
10. The women were Holy and reverent. (Acts 17:4)
11. Cornelius fasted and received a vision. (Acts 10:22)

12. Jesus gave everything for us even though He was innocent! (John 5:30; Acts 3:14; 7:52)

APPLICATION:
1. Are you walking in honor in your life?
2. Choose honor over worldly pressures to advance.

PRAYER:
Lord, I repent for not walking in Biblical honor. Amen.

SEPTEMBER 14
HONOR BRINGS A BLESSING

Exodus 20:12
"...upon the land which the LORD thy God giveth thee." (KJV)

What is the first Commandment with blessing? Honor! It speaks of honoring your parents and it is repeated in the New Testament in Ephesians 6. What is seemingly missing the most in America, today? Honor, especially where honoring parents is concerned.

We are in a time of scandals at every level of society: corporate, CEO's, bank presidents, university presidents and politicians, who talk about honor, but do not even seem to know what it is. Those who rule and lead must be just and honorable.

Honor is out of step in today's world. It is expected and accepted for people to cheat, deceive and lie. In the last quarter of 1999, a new British company opened its doors under the name, "The Alibi Agency." This business was created to provide elaborate alibis for married people who want assistance hiding extramarital affairs from their spouses. For 32 dollars to 40 dollars per use, they will send a falsified invitation to a convention, an imaginary hotel room and a prearranged phone number, which is monitored by an operator who screens all incoming calls. Alibi's director said, "Our clients tell us they'd cheat with or without us, so we provide a necessary service that lets them get away with a casual dalliance without risking the love of their long-term partner." It seems the message is, "It does not pay to be truthful!"

Still, there are great benefits for those who choose honor over deception. The scriptures point out the just and honorable shall prosper in the long run. (Job 27:16-17; Proverbs 13:22) Even our house is blessed. (Proverbs 3:33) Our marriage is blessed. (Hebrews 13:4) We will have blessings and a blessed memory, both mental and memorial (heritage). (Proverbs 10:6-7) No evil will happen to us. (Proverbs 12:21) We may fall, but we shall arise! (Proverbs 24:16) The just shall live by faith. (Habakkuk 2:4; Romans 1:17; Galatians 3:11; Hebrews 10:38)

Despite the unpopularity of being honorable, we should be the best examples possible. Honor is Godly, and Godliness is profitable!

APPLICATION:
1. Are there areas you need to be more honorable in?
2. Are you willing to suffer to be a person of honor?

PRAYER:
Lord, I will choose to honor you and be honorable, even if it is unpopular. Amen.

SEPTEMBER 15
A BLESSING FOR THE WHOLE FAMILY

Genesis 24:51-52

"Behold, Rebekah is before thee, take her, and go, and let her be thy master's son's wife, as the LORD hath spoken. And it came to pass, that, when Abraham's servant heard their words, he worshipped the LORD, lowing himself to the earth. And the servant brought forth jewels of silver, and jewels of gold, and raiment, and gave them to Rebekah: he gave also to her brother and to her mother precious things." (KJV)

God's desire when two families are joined through a marriage is for everyone to be blessed. By Rebekah becoming Isaac's wife, she brought a blessing not only on her own life, but also on the life of her whole family. Rebekah was a very beautiful woman who first caught the eye of Isaac's servants. However, there was something else about her, which struck Isaac's eye—Rebekah believed in the same God he served. This was critically important because it was not advisable to take wives of strange gods. It was believed to break the promise of God's covenant with His people.

When my daughter Rebecca was born, she brought a blessing to everyone, especially me. She was my firstborn child. I was still a young man of only 18 and had my own growing up to do, and she definitely helped me do it! Due to certain circumstances I found myself a single dad for over a year, trying to raise a beautiful, little blonde-haired girl. I did not know how to brush her hair, dress her in the right colors or how to cook anything except macaroni and cheese and sloppy joes. Still, with God's help, we made it! Children are a blessing, even when marriages do not survive. They are the victims of the fallout and they need even more attention and understanding than ever.

As Rebecca grew, we formed as special bond. We both loved music, we both were neat freaks and we both loved playing video games. Some of the best days of my life were times spent in front of the TV playing *Super TecmoBowl* and *Mario Brothers*! She was also a very good student and the first member of our family to earn a college degree. She graduated from the University of Tennessee with honors.

If you are blessed to have children, do not ever look at the time you spend with them as wasted. They are a blessing to the whole family!

GRANDCHILDREN TOO! ♡ Devon coming to dinner tomorrow!

APPLICATION:
1. Make some special time this week with your kids.
2. Recognize the uniqueness of your children.

PRAYER:
Lord, thank you so much for children! Amen.

287

SEPTEMBER 16
NOW I LAY ME DOWN TO SLEEP

Proverbs 3:24

"When thou liest down, thou shalt not be afraid: yea thou shalt lie down, and thy sleep shall be sweet." (KJV)

Sleeplessness is a very serious physical phenomenon. There are many possible causes of insomnia. Sometimes there is one main cause, but often, several factors interacting together will cause a sleep disturbance. The causes of insomnia include: psychological, physical and temporary events or factors.

We all have episodes where our sleep is less than perfect. Insomnia involves sleep problems including difficulty falling asleep, staying asleep or poor quality of sleep. Insomnia should not be confused with sleep deprivation. You can develop sleep deprivation if you are not getting enough sleep, due to a lack of opportunity to sleep.

If you have insomnia or suspect you do, you can take comfort in the fact you are not alone. According to a national survey, 54 percent of adults said they have experienced at least one symptom of insomnia at least a few times a week.

While insomnia is a nighttime problem, it may cause daytime issues as well. People with insomnia often complain about: fatigue and daytime sleepiness, moodiness, irritability or anger, lack of concentration, poor memory, upset stomach, mistakes and accidents at work or while driving. Seeing a doctor is not wrong. God gave us doctors and medicine to give help. While there are medications that can help, the Word of God has a cure for insomnia as well. Psalms 4:8 says: *"I will both lay me down in peace and sleep: for thou, LORD, only makest me dwell in safety."* (KJV) Psalms 127:2 states, *"It is vain for you to rise up early to sit up late, to eat the bread of sorrows: for so he giveth his beloved sleep."* (KJV) Ecclesiastes 5:12 reads, *"The sleep of a labouring man is sweet, whether he eat little or much: but the abundance of the rich will not suffer him to sleep."* (KJV) Jeremiah 31:26 says, *"Upon this I awaked, and beheld; and my sleep was sweet unto me."* (KJV)

If you are having trouble sleeping, read the Word of God and stand on it. Your sleep will be sweet!

APPLICATION:
1. Be sure to meditate on the Word for your sleep.
2. Pray every night before going to bed.

PRAYER:
Lord, thank you for a good, restful night of sweet sleep! Amen.

SEPTEMBER 17
CLOTHED WITH HUMILITY

I Peter 5:5-6

"Likewise, ye younger, submit yourselves unto the elder. Yea, all of you be subject one to another, and be clothed with humility: for God resisteth the proud, and giveth grace to the humble. Humble yourselves therefore under the mighty hand of God, that he may exalt you in due time." (KJV)

Do you know humility is like a garment or a piece of clothing that can be put on? Sometimes we do not feel like wearing it; we want to put on our angry clothes, spiteful clothes or our prideful clothes because they are more in fashion. Yet, humility always fits and is always in style.

Humility is *egkomboomai* (eng-kom-bo'-om-ahee) in the Greek and is always in the middle voice. It is passive alone until desired and activated. The definitions are: "a knot or band by which two things are fastened together; to fasten or grid one's self." This was referring to the white scarf or apron of slaves, which was fastened to the belt of the vest distinguishing slaves from free men, hence identifying them as servants. To walk and live in humility is to be in submission to those whom you are placed in the midst of. I Peter 5:5 says, *"...be clothed with humility: for God resisteth the proud, and giveth grace to the humble." (KJV)* This means by putting on humility we show our subjection one to another.

Humility also suggests an aroma of helplessness. It is the quality which admits there are things we cannot do, problems we cannot solve and forces we cannot control. This "can-not" admission clashes terribly with our "can-do" arrogance.

Humility is the self-recognition everything about your life is God given and you did not accomplish the things of your life without help from those who are stronger than you.

Your job is to humble yourself; God's job is to exalt you. If you do not do your job and humble yourself and exalt yourself, then God will have to do your job and humble you. Put on your "outfit" of humility, today!

APPLICATION:
1. What are you wearing, today?
2. Hang up your pride suit and put on your suit of humility.

PRAYER:
Lord, I choose to humble myself, today, before you and those around me. Amen.

SEPTEMBER 18
THE WAY UP

Luke 1:52
"He has brought down rulers from their thrones but has lifted up the humble."
(NIV)

While God resists those who are proud, He provides grace for the humble. (James 4:6) Sometimes we do not even realize when we are walking in pride.

Don Shula, the legendary coach of the Miami Dolphins, told a humorous story about himself. People who know Coach Shula generally agree he is a very humble man, but even he remembers a day when he let humility slip. He and his wife had retreated to a small town in Maine to avoid being noticed on their vacation. While there, they went to see a movie on a messy, rainy night. When Shula and his wife walked into the theater, the handful of people there began to applaud. The famous coach whispered to his wife, "I guess there's no place we can go where people won't recognize me." When they sat down, Shula shook hands with the man on their row and said, "I'm surprised that you knew who I am." The man looked at him and replied, "Am I supposed to know who you are? We're just glad you came in because the manager said he wasn't going to start the movie unless there were at least 10 people in here!" Just about the time we think we are something, someone reminds us we are not!

God uses the humble. As one person observed, "You can't clean a toilet standing up!" Dwight Lyman Moody wrote, "A man can counterfeit love, he can counterfeit faith, he can counterfeit hope and all the other graces, but it is very difficult to counterfeit humility."

Stars are only brightly visible at night. A candle only lights a dark room. While humility is not self-exalting, it is also not self-abasing. It is having an honest estimate of who you are in Christ and then considering the value He has placed on those around you as well. Kenneth Copeland says, "Humility is knowing who you are and knowing who you are not!"

To remain humble, we must remain teachable. William Somerset Maugham said, "It wasn't until quite late in life that I discovered how easy it is to say, 'I don't know.'" Remember, the way up is first the way down.

APPLICATION:
1. Humble yourself, today, in some way as you live your life.
2. Prefer others, today, over yourself.

PRAYER:
Lord, I will decrease, today, that you may increase in my life. Amen.

SEPTEMBER 19
NOTHING BUT THE BLOOD

Hebrews 9:22
"And almost all things are by the law purged with the blood; and without shedding of blood is no remission." (KJV)

Blood is the answer for sin. When Adam first sinned in the Garden of Eden, and his and his wife's eyes were opened, God met them with the skins of the first sacrifice for man's sin. Genesis 3:21 tells us animals gave their lives for them. The importance of the blood was first introduced to impact man's life forever!

From Genesis to Revelation, the blood is the central theme in expressing God's love for man and the necessity of a sacrifice to redeem man back to his Creator.

It was offered to Cain as the only choice for obtaining salvation from sin. (Genesis 4:10) It was also the key to the release of the Israelites in Egyptian bondage on the eve of the Exodus of their Passover to dissuade the Angel of Death from taking their first-born. (Exodus 12:3-7; 11-13)

There are four benefits of the blood. First, it clears the conscience. (Hebrews 9:13-14) The blood of animals was able to purify the flesh of an unclean person. However, the blood of Christ is able to purge the conscience from dead works, i.e. sin, to serve the living God. The animal sacrifices could not do this. For the daily annual sacrifices constantly reminded them of sin. (Hebrews 10:3)

The second benefit is it provides a purging of the past. Forgiveness demands blood! (Ephesians 1:7) His blood superseded any demand placed upon it!

The third benefit is it purifies us to stand in His presence. Exodus 24:5-8 tells us the Old Covenant was instituted with blood. Everything of significance was literally soaked in blood, half on the altar, half on the people and the scroll.

The final benefit is it is a settles solution. Hebrews 9:23-28 tells us there is just one of two places for your sin—either your sin is on you or it is on Christ. The blood has settled the account. Nothing, but the blood!

APPLICATION:
1. Remind yourself the blood is enough for your sin.
2. Your past is rescinded; you are free in Him!

PRAYER:
Lord, thank you for the sacrifice of your Son for my sin. I receive cleansing that only comes through the blood! Amen.

SEPTEMBER 20
BECOMING GOD'S MASTERPIECE

II Timothy 2:20-21

"In a wealthy home there are dishes made of gold and silver as well as some made from wood and clay. The expensive dishes are used for guests, and the cheap ones are used in the kitchen or to put garbage in. If you stay away from sin you will be like one of these dishes made of purest gold-the very best in the house-so that Christ himself can use you for his highest purposes." (TLB)

Every vessel has a specific designation. Every vessel is made to contain a particular object. The contents determine the value of the vessel. Ordinary vessels become pricey when the contents are valuable.

There was a very wealthy man who had only one child, a son whom he dearly loved. The man's wife died giving birth to his son. Everything he did, he did with the thought of his son's future in mind. A few years passed and the man became ill and passed away. At the reading of his will, only the servant of the house was present to represent the child. The servant was addressed first and told she could choose any one item in the house as thanks for her faithfulness to the family. Without hesitation, she chose a portrait of the son that had been painted and placed over the fireplace in the study. After this announcement, the lawyer gave instruction she should take it down and look on the back for a special message. The message read, "He who chooses my son, inherits all."

If you have chosen His Son, you have chosen the masterpiece of Heaven. You have, with Him, inherited all! Yet, something else has also taken place; now you are His child, His son, His daughter! You have become His masterpiece!

We are all vessels in the household of God; vessels to be filled with His glory and His presence. We are vessels set apart for God, not self, and are usable unto God. God has gifted you for good works, not to squander the things of God. You are pricey, not worthless! You are in the process of becoming God's Masterpiece.

APPLICATION:
1. Ask God to fill you with His glory, so you will be a vessel that can quench the thirst of others.
2. Do not let the enemy convince you that you are worthless.

PRAYER:
Lord, thank you for making me into your masterpiece. Amen.

SEPTEMBER 21
BEING MADE OVER

Jeremiah 18:4
"And the vessel that he made of clay was marred in the hand of the potter: so he made it again another vessel, as seemed good to the potter to make it." (KJV)

One of the most attractive things about the Gospel is the reality of being able to start over. We have the opportunity to be "born-again," to be made over. God loves to take the damaged vessel of our lives that we offer to Him and place it back on the potter's wheel to refashion it and make it even better.

He is the Potter. The Potter is the artist. The Potter determines the expected outcome. He always has the best in mind for the vessel. He spends His time thinking about the finished product and is not dismayed when it becomes cracked and marred. He has confidence it can still be reshaped and be beautiful again. As the Potter molds or shapes the clay on the potter's wheel, sometimes defects appear. The Potter has power over the clay, to permit the defects to remain or reshape the pot. When we are being inspected and reformed, it is not always comfortable, but the Potter is not concerned about momentary discomfort. He is making a masterpiece.

The Potter adds water (the Word) to the clay to ease the discomfort while it is still in the forming stage. Then, there is the drying process: waiting. The Artist has not forgotten about the artwork. Then, there is a coloring process, time to add details— the details which distinguish it from the others.

Finally, it is time for the Artist to put His name on it. God has to wait before He can put His name on you until you have fully submitted. Then, with His name on you, you are finally a signature art piece of His making. You are put into an oven to be fired. If you can stand the heat, you are almost ready to shine. Sometimes the vessel even breaks in the fire and must be reformed. However, you cannot be a masterpiece without exposure to the fire. Next is glazing. God, then, has you ready for use—not just for display. God is ready to unveil you to the world!

APPLICATION:
1. Place yourself, today, in the hands of the Potter.
2. Do not resist the process! When the heat comes, stay in the fire and be confident that at just the right time, you are coming out!

PRAYER:
Lord, shape and mold me after your will. I am the clay, you are the Potter. Amen.

SEPTEMBER 22
ARE YOU READY TO BE A CHAMP?

Psalms 19:4-5
"...in the Heavens has pitched a tent for the sun, which is like a bridegroom coming forth from his pavilion, like a champion rejoicing to run his course."
(NIV)

What is a champion? The word *champion* means "a person who has defeated all competing opponents so as to hold first place, one who is crowned the sole victor over all competition."

Champions are not born. The challenges of life reveal the champion is on the inside of us. God has already won for us, but we are still to fight the good fight of faith.

Champions have certain traits setting them apart from other competitors. The following is a list of seven traits of a champion: First, champions cannot be bought. Joe DiMaggio had a year where he hit under .300. He went to management and demanded a pay cut: "I looked him straight in the eyes and said, 'I'm taking a 35,000 dollar cut.'" Maybe that explains why he never again hit below .300. Second, champions do not cave into criticism. Jacques Plante, a former stand-out goalie for the Montreal Canadians, said of his career: "How would you like it in your job if every time you made a small mistake, a red light went on over your desk and 15,000 people stood up and yelled at you?" Third, champions set a higher standard than all others. Michael Jordan shared an insight he gleaned from the Olympics: "I saw some Dream Teamers dog it in practice before the Olympics. I looked at them, and I knew that's what separates me from them." Fourth, champions seize the moment and opportunity. (I Samuel 17:40-50) David saw the reward, not the opposition! Fifth, champions do not let fear control them. (Job 2:24) The only mistake Job made was to open the door to the Devil through his fear. Sixth, champions are committed. (Job 5:8-9) Jimmy Johnson, former Championship coach of the Dallas Cowboys, observed, "I played for a National Championship team, I coached a National Championship team and I coached a Super Bowl team. There's a common thread in all three: quality people who are committed to do their best." Seventh, champions never consider the cost too high. (II Corinthians 5:21) By risking all, there are no limitations for the reward! Are you ready to be a champion?

APPLICATION:
1. Apply the traits of champions to your life.
2. Are you becoming a champion?

PRAYER:
Lord, help me be the champion I am meant to be. Amen.

SEPTEMBER 23
TAKING THE TITLE

I Samuel 17:23-26

"As he was talking with them, Goliath, the Philistine champion from Gath, stepped out from his lines and shouted his usual defiance, and David heard it. When the Israelites saw the man, they all ran from him in great fear. Now the Israelites had been saying, 'Do you see how this man keeps coming out? He comes out to defy Israel. The king will give great wealth to the man who kills him. He will also give him his daughter in marriage and will exempt his father's family from taxes in Israel.' David asked the men standing near him, 'What will be done for the man who kills this Philistine and removes this disgrace from Israel? Who is this uncircumcised Philistine that he should defy the armies of the living God?'" (NIV)

To defeat the champion is not easy, but there are things that will happen for us only when we are willing to face the challenge. The MVP of the Super Bowl always appears at Disney World in Orlando, Florida, and is honored in their famous, daily Disney parade. The NCAA Basketball Champions get to cut the basketball nets down in the gym they win the championship in. The President of the United States invites the entire championship teams of all the major sports to be special guests at the White House.

Still, it takes a special determination to take down the champion. Motivation must be more than what is normal. The reward must be greater than the usual. David knew this was his shining moment of opportunity, an opportunity that would never be possible by just tending sheep. He realized all of those days and nights spent defending the sheep from predators might have been moments of training, training for this moment in time. Yet, he needed something to convince him it was worth the risk of going up against the giant, Goliath. The future of his family, his friends and his own personal hopes were possible, only if he dared to challenge the champion. He accepted the challenge and depended on his past experiences and his faith in his Creator to be the difference. Sometimes, we must face the champion. There is no other path that leads to our dreams and our destiny. We must remember whatever we lack in ability, we can overcome through faith!

APPLICATION:
1. Do not run from your challenges.
2. Seize the moments with the help of God.

PRAYER:
Lord, I am ready to take the title! Amen.

SEPTEMBER 24
LIVING A TRIUMPHANT LIFE

Isaiah 50:7-8
*"Because the Lord God helps me, I will not be dismayed; therefore, I have set
my face like flint to do his will, and I know that I will triumph…
Who will dare to fight against me now?"* (TLB)

Reginald Wallis said, "The triumphant Christian does not fight for victory; he celebrates a victory already won; the victorious life in Christ's business, not yours." We have truly been given the ability to live triumphantly now, not just when we arrive in Heaven. However, there are many defeated Christians. Why? I believe it is because we do not maintain the following things: First, praise. Psalms 106:47 says, *"Save us, O LORD our God, and gather us from among the heathen, to give thanks unto thy Holy name, and to triumph in thy praise."* (KJV) Second, praying in the Spirit. (Jude 20; Romans 8:26-28) All prominent New Testament believers spoke in tongues. Paul prayed in tongues. (I Corinthians 14) Jesus' brothers prayed in tongues, and Mary did as well. (Acts 1:14; 2:1-4) Third, is the departure from sin. Colossians 2:13-15 says, *"You were dead in sins, and your sinful desires were not yet cut away. Then he gave you a share in the very life of Christ, for he forgave all your sins, and blotted out the charges proved against you, the list of his commandments which you had not obeyed. He took this list of sins and destroyed it by nailing it to Christ's cross."* (TLB) Fourth, keeping the right attitude. I Samuel 10:9 says, *"As Saul said goodbye and started to go, God gave him a new attitude, and all of Samuel's prophecies came true that day."* (TLB) You have to do your part in determining your attitude. Fifth, it is your destiny! I Samuel 17:51-52 says, *"…When the Philistines saw that their champion was dead, they turned and ran. Then the Israelis gave a great shout of triumph and rushed after the Philistines, chasing them as far as Gath and the gates of Ekron."* (TLB)

Psalms 58:10 says, *"The godly shall rejoice in triumph of right; they shall walk the blood-stained fields of slaughtered, wicked men. Then at last everyone will know that good is rewarded, and that there is a God who judges justly here on earth."* (KJV) You can live a triumphant life!

APPLICATION:
1. Decide to live triumphantly!
2. Do not settle for defeat.

PRAYER:
Lord, I will live a triumphant life now! Amen.

SEPTEMBER 25
ORIGINAL CONDITION

Joel 2:25
"And I will restore to you the years that the locust hath eaten, the cankerworm, and the caterpillar, and the palmerworm, my great army which I sent among you." (KJV)

God is a restoring God. From the very beginning, it has always been the Father's desire to restore things to their original state. He started with a perfect man; He will finish with one. He started with a perfect city; He will finish with one. He started as sole Lord and God of all men; He will finish as the one true God.

God had an original plan for you before you were born. However, Satan caused you to stray from it. God wants to restore you to your original state with no trace of damage. It is like a paint and body repairman who receives a wrecked car. He works feverishly to restore it to the condition prior to the damage.

Restoration is a healing process. God has made an investment into your life. He has provided what is necessary to help you recover from the damages in this life caused by sickness, divorce and injustices. God is looking to restore, not destroy! Isaiah 42:3 tells us, *"A bruised reed shall he not break, and the smoking flax shall he not quench..."* (KJV) The reeds that grew along the river were used for flutes for music. The bruised or damaged ones were tossed aside and not used. However, God specializes in repairing, restoring and putting back into use again.

There are at least seven things God will restore. The first is a restored wife, or spouse. (Genesis 20:14) Abimelech restored Sarah to Abram. The second is restored money. (Genesis 42:28) Joseph restored grain and money to his brethren in their sacks. The third is restored cities. (I Samuel 7:14) Samuel ruled and the Philistines were overthrown. The fourth is a son restored to life and all. (II Kings 8:1-6) Elisha restored the widow's son. The fifth is restored people. (Ezra 6:1-5) People restored in the Kingdom. The sixth is sick bodies restored to health. (Matthew 12:13) Jesus restored the man with the withered hand. God takes the withered and brings it back to life. The seventh is a restored mind. (Psalms 23:3) He restores your soul.

God wants you to be restored to your original, intended condition!

APPLICATION:
1. Place the brokenness of your life before Him.
2. Accept His healing.

PRAYER:
Lord, please restore every crack and broken part of my life. Amen.

SEPTEMBER 26
GOD'S RESTORATION PLAN FOR YOU

Jeremiah 30:17
"For I will restore health unto thee, and I will heal thee of thy wounds, saith the LORD; because they called thee an Outcast..." (KJV)

Restoration means "to recover from loss or damage." God is the great restorer of our lives. In the worst moments of our lives, He brings His restoration to us. Psalms 23:3 says, *"He restoreth my soul: he leadeth me in the paths of righteousness for his name's sake."* (KJV)

But we have steps we are responsible for if we are to be fully and completely restored. First, you must overcome adversity, or the Devil. Proverbs 24:10 says, *"If thou faint in the day of adversity, thou strength is small."* (KJV) You are a poor specimen if you cannot stand the pressure of adversity. Someone asked their pastor, "Pastor, pray that I won't have any trouble with the Devil." "Do you want me to pray that you die?" the pastor responded. Second, we must be patient. Psalms 37:34 says, *"Don't be impatient for the Lord to act! Keep traveling steadily along his pathway and in due season he will honor you with every blessing, and you will see the wicked destroyed."* (TLB) Galatians 6:8 says, *"For he that soweth to his flesh shall the flesh reap corruption; but he that soweth to the Spirit shall of the Spirit reap life everlasting. And let us be weary in well doing: for in due season we shall reap, if we faint not."* (KJV) Patience always produces fruit. Third, you must keep your heart set on the Word and act on it. (Leviticus 26:3-10) The Word is the most powerful restoring agent on the earth today. Fourth, you must be where God wants you to be. Elisha would not let Elijah out of his sight. Fifth, you must get someone who knows how to pray in faith with you. (Hebrews 13:18-21) Agreement brings a finish to your faith. Sixth, you must fast. (Isaiah 58) Fasting brings things back to life that have died! Last, you must expect something good to happen to you. (Acts 3) When you have an expectation, every limit set upon you before loses its grip on your life.

APPLICATION:
1. Follow the steps of restoration.
2. No matter your past damage, consider the re-Creator!

PRAYER:
Lord, I am ready for you to restore my life back to its intended condition. Amen.

SEPTEMBER 27
KNOWING WHAT YOU BELIEVE

Mark 9:23
"Jesus said unto him, If thou canst believe, all things are possible to him that believeth." (KJV)

Jesus had a doctrine He preached. *Doctrine* is from the Greek word *didaskeleeha*, which means "instruction, precepts, tested instruction." He only preached tested instruction; things that had been tried and found as absolute truth. What made Jesus' preaching different from any before Him was that His doctrine was accompanied by authority. His Word changed His surroundings and the surroundings of those around Him. He cleansed the temple. (Mark 11) He disclaimed religion. (Mark 12:28) His Word had power! Jesus knew what He believed and knew it would bring out the impossible.

There is a greater need for sound doctrine, today, than ever before. There is a greater need of Christians whose opinions are free from any mixture of error. There is a greater need to be grounded in the scriptures, which provide the faith for the impossible to become reality. What you believe will determine what you receive in life either good or bad.

Everybody believes something. Yet, how do we arrive at the things we believe? Your beliefs are formed by the influences in your life: by those you allow to speak into your life, by the things you place in front of your eyes and by the things that you give heed to.

How do we cut out the unbelieving doctrines of philosophy and people who disregard God? By cutting off evil communications. According to I Corinthians 15:32-33, our manner of life becomes corrupt when we allow people with unbelief to become people we purposely associate with and take heed to. Secondly, we must not accept the traditions of men as the will of God. (Mark 7:13) We must have a responsibility to investigate and know our source. (II Timothy 3:10, 16-17; 4:3; Ephesians 4:14) The traditions of men are the only things listed in the Bible making the Word of God ineffective! Be sure that you cling to and place the Word of God as the final authority of your life. Do not let anyone or anything else be the cornerstone of what you believe!

APPLICATION:
1. Choose God's Word over the opinion and view of all others.
2. Stand on the authority of God's Word when in doubt.

PRAYER:
Lord, I will place your Word in the center of my belief system. Amen.

SEPTEMBER 28
LIVE THE REAL LIFE

Galatians 2:20
"I have been crucified with Christ: and I myself no longer live, but Christ lives in me. And the real life I now have within this body is a result of my trusting the Son of God, who loved me and gave himself for me." (NIV)

God is the only giver of real life. Until you lose your life in Him, you will never find it! There are numerous scriptures pointing out real life is only available through Jesus Christ.

Consider these scriptures from the Living Bible:

Colossians 3:3-4 states, *"You should have as little desire for this world as a dead person does. Your real life is in Heaven with Christ and God. And when Christ who is our real life comes back again, you will shine with him and share in all his glories."* The real life in Him brings real blessings to us. Romans 5:1 says, *"So now, since we have been made right in God's sight by faith in his promises, we can have real peace with him because of what Jesus Christ our Lord has done for us."* The real life He wants for you is found in His Word. Everywhere Jesus went, He preached the Gospel to those He came in contact with. Proverbs 4:13 says, *"Carry out my instructions; don't forget them, for they will lead you to real living."* Real love is only given through Him. The world offers its love as long as you do not disappoint it, but His love is everlasting. Real love is what He is, not what He does. I John 3:16 says, *"We know what real love is from Christ's example in dying for us. And so we also ought to lay down our lives for our Christian brothers. I John 4:10 reveals, "In this act we see what real love is: it is not our love for God but his love for us when he sent his Son to satisfy God's anger against our sins."* He is the only real God. Jeremiah 16:20 says, *"Can men make God? The gods they made are not real gods at all!"* God is preparing us for our real home. Hebrews 11:14 says, *"And quite obviously when they talked like that, they were looking forward to their real home in Heaven."* Your real life is in Him!

APPLICATION:
1. Do not be fooled by the life the world offers.
2. Find your real life in Him!

PRAYER:
Lord, I thank you for the real life I have in you! Amen.

SEPTEMBER 29
THE UNBREAKABLE FORCE

Matthew 12:29-30

"Or how can a person go into a strong man's house and carry off his goods (the entire equipment of his house) without first binding the strong man? ...He who is not with Me (definitely on My side) is against me, and he who does not (definitely) gather with Me and for My side, scatters." (Amplified Bible)

There is an unbreakable force. What is it? It is the force of unity. When two or more people come together, the task or challenge is greatly diminished and success is inevitable. Yet, how do we come into unity? First of all, we must promote and support the people who already are in our lives. We need to be cheerleaders for each other. The people who competed against Michael Jordan in little league, etc., do you think they supported him? No! The same people now boast about knowing him and coaching him! Yet, where were they when he needed them? Everyone has greatness in them which can only be brought out by support and unity.

Second, while everybody has their own particular area of expertise, we still have so much to learn from each other. Jesus did not just get carpenters to help Him. He got doctors, tax collectors, fishermen and political zealots. He surrounded Himself with people who had skills He did not possess. Yet, later we see all of the disciples fishing and Peter taking care of tax problems. We have so much we can learn from each other.

What will stop us from learning from and supporting each other? The enemy uses five things. First, not understanding each other. Dr. Martin Luther King, Jr. said, "We hate each other because we do not know each other!" Second, not trusting each other. When we fail to give those around us the benefit of the doubt, we reduce their abilities to be a blessing to us. Third, jealousy. Jealousy can cause the greatest of friends to become opponents instead of adversaries. Fourth, not taking any risks. If we stay in our comfort zone and do not make any concessions for each other, we miss some of the things we need in our lives. Fifth, not giving each other a chance. When we assume we know each other and draw negative conclusions, we do not allow God to show us another side of who He is. Remember, together we are unbreakable!

APPLICATION:
1. Try breaking 50 popsicle sticks at once, then try breaking just one.
2. Intentionally put yourself in unity with those you love.

PRAYER:
Lord, I will be in unity and be unbreakable! Amen.

SEPTEMBER 30
YOU HAVE SOMETHING TO GIVE

Exodus 3:4
"And when the LORD saw that he turned aside to see, God called unto him out of the midst of the bush, and said, Moses, Moses. And he said, Here am I."
(KJV)

Moses' life was down, up, down and up again. Before he was a keeper of God's people, his faithfulness to lead was tested when he was a keeper of sheep. One year later, the place he had tended sheep, was the very place he led the children of Israel out of 430 years of bondage.

God spoke to Moses where he was. God is always speaking to us where we are if we will listen. God took advantage of the things Moses already possessed. Moses knew the Egyptian language and their way of thinking. He was the most qualified to go before Pharaoh. God does not ask us for what we do not have, He asks us for what we do have. Moses discovered that when you go, God goes! God told Moses He had come down to deliver Israel. Moses had been anxious at one time to do it, but self-doubt set in. God reaffirmed Moses' doubts. He told him His presence would be with him. (Exodus 3:12) Additionally, God used what Moses had in his hand. God told Moses to throw down his stick. He did and the result was he shook Egypt.

When Moses stretched out his hand, he stretched out the hand of God. When we stretch our gifts, we stretch out the hand of God. God anoints people, not things. We are carriers of the anointing. Christians, Christ, the anointed one and His anointing all negate the antichrist spirit!

What you have is always enough. The little boy with the two piece fish dinner gave his lunch away and thousands were fed. By giving out what he had, he received back twelve full baskets. It is not what we keep, but what we give away that is anointed. Everybody has something to give.

APPLICATION:
1. Offer what you have, today, to someone in need.
2. Make it your own special charge to be a difference maker for someone else.

PRAYER:
Lord, I know you have placed something inside of me to bless others. I will give it to you to be used for others. Amen.

OCTOBER 1
A REAL SON

Romans 8:14-17
"For as many as are led by the Spirit of God, they are the sons of God. For ye have not received the spirit of bondage again to fear; but ye have received the Spirit of adoption, whereby we cry, Abba, Father. The Spirit itself beareth witness with our spirit, that we are the children of God: And if children, then heirs; heirs of God, and joint-heirs with Christ…" (KJV)

There is nothing like having a son who can be guided and taught. Sons are an extension of a father's heart. Most fathers are hopeful their sons will be able to avoid their mistakes and become better men than they are.

When I married my wife, Ginger, in 1982, we each had a child from a previous marriage. I had a daughter and Ginger had a son. We had the vision of one big happy family. We were dreaming! They did not adjust well to each other or to the "other" parent. Thank God for His grace!

Because Ginger's son's father was still in the picture, I was careful not to try to take his place. It caused more confusion and damage than I realized. We had a lot of conflict, especially throughout his teen years. I was not prepared for the challenge, and looking back, could have handled things better. We did have some good times like little league baseball, Stryper concerts and playing video games. Later, we even played together on the church softball team.

Many years later, in 2006, I did something I should have done 25 years ago. When our son, J.T., was 30, I adopted him and changed his last name. He became a legal heir, my son by name—my name!

The same thing happened for us when we made Jesus the Lord of our lives. The Father legally adopted and grafted us into His family! There are no "step children" in His Kingdom. We are now His children. We belong. We are His children!

APPLICATION:
1. Remember, you are a real child of God.
2. If you have step-children, or are a step-child, remember, step-children are real offspring!

PRAYER:
Lord, thank you for accepting me as your real child! Amen.

OCTOBER 2
REMOVING THE BOUNDARIES

Job 14:5

"Seeing his days are determined, the number of his months are with thee, thou hast appointed his bounds that he cannot pass." (KJV)

Do you recall how elephants react in captivity? When a baby elephant is kept in captivity, it must first be chained to a steel rod, which is deeply placed into the ground. It sets its boundaries. By the time it is grown, it can be tied with a rope to a wooden stake. It will not break free, although it has increased in physical strength.

The believer is much like this. We have certain boundaries we are tied to for much of our life. Even after we are freed, we are fearful to go outside of our previous boundaries. God wants us to stretch our boundaries!

What is a boundary? It is defined as "something that indicates confinement or limits." It suggests the impossible. A boundary is a line of demarcation.

God stretches the boundaries of His people. We are to look beyond our pasts. He has prepared us for a limitless existence. In Exodus, the people had to leave to find it. They were to believe there was a better future. They would be face to face with their enemies. It was risky, but the risk was worth it because they moved the boundaries of their lives.

There was a young boy who was always catching and caging things. He particularly loved the sound of the mockingbird. He decided to catch one and keep it, so he could hear it sing anytime. He found a very young mockingbird and placed it in a cage outside his home. On the second day, he saw a mother bird fly to the cage and feed the young bird through the bars. This pleased the little boy; however, the following morning he found the bird dead. Later, the boy was talking to the renowned ornithologist, Author Wayne, who told him, "A mother mockingbird finding her young in a cage, will sometimes take it poisonous berries. She evidently thinks it is better for the one she loves to die, rather than live in captivity."

God will help you remove your boundaries. God has invited us to a limitless life. You must remove yourself from your limits and boundaries.

APPLICATION:
1. Do something to move the self-imposed boundaries of your life.
2. Ask God to show you what He has in mind for you.

PRAYER:
Lord, I will not settle for less than where you want my life to be. Amen.

OCTOBER 3
CHANGES ARE COMING

Isaiah 9:10
"The bricks are fallen down, but we will build with hewn stones: the sycamores are cut down, but we will change them into cedars." (KJV)

Change precedes disaster. Consider the Titanic. It is a well-known fact the huge ship was mortally wounded by an iceberg. The Titanic's fate could have easily been prevented, if the captain had taken heed to the six separate warnings he received about icebergs. The ship had been counseled to change course and take the southern route, but instead the captain chose to ignore this advice. As Gary Smalley noted, "If you change course when warned, you can avoid disaster and then celebrate the voyage."

Jesus was an agent of change. Matthew 3:1-10 and Mark 1:27 show Jesus caused even devout religious people to wonder, "What new doctrine is this?" God was looking for a change and used John the Baptist to reach the "outsiders." The old order was not being done away with; it was being modified.

Change means "a transformation or modification; alter, modify, make different, shift, recast, restyle, remodel, reorganize, reform, revolutionize."

Leviticus 27:33 reveals some changes are for the good because they are Holy! Consider where you are today. Did you think you would be at this place 20, 10 or even 5 years ago? What would have happened to your life had you not gone through some changes? Most people overestimate what they can do in a week, and underestimate what they can do over a lifetime. We must be in a place where change can come. In Acts 2:1, the Holy Spirit brought change. We must continue to change into His image.

You can change. Everywhere you go, people in the know—know! There are some changes coming. If you humble yourself before the Lord, He will lead you to your destiny. Then, with the help of His Spirit, your change will come!

APPLICATION:
1. Allow the changes God has for you to take place.
2. Follow the leading of His Spirit.

PRAYER:
Lord, I am ready for you to change my life. Amen.

OCTOBER 4
ARE YOU COMMITTED?

I Peter 4:19
"Wherefore let them that suffer according to the will of God commit the keeping of their souls to him in well doing, as unto a faithful Creator." (KJV)

True commitment requires four things: surrender, sacrifice, support and steadfastness. First, commitment suggests surrender. (Luke 12:48) Currently, many Christian teenagers are wearing a popular, new t-shirt. On the front, it has the word "loser" on it. On the back is the scripture of Jesus' words found in Matthew 10:39, *"Whosoever loses his life for my sake finds it!"* (KJV) Seth Wilson said, "It doesn't take such a great man to be a Christian, it just takes all there is of him."

Commitment suggests sacrifice. (Philippians 2:17) There is a story about a pig and a chicken that walked down the street together. As they walked along, they read a sign advertising a breakfast to benefit the poor. The chicken said to the pig, "You and I should donate a ham and egg to the breakfast." The pig replied, "Not so fast! For you it would just be a contribution, but for me it would be a total commitment."

Commitment suggests support. (Acts 20:35) Support requires all of your efforts and energy. On October 13, 1962, a little boy was born in Starkville, Mississippi. His father was a bricklayer. As the young boy grew and matured, he and his brothers would go with their father to the job site to help out. As he continued to grow, he joined his father on the platform, while his younger brothers would throw bricks up, one-by-one for him to stack for his dad. The boy never dreamed or realized all of his efforts and energy was preparing him for more. While catching brick after brick he had developed skills, which later in his life, resulted in success. He attained a professional football career more prolific than any other NFL receiver. Who is this NFL player I am referring to? Jerry Rice.

Commitment suggests steadfastness. (I Timothy 6:20; II Timothy 2:12-14) Commitment means God can count on us. Commitment in the face of conflict produces character. Look at your life and where it is now. God has committed everything for you. Are you committed to Him?

APPLICATION:
1. Commit yourself to Him in a greater way.
2. Find ways to increase your commitment to those you love.

PRAYER:
Lord, I commit everything to you, today, and hold nothing back. Amen.

OCTOBER 5
SAY THE RIGHT THINGS

Proverbs 18:21
"Death and life are in the power of the tongue: and they that love it shall eat the fruit thereof." (KJV)

Right words create an atmosphere where God can and will abide. In his book, *Sabbath Time*, Tilden Edwards tells about a family with teenage children who decided as part of their Sabbath commitments, they would not criticize each other on Sundays. As the months went on, they kept this commitment. They realized more and more of their children's friends were coming to their home to hang out on Sundays. No one in the family had discussed this commitment with anyone outside of the family, but somehow other teenagers knew this home was a good place to be.

Speaking positive words, instead of negative words, brings the presence of God into our lives. Additionally, after we pray it is essential we continue to speak the positive things of God's Word. What we say after prayer is critical. Too often, we negate our prayers with what we say. We must speak out what we desire. Do not talk about your problems. Talk to them!

Matthew 12:34 and II Corinthians 4:13 show us after we pray, what we believe will come out of our mouths — no matter what we have prayed.

We must call those things that be not as though they were, after we pray. We can persuade our hearts if we speak it enough. (James 1:26) We must bridle our mouths until only what we desire comes out.

There must be a continuation of what we believe. (John 8:21-32) We must hold onto our confession. (Hebrews 10:23) We must keep sound words. (II Timothy 1:12-15; Psalms 19:14)

Amos 5:14 reveals God will be with you as you have spoken. When times are uncertain, your words must remain the same. Your words will determine your outcome. Job's words got him into trouble. (Job 7:11; 10:1) Job's words got him out of trouble. (Job 42:1-7) The chaos of his life was restored when the words were restored.

What you say after you pray will determine your success or your failure. So, what do you say?

APPLICATION:
1. Be sure to say the right things after you pray.
2. Do not let anything come out of your mouth that is against your will.

PRAYER:
Lord, forgive me for not saying the right things after I pray. Amen.

OCTOBER 6
WHY FIGHT?

Deuteronomy 20:10
*"When thou comest nigh unto a city to fight against it, then
proclaim peace unto it."* (KJV)

After 125 years, the infamous feud between the Hatfields and McCoys came to a close. Sixty descendants of the original clans gathered on Saturday, June 14, 2003, in Pikefield, Kentucky, to sign a document declaring an official end to more than a century of hatred and bloodshed. Most think the feuding between the McCoys of Kentucky and the Hatfields of West Virginia began in 1878, when Randolph McCoy accused one of the Hatfields of stealing a hog. The Hatfields won the "hog war," when a McCoy cousin sided with the opposing clan. Feelings festered and other incidents occurred, which finally resulted in the shooting death of Ellison Hatfield in 1882. Retaliation bred retaliation until the feud claimed 11 more family members over the next 10 years. Subsequent conflicts between the two clans have involved court battles over timber rights and cemetery plots.

The treaty calling for peace reads, "We do hereby and formally declare an official end to all hostilities, implied, inferred, and real, between the families, now and forevermore. We ask by God's grace and love that we be forever remembered as those that bound together the hearts of two families to form a family of freedom in America." Reo Hatfield, who first thought of the ceremony said, "We're not saying you don't have to fight because sometimes you do have to fight. But, you don't have to fight forever." Although the treaty was largely symbolic, both the governor of Kentucky and the governor of West Virginia were present for the nationally televised ceremony. (American Profile, CBS News.com)

How do conflicts like this originate? Conflicts originate when we demand our own way, and refuse to allow those around us to be human and make mistakes. When we refuse to compromise based on principles over relationships, conflicts breed and it becomes harder to find a way to a resolution.

Most battles we find ourselves in could easily be resolved if we would just be more patient. So the question is, "Why fight?"

APPLICATION:
1. Are you in a conflict? Look for a resolution.
2. Stop all opportunities for a fight.

PRAYER:
Lord, I repent for fighting unnecessarily. Amen.

OCTOBER 7
THINGS THAT COME BEFORE FAITH

Galatians 5:22
"But the fruit of the Spirit is love, joy, peace, longsuffering, gentleness, goodness, faith..." (KJV)

Faith is only one important part of the fruit of the Spirit. It is amazing how many attributes are listed before faith or faithfulness in Galatians 5:22. It reveals many "faith" people are not ever going to get to where they should, although their confession is right. You must have the fruit of the others listed before faith can ignite and begin to blossom. It is interesting faith or faithfulness is seventh on the list of nine! Love always comes before faith. (Galatians 5:6) Joy is the fuse to your faith. It rejoices in all circumstances. Peace precedes faith, and places God's divine order in your life. Longsuffering assures your faith will not bend. You will not be moved after you act on faith. Gentleness opens the door for faith. It places a premium on someone else's need or desire before your own. Goodness gives confidence to the faith that God desires our desires.

All of these lay the foundation for the right kind of Bible faith. Too often, we place all of our weight on our faith and wonder why things do not turn out the way we want them to. We do not walk in love. We allow the joy of our lives to be easily taken away from us. We lose our peace without reason. We become impatient and do not endure hardships. We become rude and unkind towards people God has placed in our life. We fail to have good works alongside our faith.

Our fruit is incomplete. We have only one slice of the whole fruit. When we take the time to develop the other areas of our life where the fruit of the Spirit is concerned, we strengthen our faith and place a foundation under it. The foundation will hold up, even in times of greatest pressure.

Do not be underdeveloped in your faith. Grow a garden with all of the different nutrients that produce miracle working faith!

APPLICATION:
1. Be sure to develop the other areas of your faith.
2. Do not allow your faith to stand alone. Use the "whole fruit," instead of one "slice" of it.

PRAYER:
Lord, I purpose to grow up into you in all of the fruits of the Spirit. Amen.

OCTOBER 8
FAITHFULNESS IS GREAT

Lamentations 3:21-23
"This I recall to my mind, therefore have I hope. It is of the LORD'S mercies that we are not consumed, because his compassions fail not. They are new every morning: great is thy faithfulness!" (KJV)

You cannot separate faith and faithfulness. You cannot walk in real Bible faith and see results without being faithful. This faithfulness must transcend circumstances. It must transcend people in your life, whether they choose to serve God or not!

We live in a day of unfaithfulness: saints compromising and ministers failing. Unfaithfulness tears at the heart of Christianity and diminishes our ability to convince the world of their need for Christ. When we fail to be faithful, we are failures. As long as we are faithful, we are not failures!

Your faithfulness will be tested. A faith that has not been tested cannot be trusted. Everyone in the Kingdom will be rewarded according to their faithfulness. (I Samuel 26:23) The Bible contrasts David's faithfulness and Saul's faithfulness. Proverbs 28:20 says faithfulness is rewarding. There are four things faithfulness will produce. First, faithfulness drives out the enemy in your land and gives you your inheritance. Second, faithfulness gives you the strength to wait. Third, faithfulness helps you overcome your deficiencies. Fourth, faithfulness places you before God.

Joshua 14:1-12 tells us Caleb's faithfulness brought him to God's promises. Canaan was controlled by the Israelites, although much land and several cities still needed to be conquered. Joshua told the people to include both conquered and unconquered lands in the territorial allotments. (Joshua 13:7) Caleb was now 85 years old; this was 45 years after his first mission into Canaan. His faithfulness was rewarded. Today, you are surveying the land, which one day you will possess, if you are faithful.

Do not be like the world. Be faithful unto Him as He has been faithful unto you. Faithfulness brings greatness!

APPLICATION:
1. Decide, today, to be faithful in all of your endeavors.
2. Remember, faithfulness is always rewarded.

PRAYER:
Lord, I will be faithful to you and your Word at all times! Amen.

OCTOBER 9
DO NOT QUIT

Jeremiah 20:7-9

"O Lord, you deceived me when you promised me your help. I have to give them your messages because you are stronger than I am, but now I am the laughingstock of the city, mocked by all. You have never once let me speak a word of kindness to them; always it is disaster and horror and destruction. No wonder they scoff and mock and make my name a household joke. And I can't quit! For if I say I'll never again mention the Lord—never more speak in his name—then his work in my heart is like fire that burns in my bones, and I can't hold it any longer." (TLB)

I was in an elevator a few years ago when I encountered a man whom I had known for many years. We had worked on several construction job sites together when I was employed as a house painter. I had worked full-time painting houses and was also a minister. Knowing this, he asked, "Are you still preaching?" I answered emphatically, "YES!" I was annoyed he would even ask. However, upon reflection I considered the number of people who had quit throughout the years—even preachers.

Today's message is a simple one. Do not quit! Acts 18:9-11 says, *"One night the Lord spoke to Paul in a vision and told him, 'Don't be afraid! Speak out! Don't quit! For I am with you and no one can harm you. Many people here in this city belong to me.' So Paul stayed there the next year and a half, teaching the truths of God."* (TLB)

Do not let discouragement get you down. If discouragement is the loss of courage, hope and all strength, then we need a dose of encouragement. Encouragement is to be filled with courage and hope, and to be strengthened within our hearts.

God encouraged Joshua He would be with him just as He was with Moses. Jesus told Peter He was going to pray for him and He would be the rock. Jesus knew Peter's immanent failure was only temporary. He was encouraging him, the same way He does us. Do not quit!

APPLICATION:
1. Be encouraged. God has better days ahead for you.
2. Do not let setbacks seem fatal. God will make a way for you to overcome, so you can be victorious in the near future.

PRAYER:
Lord, I believe you are planning better things for me. I will not quit. Amen.

OCTOBER 10
BAA BAA SHEEP

John 10:11-16
"I am the Good Shepherd. The Good Shepherd lays down his life for the sheep.
A hired man will run when he sees a wolf coming and will leave the sheep,
for they aren't his and he isn't their shepherd. And so the wolf leaps on them
and scatters the flock. The hired man runs because he is hired and has no real
concern for the sheep. I am the Good Shepherd and know my own sheep, and
they know me, just as my Father knows me and I know the Father; and I lay
down my life for the sheep. I have other sheep, too, in another fold. I must bring
them also, and they will heed my voice; and there will be one
flock with one Shepherd." (TLB)

Most of us do not understand the relationship between a shepherd and his flock of sheep. Shepherds must be totally devoted to the welfare of the sheep at all times. Shepherds are responsible for leading, feeding and most importantly, protecting the flock.

Factually speaking, sheep are not known for their wits. They are easily distracted and easily misled. They will be with the flock one minute and be lost the next. They constantly wander away from the natural safety of being with a group and occasionally wind up in the clutches of a wolf. Because of this tendency, it is crucial for the sheep to remain connected to the others and be well acquainted with the leading of the shepherd to survive. They must stay within the earshot of the shepherd when he speaks out to them. If they are truly connected, they can distinguish the shepherd's voice from all others. When they are able to do this, they are invariably led to the plushest, most serene pastures to graze and the most clear, pristine brooks to drink without fear or danger.

This should remind us, today, how valuable the shepherds are God has placed in our lives. As long as we are sheep who listen to their voice and follow their lead, we will be fat, safe and sassy! Thank God for the Great Shepherd who has appointed shepherds to lead and keep us as we travel life's road!

APPLICATION:
1. Take time to thank God for the shepherds He has placed in your life.
2. Make it a point to pray for your shepherds on a daily basis.

PRAYER:
Lord, thank you for the shepherds you have placed in my life. Amen.

OCTOBER 11
SEVEN REASONS WE MUST FINISH THE RACE

Luke 14:28-30

"For which of you, intending to build a tower, sitteth not down first, and counteth the cost, whether he have sufficient to finish it? Lest haply, after he hath laid the foundation, and is not able to finish it, all that behold it begin to mock him, Saying, This man began to build and was not able to finish." (KJV)

All of us have a race that is set before us. Yet, we may not consider that our finishing the race is not just for our benefit, but for the benefit of those who are in our lives. (Hebrews 12:1-2) We have been given examples. There are people in the grandstands of this room who have run the race you are running and have won. They are the proof the finish line is within reach. When you are in the middle of a hard race, it seems time slows down. What is it that gets you up again? The magnetism and joy of the finish line.

There are seven reasons we must be determined to finish. First, others have planted a field for us to harvest. (John 4:37-38) Second, how and if we finish will affect others. (I Corinthians 9:27) We are not just running for ourselves; we are running for those who are just behind us! Third, we must remember there is a prize for running. (Hebrews 10:23) Fourth, we must follow the path of the righteous and not the path of the crowd. (I Corinthians 9:24) Our finish line is different from the world. We are running for the same finish line Jesus ran for. Fifth, it is crucial we run our own race and not someone else's. (I Thessalonians 4:11) I have seen people get swept up in other people's call and miss their own. Sixth, we must not let a fall be the way our life is determined. (Proverbs 4:10-12) Everyone falls, but there are those who get up after they fall. Seventh, you must be determined if only one finishes, it will be you! (Jude 24) Your motto must be, "I will not just be in the race. I will finish!"

When all is said and done, it is not so much about how you began or how you did in the middle, but rather how you finished. No matter what may be going on now, you can still turn things around. You have several good reasons to finish, and finish well!

APPLICATION:
1. If you are thinking about quitting, do not!
2. Remind yourself finishing affects others.

PRAYER:
Lord, help me finish strong! Amen.

OCTOBER 12
THE BENEFITS OF FAITHFULNESS

Deuteronomy 7:9
"Know therefore that the LORD thy God, he is God, the faithful God,
which keepeth covenant and mercy with them that love him and keep his
commandments to a thousand generations." (KJV)

God is faithful! The reason God can call those things that be not as though they were is because He is faithful. Faithfulness activates your faith. Without faithfulness, all we have are unreliable formulas. David could face Goliath because he had been faithful with the sheep against the lion and bear. He did not have to crank up faith. He already had faith in Him and His faithfulness.

Faith and faithfulness are synonymous. What is faith? It is developing the ability to predict what God will do. Jonah did not want to prophesy doom over Nineveh. Why? Because He knew God would forgive them. When you really know someone, you can predict what they will say or do.

My wife knows me better than anyone. She can predict my actions every time. Peter walked on water because he knew the faithfulness of Jesus would allow him to and would not let him drown. (Matthew 15:28-32) He could predict what Jesus would do.

Sometimes you have to talk yourself into faith—remind yourself what God will ultimately do, like David did! You cannot be faithful overnight, but you can begin. Faithfulness is worked out in times of uncertainty and conflict. Faithfulness will help you to overcome the deficiencies of your life.

Do not let someone else's unfaithfulness stop you from being faithful. God is looking for a few good men and women. Proverbs 20:6 asks, *"Who can find a faithful man?* (NKJV) If you are faithful over few things, you will be the ruler over many! (Luke 16:10-13)

APPLICATION:
1. Decide to be faithful over what and where you are.
2. Do not let the unfaithfulness of the world keep you from being faithful!

PRAYER:
Lord, help me maintain my faithfulness at all times! Amen.

OCTOBER 13
COME CLEAN

I John 1:8-9

"If we say that we have no sin, we deceive ourselves, and the truth is not in us. If we confess our sins, he is faithful and just to forgive us our sins, and to cleanse us from all unrighteousness." (KJV)

Is there a difference between forgiveness and cleansing? *Forgiveness* is from the Greek word, *af-ee-ay-mee*, which means "to send away, to let go, to disregard, not to discuss now, to give up, to remit, to leave; go way from one, in order to go to another place; to depart from one and leave him to himself so that all mutual claims are abandoned; to go away leaving something behind." Forgiveness is to disconnect from an offence and release the offender. However, the spot of offence is not completely eliminated unless there is a cleansing.

What does it mean to be cleansed? *Cleansed* comes from the Greek word, *kath-arid-zo*, which means "to purify, to remove the stain; to have all stains removed, absolve, eradicate; to come clean."

When we come to God with the stain of our sin on our lives, He does more than just forgives us. He cleanses the stain of the sin from our lives and gives us an opportunity to be spotless! When it is within our own power to set things right with a person we have an offence with, it is imperative we do so. We may not be cleansed until we ask others for forgiveness. (Mark 11:24-26; Matthew 6:9-15)

True Bible cleansing comes when we attempt to set things right, not just in God's sight, but also in the sight of those we have hurt. Do not just repent to God for speaking harshly to someone; tell the person you were wrong. A cleansing will follow!

Cleansing is likened to the O.T. Laver, which was a bronze basin on a stand, like a bird bath. It was made from mirrors of women. (Exodus 38:8) It was located between the altar of sacrifice and the doorway to the Tabernacle building. The priests were to wash in it before ministering to the Lord. The penalty for failing to wash was death! The Laver was for cleansing. Only the cleansed could truly enter His presence.

Today, if we are forgiven and God has cleansed us, we need to also come clean before those we have injured. When we do, we will truly be clean!

APPLICATION:
1. Be sure you have come clean before God.
2. Be sure you have come clean before those in your life.

PRAYER:
Lord, thank you for forgiving and cleansing me. Amen.

OCTOBER 14
THE ART OF FORGIVENESS

I John 2:12
"I write unto you, little children, because your sins are forgiven you for his name's sake." (KJV)

Recently, a survey was made of 200 married adults in regards to forgiveness. The researchers were wondering how one's ability to forgive others would affect his/her marital satisfaction and personal well-being. The results were astounding! This research suggests there is a huge relationship between marriage satisfaction and forgiveness. In fact, it appears as much as one third of marriage satisfaction is related to forgiveness.

Not only does the ability to forgive impact the marriage relationship, it was significantly related to personal emotional distress. As forgiveness ability increased, individuals reported fewer symptoms of depression, anxiety and fatigue.

There is an art to forgiveness. It takes on the shape and beauty of the Creator. It paints over an ugly canvas with light and color. It changes the landscape of everything and everyone around it.

Mahatma Gandhi said, "The weak can never forgive. Forgiveness is the attribute of the strong." Truly, to be successful in life and relationships, you have to be a quick and frequent forgiver. Forgiveness is for those who are mature and follow closely in the footsteps of Jesus. We must remember forgiveness does not make the other person right; it makes you free. Power and healing are results of forgiveness.

We live in an age of seared consciences. Once, a shoplifter wrote a letter to a department store. It said, "I've just become a Christian and I can't sleep at night because I feel guilty. So, here is 100 dollars I owe you." He signed his name, and added a little postscript at the bottom, "If I still can't sleep, I'll send you the rest."

We have to understand the art of forgiveness is the ability to see, admit and correct our shortcomings and offences when possible. When we are able to do this, we have truly become an artist.

APPLICATION:
   1. Practice the art of forgiveness, daily.
   2. Correct the weakness of unforgiveness, today.

PRAYER:
Lord, it is my desire to master the art of forgiveness. Amen.

OCTOBER 15
TWO BECOME ONE

Ephesians 5:31-32
"For this cause shall a man leave his father and mother, and shall be joined unto his wife, and they two shall be one flesh. This is a great mystery: but I speak concerning Christ and the church." (KJV)

Adam had a need in the Garden of Eden, which could only be met through another human being, a woman named Eve. Adam seemingly had everything. He walked with God in the cool of the day. He was protected. He was provided for. He should have been fulfilled. However, not even God could totally fulfill him! After Adam saw the pairing of the animal kingdom, he knew something was not quite right.

When God used some of Adam's DNA to *banah* (skillfully form) Eve, He took her to Adam and pronounced her as his helpmeet (helpmate). This word means to complete something that was incomplete. She would be the missing part. She would cause him to be able to reach the heights of his existence. He would not be able to do it without her. Despite the interference of the Devil and the fall of mankind, the principle remains true. It was repeated by Jesus and Paul. (Matthew 19:5-6; Ephesians 5:31-32)

What about two becoming one flesh? The Bible says marriage is honorable in all and the bed undefiled. (Hebrews 13:4) There is more than just a physical merging that takes place in the marriage bed. It symbolizes the total completion of two people becoming one. It should reflect everything else about the relationship and should not simply be about sexual satisfaction. It should be the surrender that comes from the mutual love and devotion demanded of true Bible marriage. Paul likened it to the relationship of Christ and the Church. When you became a Christian, you became one with Christ. Paul called it mysterious. It is the most powerful relationship on earth. Even more powerful than the relationship between parents and children.

I thank God every day for Ginger, my wife. She has truly completed me. Without her, I could have never become what God intended for me to be. If you are married, allow God to help the two to become one!

APPLICATION:
1. If you are married, do something special for your spouse, today.
2. If you are single, ask God to bring you your helpmate.

PRAYER:
Lord, help me be one with my spouse as I am with you. Amen.

OCTOBER 16
LOVE THEM TENDER

Ephesians 5:25; 28-29
"Husbands, love your wives, even as Christ also loved the church, and gave himself for it… So ought men to love their wives as their own bodies. He that loveth his wife loveth himself. For no man ever yet hated his own flesh; but nourish and cherisheth it, even as the Lord the church…" (KJV)

In two full pages of advertisements, the Japanese government declared its desire to right wrongs committed in World War II. Asian Women's Fund, led by former Japanese Prime Minister, Tomiichi Murayama, placed the ads to announce the offer of atonement payments to "comfort women." During the war, women were forced to provide sexual services to the members of Japan's wartime military. In an effort to make atonement, the organization sent donations, messages and letters of apology from the Prime Minister to hundreds of former "comfort women."

As a pastor, at least one in every two women who ask for council confesses to having been sexually violated in some way. Many times it affects every relationship they have with men for the rest of their lives. Too often, in today's world, women are used and swept to the side. They have deep wounds of mistrust and low self-esteem they may never recover from. Because they have been physically, emotionally and sexually violated, many never find the right person.

If you are a man, God has charged you, especially husbands, to be loving, patient and tender, particularly if you are married to one of these wounded women. I Corinthians 13 states love is patient. Love never fails! Take the time in your relationship to understand deep bruises and let God show you how you can be involved in their healing. If you follow God's plan, you can have a long, exciting physical relationship.

APPLICATION:
1. Ask God for wisdom and patience in your relationships.
2. Treat your spouse with tenderness.

PRAYER:
Lord, forgive me for being impatient with my spouse. Amen.

OCTOBER 17
UNDER THE INFLUENCE

Matthew 5:13
"Ye are the salt of the earth: but if the salt have lost his savour, wherewith shall it be salted? It is thenceforth good for nothing, but to be cast out, and to be trodden under foot of men." (KJV)

What is influence? *Influence* is defined as "The capacity or power of persons or things to produce effects on others by intangible means. The power to persuade or obtain advantages resulting from one's status, wealth, position, etc. To have weight, sway, power over, pull pressure, hold, mastery, domination. The ability to positively or negatively affect the actions and traits of another or the outcome of events."

Although the word is not in the Bible, there are many examples of influence, both good and bad. Satan influenced Eve. Eve influenced Adam. Abraham influenced Lot. Lot's wife could not influence Lot. Influence can be bad or good.

Everyone is influenced by a number of different factors. We all like to think of ourselves as independent people. Yet, the truth of the matter is every day someone or something is influencing us. It could be the lyrics of a song we hum along to, a program we watch on TV, an article we read in the paper or something we are told in conversation. Like it or not, we are all under some kind of influence. Alfred Lord Tennyson said, "I am a part of all that I have met."

Here are five things shaping who you are:

1. Your family or parents. (Deuteronomy 6:6-9)
2. Your surroundings. (Exodus 2:11) Moses thought he was an Egyptian because of his surroundings.
3. Your acquaintances. (I Corinthians 15:33 NIV) People at work, school or in your neighborhood can influence you. Their traits are introduced on a repetitive scale.
4. Your friends, those you choose to spend time with voluntarily. (Proverbs 17:17)
5. Your culture. (I Corinthians 7:31) Those you view as successful, and the trends and fads of the day.

No matter who we are, we are people under the influence.

APPLICATION:
1. Examine the influences over your life.
2. Eliminate the negative influences by following the Word of God.

319

PRAYER:
Lord, help me to use the influence I have for good only. Amen.

OCTOBER 18
WHICH WAY WILL YOU GO?

Job 31:21-22
"I have raised my hand against the fatherless, knowing that I had influence in court, then let my arm fall from the shoulder, let it be broken off at the joint."
(NIV)

An accurate proverb states, "People travel together; no one lives detached and alone." This proverb expresses the importance others have in our lives. Other's influence establishes whether we are walking towards the will of God or the will of the Devil. We cannot allow ourselves to be influenced by the wrong people. Additionally, we have to be a right influence for others who are lost.

J. Oswald Sanders wrote in his book, *Spiritual Leadership*, "If those who hold influence over others fail to lead toward the spiritual uplands, then surely the path to the lowlands will be well worn." We must be willing to be trailblazers for God and be willing to become more like Him. We must be willing to influence others to be like Him as well!

There are five reminders regarding influence. The first is who you want to please most in life is going to determine how much and what kind of influence you have. If you choose to try to please your spouse, your boss and your friends, you will have only a limited influence on their lives. This will ultimately lead to frustration and failure. (Galatians 1:10) The second reminder is to look for people who will bring out your best, not your worst! Jesus had a way of bringing out the best in others during his time on earth. Third, you must subtract from your life to have more. Do not be afraid to part ways with those who are bad influences in your life. (Galatians 5:9) Fourth, remember, walking with God distances you from the influences of others. (Romans 8:1-2; II Corinthians 5:7) Last, choose to be a servant of Christ. Matthew 6:24 says, *"No one can serve two masters; for either he will hate the one and love the other..."* (TLB) In the end, you will be glad for the sacrifices you make for Him!

We must never minimize the power of influence for either good or evil. Long after we are dead and gone, our influence will live on. Will you influence or be influenced? Which way will you go?

APPLICATION:
  1. Are you presently being influenced more than you are influencing?
  2. Which way are you going in the area of influence?

PRAYER:
Lord, I will use my influence for your Kingdom. Amen.

OCTOBER 19
YOUR FUTURE IS IN YOUR HANDS

Matthew 7:13-14

"You can enter God's Kingdom only through the narrow gate. The highway to Hell is broad, and its gate is wide for the many who choose that way. But the gateway to life is small, and the road is narrow, and only a few ever find it!"
(NLT)

Not everyone finds the life God intends for them. It is a narrow way. *Narrow* in Greek is *thlibo* (thlee'-bo), which means "to press a compressed way, affording little room; narrow quarters; limited in range or scope; lacking breadth of view or sympathy." Because it is not an easy path, few people choose it and even fewer follow it.

Consequently, few people ever truly find the future that fulfills their lives. There are things we can do to find our future. We can obey the Word of God. (Deuteronomy 32:46-47) When we do what God says, it prolongs our lives. We can stand through difficult times with a good attitude. (Proverbs 24:10) John Maxwell said, "When confronted with a difficult situation, a person with an outstanding attitude makes the best of it while he gets the worst of it. Life can be likened to a grindstone. Whether it grinds you down or polishes you, depends on your attitude." We can demonstrate our devotion by drawing closer to Him. *"For as you know him better, he will give you, through his great power, everything you need for living a truly good life."* (II Peter 1:3 TLB) We can choose to receive God's correction. (Job 5:17-26) There is ascension when we learn from correction.

The Bible tells of many people God brought to their future. He told Abraham to "look and see." (Genesis 12, 15) Abraham went from being fatherless to the father of our faith! He told Noah to build an ark. (Genesis 6) Noah went from preacher to progenitor of mankind. He led David to Samuel. David went from a kid who kept sheep to the King of Israel. He led Joseph from being a throw away to being second in line to the throne. He took Peter from the reed that choked under pressure to the rock of the Church.

Which road will you take? Your future is in your hands!

APPLICATION:
1. Make a decision to stay on the narrow way.
2. Do not let the pressures of life cause you to take another way.

PRAYER:
Lord, lead me and I will follow you on the narrow way. Amen.

OCTOBER 20
GENTLE ON MY MIND

Galatians 5:22-23
"But the fruit of the Spirit is… gentleness… against such there is no law." (KJV)

Robert Browning said, "The great mind knows the power of gentleness." *Gentleness* is from the Greek word *chrestotes* (khray-stot'-ace). It means "to put on an open display and practice moral goodness, integrity and kindness towards all, including those who have suffered harshness."

Gentleness is a part of God. Jesus was our example of this. In II Corinthians 10:1, Paul points this out, *"Now, I Paul myself beseech you by the meekness and gentleness of Christ…"* (KJV) Jesus certainly displayed gentleness to people whom others trampled on.

Gentleness is voluntary humility, becoming lowly on purpose. Gentleness is a part of greatness. When we display gentleness and kindness to those who have been treated unkindly, we display who the Lord really is. God is merciful to those who are kind. The Church needs builders and workers, not a wrecking crew. Seek to help others in a spirit of gentleness.

Henry Drummond said, "Life is short and we never have enough time for gladdening the hearts of those who travel the way with us. O, be swift to love! Make haste to be kind. The greatest thing a man can do for his Heavenly Father is to be kind to some of His other children."

We need a deeper revelation of who our Heavenly Father really is. James 1:12-17 points out He is not harsh through tests and trials. Instead, He brings every good and perfect gift into our lives. Without an understanding of gentleness, we will never fully understand or trust God as our Father! Understanding the gentleness of God is the secret to true success in life. When we encounter difficulties and contradictions, we should not attempt to break them, but instead, bend them with gentleness and time.

Romans 2:4 tells us, *"Or despisest thou the riches of his goodness and forbearance and longsuffering; not knowing that the goodness of God leadeth thee to repentance?"* (KJV) It is His goodness, which leads us back to Him when we stray. No one in the world can ever treat us with the goodness and kindness He treats us with.

APPLICATION:
1. Decide, today, to show the goodness of God to someone in need.
2. If you have strayed, let His goodness lead you back.

PRAYER:
Lord, thank you for being good to me all of the time! Amen.

OCTOBER 21
GRACE PERIOD

Genesis 6:5-8

"And GOD saw that the wickedness of man was great in the earth, and that every imagination of the thoughts of his heart was only evil continually. And it repented the LORD that he had made man on the earth, and it grieved him at his heart. And the LORD said, I will destroy man whom I have created from the face of the earth... But Noah found grace in the eyes of the LORD." (KJV)

Unrepentant sin produced a need for purging. Immorality endangered redemption. It jeopardized the plan of God. It caused God to take drastic measures to preserve the promised seeds by sending a flood. Still, God gave a grace period to earth's inhabitants of over 100 years. God called Noah to preach righteousness. They should have reaped then, but God extended His grace. Noah found grace. It is something that must be sought The expression "find" or "found grace" is mentioned 28 times in the Bible.

What is grace? Grace is the extension of God's mercy after the time to harvest has come. It is the giving of more time to correct and repent even after the time of justice has come.

Grace provides space—space for you to get things corrected. (Romans 5:1-2; 19-21) Again, grace is the extension of God's mercy after the time to harvest has come. It is likened to an insurance policy that has expired, but still contains a grace period to get it reinstated. The way you know you are in grace is when you are still enjoying the blessings of God after being disobedient.

Peter was walking in grace until Pentecost. He had collided with the plan of God numerous times during the time of Christ. Peter had denied Christ three times when he was needed the most at His side. He had disappeared when Jesus was crucified, but the grace of the Lord presided over him until he was converted at Pentecost.

Because everything is governed by spiritual law, God has to allow the process of sowing and reaping. Yet, the one thing He has in reserve against even law, is His grace! Thank God for His grace period!

APPLICATION:
1. Be sure to thank God for His grace, today.
2. Show the grace He has bestowed on you to others, today.

PRAYER:
Lord, thank you so much for your grace. May I never abuse it! Amen.

OCTOBER 22
THE APPEARANCE OF GRACE

Genesis 39:4
"And Joseph found grace in his sight, and he served him: and he made him overseer over his house, and all that he had he put into his hand." (KJV)

Phillip Yancey said, "Grace means that God already loves us as much as an infinite God can possibly love." The popular rock band, U2, has a song entitled *Grace*. It says, "Grace finds beauty in everything… Grace makes beauty out of ugly things." Grace brings the possibility of making something beautiful out of something revolting. It is hard to accept, hard to believe, hard to receive and even harder to extend. Why did grace appear? Grace appeared to answer the problem of sin. The appearance of sin demands the appearance of grace. (Romans 5:20) Grace produces a scandal. In his book *What's So Amazing About Grace*, Phillip Yancey brilliantly points out the nature of grace is scandalous. Just when people think someone has been caught, God extends His grace to them!

Grace shocks us in what it offers. It is truly not of this world. It frightens us with what it does for sinners. Grace teaches us God does for others what we would never do for them. In John 8:1-11, an adulteress would have been stoned for her crime/sin under Moses' Law, had it not been for grace. The law was so perfect, even Moses or David could not have been saved by it. They were murderers!

Not too long ago, there was a baby found alive in a Savannah, Georgia, dumpster. They decided to call her "Baby Grace." Amidst the stench of rotting food and household refuse, was this innocent creature named Grace. Where do you generally find grace? In the midst of the stench!

Jesus did all the work when He died on the cross. (Ephesians 2:1-8) An equation I appreciate is mercy plus love equals grace!

Grace is a gift which costs everything to the giver and nothing to the receiver. It is given to those who do not deserve it, barely recognize it and hardly appreciate it. This is why God alone gets the glory in our salvation. That is why grace appeared!

APPLICATION:
1. Are you showing the grace of God to others regularly?
2. Do you thank God for His grace, daily?

PRAYER:
Lord, I will walk in the grace you have shown me. Amen.

OCTOBER 23
HAPPY BIRTHDAY

Ezekiel 16:4-7
"And as for thy nativity, in the day thou was born… None eye pitied thee, to do any of these unto thee, to have compassion upon thee; but thou wast cast out in the open field, to the lothing of thy person, in the day that thou wast born. And when I passed by thee, and saw thee… I said unto thee.. Live; yea I said unto thee when thou wast in thy blood, Live. I have caused thee to multiply as the bud of the field, and thou hast increased and waxen great, and thou art come to excellent ornaments…" (KJV)

What day of the year is your birthday? Mine happens to be today! When I was born, I do not think it was a day of much celebration. My mother was nearly 43 years old and unwed in 1958. I was the last of nine birth children. I do not think I was in the planning nine months before. If abortion had been legal, I would have most likely been aborted. I was just another child born to a very poor, unwed woman, with no visible means of support, on the poor side of town without a future. BUT GOD!!!

As a small child, I felt inside I had a special purpose. I was not raised in church, so I did not know what it was or how to find it. BUT GOD! God has a way of introducing Himself to you when you do not even know He exists.

I had a natural knack of being comfortable with people. I would perform for people who visited our home by lip-synching to Beatles songs. I was never nervous. I was excited about being in front of people. God was preparing me for the day when I would offer this "gift" to Him and His Kingdom. That time finally came. The 23rd of October became the birthday of someone who made a difference in the lives of others. BUT GOD! God found a way to work through my many weaknesses and flaws and use the best for good!

What is your birthday? It is a very special day to Him. He wants to take your life and turn your birthday into a day others celebrate, too! Happy Birthday!

APPLICATION:
1. Decide to make your birthday a day for others to celebrate.
2. Let God use the best inside of you to help others.

PRAYER:
Lord, thank you for my birthday. May I cause it to be a day others have a reason to celebrate. Amen.

OCTOBER 24
THE GREAT PHYSICIAN

Psalms 107:20
"He sent his word, and healed them..." (KJV)

God has always been in the healing business. Healing was introduced in the Old Testament and magnified when Jesus appeared in the New Testament.

While serving as an associate professor at Harvard Medical School, Dr. Herbert Benson authored a book entitled, *Timeless Healing: The Power and Biology of Belief.* In this work, which is the culmination of 30 years of research, Dr. Benson maintains the conviction "human beings are wired for God." He notes until 150 years ago, there was no separation between belief and healing. We have since begun to replace our belief systems with medical systems. Healing is now attributed to pills and surgery, rather than the combined efforts of medicine and faith. Benson reminds the reader placebos are effective in 30 to 90 percent of the cases. We have come to discount the placebo effect and say, "It's all in your head." He says, "In truth, we should be paying more attention to it." The medicine is in our "head" (faith). It must not be replaced by pharmaceuticals or surgery, but returned to its position as a complementary tool in the process of healing. Benson sees belief as one of three legs on a stool with medicines and surgery comprising the other two. We should not discount the fact that Jesus told the one grateful leper, *"Your faith has made you well."* (Luke 17:19 NKJV) Faith in the Great Physician is the best resource in your medicine cabinet.

If God is the Great Physician, then why do people get sick and not recover? There is a curse still on our flesh. (Genesis 2:8-15; 3:17-19) People lack the knowledge healing is provided. (Mark 3:1-5) People lack the belief healing is the will of God. (Matthew 17:14-20) Some continue to disobey. (Psalms 107:17-20) Some have a lack of demand placed on their faith. (Matthew 9:20) People fail to properly take care of their bodies. Some fail to recognize the significance of communion. (I Corinthians 10:16)

Doctors are an extension of Heaven, but He is still the Great Physician!

APPLICATION:
1. If you are sick, do not just call on your doctor. Call on Him!
2. Trust Him, today, to heal you from all of your sickness.

PRAYER:
Lord, I believe you are my healer, today, tomorrow and forever! Amen.

OCTOBER 25
BUILD A STRONG FOUNDATION

Job 11:18-20

"You will be secure, because there is hope; you will look about you and take your rest in safety. You will lie down, with no one to make you afraid, and many will court your favor. But the eyes of the wicked will fail, and escape will elude them; their hope will become a dying gasp." (NIV)

When my children were younger, we made it a point to make Christmas special. Money was limited, so we bought our children several small gifts and one "big" (more expensive) gift. On Christmas morning, the kids would open all of their presents first, and then they would empty their stockings last. Hidden in each of their stockings was a clue. Each clue, led to another clue. The clues required them to go from inside the house to outside, upstairs to downstairs, until the last clue led them to their "big" present. This practice became one of our family's traditions.

Every year the kids hoped they would receive their "big" gift. However, they had faith my wife and I would provide it. Without hope, they would not have been as excited or appreciative when they received the gift.

Without a good understanding of hope, our faith will never achieve the greatness it was meant for. It is almost as if people think they can "skip" hope and go straight to faith. (Romans 15:13) Hope is the foundation for your faith, the anchor of the soul. (Hebrews 6:19) Romans 4:17-18 says Abraham believed in hope even when his reason for hope ran out! He believed the power of his hope would be enough to connect his faith to the level of being willing to sacrifice Isaac. We must find a way to believe in the power in hope!

Hope gives faith direction. It causes faith to have aim. Hope is a goal setter. As Charles Capps said, "The thermostat will only produce what you set it on. Faith is the power, but hope is the thermostat!"

Hope provides us with the confidence that no matter how desperate things may be right now, we are God's children and we are destined to win!

APPLICATION:
1. Are you hoping for God to do something in your life right now?
2. Do not let discouragement overwhelm you. Put your hope in Him!

PRAYER:
Lord, I place my hope in you and am confident in all you can provide! Amen.

OCTOBER 26
HOPE, THE PATHWAY TO YOUR FUTURE

Philippians 1:3-6
"I thank my God every time I remember you. In all my prayers for all of you, I always pray with joy because of your partnership in the gospel from the first day until now, being confident of this, that he who began a good work in you will carry it on to completion until the day of Christ Jesus." (NIV)

When Jerome Groopman diagnosed patients with serious diseases, the Harvard Medical School professor discovered all of them were "looking for a sense of genuine hope and indeed, that hope was as important to them as anything he might prescribe as a physician." After writing a book called, *The Anatomy of Hope*, Groopman was asked for his definition. He replied, "Basically, I think hope is the ability to see a path to the future...You are facing dire circumstances, and you need to know everything that's blocking or threatening you. And then you see a path, or a potential path, to get to where you want to be. Once you see that, there's a tremendous emotional uplift that occurs..." The doctor confessed, "I think hope has been, is and always will be the heart of medicine and healing. We could not live without hope." Even with all the medical technology available to us now, we still come back to this profound human need to believe that there is a possibility to reach a future that is better than the one in the present."

Hope is a pathway to your future. Dutch Sheets said, "You don't have to be well to hope, but you have to hope to become well!" Hope breeds life. Hope produces something better! (Zechariah 9:12) We know hope deferred makes the heart sick. (Proverbs 13:12)

Thomas Fuller said, "If it were not for hopes, the heart would break." One of my favorite movies is *The Shawshank Redemption*. In the movie, Andy says to Red, "Get busy livin', or get busy dying!" Red responds, "There's no place for hope inside of a prison!" For the person who has stopped hoping, failure is inevitable. Just take the pathway of hope and it will take you to your future!

APPLICATION:
1. Are you getting your hopes up?
2. Get busy living!

PRAYER:
Lord, I will put my hope in you and live! Amen.

OCTOBER 27
TAKE FLIGHT

Ephesians 4:3
"Endeavoring to keep the unity of the Spirit in the bond of peace." (KJV)

A flock of birds had spent an entire day flying south for the winter. Along the way, several of the birds began to get hungry. They spoke to their leader and said, "We are hungry. When can we stop for food?" The leader replied, "When we see a field of grain, then we will stop and feast before carrying on." It was at that time, a member of the flock spotted a patch of rice scattered on the ground. "Here's some food! There's rice on the ground! Let's stop here," the bird said. The rest of the flock concurred this is where they should stop for food. Under the pressure of his flock, the leader agreed this is where they would stop to feast.

As the birds began eating the rice scattered on the ground, a large net fell upon them, and the birds were trapped. In panic, the birds began anxiously flapping their wings, trying to get out. When the leader observed this was not going to free his flock, he quickly and directly instructed them, "Stop! If we are not in unity, this net will never lift. We must flap our wings together to get this net to lift!" So, the flock began to flap their wings simultaneously. Just as the leader had predicted, the net began to lift and the birds began to take flight.

Unity is the key to the Christian faith. In Romans 15:5-7, Paul confronted the Roman Church to be in unity, to be like minded. This was a foreign concept.

What will it take to become unified? We must become aware of each other. (I Corinthians 10:24) We should live to lift up someone else. We should lay down our lives for those who are in Christ. (I John 3:14-15) We should learn to walk together. (Jeremiah 3:18; 50:4) We should look at people the way God does. (Romans 2:10-11) If we choose to look hard enough, we will undoubtedly find something we have in common with others. We can lift up those around us and become stronger because we are unified.

APPLICATION:
1. Find common bonds of unity.
2. Lift up those around you.

PRAYER:
Lord, help me to lift up others and be in unity with those around me. Amen.

OCTOBER 28
THE PAYOFF OF PATIENCE

Isaiah 40:29-31
"He giveth power to the faint; and to them that have no might he increaseth strength. Even the youths shall faint and be weary, and the young men shall utterly fall: But they that wait upon the LORD shall renew their strength; they shall mount up with wings as eagles; they shall run, and not be weary; and they shall walk, and not faint." (KJV)

Benjamin Franklin said, "He that can have patience can have what he wills." Luke 21:19 says, *"By your patience, possess your souls!"* (KJV) Patience is an active endurance of opposition, not a passive resignation. *Patience* and *patient* are used to translate several Hebrew and Greek words. Patience is endurance, steadfastness, long-suffering and forbearance. It also means constancy regardless of circumstances. There is payoff for patience. Joseph is the greatest example of Bible patience in the Bible. Noah waited even longer. Like Joseph, he was given no reason to believe what God had spoken to him. Yet, Joseph's circumstances did not become neutral; they became worse after God spoke to him. However, he persevered and never lashed out at God. Acts 7:9-10 reveals that God was with him in his afflictions.

Someone wise said, "A delay is better than a disaster!" In Isaiah 30:18, Israel wanted to sprint ahead and it cost them! A Persian Proverb states, "All things are difficult before they become easy."

There are two keys to using your patience. One key is to follow people who have walked through to the end. (Hebrews 6:12) Secondly, never, never, never give up! Today is not won by old victories nor lost by old defeats. I like this saying, "With patience, a well can be dug with a spoon."

Jesus was patient with people. He was patient with Peter. There was eventually a payoff! If you continue to wait on the Lord, He will release things into your life you have been waiting for. Regardless of what it seems, there is a payoff for patience.

APPLICATION:
1. Do not be impatient. Wait!
2. Trust God is working out things you cannot see.

PRAYER:
Lord, I will be patient with the process you have working in my life. Amen.

331

OCTOBER 29
FINDING PEACE

II Thessalonians 3:16
"Now the Lord of peace himself give you peace always by all means. The Lord be with you all." (KJV)

There was a very extensive survey conducted across the United States by a leading polling agency. The survey examined every age group, every social group and every financial group. There were many questions pertaining to modern life in America. However, the chief question was, "What is it that you would choose to have over any other one thing?" The answer astoundingly was not riches, fame or popularity. The overwhelming majority of people said they most desired peace in their lives!

Peace is the will of God for every believer. He wants to bring a calmness that supersedes every storm, every disappointment and every setback. Dwight L. Moody made this observation, "A great many people are trying to make peace, but that has already been done. God has not left it for us to do; all we have to do is enter into it."

Peace is the deliberate adjustment of our life to the will of God. We have mistaken the lack of trouble as peace. If that is true, then one incident can take away our peace. If we depend on our relationships to give us peace, the other person can take it away. The same is true if we are depending on our peace being in our job, family, etc. It can be quickly taken away. I remember vividly the 1999-2000 sports season. The University of Tennessee football team won the 1998 NCAA National Championship, in January, 1999. (I am a BIG UT fan.) The St. Louis Rams won the Super Bowl. (I am a life-long Rams fan.) The Los Angeles Lakers won the first of three consecutive NBA titles (I am also a life-long Lakers fan.) Oh, what a great, peaceful sports year! However, just a few short years later, the Rams were the second worse team in the NFL. The University of Tennessee did not even make it to a bowl game and had to hire a new coach. The Lakers lost in the finals to their rivals the Boston Celtics. Any peace you get from temporary things is temporary!

We must always remember when we find Christ, we find permanent peace!

APPLICATION:
1. Be sure to look for peace in eternal things.
2. Remember, our peace is found in His will for our lives!

PRAYER:
Lord, I desire to have the peace that only you can provide in my life. Thank you for filling me with it. Amen.

OCTOBER 30
LASTING PEACE

Numbers 25:12-13
"Wherefore say, Behold I give unto him my covenant of peace: And he shall have it, and his seed after him..." (KJV)

I heard a preacher tell this funny story: "There was Kentucky mountaineer fighting overseas in WWI who kept getting nagging letters from his wife back home. He was too busy fighting to write letters, even to his wife. At last, angered by his wife's scolding letters, he sat down and wrote her, 'Dear Nancy, I been a-gittin' yore naggin' letters all along. Now I want to tell ye, I'm tired of them. For the first time in my life, I'm a fightin' in a big war, and I want to enjoy it in peace as long as it lasts!'"

Peace is the ability to be settled at all times, even when things are unsettled around you. It is not avoiding an issue which demands a resolution or appeasing an individual who needs to be confronted. Proverbs 10:10 says, *"...Bold reproof leads to peace."* (TLB) There was a widow who had "Rest in Peace" inscribed on her husband's tombstone. When she found out he left her out of his will, she added, "'Til I Come!"

How do we obtain peace? Obedience to God brings peace. (Isaiah 48:17-20) God teaches and directs us to an overflowing, always reachable peace when we obey Him. Faith produces peace. (Mark 4:35-40) Jesus reproved the disciples for not using their faith to calm the storm and bring about peace. The absence of faith is the absence of peace. Worship produces peace. Gideon listened to God and then built an altar to Jehovah Shalom. (Judges 6:11-24) It was so powerful even Ophra appeared. Renewing your mind to things of God produces peace. (Isaiah 26:3) When you meditate on the things God says about you, even your mind achieves peace!

Real Bible peace will take you through everything life offers. It will stand up in the fiercest storms and be present when trouble is closing in. The Prince of Peace offers more than just peace; He offers lasting peace!

APPLICATION:
1. Are you obeying God? Are you walking in faith?
2. Worship God in the storm and renew your mind in Him.

PRAYER:
Lord, I will follow you and seek the peace only you can offer! Amen.

OCTOBER 31
TRICK OR TREAT?

II John 1:7
"For many deceivers are entered into the world, who confess not that Jesus Christ is come in the flesh. This is a deceiver and an antichrist." (KJV)

We are living in an age of great deception. Because of spiritual hunger, people are seeking spiritualism more than ever, but not seeking God. Is this a possible "treat" or another "trick" of the enemy?

Spiritualism outside of God brings judgment. Worshipping creation is forbidden. Mediums and psychics are not agents of God, regardless of how many scriptures they paste on their practices' advertisements. They are not dealing with God's Spirit, but with familiar spirits.

Familiar spirits, and those who operate with them, are not from God. (Leviticus 19:31) Do not give them any fame or attention. Predicting behavior or destiny from the moon, sun and stars is not the way God will guide you.

Yet, how do these people sometimes know things about us? Palm readers, fortune-tellers, astrologers, mediums, etc. are in contact with a darker spirit realm which has become familiar with you, your life and habits. If they are not out and out charlatans (most are), they relay the information they are shown through this dark spirit realm.

The Bible is very clear about not following people who follow the occult. (Isaiah 8:19-22; Deuteronomy 18:10-12) We must be able to discern the good and the evil. (Deuteronomy 18:20-22) Saul was fooled by a familiar spirit. (I Samuel 28:3) Saul had been ordered not to have anything to do with this, and he eventually lost his throne and his life! (I Chronicles 10:13-14)

Familiar spirits have no power to deliver. (Isaiah 47:13) If these things were as grand as they portray themselves, then the lands they originate from would not be desolate!

Although there is much spirituality around you, do not accept it is all from God. Only God can "treat" us with His blessings. Do not be tricked!

APPLICATION:
1. Do not participate in false spirituality of any kind!
2. Trust God to speak to you and lead you.

PRAYER:
Lord, deliver me from the tricks of darkness and its effects. Amen.

NOVEMBER 1
ADDITION BY PRAYER

II Kings 20:1-5
"In those days was Hezekiah sick unto death. And the prophet Isaiah
the son of Amoz came to him, and said unto him, Thus saith the LORD, Set thine
house in order; for thou shalt die, and not live. Then he turned his face to the
wall, and prayed unto the LORD... And it came to pass, afore Isaiah was gone
out into the middle court, that the word of the LORD came to him, saying, Turn
again, and tell Hezekiah the captain of my people, Thus saith the LORD, the
God of David thy father, I have heard thy prayer, I have seen thy tears:
behold, I will heal thee..." (KJV)

Hezekiah had conquered kingdoms and kings. He had seen many battles he was triumphant in. However, this time, only help from Heaven was able to bring him the victory. When he turned and prayed, he changed the will of God for his life and prolonged his life. God added 15 years to his life.

God has a plan, a promise and a purpose for your life. He promises us days. In Psalms 90:8-10, it is 80 years. In Genesis 6:3, your days shall be 120 years. However, our prayer life will determine how many of those days are added to our lives.

Benjamin Franklin once said, "Do you love life? Then do not squander time for that is the stuff that life is made of." Another quote by an unknown source reads, "The tragedy of life is not that it ends so soon, but that we wait so long to begin it."

Prayer brings the addition of time to our lives, which we cannot add ourselves. Whenever we spend time in prayer, we are expanding the presence of God in our lives. Then, when we need help from Heaven, we are able to make withdrawals! We slow time making it our servant. We are no longer slaves to time.

God is the only one who can add time back to your life. He says He will do it in Joel 2:24-28. He will add the years hurt, loss, divorce and disappointment have stolen away. The question is, "Will you pray?"

APPLICATION:
1. Be sure to give yourself to God in prayer everyday. He will give you the time back.
2. Trust God! He is listening to your prayers.

PRAYER:
Lord, please add back the stolen time to my life. Amen.

NOVEMBER 2
OVERCOMING THE STRESS

John 16:33
"I have told you all this so that you will have peace of heart and mind. Here on earth you will have many trials and sorrows; but cheer up, for I have overcome the world." (TLB)

Most of life's problems are common; they are not extraordinary. Yet, even daily problems unmanaged, produce stress. What is stress? It is best defined as unusual strain, tension, anxiety, force, burden or pressure.

The fact is most leading medical clinics report 80 to 85 percent of their total caseload is due directly to worry and anxiety. Many experts say coping with stress is the number one health priority of our day. One leading physician has stated, in his opinion, 70 percent of all medical patients could cure themselves, if only they got rid of their worries and fears. We know medical science has closely tied worry to heart trouble, high blood pressure, ulcers, thyroid malfunction, migraine headaches and a host of stomach disorders, among others.

There are many people, today, who are overwhelmed with life. Psalms 61:1-2 says, *"Hear my cry, O God; attend unto my prayer. From the end of the earth will I cry unto thee, when my heart is overwhelmed: lead me to the rock that is higher than I."* (KJV) Only God can truly help us overcome the stresses of life when we get to the level of being totally overwhelmed.

There are other Psalms we can get some relief from, such as Psalms 77; 142:1-7; 143. Proverbs 3:6 says, *"...in all your ways acknowledge Him, and He will make your paths straight."* (NIV)

There are some practical things you can do, as well as spiritual, that will help you overcome your stress. First, plan days realistically. Second, pace your life according to importance. Third, slow down! Fourth, make plans for relaxation. Fifth, do not feel guilty when you do things other than work. Finally, deal with things with your faith as well as your experience!

Jesus is the example we can overcome now, in this present, crazy world. You do not have to be stressed out. You can be blessed out!

APPLICATION:
1. Follow the steps listed above.
2. Spend more quiet time with God.

PRAYER:
Lord, I give you all of my worries and cares. Help me to manage what I can manage. Amen.

NOVEMBER 3
TEMPER, TEMPER

Romans 7:18-19

"For I know that in me (that is, in my flesh,) dwelleth no good thing: for to will is present with me; but how to perform that which is good I find not. For the good that I would I do not: but the evil which I would not, that I do." (KJV)

Temperance is the last of the fruits of the Spirit. (Galatians 5) No wonder Paul left this one for the last one listed. Temperance comes from the Greek word *egkrateia* (eng-krat'-i-ah). It means "self-control, forbearance, self-discipline, restraint, discretion, prudence; abstention, self-denial."

Our flesh does not like restraints. Seatbelts are in your car for your protection. They restrain you in the event you are in an accident. They do not put themselves on you; you must voluntarily place one on yourself. They are preventive. They keep you from the possibility of great harm.

Temperance is solving the problem of acting like yourself. It provides you with the opportunity to be patient when things are uncertain.

We develop self-control through comparing our desires and God's desires for us. Temperance is choosing God's desire for our lives. The big question for all of us is, "Who is in control of my life?" The fallen state of humanity makes it impossible for us to control our sinful desires. The Bible reveals even the Apostle Paul was not able to remain in control of himself at all times.

How do we turn our desires into His? We must trust God enough to die—die to ourselves, die to our emotions and die to our desires. (Romans 6:11-14) The Holy Spirit enables us to accept this solution. The Holy Spirit provides us with self-control or temperance. It is not enough to have a law against something; there must be something inside which legislates and guides.

The next time your flesh tries to get you to go against God, turn to the Spirit. He will help you overcome the temptation and give you the strength to solve your temper's temper!

APPLICATION:
1. Submit yourself to Him, today.
2. Seek His help if your flesh is controlling you in a certain area.

PRAYER:
Lord, please give me the strength to stand up against my flesh. Amen.

NOVEMBER 4
CHILDREN OF CHOICES

Romans 1:18-19, 28, 32

"The wrath of God is being revealed from heaven against all the godlessness and wickedness of human beings who suppress the truth by their wickedness, since what may be known about God is plain to them, because God has made it plain to them... Furthermore, just as they did not think it worthwhile to retain the knowledge of God, so God gave them over to a depraved mind, so that they do what ought not to be done... Although they know God's righteous decree that those who do such things deserve death, they not only continue to do these very things but also approve of those who practice them." (NIV)

People without God are most likely to make their moral and ethical decisions on the basis of whatever feels right or comfortable in a situation. Their choices are guided from a source apart from God. They feel religion is for older adults.

Choices always bring consequences. In II Samuel 11:1, David made a choice to stay home and not go to battle. He sent someone else to fight for him. The mighty warrior quit, rested and relaxed. This proved to be a poor choice. The consequences of this one little choice haunted David all the days of his life. David only lived to be 70. He spent only half of his life in God's will. Sin and regret will often follow choices made apart from God.

What chain of events came forth out of the simple choice to stay home when God wanted David with his men? David lusts for Bathsheba to the degree he commits adultery and conspires to murder. A baby boy is born, but David has to bury him. Bathsheba's grandfather, Ahitophel, was in great disappointment. As a result, Ahitophel sets his house in order. He ties a hangman's noose and ends his life. David's daughter, Tamar, quit wearing the colored virgin dress. Absalom kills Amnon for the sexual sin to his sister. David goes five years without seeing his handsome son. All these tears are traced back to the one sad day, the General, the King, decided not to report for active duty. Do not underestimate the effect your choices may have!

APPLICATION:
1. Ask God to help you make good decisions each day.
2. Let His Spirit lead and guide you.

PRAYER:
Lord, I will listen to you. I choose your way and not mine. Amen.

NOVEMBER 5
WALKING IN THE WILL OF GOD

Psalms 32:8

"I will instruct you and teach you in the way you should go; and I will guide you with My eye…" (NKJV)

One of the most inspiring truths in all the Bible is the fact God has a plan for every life. There is a divine blueprint. It matters where you work, where you go to college, who you marry and what career you choose because God has a plan for your life.

God does not only call preachers. His divine will applies to all of us. We all must seek the face of God and find out the plan He has designed just for us! Despite our upbringing and background, when we give our plans to Him, He is able to bring the best out and help us find the right path for our lives.

John Wesley's mother had one baby per year for 21 years. He was one of seventeen who survived. He grew up in England where the Gospel of Grace had been forsaken, and the nation was following the doctrine of salvation by works. John Wesley was also brought up this way.

He believed if he punished himself enough and did enough penance, it would seal his fate in Heaven. Each morning, he arose around 4 a.m. and swam in an ice-cold river as a proof of denial. He ceased to be jovial and did not listen to jokes, nor did he tell them. It is said he walked 150 miles to college and it took nearly a week. At college, he discovered Bible grace from George Whitfield. There, he became born-again and used his experience to bring alive again the doctrine of Salvation by Grace. It turned the nation and the world back to God. He believed in a God directed life and God directed future.

Walking in the will of God begins by acknowledging God has a plan for your life. Then, you must commit yourself to discovering and following that plan. You will find the plan in the Word of God, and you will be directed by walking in the Spirit. When you choose to do His will, He will help you make good decisions which will take you closer to the center of it. He will begin to place everything you need in your life to be successful. Then, you will be able to say you are walking in His will!

APPLICATION:
1. Be sure you are submitting your plan to Him.
2. Be willing to make any changes needed.

PRAYER:
Lord, help me understand the things you have in mind for my life. Amen.

NOVEMBER 6
THE TEN COMMANDMENTS

Deuteronomy 10:4
"And he wrote on the tablets, according to the first writing, the ten commandments, which the LORD spake unto you in the mount out of the midst of the fire in the day of the assembly: and the LORD gave them unto me." (KJV)

Today's verse describes the second writing of the Commandments after Moses had previously broken the tablets. It is symbolic that although the Commandments were broken, it did not mean that they were done away with.

Some facts about the Commandments are: There were actually 613 given in the law, but 10 were the foundation from which all the others flowed. They were given about 50 days after the Israelites came out of Egypt, which symbolized the feast of Pentecost. (Exodus 19:10-23) They were first spoken by God in Exodus 20, and later written in stone by His finger in Deuteronomy.

Although born-again believers are not under the law which is performance based only, (Romans 6:15) nine of the ten are repeated in the New Testament with added stipulations, which are even higher than those given in Exodus 20. An example is Matthew 5:27-32, which states to look lustfully, is the same as adultery; whereas in the Old Testament, it was a purely physical act.

The Commandments were a code of wisdom. God set up some house rules. These rules were given not only to govern by, but to provide, protect and to prosper those who followed them. In the New Testament we are introduced to the law of love. Love and law are not opponents, but allies. Law needs love as its motive. Law without love results in Pharisaism, which places principles before people. With Pharisaism, one can be perfectly good without actually loving one's neighbor. Additionally, love needs law as its eyes, for love is blind even to things that are irresponsible.

Only as we observe the limits set by God's law can we really become what we are meant to be. God's Ten Commandments are not just the law, they are the way!

APPLICATION:
1. Are you following His Commandments?
2. Do you keep the Commandments He has spoken over you?

PRAYER:
Lord, forgive me for not keeping your Commandments. Amen.

NOVEMBER 7
RELATIONSHIP COMMANDMENTS

Exodus 24:12
"And the LORD said unto Moses, Come up to me into the mount, and be there: and I will give thee tables of stone, and a law, and commandments which I have written; that thou mayest teach them." (KJV)

All the Commandments were about relationships. The first four were about a relationship with God. The last six were about a relationship with God's people, hence the reason for two tablets.

Here is a breakdown of the Commandments: First Commandment, *"Thou shalt have no other gods before me."* (Exodus 20:3; Deuteronomy 6:1 KJV) The people were introduced to many gods, but there was only one true God. Jehovah reminds them all that is good, and all that is made is from the one God.

The Second Commandment, *"Thou shalt have no idols before me."* (Exodus 20:3 KJV) God is saying not to have any physical representation or worship any likeness of Him (in Heaven) or anything He created (on earth). (Exodus 20:22-26 KJV) God does not want to share you with anyone.

The Third Commandment, *"Thou shalt not take the name of the Lord thy God in vain."* (Exodus 20:7 KJV) The Hebrew meaning of *vain* is "empty, false, or falsely." This Commandment means not to say anything false about God or attach anything false to His name. (Job 38-41; 42:7) To *misuse God's name* literally means "to lift it up to or attach it to emptiness."

The Fourth Commandment, *"Remember the Sabbath and keep it Holy."* (Exodus 20:8 KJV) Remembering something is more than just calling it to mind and doing nothing; you have to do something. In this case, it was to remember God rescued the Israelites.

All of these first four Commandments pertain to our relationship with God. Each of them is critical to our ability to follow through with obedience to God's way of doing things. Each one of these Commandments brings a blessing to those who choose to follow them!

APPLICATION:
1. Be sure to check these Commandments and decide if your relationship with God is in tact.
2. Be sure to consider the great blessings which accompany obedience.

PRAYER:
Lord, I pledge to obey your Commandments. Amen.

NOVEMBER 8
FOLLOWING THE COMMANDMENTS

Matthew 19:17
"...but if thou wilt enter into life, keep the commandments." (KJV)

The Ten Commandments were about relationships. The first four relate to our relationship with God: 1. Thou shalt not worship other gods. Worship only the one true God, the one who caused everything to be. 2. Thou shalt have no idols before me. 3. Thou shalt not take the name of the Lord thy God in vain. 4. Remember the Sabbath and keep it Holy. (Exodus 20)

The next six relate to human relationships: 5. Honor your father and mother. This is the first Commandment with promise according to Ephesians 6. It is based on the father-child relationship we have with God. 6. Thou shalt not kill. Most Bible scholars agree the word *kill* refers to murder. It is the intentional, malicious act of taking another human being's life without regard or regret. It is considered heinous and God spoke about its severity when the first murder took place in the Bible in Genesis 4. 7. Thou shalt not commit adultery. Adultery is considered any sexual relationship outside of marriage. It is destructive not only because of the physical breach it brings, but also the spiritual. It breaks a solemn covenant God intended to be sealed in the marriage bed and should not be compromised. It is a breach of faithfulness and brings destruction to the relationship God said no man should sever. 8. Thou shalt not steal. Stealing was considered sometimes a capital offence. Stealing is to take something that is not your own personal property. God has promised to bless and take care of His people, so stealing reveals lack of belief and hard work. 9. Thou shalt not bear false witness. This means lying against your neighbor. It reveals you are untrustworthy and unreliable. It disqualifies you from God's best because He said if we are going to follow Him, we must do so in Spirit and in truth. 10. Thou shalt not covet thy neighbor's goods. This deals with jealousy and desire for something that belongs to someone else. One priest remarked: "It's the only sin I never hear confessed!"

These Commandments are for our good and benefit. Despite the unpopularity of the Commandments, we must be willing to obey God by following them!

APPLICATION:
1. Check yourself to be sure you follow each one.
2. Commit to following the Commandments, daily.

PRAYER:
Lord, help me follow the things you have commanded. Amen.

NOVEMBER 9
THE BLESSING OF THE TEN COMMANDMENTS

I John 5:2-5
"By this we know that we love the children of God, when we love God, and keep his commandments. For this is the love of God, that we keep his commandments: and his commandments are not grievous." (KJV)

Probably the most misunderstood part of the Ten Commandments is they are for our good. Each one brings with it a special blessing when we act upon them. The Commandments were given as a guidepost. They were not a way to enter into Heaven; this was accomplished only through His blood. The Commandments helped condition the human spirit into the image of God.

The Commandments were fulfilled by Jesus. (Matthew 5; Hebrews 10:1-20) He brought the law under His own blood and did away with the ongoing, temporal sacrifice of animals. He paid the full price for redemption and provided grace to the repentant.

Though believers today are not under the Law (Romans 6:15), they are under obligation to abide by the Holy standards represented in the Ten Commandments. Nine of the Ten Commandments are repeated in the New Testament with added stipulations, which are considered even higher than those in Exodus 20:3-17.

The one not repeated is the command to keep the Sabbath; however, the first day of the week is to be set aside for worship in commemoration of the Savior's resurrection. Jesus' disciples were persecuted for not observing the Sabbath, or *shabat* in the Hebrew. What was Jesus' response? Mark 2:27-28 say, *"And he said unto them, The sabbath was made for man, and not man for the sabbath:Therefore the Son of man is Lord also of the sabbath."* (KJV)

Jesus revealed all other Commandments were for the benefit of God's people. He simplified them by stating in Matthew 22:37-40, *"Jesus said unto him, Thou shalt love the Lord thy God with all thy heart, and with all thy soul, and with all thy mind. This is the first and great commandment. And the second is like unto it, Thou shalt love thy neighbour as thyself. On these two commandments hang all the law and the prophets."* (KJV)

APPLICATION:
1. Are you obeying His Commandments?
2. Believe God for the blessings accompanying them.

PRAYER
Lord, thank you for the blessing of your Commandments. Amen.

NOVEMBER 10
ADOPTED BY GOD

Romans 8:15-16

"For ye have not received the spirit of bondage again to fear; but ye have received the Spirit of adoption, whereby we cry, Abba, Father. The Spirit itself beareth witness with our spirit, that we are the children of God:" (KJV)

God has purposely brought us into His family. This act was a response to the effects of sin and death. He dealt with our past. He deals with our present. He has dealt with our future. He removed the wall that kept us outside of His care.

What does adoption for the believer mean? The Greek word for *adoption* is *huiothesia*. It means "that relationship which God was pleased to establish between Himself and the Israelites in preference to all other nations; the nature and condition of the true disciples in Christ, who by receiving the Spirit of God into their souls become sons of God."

In her book *Does God Believe in Adoption?* Kay Green points out that even though the Bible uses the word *adopt* only about five times, it refers to the concept of adoption surprisingly often. Additionally, when it does, the Bible always presents adoption as a positive, gracious act, which is part of God's plan. Moses, for example, was adopted by Pharaoh's daughter. (Exodus 2:1-10) His adoption, though sad for his Israelite parents, was part of God's overall plan for the deliverance of Israel from Egypt. Esther was also an adoptee. We are told when her parents died, Mordecai, her cousin, took her as his own daughter and adopted her. (Esther 2:15) This adoption also led to a wonderful deliverance of the people of God.

Yet, by far, the most important adoption story of all is the one pertaining to you and me. God chose to adopt us into His family. We are no longer orphans. Paul spoke of adoption to assure all believers would be able to enter into God's family legally. We have been adopted by God!

APPLICATION:
1. Stop and think, "I am a child of God by His choice!"
2. Do not ever consider yourself less than a part of His family.

PRAYER
Lord, thank you so much for accepting me as a child of your own. Amen.

NOVEMBER 11
THE AUTHORITY OF THE BELIEVER

Matthew 28:18-19
"And Jesus came and spake unto them, saying, "All power is given unto me in Heaven and in earth. Go ye therefore..." (KJV)

Faith, love and authority are the three necessary attributes of a successful Christian. You may have faith, but without an understanding of your authority, you will never utilize it to its fullest potential. You may have love, but without an understanding of your authority, you may never walk in it to its fullest degree. Authority is the measure of your position in God's Kingdom on the earth.

Authority must be given. It has an originator. (II Corinthians 10:8) God's desire was to transfer His power to the earth. In Genesis 1:26, Adam and Eve were given supreme authority over the earth. This authority was the envy of Lucifer. He deceived mankind for it. (Ezekiel 28; Isaiah 14; Daniel 10:13; Jeremiah 4:23) The fall meant man no longer possessed his God given authority.

Jesus came to restore the power and authority to the earth, to place it back in the hands of believers. The disciples experienced this authority. (Mark 6:6-7; Luke 9:1; Matthew 10:1) One of the last things Jesus did before returning to Heaven was to direct the disciples to Jerusalem where they would be *"endued with power from on high."* (Luke 24:49 NKJV)

We have been given the same authority. The Devil is under your feet! (Ephesians 1:17-23) The Church is in charge! (Ephesians 2:1-7) We are destined to win! (II Timothy 4:18; I John 4:4, 17; 5:4-5) This authority is for now, today—this moment!

We have been deputized to carry out the Gospel. To be *deputized* means we have delegated authority. It means "to act as a substitute with the authority to act; to be second in command; one who takes charge when the one who has ultimate authority is absent." We can use His name and His authority, and the powers of darkness must bend!

It is time we take up this authority and begin to regain what has been lost. (Luke 19:10) We are believers with His authority!

APPLICATION:
1. Are you walking in the authority He has given you?
2. Do you use His name to bring His will to the earth?

PRAYER:
Lord, I will use the authority you have given me to break the powers of darkness. Amen.

NOVEMBER 12
LOOKING FOR GREENER PASTURES

I Timothy 6:6
"But godliness with contentment is great gain." (KJV)

Contentment is a learned behavior. We are conditioned to want something we cannot have. Lot was given a choice and chose what seemed to be the greener pasture. This attitude was felt throughout his family when God saw the sin of Sodom and Gomorrah. Even his wife loved the city more than him. By looking for greener pastures and being discontent, he led his family into destruction.

What does it mean to be truly content? It means sustained fulfillment can never come from the outside. What we gain is not what is important; it is what we pursue that is important. Contentment is the ability to take your present circumstances and be settled with them.

What causes discontentment? Why do people leave their spouses and families? (Hebrews 13:5) They are looking for greener pastures and chasing after the pot of gold at the end of the rainbow.

There are two major reasons for being discontent. First, lusting after something someone is or has that you desire. Second, it is not being where God wants you. When you start comparing your life with someone who has something you do not have, you begin to get discontent. Comparison is dangerous and can cause you to forget about the good things already present in your life.

Also, when we are out of the will of God, we become discontent. We know deep within us something is missing. We try to fill our lives with things that dull us to the conviction of the Holy Spirit. Somehow, we believe we can find fulfillment in something other than God's will.

One very wise person said, "Contentment is not having what you want, but wanting what you have." One thing is for sure, contentment is a Godly quality which produces great peace. True contentment will produce Godliness in our lives!

APPLICATION:
   1. Be sure you are not discontent with what you have.
   2. Count the things God has done for you and is doing for you.

PRAYER:
Lord, forgive me for not being content with what you have given me. Daily, I will count the blessings of my life! Amen.

NOVEMBER 13
GET OUT OF THE BOAT

Matthew 14:25, 28-29

"And in the fourth watch of the night Jesus went unto them, walking on the sea... And Peter answered him and said, Lord, if it be thou, bid me come unto thee on the water... And he said, Come. And when Peter was come down out of the ship, he walked on the water, to go to Jesus." (KJV)

The easiest thing to do when you read this passage is to look at the fact Peter took his eyes off of Jesus and began to sink. However, what about the other 11 disciples? None of them even got out of the boat! They chose the supposed safety of the boat from the storm over the presence of Jesus as Protector. Peter took a risk none of the others even considered. Eventually, Peter would become one of the greatest figures in Christian history.

You have to trust God will take care of you. You have to believe there is something higher you can reach for with His help.

In *The Autobiography of Benjamin Franklin*, a quote by Ulysses S. Grant written before the Battle of Cold Harbor in 1864 appears, "If you see the President, tell him whatever happens there will be no turning back."

Alex Haley, author of *Roots*, said of the slave, Kunta Kinte, after his foot was cut off as punishment for trying to escape, "I'm gonna do better than learn to walk. I'm gonna learn to run."

There are some things you can only do if you are willing to risk the safety of your present surroundings. You have to walk by faith and not by sight! I read a quote of an actor in a recent playbill who said, "If you are willing to leap, a net will appear!" This does not mean being reckless, but it does mean trusting God when He beckons you to go to a higher place.

As Dag Hammarskjold said, "When the morning's freshness has been replaced by the weariness of midday, when the leg muscles quiver under the strain, the climb seems endless, and suddenly, nothing will go quite as you wish—it is then that you must not hesitate!"

APPLICATION:
1. Look carefully at where you are.
2. Are you willing to get out of the boat and walk to Him?

PRAYER:
Lord, I will trust you and get out of the boat and walk to you! Amen.

NOVEMBER 14
WHICH DIRECTION ARE YOU GOING?

Jeremiah 7:23-24

*"But I gave them this command: Obey me, and I will be your God and you will
be my people. Walk in all the ways I command you, that it may go well with
you. But they did not listen or pay attention; instead, they followed the stubborn
inclinations of their evil hearts. They went backward and not forward."* (NIV)

In Louis Carroll's book, *Alice in Wonderland*, Alice comes to a fork in the
road and does not know which way to turn. She sees the grinning Cheshire Cat
and asks which direction she should take. The cat replies, "That depends a good
deal on where you want to get to."

Are you going in the right direction? Jeremiah was given a warning for Israel.
It was to be clearly stated. It was to be where God's people gathered. They were to
amend their ways. They were going in the wrong direction. They were proceeding
toward an unwanted destination. They were given false directions. They were
depending on what they thought were dependable signs around them.

I was with some friends in Atlanta, Georgia, many years back. We were traveling to a Christian convention at the Omni for the opening session. We had not
traveled into this city before. We asked for directions before we left our hotel. We
left early to beat some of the traffic. The traffic was not the problem we encountered. After traveling about an hour, we saw a sign that said: "Omni, 75 miles!" We
were going in the wrong direction! Although we were moving, we were moving
away from our destination.

There is nothing more upsetting than to realize you have been going in the
wrong direction. In the 1932 Rose Bowl, Roy Riegels of UCLA, against Georgia
Tech, scooped up a fumble and made his way to the end zone. However, it was
not a touchdown. On his way to what he thought was a score, Riegels lost his
bearings and ran the wrong way. For the rest of his life, he was not known for
his remarkable athletic abilities. He never escaped the reputation as Roy "Wrong
Way" Riegels.

The question today is, "Are you going in the right direction?"

APPLICATION:
1. Be sure you are not going to an undesired destination.
2. Be sure you are getting directions from the right sources.

PRAYER:
Lord, redirect me if I am going in the wrong direction! Amen.

NOVEMBER 15
STOPPING FEAR

Joshua 10:8, 25

"And the LORD said unto Joshua, Fear them not: for I have delivered them into thine hand; there shall not a man of them stand before thee...And Joshua said unto them, Fear not, nor be dismayed, be strong and of good courage: for thus shall the LORD do to all your enemies against whom ye fight." (KJV)

We are told the four greatest impelling motives in life are fear, hope, love and faith. We are also told the greatest is fear. It is first in order, first in force and first in fruit.

The Bible reveals plenty about fear. The word *fear* is mentioned 266 times in scripture and the word *afraid* is mentioned 223 times. The first time fear is mentioned is Genesis 3:10 and the last time it is seen is Revelation 19:5. From beginning to end, fear had to be dealt with.

God spoke to Joshua, and Joshua dealt with his fear. Then, Joshua spoke to His people and dealt with their fear. We cannot help others paralyzed with fear if we do not deal with our own fears.

You have been redeemed from fear. (Isaiah 43:1-5) When I got this revelation, it chased away the fears of my life. Harry Emerson Fosdick pointed out, "Fear imprisons, faith liberates; fear paralyzes, faith empowers; fear disheartens, faith encourages; fear sickens, faith heals; fear makes useless, faith makes serviceable—and, most of all, fear puts hopelessness at the heart of life, while faith rejoices in its' God."

Max L. Lucado said about fear, "His modus operandi is to manipulate you with the mysterious, to taunt you with the unknown. Fear of death, fear of failure, fear of God, fear of tomorrow-his arsenal is vast. His goal? To create cowardly, joyless souls. He doesn't want you to make the journey to the mountain. He figures if he can rattle you enough, you will take your eyes off the peaks and settle for a dull existence in the flatlands!"

We have the tools to fight fear. We have God's Word. We have our faith in Him. We have His armor. We have each other. It is up to us! We must put a stop to fear!

APPLICATION:
1. Are you dealing with fear in your life?
2. Be sure you use your faith to stop it in its tracks!

PRAYER:
Lord, with your help I will not fear! Amen.

NOVEMBER 16
GOD WILL BALANCE THE SCALES

Psalms 89:14
"Justice and judgment are the habitation of thy throne: mercy and truth shall go before thy face." (KJV)

Sometimes it seems God has gone to sleep. It seems as though He has forgotten His people who try to live right and promoted those who have no regard for Him. However, the scales will be balanced.

Some Bible examples to consider are: 1. Haman, who was full of evil, was in the court of the king, while faithful Mordecai sat in the gate. 2. Courageous giant killer, David, wandered in the mountains, while corrupt and murderous Saul reigned in state. 3. Powerful prophet, Elijah, was alone and desolate in the cave, while vindictive, Jezebel, was boasting in the palace. Yet, Mordecai was spared and Haman was hanged on the scales he had prepared for Mordecai. David unseated Saul as King, so Saul commits suicide. Elijah was swept up into Heaven with the chariot of God and Queen Jezebel was thrown out her window to her death by her servants.

God is with those who seem to be forgotten. (Psalms 9:18; 12:5; 40:17; 41:1-4) Those whom people think are forgotten and abandoned are just a prayer away from promotion. Meanwhile, the people who think they are with the winning team, today, may not realize they are with those on their way down.

The days before God delivered the enslaved children of Israel from Egypt, Pharaoh and Egypt were the most powerful leader and nation in history. Yet, God was about to balance the scales.

How do you position yourself to have the scales balanced in your favor? First, trust God to promote you. (Mark 9:35; Luke 13:30) Second, develop a servant's heart. (Matthew 23:11) Third, have patience in the process. Patience is knowledge the laws of God will be enforced.

This popular quote describes it well, "When the wheel turns, those who are lowest rise, and the highest sink." God will balance the scales!

APPLICATION:
1. Are you anxious about your life?
2. Be sure you trust God to balance the scales of justice in your favor.

PRAYER:
Lord, forgive me for not trusting you for my justice. Amen.

NOVEMBER 17
JUSTICE FOR ALL

Jeremiah 23:5
"Behold, the days come, saith the LORD, that I will raise unto David a righteous Branch, and a King shall reign and prosper, and shall execute judgment and justice in the earth." (KJV)

Although it seems like justice is not served, God keeps excellent records. God sees the long range effects of the decisions people make. He factors in their faithfulness and their lack of faithfulness. Still, there are things we can do to bring justice to our own lives:

First, by staying in the Word. (Nehemiah 8:18) The Word applies pressure on the justice system of Heaven. Second, by doing the right thing. (Hosea 10:12) Although it initially seems doing the right thing does not pay, it always pays ultimately! Third, by blessing the house of God. (Leviticus 23:10) Every time you do something to promote God's Kingdom, you sow into your own future. Fourth, by accepting constructive criticism. (Proverbs 3:11-12) When we reject correction, we delay the process. We cannot get to our destiny without it. Fifth, by taking notice of God's provision for other things. (Matthew 6:24-33) We must observe the way God attends to the seemingly insignificant things around us. They are a sign God is seeing you and will provide for you. Sixth, by sowing consistently. (II Corinthians 9:6; Isaiah 55:10) Sowing is the absolute sign we trust God keeps His promises. When we give, we show we believe it is only a matter of time before the breakthrough. Finally, by maintaining your vision in uncertain times. (Job 4:4-6) When the storms come, and they will, we must maintain our faith in Him. We must realize every storm has a life span. Although it may seem like it, no storm will last forever!

God has an equity system that never fails. Even those whose lives seem to be cut off early, go immediately to a great Heavenly reward! God is a God of truth and justice. He has justice for all!

APPLICATION:
1. Do a check list of the things you are responsible for.
2. Be patient! Today, may be your day of breakthrough!

PRAYER:
Lord, thank you for your faithfulness and justice! Amen.

NOVEMBER 18
LIVING A SATISFYING LIFE

Psalms 91:16
"With long life will I satisfy him, and shew him my salvation." (KJV)

Brooke Shields commented on why she wanted to become spokesperson for a federal anti-smoking campaign. She said, "Smoking kills. If you're killed, you've lost a very important part of your life."

Mark 1:1 denotes the Gospel as being the Good News about Jesus Christ. In Mark 1:14-20, the disciples were not content with the life they were living. They willingly forsook their businesses. They were not failing in business. They were failing to live their life well. They willingly forsook their families for a season. They were not failing in family. Their families alone were not fulfilling enough. They were looking for something to ignite their life. It is that certain something inside of each person, which cannot be explained or dampened. People search outside of their present life for something more. They are looking for their destiny.

There are two kinds of life: The first is ordinary or the expected. It is planned by someone other than you and mostly unfulfilling. The second is extra-ordinary or beyond expectations. It is finding the life which was created for you. I like what Charles Lindbergh said, "It is the greatest shot of adrenaline to be doing what you've wanted to do so badly. You almost feel like you could fly without the plane."

The saddest people in the world are those who deep down inside know their lives are meant for something else. God's own people wandered around the place He had designed for them, but never entered into it. They were instructed to go, but did not follow. (Exodus 14:1-3) Instead, they went back to the expected.

God has provided all of us with the possibility of an exciting and fulfilling life. A life He breathes on and causes to become everything we could hope for. He wants you and me to live a satisfying life!

APPLICATION:
1. Are you living the life God has for you?
2. Are you obeying Him, so you can walk in His best for your life?

PRAYER:
Lord, I want the life you have planned for me. If I am out of your will, lead me and show me how to walk in it to its fullest! Amen.

NOVEMBER 19
YOU DO NOT HAVE TO BE LONELY

Psalms 68:6
"God sets the lonely in families, he leads forth the prisoners with singing; but the rebellious live in a sun-scorched land." (NIV)

Have you ever felt like you did not fit in or belong, like you were not meant to be a part of something or someone's life, or you were meant to live alone? There is a place just for you.

Lee Strobel writes, "People today will admit any problem - drugs, divorce, alcoholism - but there's one admission that people are loath to make, whether they're a star on television or someone who fixes televisions in a repair shop. It's just too embarrassing. It penetrates too deeply to the core of who they are. People don't want to admit that they are (sometimes) lonely. Loneliness is such a humiliating malady that it ought to have its own politically correct euphemism: 'relationally challenged,' or its own telethon, anything to make it safer to confess. Right now loneliness is a taboo, an affliction of losers and misfits, and - to be honest - of respectable people like you and me."

God desires to arrange your life in a meaningful way. He wants to make a place for you, your gifts and your personality—a place where you are loved, appreciated and respected. He wants to loosen you from the chains of expectation. He wants you loose from the expectations of those around you—expectations which seem to exclude you from others. As one weary wife, tired of relocations for her husband's career explained, "I got so tired of saying 'Good-bye,' that I stopped saying 'Hello.'"

You need to first of all understand God is the only one who can cure your loneliness. Having a lot of people in your life is not the answer. You can be in a room full of people and still be lonely. The fulfillment that comes from belonging to the family of God, of having a Father you know personally and knowing He will never abandon or forsake you is the only way to overcome loneliness.

Today, stop and talk to Him. He is always listening to His people. He always has time for you. You do not have to be lonely anymore!

APPLICATION:
1. Make some time, today, to let God speak to you about your life.
2. Receive the love and assurance from Him, which only He can give.

PRAYER:
Lord, I know I do not have to be lonely anymore. Thank you! Amen.

NOVEMBER 20
QUENCHING THE THIRST

Isaiah 29:8
"It shall even be as when an hungry man dreameth, and, behold, he eateth; but he awaketh, and his soul is empty: or as when a thirsty man dreameth, and, behold, he drinketh; but he awaketh, and, behold, he is faint, and his soul hath appetite..." (KJV)

There was a young salesman who was disappointed about losing a big sale. He talked with his sales manager and lamented, "I guess it just proves you can lead a horse to water but you can't make him drink." The manager replied, "Son, take my advice: your job is not to make him drink. Your job is to make him thirsty." It is the same way with evangelism. Our lives should be so filled with Christ that they create a thirst for the Gospel.

There is no question we are living in a land where people eat, but they are still hungry. They drink, but their thirst is not quenched. We have what they need! We have been to the well where living water flows. We have drunk from the fountain that provides refreshment and life to the weariest of souls. We have been fed by the Creator of the universe.

It is time for us to lead them to the well, to take them to the fountain. Without someone to guide them and care enough to help them, many will die of dehydration and starvation. Most of them will not go unless we provide them with a taste of what we have tasted. It is our commission to share the goodness which has been shown to us. We must let them know there is a place that has what they need; therefore, they do not need to look to drugs, alcohol or sex to fill them. There is a place for them.

Sometimes it is good to remind ourselves of what it was like before we drank from the stream. Think about how desperate we were. Reflect on how refreshed our lives became after we drank! We can develop a heart for those we see perishing around us.

Take the time to look around you. What do you see? How many more have to perish of thirst and hunger before we take it upon ourselves to bring them to the living water?

APPLICATION:
1. Make a note of those you are in closest contact with who are thirsty and hungry.
2. Pray for them. Then, lead them to the water!

PRAYER:
Lord, give me a heart for the thirsty and hungry! Amen.

NOVEMBER 21
OVERCAME OR OVERCOME

John 16:33
"These things I have spoken unto you, that in me ye might have peace. In the world ye shall have tribulation: but be of good cheer; I have overcome the world." (KJV)

In today's world, we talk about many types of survivors: cancer survivors, abuse survivors, tornado survivors, earthquake survivors and the list goes on and on. It is great to be a survivor, but I want to do more than just survive. The Bible does not use the word *survivor*, but it does use the word *overcomer*.

What does it mean to be an overcomer? The Greek root word of *overcome* means "to prevail, to pass over, to gain the victory." The Japanese word for it is *nike*. It means: "to conquer, best, get the better of, master, surmount, vanquish, defeat, beat, lick, suppress, overthrow, put down, overwhelm, overpower, subdue, crush, quell, prevail over, triumph over, win over, transcend."

We will have obstacles to overcome: our past, our weaknesses and the trials of life. Yet, the Word has an answer for every one of them. We are given the tools we need to not only survive, but to also overcome!

Helen Keller, who became famous for the difficulties she overcame being born blind, made an amazing observation. She said, "The marvelous richness of human experience would lose something of rewarding joy if there were not limitations to overcome. The hilltop hour would not be half so wonderful if there were no dark valleys to traverse." It is the difficulties in life, which give us the opportunity to know what it is like to have victory.

You do not become an overcomer by trying. You become an overcomer by trusting and believing God is who He said He is. He is the great "I Am," and He is able to help you in any difficulty, any circumstance.

How can we live like overcomers? I John 4:4 states, *"You are of God, little children, and have overcome them, because He who is in you is greater than he who is in the world."* (NKJV)

If you have been born-again, you have already been made an overcomer in Him. It is time we overcome and not allow trials to overcome us!

APPLICATION:
1. Stop the attacks of the enemy, today, by declaring you are an overcomer.
2. Use the blood, the name of Jesus and your own testimony.

PRAYER:
Lord, I boldly declare I am an overcomer! Amen.

NOVEMBER 22
THE GOD FACTOR

Matthew 9:27-29
*"And when Jesus departed thence, two blind men followed him, crying, and
saying, Thou Son of David, have mercy on us. And when he was come into the
house, the blind men came to him: and Jesus saith unto them, Believe ye that I
am able to do this? They said unto him, Yea, Lord. Then touched he their eyes,
saying, According to your faith be it unto you."* (KJV)

We must always consider the God Factor! We are only as limited as our confidence in Him. There is an answer beyond our capabilities, strength and power. If we are merely left to what we can accomplish, then no matter how great it may seem, it will be short of what God had in mind for us!

The sum of our lives is greater than what is seen. Many times people look at the sum of their lives and determine their lives are advancing to a certain destination, but they do not factor in the God Factor!

Ephesians 3:20 says, *"Now unto Him who is able to do exceeding, abundantly above all that we ask or even think, according to the power that worketh in us."* (KJV)

When the two thieves were hanging on crosses beside Jesus, everyone saw three doomed humans. However, what they did not know was two of the three would be redeemed because of the God Factor!

The God Factor will change everything in your life. Deuteronomy 11:25 reveals God will cause those around you to fear you. Joshua 1:5 says no man will be able to block you from the things God desires for you. Acts 2:32 states God will cause you to be built up. Romans 4:18-22 reveals God is able to bring promises to pass in your life. I Corinthians 10:10-13 says God is able to make an escape route for you from the worst circumstances.

The God Factor is enough to bring you to the finish line. Do not let the world convince you that you will not make it!

APPLICATION:
　　1. Do not get discouraged about setbacks—they are temporary.
　　2. Consider the God Factor!

PRAYER:
*Lord, I choose not to let the world or my circumstances keep me from the victory.
I will consider the God Factor! Amen.*

NOVEMBER 23
THE CURSE OF PERMANENT POTENTIAL

Jeremiah 1:5
"Before I formed you in the womb I knew you, before you were born I set you apart." (NIV)

We see it all of the time, the curse of permanent potential. Consider the people you think have or had potential: gifted athletes who never meet expectations, great singers who rise quickly and fall even more quickly, people you went to school with who were voted the "most likely" to succeed and lived fast and died young, brilliantly minded students who fade into the background of society without any accomplishments and family members everyone predicts will place credibility back in the family name, who instead just bring more shame. They all have something in common.

In the Bible, Saul, Samson and Judas all had potential, but never really reached it. What is potential? Webster's says it is "possible, as opposed to actual: the potential uses of nuclear energy; expressing possibility; a latent excellence or ability that may or may not be developed."

First, recognize realized potential is not necessarily to be equated with natural success. The *Executive Digest* made an interesting observation concerning the potential price tag of success. The periodical reported, "The trouble with success is that the formula is the same as the one for a nervous breakdown." Potential realized is discovering (un-covering) pre-existing qualities and abilities, and finding what God intended for you to do with them.

There are people who discovered their potential. They seemed to come out of nowhere. They were not predicted to have success, but they connected with their ability, their talent or their call, such as David, Abraham and Gideon. We would call them overachievers. But are they really? God had previously deposited gifts in them, which they were unaware of. It took an encounter with God to bring them to the surface.

Do not be a person who falls under the curse of permanent potential. Let God show you the path, which takes you to your victory and brings the best out of you!

APPLICATION:
1. Check yourself. Are you living up to your potential?
2. If not, begin by going after God's best for your life, today.

PRAYER:
Lord, I will not fall short of the things you desire for my life. With your help, I will live up to my potential! Amen.

NOVEMBER 24
THE GREATNESS INSIDE OF YOU

I John 4:4
"Ye are of God, little children, and have overcome them: because greater is he that is in you, than he that is in the world." (KJV)

Everyone has something inside of them they are running from that is God imparted. There are hidden things inside of us. We have grossly underestimated our value. God has made an investment into us, which we have yet to realize. We have untapped potential waiting to be brought forth.

There are keys to unlocking your potential: First, you must live a joyous life. Joy is a key to unlocking potential. If you do not have a joyous spirit about your life, you will miss most of what is inside of you. Next, you must point out the potential in others around you. By releasing others to find their own potential, you raise your own potential, thus provoking the blessing of God on your life. Third, you must understand God's unwearying love. (Titus 3:3-4) When you have someone who loves you through all of life's adversities, it keeps you pressing to be better. Fourth, you must refrain from a sinful life. (II Samuel 12:1-8) Someone said, "More people are bitten trying to let go of snakes than when they grab them." You cannot get trapped in a life of sin. Sin slows down your life and causes you to miss what is really inside of you. Fifth, you must be committed to finish your assignments. (Nehemiah 4:1-6; II Timothy 4:6-8) It is critical you take every moment of your life and treat it as the most important moment. When you are faithful over little, much comes forth! Napoleon Hill said, "It's not what you are going to do, but it's what you are doing now that counts." Resolve, today, to drop the motto of the masses, "One of these days..." An English Proverb says, "One of these days means none of these days." Next, you must keep your faith in God. (I Corinthians 4:2) You must keep your faith in times of uncertainty. It will lead you to better days and bring out the best inside of you. George Eliot said, "It is never too late to be what you might have become." Finally, you must develop your character. Remember, character is who you are when no one is looking. Be dependable! God unlocks greatness when you live in integrity. Let God show you the greatness inside of you.

APPLICATION:
1. Remind yourself, today, He is inside of you!
2. Do not underestimate what God has placed within you!

PRAYER:
Lord, help me to live up to the greatness inside of me. Amen.

NOVEMBER 25
GOD'S PROMOTION SYSTEM

Psalms 75:6-8
"For promotion and power come from nowhere on earth, but only from God. He promotes one and deposes another." (TLB)

Motivational speaker Joe Girard said, "The elevator to success is out of order. You'll have to use the stairs, one step at a time." There is no quick way to any promotion or success. God is very deliberate. He is very methodical. Yet, He is also very faithful.

God desires to promote His people. (Joshua 1:8; Psalms 75:5-7; Proverbs 3:34-35; 4:5-10) These scriptures reveal three things about promotion: First, sustained promotion comes from God alone. People rise quickly and fall quickly without God, but He alone can sustain success in someone. Secondly, wisdom and understanding are pre-requisites to Godly promotion. God is slow to promote someone who is foolish and careless. The only way up is down. Unless we become less "agenda driven" and more "God driven," we will fall woefully short of the place of promotion God has for us! Thirdly, promotion comes when we grow. We are always in the disciple process. To be a disciple means to grow, and growth means entering new territory. John was a perfect example of a disciple. John was faithful beyond the others. This was evident throughout his writings. John trusted Jesus enough to remain anonymous in his own Gospel. In John's Gospel, he never mentions himself by name. When we yield ourselves to become His disciples, we are moving into the next promotion He has for us.

God chooses the unlikely to promote. (I Corinthians 1:25-28) Three people God promoted are: 1. Joseph, who never gave up on his dreams. Joseph was promoted everywhere he went. He remained committed to God. 2. Joshua, who faithfully served Moses. Joshua was never promised anything. It was he who was promoted to take Israel to the Promised Land, and not Moses! 3. Moses, who trusted God to promote him. He forsook pleasure for promotion from God. He knew God was a better promoter than Pharaoh.

Although the world offers methods of promotion, only God is able to help you sustain success!

APPLICATION:
1. Do not take the worlds "shortcut" to promotion.
2. Trust God to put you in the right place at the right time!

PRAYER:
Lord, I will believe you for my next promotion! Amen.

NOVEMBER 26
PLENTY TO BE THANKFUL FOR

Colossians 3:15
"And let the peace of God rule in your hearts, to the which also ye are called in one body; and be ye thankful." (KJV)

Giving thanks is a language that gets God's attention. We enter His gates with thanksgiving. (Psalms 100:4) In ancient times, it was difficult to enter into the king's presence, but a show of gratitude opened the door. The Mosaic Law set aside three times each year when the Israelites gathered together to celebrate and give thanks. It was important for God's people to have appointed times for these celebrations and to give thanks.

We should always be a person who gives thanks. We should always be in a thankful posture towards God. Even when things are not going our way, we should increase our thanksgiving for what God has done and what He will do.

We should thank Him in the good times. (Psalms 103:1-5) William Shakespeare said, "I can no other answer make but thanks and ever thanks." We should thank Him in the hard times. (Psalms 119:62) A Jewish proverb says, "If men thanked God for good things, they wouldn't have time to complain about the bad." We should thank Him for what He has done. (Psalms 66:16) A Chinese proverb says, "When you drink from the stream, remember the spring." We should thank Him for what He is currently doing. (Psalms 68:19) There is more being done presently on our behalf than our senses can discern. We should thank Him for what He will do. (Philippians 4:6-7)

Robert Herrick said: "Thanksgiving invites God to bestow a second benefit." When you thank God first, He always returns you with a blessing. (I Chronicles 16:8, 34-35, 43)

Psalms 50:13-15 in The Living Bible tells us what God really desires from His people, *"No, I don't need your sacrifices of flesh and blood. What I want from you is your true thanks; I want your promises fulfilled. I want you to trust me in your times of trouble, so I can rescue you, and you can give me glory!"* We have plenty to be thankful for!

APPLICATION:
1. Be sure to stop on more than one occasion, today, and thank God.
2. If you are going through a trial, thank Him even more!

PRAYER
Lord, I will not grumble and complain, but I will thank you for all you have done, all you are doing and all you will do for me! Amen.

NOVEMBER 27
WHO ARE YOU?

Acts 19:13-15
"Then certain of the vagabond Jews, exorcists, took upon them to call over them which had evil spirits the name of the Lord Jesus, saying, We adjure you by Jesus whom Paul preacheth. And there were seven sons of one Sceva, a Jew, and chief of the priests, which did so. And the evil spirit answered and said, Jesus I know, and Paul I know; but who are ye?" (KJV)

Demons have the ability to identify people and their standing or lack thereof in God's Kingdom. They have a personal history with Jesus. They knew they were overmatched when His presence was revealed. Jesus exhibited His absolute power over them. They quickly identified who Paul was. Paul had firm confidence in who he was in Christ. He had demonstrated publicly he was not who he once was.

The seven sons of Sceva were imposters. They had no connection with Christ. They were impersonators. When they tried to exorcise the demons, they were overpowered and their clothes were stripped off of them until they fled in terror, naked!

Where is the body of Christ in relation to this event? Are we like Paul? Do we overcome, overpower, overwhelm and humiliate the Devil? Or are we overmatched? Do we know who we really are in Christ and cast the Devil out? Or do we simply put up with the Devil's attacks?

God intends for His people to be like Paul. It is not God's will for His body to be beaten and destroyed again! We have been given powerful weapons to fight with. Here are five reasons we should not be overcome, overpowered, overwhelmed and humiliated: 1. His Name. (Luke 10:17-19) 2. His blood. (Revelation 12:11) 3. His Word. (Psalms 119:89) 4. His joy. (John 15:11) 5. His authority. (Luke 19:17)

It is time for us to realize who we are and not have anymore mistaken identity, or being: overcome, overpowered, overwhelmed and humiliated!

APPLICATION:
1. Truthfully evaluate your life in the present. Are you overtaking the enemy or is he overtaking you?
2. Be sure to keep yourself in line with God's Word and authority.

PRAYER:
Lord, teach me your ways that I might drive out the Devil. Amen.

NOVEMBER 28
FINDING THE RIGHT SPOUSE

Proverbs 18:22
"The man who finds a wife finds a good thing;
she is a blessing to him from the Lord."
(TLB)

I realize this devotional seems to be out of order, but thank you for indulging me. Today is my beautiful helpmate, Ginger's, birthday. She was absolutely sent to me from God and has been the greatest blessing I could have possibly ever asked for!

She is everything a Biblical wife could be. She loves the Lord with all of her heart. She has devoted her life to pleasing Him. I have watched her stand for God during the darkest times of her life. Even before I met her, she had already endured the tragic death of a child. She had already gone through the most important years of a young girl's life, and her dad was murdered when she was 14. She had already suffered through a horribly painful marriage with a very abusive husband. Most people would have long before quit. However, the depth of her faith was so well rooted. She kept her faith, despite all of these painful times.

When we met nearly 30 years ago, she was an anchor, a strong reflection of God. I was the one who needed someone with great strength. I did not realize at that time how big and heavy the call on my own life was. Had I married someone weak or untested, my calling and ministry would have never gotten off of the ground. She worked laboriously at a secular job for years, raised our three children with me and somehow put up with me as I grew up as a man, father, husband and a man of God!

If you are looking for a mate, there are some steps which will lead you to them or them to you. First of all, seek God first! Do not seek a mate. When Ginger and I met, we were both very content being alone with God. Second, be sure the person you consider has the same vision for life you have. If he/she does not, then trouble is inevitable, no matter how strong your feelings may be. Finally, pray for God to show you who the person is. It is your responsibility to be the person they need as much as it is for them to be the person you need!

APPLICATION:
1. If you are unmarried, seek God first and be content with Him.
2. Do not allow your feelings to be connected with someone who does not share your dreams and values!

PRAYER:
Lord, give me the right spouse, the one you have for me! Amen.

NOVEMBER 29
WHO DO YOU THINK YOU ARE?

Philippians 3:4
"Though I might also have confidence in the flesh. If any other man thinketh that he hath whereof he might trust in the flesh, I more:" (KJV)

The question must be answered, "Who do you think you are?" The Bible is the answer book for believers.

In Matthew, you are the one God sent His Son for to redeem your sins. You are the one He saw as a pearl and a treasure hidden in the field. He purchased the field with His life for you. In Mark, you are the one He gives 30, 60 and 100 fold returns to. He gives mountain-moving faith to you and will ride with you to the other side. In Luke, you are the one He was born unto. You are the one He was anointed to deliver from poverty, to heal from broken heartedness, to deliver from captivity, to set free from all forms of blindness, to mend the bruises and set totally free. In John, you are the one He gave power to become a son or daughter of God. He turned the water of your life into wine and prayed for you to be one with Him. You are the one He promised to return for and has reserved a place in Heaven for. In Acts, you are the one He baptizes with the Holy Ghost and promises to save all of your family. In Romans, you are the one He justified by faith, forgave by grace and were made to be the righteousness of God. In I Corinthians, you are the one He gave the ministry gifts and the nine gifts of the Spirit to. In II Corinthians, you are the one He comforts in all of your trials. He says you can walk by faith and not by sight. In Galatians, you are the one He blessed with faithful Abraham. You were named His seed and became an heir according to the Promise. In Ephesians, you are the one He has made to sit together with Him in Heavenly places. He gave the secrets of a successful marriage to you. In Philippians, you are the one He humbled himself as a servant to and gave you the strength to do all things.

APPLICATION:
1. Do not speak defeat about your life.
2. Line your life up with what God says about you.

PRAYER:
Lord, I confess I am all that you said I am! Amen.

NOVEMBER 30
REALIZING WHO YOU ARE

I John 2:14

"I have written unto you…because ye have known him that is from the beginning. I have written unto you…because ye are strong, and the word of God abideth in you, and ye have overcome the wicked one." (KJV)

The Word of God not only reveals who you are, but what you are capable of being. The following list is a continuation of "who you are" in the New Testament.

In Colossians, you are the one He redeemed by His blood and whose life has been hidden in Him. In I Thessalonians, you are the one He delivered from the wrath to come and promised to return for. In II Thessalonians, you are the one He called to His glory and gave His peace to. In I Timothy, you are the one He gave abundant grace. He has promised you a life, yet to come. In II Timothy, you are the one He called with a Holy calling. He made you to be a vessel of honor. In Titus, you are the one He gave the hope of eternal life, and He appears to you with kindness and love. In Philemon, you are the one He gave every good thing to. You are refreshed in Him. In Hebrews, you are the one He gave ministering angels to and are invited boldly to His throne room. In James, you are the one He gave every good and perfect gift to. He promised not to tempt you with evil. In I Peter, you are the one He has begotten again with a lively hope, and you are redeemed by His blood. In II Peter, you are the one He gave exceeding, precious promises to. He shows His longsuffering to you. In I John, you are the one He cleanses from ALL sin. He shows His great love to you. In II John, you are the one He gives a full reward. In III John, you are the one He desires to see prosper and be in health even as your soul prospers. In Jude, you are the one He builds up when you pray in the Holy Ghost. In Revelation, you are the one He made a king and priest. He fought and defeated the false prophet, the antichrist, the beast and the Devil for you. He prepared a city for you, which has no tears, no fear, no hurt, no pain, no crying, no sorrow, no darkness, no death and no end. You will receive a glorified body, see Jesus and see your loved ones who knew Him again!

APPLICATION:
1. Pray the Word of God over your life.
2. Rehearse the Word of God about your life.

PRAYER
Lord, I will walk in the Word of who I am! Amen.

DECEMBER 1
SECOND HALF COMEBACK

Hosea 14:1-5
"O Israel, return unto the LORD thy God; for thou hast fallen by thine iniquity. Take with you words, and turn to the LORD: say unto him, Take away all iniquity, and receive us graciously: so will we render the calves of our lips... I will heal their backsliding, I will love them freely: for mine anger is turned away from him." (KJV)

I have been an avid sports fan since I was a boy. I have watched hundreds of games. Some of the games seemed over almost as soon as they started.

One such game was in 1987 when Austin Peay State University, located in Clarksville, Tennessee, was playing Morehead State in the opening round of the 1987 Tournament. Although APSU was favored and had home court advantage, they played terribly and were behind by 23 points with only 8 minutes to play. I was about to leave, but I am glad I did not! Over the next 8 minutes, APSU mounted a furious rally and won the game at the end! They went on to win the Ohio Valley Conference Tournament, and then went on to the NCAA Regional Finals in Birmingham, Alabama. They upset 10th ranked Illinois in the first round and lost to eventual Final Four, Providence, in double overtime, whose coach was Billy Donovan. Coach Donovan is now the current coach of the two time National Champions, Florida Gators!

Many times, it looks like our lives have hit an impasse. We may have experienced a major setback. However, if we hold onto our faith, God is able to help us make a "second half" comeback!

There are five ways to make a comeback: The first way to make a comeback is to put God first. Israel once and for all gave up her fondness for man-made idols as her god. The second way to make a comeback is to pray. Prayer turns things around. The third way to make a second half comeback is to disavow your past and distance yourself from any form of it. The fourth way to make a second half comeback is to point out the goodness of God. Proclaim His desire to bless and His record of blessing. The fifth way to make a second half comeback is to depend on God for safety and protection. God is able to deliver His people from any and all distress!

APPLICATION:
1. Do not give up! No matter how bad things are now.
2. Trust God to give you the things you need to rally.

PRAYER:
Lord, I believe my best days are not behind, but ahead of me! Amen.

DECEMBER 2
FOLLOWING UP ON YOUR SEED

Job 39:12
"Wilt thou believe him, that he will bring home thy seed, and gather it into thy barn?" (KJV)

What is your responsibility after the seed is planted? Do you just merely wait and hope, or are there things you must do to see it produce?

Does the farmer plant and then sit for two, three or four months No! Yet, many people seem to think after they have given (planted) their work is over.

We must maintain our lives on a daily basis to see the harvest. (Mark 4:26-29) The seed will not be determined by what we know, but rather what we believe. The seed contains a mystery method of producing. The earth takes on the responsibility for the seed once it is placed within it. The principle of the seed, time and harvest goes into effect. Still, without help from the outside elements, the harvest can be severely affected or destroyed.

We have a responsibility to ensure the harvest makes its way from the field to the barn of our lives. How do we do it? Everything starts with our trust in the Word of the Lord. There are hindrances to the production of the seed. First, Satan disputing the harvest. He disputes our right to reap. Second, affliction and tribulation. The pressure to give up and not wait patiently for the harvest. Third, persecution and testing of virtue. We wonder, "Is it worth it?" Fourth, deceitfulness of riches and the delusion another way is more profitable. We begin to invest in the world and not the Word's method of prosperity. Finally, lusts of other things. Our longing for something else becomes greater than our longing for the things we have seeded for.

The purpose for the harvest is to be positioned to be a blessing. (Mark 4:30-32) God has given us the method whereby we can be blessed and be a blessing. Jerry Savelle said: "You may not always have what you need, but you are never without the seed that will produce it!" He allots seed to the sower. (II Corinthians 9:10) It is time we see our seed all the way from the field to the harvest. No more crop failures!

APPLICATION
1. Have you sown your seed in faith with nothing wavering?
2. Are you determined to do what it takes to see it all of the way to the barn?

PRAYER:
Lord, I will watch over the seeds I have planted and see the harvest! Amen.

DECEMBER 3
MOVED WITH COMPASSION

Matthew 9:36

"But when he saw the multitudes, he was moved with compassion on them, because they fainted, and were scattered abroad, as sheep having no shepherd."
(KJV)

When you closely examine the circumstances of Jesus' life and this moment of compassion, you will discover He was still trying to recover from the murder of John the Baptist at the hands of Herod. John the Baptist was not only His cousin, but also considered the greatest prophet ever by Jesus. He baptized Jesus in water. He paved the way for the ministry of Jesus and gave his life for the Gospel. Jesus' healing ministry was based on His compassion for the people. The result of Jesus not being moved with grief, but rather being moved with compassion was an outbreak of miracles.

What is compassion? Webster's defines it as "a feeling of deep sympathy and sorrow for someone struck by misfortune, accompanied by a desire to alleviate the suffering; mercy. Synonyms: heart, humanity."

Compassion is more than a just a feeling of sympathy or empathy, it is a spiritual direction. It has a depth, which will not easily release you.

Compassion is a feeling that takes you past feeling sorry. It is not a religious right. Many people do things of spiritual habit. *Compassion* comes from the Greek word, *splangkh-nid'-zom-ahee*, which means "to be moved as to one's bowels, have compassion (for the bowels were thought to be the seat of love and pity), or the spleen innermost."

God is full of compassion. Psalms 112:4 says, *"Unto the upright there ariseth light in the darkness: he is gracious, and full of compassion, and righteous."* (KJV)

We are called to be more like Him. We should be moved with compassion even when we are hurting. It produces the miraculous!

APPLICATION:
1. Take the time, today, to look at the plight of those around you. Let compassion move you.
2. Even if you are hurting, reach out and ease the pain of someone else. Healing will come to you.

PRAYER:
Lord, stir the compassion up in me to help others. Amen.

367

DECEMBER 4
ARE YOU READY TO FORGIVE?

Psalms 86:5

"For thou, Lord, art good, and ready to forgive; and plenteous in mercy unto all them that call upon thee." (KJV)

How many times have you been mistreated, hurt or betrayed? When those things happened to you, did you harbor the hurt or did you look for a way to forgive?

I had something really hurtful happen to me many years ago. In fact, I was so angry I considered how I could retaliate and get even.

I considered myself to be good. Yet, I eventually realized one of the only things making us, as Christians, different from the world is, we are forgivers. The only way the world can see the value of forgiveness is to see us exhibit it in painful situations.

I had to remind myself of the many times I had been forgiven when I had sinned or made mistakes. I had to remind myself when I least deserved to be forgiven, was when I was forgiven the most. I decided to pray for those who had hurt me. When I prayed for their freedom, my freedom came to me.

When we operate in forgiveness, we become freer in our own lives. This is why the Bible says, *"...Forgive and you will be forgiven."* (Luke 6:37 NIV)

APPLICATION:
1. Have you truly forgiven those who have you hurt you?
2. Consider the times you have been forgiven for things you have done.
3. Pray for those who have spitefully used you.

PRAYER:
Lord, I make a decision, today, to forgive those who have hurt me. Please forgive me for being slow to forgive others. Amen.

DECEMBER 5
DO THE RIGHT THING

I Chronicles 29:12
*"Both riches and honour come of thee, and thou reignest over all; and in thine
hand is power and might; and in thine hand it is to make great, and to give
strength unto all." (KJV)*

Most people are aware of the chivalry which existed when the Titanic sank in April, 1912. Out of honor and respect for the courageous men who declared, "Women and children first," an organization was created in 1997 called The Christian Boy's and Men's Titanic Society. These men gather once a year for a dinner in San Antonio, Texas, on April 14, and in Washington, D.C., on April 15. The two events are set up in conjunction with the dates of the iceberg collision and the actual sinking. At these dinners men are encouraged to be courageous, Godly protectors of their families and to practice old-fashioned chivalry.

Honor causes you to do the right thing, no matter what. Honor means the cause becomes greater than the personal loss it may cost you. (Proverbs 21:15) George Macdonald said, "When one seeks the honor that comes from God only, he will take the withholding of the honor that comes from men very quietly indeed." Honor also causes you to believe in something or someone. (John 14:1-2) It causes you to put yourself second and become unconcerned with your own agenda. (Romans 12:10) Honor causes you to defend something with the utmost loyalty. (II Samuel 23:11) It brings integrity. (Proverbs 25:19; Luke 16:10)

We should show deference and preference to certain people God places in our lives. People who should be honored are: first and foremost God. Psalms 71:8 says, *"All day long I will praise and honor you O God for all that you have done for me."* (TLB) Second, the authorities should be honored. I Peter 2:13-14 says, *"Submit yourselves to every ordinance of man for the Lord's sake..."* (NKJV) Next, we are to submit to our spouse. Ephesians 5:21 says, *"Submitting yourselves one to another..."* (KJV) Fourth, we should submit to our parents. This is referenced in many places throughout Bible including: Exodus 20; Ephesians 6; Deuteronomy 5:16; Matthew 15:4; 19:19. Next, we are to submit to our employer. I Peter 2:18 says, *"Servants be subject to your masters."* (KJV) Sixth, we are to submit to the elders. I Timothy 5:1 says, *"Rebuke not an elder..."* (KJV) Last, but not least, we are to submit to our Pastor (Double honor - honorarium). The Bible says we should look for ways to honor those to whom honor is due.

APPLICATION:
1. Are you giving honor to those who deserve it in your life?
2. Are you doing the right thing when under pressure?

PRAYER:
Lord, I will honor those you have placed in my life. Amen.

DECEMBER 6
FAITH IN THE FAST LANE

Amos 9:13
"'Yes indeed, it won't be long now.' God's Decree. 'Things are going to happen so fast your head will swim, one thing fast on the heels of the other. You won't be able to keep up...'" (The Message)

We are truly moving into a different time in history, a time when God is bringing all things to a climax. However, this does not mean it is all bad! The Church the Lord is returning for will not be a broken down, hapless Church, but a glorious one, as written in Ephesians 5:27, *"That he might present it to himself a glorious church, not having spot, or wrinkle, or any such thing..."* (KJV)

As we approach the end of this present age, God has promised to speed up the harvesting process for His people. As I heard the world renowned preacher Jerry Savelle say, "God is going to accelerate things. He is going to do things speedily!" God is looking for a group of people He can trust this latter day harvest with. This group of people will not squander it on greed and lusts of the flesh and will not seek it for self-gain and glory, but rather for the glory of the Church. He is looking for a people who will take the great commission to heart. He desires a group who will look for every available resource to reach a lost and dying world. He is looking for a group who sees the spreading of the Gospel as the most important mission on planet earth.

However, for this to happen, we are going to have to take the restrictions off of our faith, so it can function at optimum levels. How do we do this? We have to sow at all times. We must keep on planting. We have to keep the weeds of doubt and unbelief from growing in our gardens and choking out the increase. If we do these things, we will see our faith move into another dimension—a place where it is not restricted any longer and is in the fast lane!

APPLICATION:
1. Honestly, check your faith. Is it in the slow or fast lane?
2. Recommit yourself in the area of giving.

PRAYER:
Lord, I am ready to move into the harvest at a greater pace. I purposely throw off all the restrictions of doubt and unbelief. Amen.

DECEMBER 7
RIGHT AGAIN

Amos 9:14

"I'll make everything right again for my people Israel: They'll rebuild their ruined cities. They'll plant vineyards and drink good wine. They'll work their gardens and eat fresh vegetables." (The Message)

Have you ever been to a run down part of a city and thought to yourself, "They may as well just bulldoze this over and do something else. There is no use in trying to rebuild, here, again!" Yet, when you visit the same spot months or years later, you see a different sight. Buildings have been repaired, resurfaced or restored. There is a new life about the area.

This is what God promises His people. He is saying to us, "I am going to bring back 'the good ole days' of your lives! I am going to help you rebuild. I am going to restore what others have given up on!" I have seen this happen in the lives of people for years. When others have walked away from them, when their lives were in shambles, God has done something new in their lives. He has resurrected the ruins of their surroundings and dreams.

I heard the story of a man who lost everything he owned in a fire. His life's work was seemingly destroyed by his charred business. As a matter of fact, his building was the only one destroyed, while surrounding buildings only suffered minor damage. Everyone expected him to move on. His business had been failing even before the fire. However, he decided this was a perfect opportunity to improve his business, which he had wanted to do for some time. He rebuilt and included more customer friendly technology and services. He also used totally different colors and décor, and even renamed his business. What was the end result? His business tripled and was more successful than ever!

Sometimes when we think things cannot be revived, we underestimate what God wants to do through our lives. We miss the fact that it just may be an opportunity to get things "right again!"

APPLICATION:
1. Take an inventory of the broken things in your life.
2. Make it a point to give those things to God and ask Him to help you rebuild the right way.

PRAYER:
Lord, I ask you to help me rebuild the things in my life that are right for me and my family. Amen.

DECEMBER 8
GOD SAYS SO

Amos 9:15
"'And I'll plant them, plant them on their own land. They'll never again be uprooted from the land I've given them.' God, your God says so." (The Message)

When things are said to us by others, the merit of the statements is always measured by those who have said them. If someone untrustworthy says to us, "Do not go to work for the next month, I am personally going to pay all of your bills," we are probably not going to believe them enough to follow their instructions. They have an unproven track record. Their words cannot be depended on.

However, we must never confuse God's words to us with those of mere men. When He speaks something pertaining to our lives, it is dependable. It is trustworthy. He has proven Himself to us, as well as others, innumerable times.

Numbers 23:19 states, *"God is not a man, that he should lie; neither the son of man, that he should repent: hath he said, and shall he not do it? or hath he spoken, and shall he not make it good?"* (KJV) Every time we have scripture revealed to us for our lives, we should not hesitate to believe it. Additionally, we should plan for it to come to pass in our lives. He has spoken to me on numerous occasions about things He has planned for me and my family. His words have never failed me when I have chosen to believe Him and not waver. God is "good" for what He says. He has the resources and ability to bring anything to pass we trust Him for and He has promised to us. His words are full of power and truth. He does not hesitate to back up His words with actions, unlike man.

What has God said to you about your life over the years? What has He spoken on the inside of you? What kinds of confirmations have you received, which verified His words to you about your life? Remember, these are not the words of a man; these are the words of God. You are destined for better things. How can you be sure? Because God says so!

APPLICATION:
1. Reflect on what God has said to you about your life that you have not seen come to pass yet.
2. Say, "These things will come to pass because He says so!"

PRAYER:
Lord, help me to remember your words about my life! Amen.

DECEMBER 9
ARE YOU WASHED?

Galatians 3:27

"For as many of you as have been baptized into Christ have put on Christ."
(KJV)

What is baptism? It comes from the Greek word *baptize*, which literally means to "be buried alive." The scriptures representing this best are Romans 6:1-6 and Colossians 2:12. It also means to be dunked or submerged.

According to Acts 8:38, it is putting on Christ, like a covenant of marriage. Alice Motyer said, "Baptism points back to the work of God, and forward to the life of faith."

Baptism signifies leaving behind the old life. Every time I baptize people, I always point out baptism is laying to rest the former life. Even the children of Israel were baptized. (I Corinthians 10:1)

Why should we be baptized? It is commanded. (Matthew 28; Mark 16) It is an act of obedience. Still, it is not conversion by itself, but the outward showing of it. According to Luke 22, the thief on the cross was not baptized, but would be joining Jesus in Paradise.

Who was baptized? The children of Israel were according to I Corinthians 10:1. The Eunuch was according to Acts 8. Our Lord was baptized according to Matthew 3. When Jesus was baptized four important things happened to Him and often will happen to believers after conversion and baptism: First, the Heavens opened. Things open to us after our obedience. Second, the Father spoke. We hear the Father's voice more clearly after our obedience. Third, the Holy Spirit descended. The power of the Holy Spirit intensifies after our obedience. Fourth, Jesus was tested and went into His ministry. We are tested and then shown what we are to do after we are obedient.

What name is to be used? (Ephesians 4:5) The greatest theological wars are fought over this question. Yet, the correct answer is both! There is Baptism in Jesus' name. (Acts 8:14; 2:38) There is also Baptism in the Father, Son and Holy Spirit. (Matthew 28:19)

Who said baptism was essential? Christ said it was essential in Mark 16:16. Peter said it was in I Peter 3:21. Philip said baptism was necessary in Acts 8:36-38. Paul also stated the same in Galatians 3:27. Are you washed?

APPLICATION:
1. If you are not water baptized, be washed in His Word of obedience.
2. Consider water baptism.

PRAYER:
Lord, thank you for allowing me to be baptized like Jesus. Amen.

DECEMBER 10
BUILDING UP THE BODY

Romans 1:11-12

"For I long to see you, that I may impart unto you some spiritual gift, to the end
ye may be established; That is, that I may be comforted together with
you by the mutual faith both of you and me." (KJV)

We are divinely connected. The first thing that happened when we became a Christian is we became a member of His body. There is a connection which takes place. You take your spot in the body. You give your strength to those who need it and receive strength from others where you need it. When the body of Christ functions in unity, it is truly a very beautiful thing. It should be the most powerful entity on the planet.

Instead of this being so, the body seems to be losing its power As Bob Lemon said, "The Church is suffering from the high cost of low power!" Why? Because we let miniscule things separate us from the power base. We let disagreements grow into offences. We let offences produce roots of bitterness. We let our bitterness cut us off from the power supply of the rest of the body.

We should look out for those around us. We should become protectors of unity. At any cost, we should be peace makers. We should be those who keep division out. The power supply is directly connected to the unity we keep. Unity accelerates the power of God. It takes the strain off of us and places it on our enemy. (Deuteronomy 32:29-30) It produces joy for everyone. (Isaiah 52:8) It causes us to come into the things God has prepared for us. (Jeremiah 3:18) It causes us to seek God for others as well as ourselves. (Jeremiah 50:4) The orphan spirit in our lives diminishes, only when we come together.

God is in the process of assembling His body, in which every person matters and everyone counts. He is building up His body!

APPLICATION:
1. Be sure you are a peacemaker.
2. Do not let anything separate you from the people God has connected you to!

PRAYER:
Lord, I will keep the peace and the unity in your body. I will not lend myself to anything that breaks your body down! Amen.

DECEMBER 11
REPORTING FOR DUTY

Acts 6:1-7
"And in those days, when the number of the disciples was multiplied, there arose a murmuring of the Grecians against the Hebrews, because their widows were neglected in the daily ministration. Then the twelve called the multitude of the disciples unto them, and said, It is not reason that we should leave the word of God, and serve tables. Wherefore, brethren, look ye out among you seven men of honest report, full of the Holy Ghost and wisdom, whom we may appoint over this business…Whom they set before the apostles: and when they had prayed, they laid their hands on them. And the word of God increased; and the number of the disciples multiplied in Jerusalem greatly…" (KJV)

During WWII, the 101st Airborne Division spearheaded some major battles in Europe. They fought in places like Bastogne, Belgium, where they were pounded with heavy artillery—then asked to advance toward Berlin against fierce opposition. Many lives were lost. Many who survived were highly decorated soldiers. Years later, one of those men was asked by his grandson, "Grandpa, when you were in the war were you a hero?" He answered, "No, but I served with some men who were." (*Band of Brothers*)

By serving, you fulfill God's purpose for your life. You were made with a specific purpose and a ministry planned for you. There are people we are commissioned to reach for the Gospel. There are many victims, but very few heroes! Eugene Rivers said it best, "The great thing about serving the poor is that there is no competition."

Remember what Frederick William Robertson said, "Do right, and God's recompense to you will be the power to do more right!" It is time to stop making excuses. It is time to stop letting someone else take the assignment meant for us. It is time for us to report for duty!

APPLICATION:
1. If you are moved to a cause, get more involved than ever!
2. Do not let the busyness of life keep you from being involved.

PRAYER:
Lord, I repent for making excuses. I will get involved in others' lives! Amen.

376

DECEMBER 12
IT IS ONLY THE BEGINNING

Ezekiel 36:11

"And I will multiply upon you man and beast; and they shall increase and bring fruit: and I will settle you after your old estates, and will do better unto you than at your beginnings: and ye shall know that I am the LORD." (KJV)

Robert Schuller said it well, "Beginning is half done." Your state of being at the present time, or at its worst, is not a true indicator of what God desires for your life. What may seem insignificant, today, may be the key to everything in your future. Anything you are facing now has already been faced, failed at or succeeded at. You are not finished, yet!

Your day of rejoicing is coming! The Kingdom of God operates on the principle of small things becoming great things. Mark 4:30-32 says, *"And he said, Whereunto shall we liken the kingdom of God? or with what comparison shall we compare it? It is like a grain of mustard seed, which, when it is sown in the earth, is less than all the seeds that be in the earth: But when it is sown, it groweth up, and becometh greater than all herbs, and shooteth out great branches; so that the fowls of the air may lodge under the shadow of it."* (KJV) Inside of the seed is a tree, on the tree is the fruit and inside of the fruit are—more seeds. This is the law of perpetual harvest. It just will not quit. You are destined to be a fruit bearer.

The key is how you deal with hard times. It is during the hard times God deals with you individually. Promotion comes from being faithful in the hard times. Small beginnings represent the time it takes to learn the basics. I had to learn as a young minister you cannot be successful without the anointing. You cannot have the anointing without spending time with God. You cannot spend time with God unless you pray. You cannot pray effectively without the Word. The Devil will not leave you unless you resist him. You cannot resist him successfully if you have pride. You cannot be humble if you do not make it through the hard times. Cheer up! The best is ahead. It is only the beginning!

APPLICATION:
1. Consider God has something just ahead for you!
2. If you are in a difficult season, trust Him to bring you out.

PRAYER:
Lord, I will not become frustrated. I will wait on you! Amen.

DECEMBER 13
FORGET NOT HIS BENEFITS

Psalms 116:12
"What shall I render unto the LORD for all his benefits toward me?" (KJV)

Reaching the end of a job interview, the Human Resources director asked a young accountant who was fresh out of school, "What starting salary were you thinking about?" The accountant said, "In the neighborhood of 100 thousand dollars a year, depending on the benefits package." The interviewer said, "Well, what would you say to a package of five weeks paid vacation, full medical and dental, company retirement fund to 50 percent of salary, executive share option, profit related pay and a company car leased every two years - say, a Five Series BMW?" The accountant sat up straight and said, "Wow! Are you kidding?" The interviewer replied, "Yes, but you started it."

God has a great benefits package for His children. He has bestowed His benefits upon us, but, too often, we neglect or forget them. He forgives all our iniquities. He is a forgiver. Our past is completely washed away. He will never again bring it up to us! He heals all our diseases. (Jeremiah 17:14) He is a healer of body, soul and spirit. He redeems our life from destruction. He steps in when the storm strengthens and delivers us. In the midst of the worst storm of his life, Job proclaimed: "I know my Redeemer lives!" He crowns us with loving kindness and tender mercies. He not only shows us mercy, but also, His kindness. When the whole world seems against us, He is good to us. He satisfies us with good things. He is a satisfier. Psalms 34:8 says, *"O taste and see that the Lord is good."* (KJV) He renews our youth like an eagle. He adds back time that has been stolen or lost. We are given our second breath to finish strong, no matter how we started. He executes righteousness and judgment on our behalf. He pleads our case and exonerates us.

We are not paupers! We have a great God who has given us great benefits!

APPLICATION:
1. Do not forget the things belonging to you.
2. Do not speak defeat. You are blessed!

PRAYER:
Lord, thank you for your many, many benefits! Amen.

DECEMBER 14
GOD WILL HONOR YOUR SEED

Genesis 8:22
"While the earth remaineth, seedtime and harvest, and cold and heat, and summer and winter, and day and night shall not cease." (KJV)

The seed is never intended to go unrewarded. There is seed. Then, there is time, time, and more time! This is where most Christians quit. After we have planted, we are not patient enough to give our seed the space to grow. However, if we do, after time, there is always harvest.

This principle has been in place since the beginning. *Seed* is mentioned 58 times in Genesis alone. It is mentioned in relation to the continuation of things. As long as you have a seed, you have a promise of more to come.

God used this principle many times. (Genesis 1:11; 12; 21; 22; 28; 29) He created fruit with seed inside of it to assure the continuation of creation. He assured the continuation of mankind and beasts after the flood by having Noah bring his family on board the Ark with the animals. He knew they had the seed of reproduction in them! There would not be another God-created man. God would never create another human being without the seed principle in play.

The answer against the Devil is the seed. (Genesis 3:14-15) When Adam and Eve gave Satan the keys to this planet, God immediately announced the seed of the woman would be the Devil's downfall, and it was.

God placed a law into motion that will never be revoked. The first covenant on earth involved seed. (Genesis 9:8-10) There can never be the establishment of a covenant without a seed.

Jerry Savelle said, "I have learned over the years that God never forgets a seed sown!" He also said, "The seed you sow will determine how far you go!" On another occasion he stated, "How you deal with seed has everything to do with how your life turns out."

Even if it seems like God has forgotten the seeds you have planted, do not be deceived. God is planning a great harvest for your life. He will honor your seed!

APPLICATION
1. Do not stop sowing. It determines your future!
2. Do not speak against your harvest.

PRAYER:
Lord, I confess a harvest for every good seed I have planted! Amen.

DECEMBER 15
DO NOT MOCK GOD

Galatians 6:7
*"Be not deceived; God is not mocked: for whatsoever a man soweth,
that shall he also reap."* (KJV)

God is so sure of the principle of seed, time and harvest; He defies people to mock it. The word *mock* or *motorize*, means to "snout, as that whence lowing proceeds; to make mouths at, i.e. ridicule." This means the harvest will have the final say. People may mock you, mouth at you or ridicule you. They may say: "God isn't on their side. They're going down!" However, if you have seed in the ground, they do not understand something is happening underground that will soon be seen. Your harvest will speak for you.

The seeds you have planted will produce the harvest you expect. There are certain areas in your life where your seed will produce: The first is in your finances. Ecclesiastes 11:6 says, *"Sow your seed in the morning and do not be idle in the evening, for you do not know whether morning or evening sowing will succeed, or whether both of them alike will be good."* (NASV) Your harvest is coming in. The second area is in your health. (Acts 3:25) You are a child of faith. The seed is in you. The third area is promotion. (Isaiah 61:8-10) God will cause the seed in you to promote you. The next area is in business. (Psalms 69:35-36) God will deliver things into your hands that have been in the possession of others. The fifth area is in your future and destiny. (Deuteronomy 11:10-14) God will cause your seed to override your past and place you in an environment you have never been in before. The sixth area is over your past hurts. (Psalms 126:5-6) God knows about every moment of struggle, hurt, disappointment and heartbreak you have suffered. He will turn your tears into tears of joy. The final area is your children. (Psalms 112:1-2; Genesis 24:60) Zechariah 8:12 says you have a promise that your physical seed will come into the Kingdom of God. No matter how far they have strayed, do not give up on the power of the seed principle!

Your time is coming! Haggai 2:18-19 says, *"Consider now from this day and upward, even from this day...Is the seed still in the barn? As yet the vine, the fig tree, the pomegranate, and the olive tree have not yielded fruit. But from this day I will bless you."* (NKJV)

APPLICATION:
1. Keep planting.
2. Remember, your harvest will silence the mockers.

PRAYER:
Lord, I believe in the power of my seed to produce now! Amen.

DECEMBER 16
IF FAITH IS ALL YOU HAVE,
FAITH IS ALL YOU NEED

II Corinthians 5:7
"We walk by faith and not by sight!" (NIV)

Hebrews 10:38 says, *"Now the just shall live by faith."* (NKJV) It is true; faith sustains our lives until the promise is performed.

There may be times in your life when you have no money, no friends and no reason to get up or to go on. Yet, if you have faith, you have what you need.

Faith breathes life into hopeless situations. Faith moves time. (Matthew 15:21-28) Faith takes you into your time. It is the answer to your life!

With every opportunity to fear, there is an opportunity for faith. (Mark 4:35-40) With every opportunity for sickness, there is an opportunity for healing. (Hezekiah) Remember, with every opportunity for poverty, there is an opportunity for prosperity. (Widow Woman) With every opportunity for failure, there is an opportunity for victory. (Job 42)

God will lead you into impossible situations where only faith will work. (Luke 8:22-25; Mark 4:35-40) He will lead you to situations where nothing else will make a difference, but faith! Faith is all you need, when you are in need. (Luke 8:40-56; Mark 5:24-34)

When you have exhausted all other options, what you believe is all that remains. Faith brings comfort. Faith turns the storms of life out to sea. Let God be true. (Romans 3:3; Job 23:11-12)

If you keep your faith, you have the answer inside of you to prevail over the worst of circumstances. I know this to be true. I have had valleys in my life as a pastor where nothing seemed to be going right. Yet, somehow, I managed to hold on to my faith. I clung tightly to what God had said about me and what He had promised. My faith guided me into paths of righteousness.

There comes a critical moment in your life when you must decide God is who He said He is, and His Word is trustworthy and the final authority.

When you choose to walk His Word by faith, you will discover faith is all you need!

APPLICATION:
1. Walk in faith starting today.
2. Protect your faith at all costs!

PRAYER:
Lord, I will walk by faith and not by sight. I will not let anything take my faith from me! Amen.

DECEMBER 17
I HAVE CONFIDENCE

Hebrews 11:1
"Now faith is being sure (confident) of what we hope for and certain (convinced) of what we do not see." (NIV)

We must keep our confidence in the Word, despite anything going on in our lives. The word *confidence* means "the steadfastness of mind, firmness, courage." It comes from the Greek word, *parrhesia* (par-rhay-see'-ah), which means "freedom in speaking, unreservedness in speech; free and fearless confidence, cheerful courage."

When we read the great Hall of Faith chapter in Hebrews, we see examples of those who used faith to get them through, and they never even saw the cross! Nothing changed for Abraham until he walked in faith! (Genesis 22:1; John 8:35; Galatians 3:5)

Faith produces the will of God for our life and His will is beyond what we expect. I understand this principle. Many years ago, my wife and I started our ministry with no money, eight people and faith in Him. Recently, we just finished paying off our first building, a state of the art multi-million dollar facility. How did we do it? By keeping our confidence in Him!

How do we keep this kind of overwhelming confidence? We keep confidence by speaking it out at all times and answering our problems with our faith. We must state our authority. This authority comes from a relationship with God. We must realize we are more than conquerors: conquerors of our weaknesses, our shortcomings and our enemies.

When everything around you suggests failure, you should confidently suggest faith! When everything around you suggests a fall, you should confidently suggest faith! When everything around you suggests fear, you should confidently suggest faith!

Paul was confident in the Gospel. Hebrews 3:6 says, *"But Christ as a son over his own house; whose house are we, if we hold fast the confidence and the rejoicing of the hope firm unto the end."* (KJV) This is the secret to your success. You must maintain your confidence at all times, to ensure protection of what you believe. So, when someone asks, "How are you going to make it?" You can answer, "Because I have confidence!"

APPLICATION:
    1. What do you have your confidence in?
    2. Do not allow your confidence to fade. Stay in His Word!

PRAYER:
Lord, forgive me for not being confident in your Word for my life! Amen.

DECEMBER 18
THE IMPORTANCE OF FAVOR

I Samuel 2:26
"And the child Samuel grew on, and was in favour both with the LORD, and also with men." (KJV)

Samuel obtained something man could not give him. He obtained the favor of God. Favor comes from a relationship with God. It is the influence of God upon man, which causes his circumstances and environment to work on his behalf. Favor is the special affection of God towards you. It releases an influence on you, so that others are inclined to like you or cooperate with you.

Favor is different from grace, although it comes from the same root word. Grace is undeserved, but the Bible is full of instruction about how we can obtain favor. (Psalms 44:3)

Favor is a necessary component for the dreams God has given you. Your dreams must be funded by your favor for them to come to pass. They are given to bless others, and it will take others to help you realize them. Favor will take you places your faith cannot and will not. Throughout the Bible, you will not find anyone who had a mission from God who did not also have God's favor.

Seven examples of those who obtained favor: 1. Joseph. He found favor with Potiphar, his jailors and eventually Pharaoh! (Genesis 39:21) 2. Daniel and the three Hebrew children were favored. Their favor eventually won the attention of the king. (Daniel 2; 3) 3. Israel was favored over Egypt. God caused the mightiest nation on the earth to bow to them. (Exodus 3:20-21; 11:3; 12:36) 4. Esther found favor in the sight of the king and God used her to deliver her people. (Esther 2:15) 5. Mary had favor. She gave birth to the Son of God! (Luke 2:26-30) She discovered when the favor of God comes upon you, the impossible is not impossible anymore. 6. Jesus had the favor of God on Him. He won the heart of the sinners and died to deliver them. (Luke 2:52) 7. The first church had the favor of God. They did even mightier acts than Jesus! (Acts 2:46-47)

If you are struggling, ask God for His favor. You will be delivered!

APPLICATION:
1. Study the scriptures concerning God's favor.
2. Speak them over your life, today!

PRAYER:
Lord, I confess that I am favored by you. Please watch over my life! Amen.

DECEMBER 19
OBTAINING GOD'S FAVOR

Psalms 5:12
"For thou, LORD, wilt bless the righteous; with favour wilt thou compass him as with a shield." (KJV)

Having the favor of God on your life can be the difference maker. When God's favor is on your life, you become irresistible. You are put in the right place at the right time. He even makes your mistakes turn in your favor!

How do you get the favor to come upon you? First of all, you must have an ongoing relationship with the Father. (I Samuel 3:10; 19) Because Samuel honored God's words, God honored His words! (Psalms 119:58)

Whoever has your ear has your life! You must also have a commitment to living a Holy life. (Proverbs 14:9) Do not be as concerned with what you do as with what you are. Integrity over time silences even the harshest critics. Another attribute attracting God's favor is service to others. (Proverbs 11:25; 12:2) To be a Kingdom builder, you must be a people builder! Jesus was the greatest people person. When they were hurt, He had compassion on them. When they were sick, He healed them. When they were lost, He saved them. When they were dead, He raised them. When they were ignorant, He taught them. When they were wrong, He corrected them.

Another necessity for God's favor is loyalty to those whom you commit to. (Proverbs 14:35; 16:15) Faithfulness is commitment to a cause; loyalty is commitment to those who lead the cause. A faithful man is for you; a loyal man is with you. A faithful man believes in tithing; a loyal man tithes. A faithful man is a church member; a loyal man will work to build the Church. A faithful man will stand by his pastor; a loyal man will stand with his pastor. A faithful man will live with his wife; a loyal man will live for her. The act probably attracting God's favor the most is staying humble by not being a self-promoter. (Proverbs 27:2) Be cognizant you are a recipient of God's favor on your life because without it, you would be nothing.

As a believer, you need God's favor to fully walk in His will. Begin today to adjust your life and your attitudes, so He can place His favor over your life!

APPLICATION:
1. Ask God for His favor.
2. Allow His Spirit to show you where you need to change.

PRAYER
Lord, I repent of not having my life in place for your favor! Amen.

385

DECEMBER 20
GREAT GRACE

Acts 4:33

"And with great power gave the apostles witness of the resurrection of the Lord Jesus: and great grace was upon them all." (KJV)

Great grace in the life of fallen humanity is probably best seen in the amazing transformation of John Newton. Newton was born in London, half a century before the American Revolution. Although his mother was a Christian, she died when he was only six and his father was an Agnostic. When John was only 11, he went to sea with his father who was a captain of a ship. He grew to be a wild and uncontrolled young man who eventually became a slave trader. He allowed horrible degradation of other human lives to be a part of his livelihood. He narrowly survived death by fever and shipwreck, and his life became dark and meaningless. He began reading the writings of the great believer Thomas Kempis. The Spirit of God began to convict him and he became a sold-out Christian. In fact, he felt the call to ministry. He was ordained in 1781 and accepted a pastorate in Olney, England. Yet, his past sins haunted him. Still, he enjoyed such a great transformation and knew something more was required of him to heal his past. This is when he sat down one night and wrote a hymn. What was the hymn? *Amazing Grace.* "Amazing grace, how sweet the sound that saved a wretch like me. I once was lost, but now I'm found, 'twas blind but now I see!"

Great grace does more than just overshadow us with mercy and forgiveness. It helps us to find a way to forgive ourselves. It leads us to a path that takes away our past transgressions and shows us our purpose. Grace provides space – space for you to get things corrected. (Romans 5:1-2; 19-21) Grace is the extension of God's mercy after the time to harvest has come. The way we know we are in grace is when we are still enjoying the blessings of God after being disobedient. We have been shown great grace! Much of the time we do not even realize to what extent that grace is given!

APPLICATION:
1. Thank God for the great grace over your life.
2. Do not abuse His grace by sinning.

PRAYER:
Lord, thank you so much for your great grace on my life! Amen.

DECEMBER 21
YOUR FREE GIFT

Acts 2:38-39

"Then Peter said unto them, Repent, and be baptized every one of you in the name of Jesus Christ for the remission of sins, and ye shall receive the gift of the Holy Ghost. For the promise is unto you, and to your children, and to all that are afar off, even as many as the Lord our God shall call." (KJV)

Dr. Carl Bates said, "If God were to take the Holy Spirit out of our midst today, about 95 percent of what we are doing in our churches would go on, and we would not know the difference."

Many people are working and working in the Church, as Rowland Hill said, "...like children on a rocking horse—it is a beautiful motion, but there is no progress."

If you do not understand there is a third person in the trinity, know who He is and what He does, you will never understand the fullness of God. The power of the Holy Spirit was necessary for the New Testament Church to be birthed. If it was necessary for the Church to be birthed, is it not then necessary for the New Testament Church to be sustained?

There is a gift after salvation. It is for every believer, today. (Mark 16:17) More people speak in tongues today than ever. It is a last days' sign. (Acts 2:17; Acts 19:1-7) If you have been born-again and water baptized, it is for you. (Acts 1:4-5; 10:44-47; 19:2) These scriptures help to point out the next step after conversion is to be filled with the Holy Ghost.

It was for then. (Acts 2:33; 10:44) It is for now. (Acts 2:38-39; John 7:37-39) It is a River. It is for all! (Acts 15:4-9)

All of the power packed scriptures Paul wrote were to Spirit-filled, tongue talking believers. They understood the fullness of God. Paul spoke in tongues and encouraged it. (I Corinthians 14:18)

How long will tongues last? They will last until Jesus comes back. (I Corinthians 13:8-12) When He returns, we will have His fullness. Until then, we have His Spirit to comfort us, to strengthen us and to lead us. (Luke 11:13)

Have you received the gift of the Holy Spirit, since you first believed?

APPLICATION:
  1. Take the time to carefully study the Word of God about this gift.
  2. Ask God for this gift; it is free to the believer!

PRAYER:
Lord, thank you for this wonderful gift of the Spirit! Amen.

DECEMBER 22
KEEPING HOPE ALIVE

Job 11:18-20
"And thou shalt be secure, because there is hope; yea, thou shalt dig about thee, and thou shalt take thy rest in safety. Also thou shalt lie down, and none shall make thee afraid; yea, many shall make suit unto thee. But the eyes of the wicked shall fail, and they shall not escape, and their hope shall be as the giving up of the ghost." (KJV)

Lewis Smedes sized up the need for hope with this statement, "But we all need to keep hope alive. Hope is to our spirits what oxygen is to our lungs. Your spirit dies when hope dies. They may not bury you for a while, but without hope you're dead." Hope is the key to your tomorrow. Keeping hope alive prevents failure.

There is a liveliness accompanying hope. Nothing is worth the cost of your hope. Hope is the inseparable companion of faith. It is the predecessor to the fulfillment of the promise. Faith produces what hope has presented. There is nothing too hard when hope is available.

Lewis Smedes also said, "This nation was built by the power of hope. No painter ever set brush to canvas, no writer ever set pen to paper, no builder ever set brick on brick, no enterpriser ever built an enterprise without having hope that he or she could do what they were dreaming of doing. We have not begun to fathom the power of hope in creating better lives for ourselves and our children."

Hope is the basis for the success of every believer. All vision you possess is dependent on your hope. Job 14:7-9 illustrates hope is a non-surrendering attitude. It fills your life until your dreams unfold.

There was young girl who dreamed she was a princess and a prince had come to take her away. She asked him, "Where are we going?" He replied, "I don't know, it's your dream!" Hope will produce your dream. Keep your hope alive!

APPLICATION:
1. Keep your hope alive by speaking God's Word for your life.
2. Do not let anyone or anything take your hope from you.

PRAYER:
Lord, I will hope and trust in your Word for my life. I will not listen to anything or anyone who tries to steal it away! Amen.

DECEMBER 23
PREPARE YOURSELF FOR HIS ARRIVAL

Matthew 3:1-3

*"In those days came John the Baptist, preaching in the wilderness of Judea,
And saying, Repent ye: for the kingdom of Heaven is at hand. For this is he
that was spoken of by the prophet Esaias, saying, The voice of one crying in the
wilderness, Prepare ye the way of the Lord, make his paths straight."* (KJV)

John the Baptist was born to Elisabeth, Mary's cousin. His father, Zechariah,
was a minister of incense in the temple. Elisabeth had been barren all of her life. It
seemed they would never have a child of their own. However, one day, Zechariah
had a visitation of the Lord while performing his duties. An angel spoke to him
and told him he would have a son. He also told him he was not to name him after
himself or any family member, but to name him John. Zechariah was stricken
dumb until John's birth to keep this pledge from being broken.

John came as a man of great passion and faith. He was unorthodox in his
lifestyle, eating habits and appearance. His message was also new and fresh. He
preached repentance! He showed the people the only way the Messiah would
come would be when God's people were repentant for their actions.

Today, we await the return of the Lord for His Church. I Thessalonians
4:14-17 says, *"For if we believe that Jesus died and rose again, even so them also
which sleep in Jesus will God bring with him. For this we say unto you by the
word of the Lord, that we which are alive and remain unto the coming of the Lord
shall not prevent them which are asleep. For the Lord himself shall descend from
Heaven with a shout, with the voice of the archangel, and with the trump of God:
and the dead in Christ shall rise first: Then we which are alive and remain shall
be caught up together with them in the clouds, to meet the Lord in the air: and so
shall we ever be with the Lord!"* (KJV)

Are you prepared for His arrival? Are you living a life He will find pleasing
when He returns?

APPLICATION:
1. Spend some time, today, honestly assessing your life.
2. If you need to repent, repent!

PRAYER:
Lord, I thank you for coming again! I will be ready! Amen.

DECEMBER 24
HIS GIFT TO YOU

II Corinthians 9:15
"Thank God for his Son--his Gift too wonderful for words!" (TLB)
"Thanks be unto God for his unspeakable gift!" (KJV)

Jesus is the greatest gift ever given! The word *unspeakable* means "indescribable, unutterable; without human ability to fathom or express." His arrival marked a time in history, which changed everything for everyone, forever! Do you know what today's date is? Every time you date a check, refer to the day and year, or the day of your own birthday, you are referring to the birth of Christ and His return! As Dorothy Sayers said, "Jesus Christ is the only God who has a date in history."

There were six different reactions to the birth of Christ: The first was Mary's reaction. She was frightened at first, but embraced God's plan for her. The second was Joseph's reaction. An angel appeared to him when he had decided to divorce Mary. Instead, he was willing to let God do things His way. The third was the reaction of the Magi. They saw His star in the east, the same direction He will come from again. They followed it with the intent of worshipping Him. Although they did not make it to His manger, they disregarded their personal danger for His sake. The fourth was the shepherds' reactions. Angels appeared unto them and they received the message gladly. They ran immediately to where He was. They told the Great News. The fifth was Herod's reaction. He was an angry, aging ruler. He lied about his intent to the Magi and was afraid of the announcement. He was jealous to the point of issuing a vicious order to murder babies who were born at that time. The last was the reaction of the citizens of Jerusalem. They were troubled like Herod. They were unconcerned to the point they would not travel five miles to see him. They were expecting a powerful messiah.

What is your reaction? Which of these examples best describe you? Are you Mary, willing to receive the Word, despite unworthiness? Are you Joseph, willing to believe the best even though the flesh suggests otherwise? Are you the shepherds, ready to drop everything which seems important and run to where He is? Are you the Magi, willing to travel a far distance just to be in His presence. Are you Herod, afraid of how He may dethrone and overtake you as king? Or, are you Jerusalem, unwilling to recognize Him as King?

APPLICATION:
1. On this Christmas Eve, who do you see Him as in your life?
2. Have you fully accepted God's gift to you?

PRAYER:
Lord, thank you so much for your unspeakable gift for me! Amen.

DECEMBER 25
GOD'S CHRISTMAS TREE

Luke 23:26, 31
"As the crowd led Jesus away to his death, Simon of Cyrene, who was just coming into Jerusalem from the country, was forced to follow, carrying Jesus' cross...For if such things as this are done to me, the Living Tree, what will they do to you?" (TLB) *"For if men do these things when the tree is green, (resists the fire) what will happen when it is dry (burns easily)?"* (NIV)

Jesus was the first Christmas tree. Jesus called himself the "Living Tree." His branches became our lives. He "lit up" the houses of our souls when we allowed Him to be placed inside.

Throughout the Bible, Jesus is consistently compared with a tree or branch. He grew forth out of the house of David. (Isaiah 4:2-3; 11:1-5) God raised Him up to bring His will to pass in our lives.

The tree was also a place of His death. The cross, or tree, was the place He gave His life. There are two Greek words used in the New Testament for the word *cross*. The first word is not used of tree. *Stauros* is "an upright pale or stake." It represented the Roman crucifixion. (Matthew 27:32; 40; Colossians 1:20; 2:14; Hebrews 12:2; Philippians 2:8) The cross is a symbol which stands for the substitutionary death of Jesus to give us life. The second word is *xulon*. This word is used for both a tree and the cross. It represents wood, a piece of wood or anything consisting of wood. It is also used for the cross. (Acts 5:30; 20:39; 13:29) It is used to depict the tree of Life in Revelation. (Revelation 2:7; 22:2; 14; 19)

Under the tree (the life and death of Jesus), there are a number of presents. The tree is evergreen. It always produces. (I Peter 1:18-19) It never dries out.

While we generally think of the wonderful birth of Jesus on this day, let us also pause to consider the ultimate reason for His birth. He was to become the Living Tree of God, which was cut down, so we might have the gift of eternal life!

APPLICATION:
1. Stop, today, and thank Jesus for being the first Christmas tree!
2. As you look at the lights on a Christmas tree, consider Him as the light.

PRAYER:
Lord, thank you for being the Living Tree for me! Amen.

DECEMBER 26
JOY TO THE WORLD

Luke 2:10-11
"And the angel said unto them, Fear not: for, behold, I bring you good tidings of great joy, which shall be to all people. For unto you is born this day in the city of David a Saviour, which is Christ the Lord." (KJV)

The message of the Gospel is joy! The pronouncement of the arrival of Jesus was one of joy. In the familiar Christmas story, the angels appeared to the shepherds and announced the birth of the Savior Jesus as good tidings of great joy — joy that fits every situation and every person. This joy is not just momentary or selective, but is for everyone, everywhere, for all eternity!

Joy in the New Testament speaks of a celebration. Brian Bill said, "If you read through the Scriptures and do a study on the topic of joy, every time you see it, it is accompanied with adjectives – great joy, exceeding joy, joy unspeakable and full of glory." This reveals joy is not mere human emotion or happiness, but Heaven sent. Tony Campolo said, "Most Christians I know have just enough of the Gospel to make them miserable, but not enough to make them joyful."

There is no question most Christians do not draw on the joy brought to us through the birth of Jesus. Isaiah 12:3 says to draw out water from the wells of salvation with joy. What is He saying here about the wells of salvation? When you get saved and give your life to Jesus, you should be experiencing joy. It is fun being saved! There is joy in Jesus. God has given us access to a never ending, bottomless well—the well of salvation. There is only one way to obtain all of what He has promised us, and it is with the bucket of joy! Billy Sunday said, "If you have no joy, there's a leak in your Christianity."

Jesus came to the world from Heaven, so we may one day leave this world and go to Heaven. Do you feel as good about the home God is preparing for you as the one that may be gone tomorrow? If you anticipate that home with joy, how wonderfully you will live in today's world even with all of its challenges. Joy to the world!

APPLICATION:
1. How is your joy in the Lord, today?
2. Consider your salvation and joy, not your circumstances!

PRAYER:
Lord, thank you for the joy you have brought to my life! Amen.

DECEMBER 27
ALL YOU NEED IS LOVE

John 3:16-17
"For God so loved the world, that he gave his only begotten Son, that whosoever believeth in him should not perish, but have everlasting life. For God sent not his Son into the world to condemn the world; but that the world through him might be saved." (KJV)

The most important thing we can learn in life is God never stops loving us! Moses disobeyed God, but God still loved him. Peter denied being one of the disciples and cursed Him, but God still loved Peter and used him to preach the first message after He ascended back to the Father. John Mark turned back and quit in the middle of a missionary journey with Paul, but Jesus still loved him and caused him to later be a blessing to the church and the Apostle Paul. David committed adultery, conspiracy and murder, but God still loved him and promised him a throne! The nation of Israel were idol worshippers most of the time and complainers the rest of the time. They were still given a divine promise in the book of Zechariah, *"For thus says the Lord of hosts: 'He sent Me after glory, to the nations which plunder you; for he who touches you touches the apple of His eye.'"* (Zechariah 2:8 NKJV)

These scriptures point out God's unconditional love for us. It holds up under any and all circumstances. Love saved us! God's love is not in any way influenced by anything we say or do.

One day C. H. Spurgeon was walking through the countryside with a friend. As they strolled along, the evangelist noticed a barn with a weather vane on its roof. At the top of the vane were the words, "God is Love." Spurgeon remarked to his companion he thought this was a rather inappropriate place for such a message. "Weather vanes are changeable," he said, "but God's love is constant." "I don't agree with you about those words, Charles," replied his friend. "You misunderstood the meaning. That sign is indicating a truth: Regardless of which way the wind blows, God is love."

APPLICATION:
1. There may be many things you are not, but you are not unloved!
2. Share the love He has shown you with someone else, today. Remember, you did not deserve it either!

PRAYER:
Lord, help me to love others as you love me! Amen.

DECEMBER 28
YOUR SEASON WILL COME

Luke 1:18-20
"And Zacharias said unto the angel, Whereby shall I know this? for I am an old man, and my wife well stricken in years. And the angel answering said unto him, I am Gabriel, that stand in the presence of God; and am sent to speak unto thee, and to shew thee these glad tidings. And, behold, thou shalt be dumb, and not able to speak, until the day that these things shall be performed, because thou believest not my words, which shall be fulfilled in their season." (KJV)

God has an appointed season for our life. God always seems to send His Word just before we come into our harvest. Every Word of God has a season attached to it for our lives!

When things seem to be at their worst, we should lean on the Word to see us through. A moment of crisis can become an opportune time for those who choose to continue to believe.

The word season in Luke 1:20 is the Greek word, *kairos*. It is "a measure of time, a larger or smaller portion of time, hence: a fixed and definite time, the time when things are brought to crisis, the decisive epoch waited for; an opportune or seasonable time; the right time."

The seasons of our lives contain three things: time, purpose and readiness. Together, each work brings us to a decisive moment, to move us into another season of our lives. We could say it is our "moment."

It takes courage to seize the moment. It takes faith to move into our season. Without an infusion of faith, we will hesitate and get stuck where we are. God always led the people to places where faith was required. We cannot change with will-power alone; we need God's Word to bridge us from where we are to where we are meant to be.

Seasons can be prolonged or diminished according to our responses to them. If we understand what God is saying to us and are willing to move in faith, we can reap in the season!

APPLICATION:
1. Ask God to help you identify the seasons of your life.
2. Trust God to show you what is next.

PRAYER:
Lord, help me move into the seasons of my life you have for me. Amen.

DECEMBER 29
GOING THE DISTANCE

II Timothy 4:6-8
"For I am now ready to be offered, and the time of my departure is at hand.
I have fought a good fight, I have finished my course, I have kept the faith:
Henceforth there is laid up for me a crown of righteousness, which the Lord, the
righteous judge, shall give me at that day: and not to me only, but
unto all them also that love his appearing." (KJV)

You are capable of going the distance! Lewis and Clark set out with a bad map, but drew a new one as they went along. They started with 33 people, and the voyage from Missouri to the West Coast took over four years. They traveled over 3,700 miles. Along the way, they were helped by a Native American guide, Sacagawea. They were able to go the distance with this help.

Those who go the distance are the winners. Winners see the prize. (Matthew 25:23) Your perseverance is the promise of the reward. If there is no reward at the end, there will be no desire to win. "Don't wish upon a star; reach for one." (Unknown) Winners are willing to pay the price. Matthew 24:13 says, *"But he that shall endure unto the end, the same shall be saved."* (KJV) No matter how much is taken from them, winners are convinced, in the end it will be worth it. Winners are not swayed by others around them, those who have left the race or those who do not enter the race. They run their own race. Winners do not let setbacks stop them. (Micah 7:8) They regroup, refocus and re-enter the race. Winners are not moved by their surroundings and circumstances. (II Corinthians 4:18) They see each moment as one moment only, and do not accept it as permanent. Winners look ahead and not behind. They do not dwell on past failures or mistakes. They convince themselves that better days are just ahead. Winners believe in themselves. They believe they have something deep inside that has not been tapped into, yet. They have yet to see the best from themselves. Will you be a winner? It is up to you!

APPLICATION:
1. Do the things you need to do and be a winner.
2. Do not accept defeat!

PRAYER:
Lord, I believe I am created to win. Help me be what you desire for me! Amen.

DECEMBER 30
BUILDING YOUR FOUNDATION

Hebrews 6:9-11

"But, beloved, we are persuaded better things of you, and things that accompany salvation, though we thus speak. For God is not unrighteous to forget your work and labour of love, which ye have shewed toward his name, in that ye have ministered to the saints, and do minister. And we desire that every one of you do shew the same diligence to the full assurance of hope unto the end..." (KJV)

We must build on the foundation laid over the course of this year. Foundations are poured with the expectancy a building will soon follow. We are urged not to keep walking over the same ground and taking the same course over, especially after we have already passed them. We need to make what we have done over the course of this year count!

Where are you now in comparison to a year ago? Has your investment of this year been a good one? (II Corinthians 8:10) Someone wise said, "As every thread of gold is valuable, so is every minute of time."

There are seven things that can make the year ahead count for you. First, do not let anything take you away from God's Word. (Luke 10:41-42) Things seemingly necessary are not as necessary as spending time in God's Word. Second, do something new. (Romans 13:11-12) The two greatest enemies people have are: regret for the past and anxiety of the future. You must learn to live in the moment. Third, do not stress over things you have no control over. (I Thessalonians 4:11) You do not have control over where you were born or to whom. You do not have control over the actions of others. Fourth, you must believe God is for you! Philippians 4:13 says in The Living Bible, *"For I can do everything God asks me to with the help of Christ who gives me strength and power."* Fifth, you must set obtainable goals. Proverbs 17:24 says, *"The perceptive find wisdom in their own front yard; fools find it everywhere but here."* (The Message) Sixth, take necessary steps towards your goals. (Matthew 5:4) Seventh, take care of your relationships. (Ecclesiastes 7:22)

If you do these things, you will have a strong building next year!

APPLICATION:
1. Make an honest assessment of this past year.
2. Ask God to help make this next year even better!

PRAYER:
Lord, thank you for helping me build on my foundation! Amen.

DECEMBER 31
BRINGING FORTH NEW THINGS

II Kings 19:3
"...This day is a day of trouble, and of rebuke, and blasphemy: for the children are come to the birth, and there is not strength to bring forth." (KJV)

There are things God is ready to birth, but up until now, there has been no strength! One of the saddest things is to carry to full term, only to be too weak to deliver.

The Church has boasted many things, but has not been able to deliver the goods consistently. We have spoken about greatness, but settled for mediocrity. We have let the words of others become louder and stronger than the Word of God. Do not rely on the world's view or opinion! It is blasphemy not to be able to bring the Word of God to fruition. We have been given everything we need. (Philippians 4:19)

There are some things God is ready to bring forth in the body of Christ, we have not brought forth before. (Judges 16:17-22) We need His strength to give birth to His plans. When we begin to walk in them, all of Heaven will get involved with us. The angels of God will become more active. The Spirit of God will move over our lives. The Word of God will come alive and begin to manifest in everything we do!

What will the results be? 1. There will be great breakthroughs financially in the body of Christ. 2. Great changes will come into our lives and the lives of our loved ones. 3. There will be some great shake-ups in those who would oppose us and hinder God's plan for our lives. 4. There will be more reports of great spiritual outbreaks moving us into the perfect will of God. 5. There will be some great prayers being answered we have been offering for years. 6. There will be a great spiritual uprise in our children. 7. There will be a great love for God and His people producing a great harvest of souls.

Do not let this next year be a repeat of this year. Even if this was a good year, God has something even better for you. If this past year was one of disappointment because you did not birth things you thought you would, do not stop pressing into the things of God. The best is just ahead!

APPLICATION:
1. Begin planning, now, for God to do something great!
2. Keep yourself before Him and ask Him to flow through you.

PRAYER:
Lord, thank you for what you will do in the year ahead! Amen.

INDEX OF ABBREVIATIONS

All scripture references are from the King James Version (KJV),
unless otherwise noted.

NKJV   New King James Version
NIV   New International Version
TLB   The Living Bible
NLT   New Living Translation
NASV   New American Standard Bible
ASV   American Standard Version
TEV   Today's English Version
ESV   English Standard Version
NET   New English Translation
AMP   The Amplified Bible
THE MESSAGE: **The Bible in Contemporary Language**

Acknowledgements

*T*here are so many people who have contributed to shaping my life as a man and a minister; space would not allow me to name them all. I would like to thank my pastors, Dr. and Mrs. Mark T. Barclay or Mark Barclay Ministries, Midland, Michigan, for their guidance, encouragement and friendship. Their support and endorsement of our lives and this book are greatly appreciated.

I would also like to thank my wonderful congregation at Faith Outreach Church for all their support throughout the years.

In addition, I would like to thank my two beautiful daughters for their tireless efforts to make this project a reality. To Rebecca, I suppose your English degree from the University of Tennessee finally paid off for me! To Rachel, I know there were numerous diaper changes and feedings for Janel while you were pushing this to the finish line. To my son-in-law, Jason, thanks for being so understanding!

About the Author

D r. William T. Luffman was born in 1958 to an unwed mother, the last of nine birth children. Despite being raised in abject poverty and becoming a high school dropout, he overcame these obstacles. In 1976, he became a born-again Christian and later the next year answered the call to ministry.

He and his wife, Ginger, of nearly 30 years, founded Faith Outreach Church of Clarksville, Tennessee, in 1989. Faith Outreach Church is one of the fastest growing churches in the state whose membership boasts nearly 2,500 members. In 2009, Dr. Luffman also founded William Luffman Ministries.

Dr. Luffman finished his formal education and earned his B.A in Theology from Zoe Bible College of Jacksonville, Florida, in 1996. He later earned his Master in Theology in 2003 and then earned his Doctorate in Theology in 2006 from Christian Bible College of Rocky Mount, North Carolina. He also holds a Doctorate in Divinity from Magister University, St. Johns, Antigua.

Dr. Luffman is ordained through Faith Covenant Ministries, Sicklerville, New Jersey, and Mark Barclay Ministries, Midland, Michigan.

CPSIA information can be obtained at www.ICGtesting.com
Printed in the USA
LVOW071311070212

267508LV00002B/4/P

9 781612 152479